The Essential West

Also by Elliott West

(coed.) *Essays on Walter Prescott Webb* (Austin, 1976)

The Saloon on the Rocky Mountain Mining Frontier (Lincoln, Nebr., 1979)

Growing Up with the Country: Childhood on the Far-Western Frontier (Albuquerque, 1989)

(coed.) *Small Worlds: Children and Adolescents in America, 1850–1950* (Lawrence, Kans., 1992)

The Way to the West: Essays on the Central Plains (Albuquerque, 1995)

Growing Up in Twentieth-Century America: A History and Reference Guide (Westport, Conn., 1996)

The Contested Plains: Indians, Goldseekers, and the Rush to Colorado (Lawrence, Kans., 1998)

The Last Indian War: The Nez Perce Story (New York, 2009)

The Essential West

Collected Essays
by Elliott West

Foreword by Richard White

University of Oklahoma Press : Norman

LIBRARY OF CONGRESS CATALOGING-IN-PUBLICATION DATA

West, Elliott, 1945–
  The essential West : collected essays / Elliott West.
    p. cm.
  Includes bibliographical references and index.
  ISBN 978-0-8061-4296-8 (cloth)
  ISBN 978-0-8061-4653-9 (paper)
  1. West (U.S.)—History. 2. Frontier and pioneer life—West (U.S.)—History. I. Title.
  F591.W4528 2012
  978—dc23

2012011193

The paper in this book meets the guidelines for permanence and durability of the Committee on Production Guidelines for Book Longevity of the Council on Library Resources, Inc. ⊗

For my children:
Elizabeth, Bill, Richard, Garth, and Anne

Contents

PART III ❀ MYTH

Illustrations

Foreword

Elliott West is the best historian of the American West writing today. If there were any argument about the issue, this collection pretty much lays it to rest. Any reader can appreciate the range and grace of these essays, as well as their imagination, humor, and insight. It might, however, take other historians to recognize the deep learning and familiarity with the archives evident in each chapter, because Elliott West wears his learning lightly. He frames knotty questions simply and clearly and makes it obvious why they matter. He never neglects the "Who cares?" question that all historians know they must answer. He writes like an angel, but he is far funnier than any angel that I have ever seen in print.

Elliott West has had a long and distinguished career, and most of the themes and concerns of that career are on display here. This book is an intellectual feast served as a series of small plates. Each displays West's skills in the various subgenres of history. Individually, they are all worth savoring. Collectively, they reveal how the writing of American history has broadened over the past quarter century or so.

Elliott West, like many of his scholarly generation, started out as a social historian and a historian of the family. The skills of the social historian—the concern with the everyday, with communities and the ordinary and extraordinary people who make them up—are on display in these pages. The governing patterns of any society are visible in the quotidian activities of its members—including, he insists, children. Other historians know this and write about them, but few with the care and insight that characterize these essays. West has an eye for stories and characters. Encounter Marie Rosa, Jean L'Archevêque, and "Ignon Ouaconisen," and you will not forget them. They lived astonishing lives, and in West's hands they become instructive lives.

Elliott West's interests have broadened over the course of his career, but he has retained the social historian's attention to the everyday and the patterns they reveal. Those interests carry over into his writings as an environmental historian. His Lewis and Clark essay, included in this collection, is a gem of environmental history. I wish that I had had the wit to compare Lewis and Clark's journey up the Missouri and down the Columbia to Mungo Park's attempt to trace the Niger River in Africa, and to draw out the lessons about environment and imperialism. I didn't, but Elliott West did, and I can't imagine anyone, from environmental historians to intelligent readers, not being entranced and instructed by the analysis.

The same ability to move between close observation and interpretation is apparent when West writes about Native Americans and Indian-white relations. He examines Indian and white interactions on the Great Plains and elsewhere with more subtlety and nuance than virtually anyone else whom I know. If a reader desires to discover largely vanished worlds, Elliott West's prose and stories are up to the task; but there is much more in these essays than evocations of past worlds. These essays deliver big ideas and large frameworks that have greatly influenced other historians.

West's big-picture ideas are so impressive and so influential because they rise out of his materials and are not imposed upon them. To read about bison, grass, and horses is to understand the ecology of the plains, how energy regimes function, and how they shape human history. As these essays show, he has been quietly and influentially rethinking the consequences of the central event of American history, the Civil War, by juxtaposing the South, the region where he lives and teaches, and the West. He writes, for example, that "the war shattered or shook institutions regulating race from coast to coast. It jumbled identities and began a time of unprecedented racial disarray." In looking at the way the triumphant North tried to remake the nation in its own image following the Civil War, he has advanced the idea of a "Greater Reconstruction" that embraced the West as well as the South.

Finally, Elliott West is a skilled cultural historian who is as perceptive as anyone when analyzing popular portrayals of the West and diagnosing their appeal. He recognizes that the enduring attraction of the West is that it has come to stand in for the country as a whole. When Americans turn to bison or Jesse James, they think with them and derive larger meanings. The stories we tell about the West interpret the country itself.

These essays are a rare treat. They are as entertaining and interesting as they are instructive. They leave you thinking.

Richard White

Introduction

It has been my astounding good fortune to have wandered into western history, and to have done it with excellent timing. I grew up assuming I would be a journalist—or a "newspaperman" as my family put it. My father was an editor in Dallas, Texas; my older brother has been a very fine travel writer for magazines; I majored in journalism. I appreciated history, and by graduation I had more hours in it than in my major. Still, I was all set to enter the newspaper life when, on a whim, I applied for graduate study in history at the University of Colorado. I loved history and I loved Colorado. What could be more sensible? For reasons that baffle me to this day, the department offered a plush fellowship, which I grabbed before anyone found me out as the fraud I was. I had not the slightest inkling that western history was the department's strength, and in fact I was flabbergasted to learn that I was supposed to specialize at all, but that first semester I took a seminar with Robert Athearn, one of the leading western historians of his day, and that was that. I caught the bug, or rather it caught me, and it has not let loose.

When I was graduated at twenty-six, much the naïf, I was unaware that my chosen area was not the hottest around. In 1971 western history was widely considered a peripheral field stuck in outmoded approaches. It was an exciting time generally. The civil rights movement, the war in Vietnam, and the cultural convulsions of the crazed 1960s had inspired a wonderful array of new work, but despite some fine scholarship afoot, the ruling opinion was that my field had little of interest to say. To put it mildly, however, that was about to change.

It began with fresh looks at western society, including an outpouring of work in women's history challenging the tradition of the hairy-chested West. There was an innovative revival of southwestern borderland studies and a flurry of western ethnic history, especially on Hispano/a topics, but directed as well at groups ranging from Czechs and Basques to Italians and Chinese. Soon afterward came an initial barrage of environmental history. At some point it dawned on people that the West was an especially inviting field to cultivate, in part, ironically, because it had been such a scholarly backwater. There was so much waiting to be done in applying new methods to answer new questions. And once those new questions were asked, it turned out that the West was inherently rich in possibilities. Pioneer society and the bizarre demographics of the mining West made for fascinating studies of western women's worlds. What better place to pursue ethnic history than the region that was, and is, the most ethnically diverse part of America? The West's breathtaking range of geography, climate, flora, and fauna made it a natural historical laboratory for environmental studies. Here, in fact, was one area where we were ahead of the curve. The dance between people and their environment had long been a central theme, certainly in the work of the men typically mentioned as the field's two great gurus, Frederick Jackson Turner and Walter Prescott Webb.

Having floated aimlessly into western history, I soon found myself caught up in some of the most provocative and original scholarship done by some of the smartest and most articulate members of the historians' guild. The shorthand term for this work was "the new western history." The phrase requires quotation marks because it refers to ideas and writing that predated cell phones and the popular use of the Internet, but at the time, in the 1980s, it sure felt new. As a friend once put it, the "new" history rearranged our mental furniture.

Like all good new work, it provoked more of the same. We are now more than a full generation past the "new" history, and the provocateurs have produced dozens of their own students whose work has extended, revised, and challenged that of their teachers. Personally, I found it impossible not to jump into the action. As family and colleagues will readily testify, I suffer from a short attention span, and I found myself jumping from topic to topic to topic, each one irresistible at the time. Of about seventy-five essays that resulted, I've chosen fourteen for this volume. Some have been previously published, some not. Gathering them together has offered a chance to wonder a bit about what lessons we can take away from the work of so many fine historians published in the past quarter century or so. I have used a few tentative thoughts to organize the essays into three sections. The divisions are necessarily crude, and any piece might sensibly be moved from one to another, but the three sections do offer a rough guide to the essays' themes, and in turn suggest some of the broader and more fruitful insights that have excited me and so many others.

The first section concerns conquest. It was a term heard quite a lot after publication of what was arguably the book most associated with the "new western history," Patricia Nelson Limerick's *The Legacy of Conquest: The Unbroken Past of the American West* (1987). Initially the focus was the simple fact of the word itself: western history was best understood not through the traditional story of pioneer trials overcome, a people uplifted, and national virtues ingrained. Rather, the West emerged through violence, dispossession, and an empire created at enormous human and environmental costs. "Conquest" remains a true enough term to describe a lot of what happened, but over the years, our understanding of it has gotten much more complicated and more resistant to easy summarizing—in short, messier.

Western conquest, for instance, was part of a much wider story of global empire-making that unfolded simultaneously in the Great Plains and Sudan, California and India. The opening essay, "Lewis and Park; Or, Why It Matters That the West's Most Famous Explorers Didn't Get Sick (or at Least Not *Really* Sick)," sets the well-known journey to the Pacific side-by-side with a coincident expedition in western Africa. This wider perspective puts the Corps of Discovery, and national expansion generally, in an illuminating and rather humbling light. The traditional and "new" histories had one point in common. The one often implied that national domination was the natural result of American superiority; the other saw it as irresistible bullying; but the two agreed that it was pretty much bound to happen. In global context, however, American conquest appears a far chancier proposition that turned on luck and on circumstances—latitudes and insects, in the case of Lewis and Clark—having nothing to do with national virtues or vices.

When we zoom in from that planetary view for a closer look, "conquest" itself turns out to be a slippery term. For one thing, there were others—French, English, Russians, Spanish, Mexicans, and the occasional Hawaiian—jockeying for control of the West. The newcomers, furthermore, did not just step in and take over. They did unsettle things profoundly, which brought plenty of trouble to Indians, most notably in the form of horrifying epidemics. But the changes triggered by contact also brought opportunity and enhanced enormously the power of some native peoples, who quickly set off on conquests of their own. Although bitter enemies, the Comanches and Sioux each took brilliant advantage of the times and together dominated an area larger than the newborn United States. "Called-Out People: The Cheyennes and the Central Plains" traces a similar story. The Cheyennes followed their own westward expansion from the Mississippi Valley into a new life as traders, hunters, and warriors. Their golden time on the plains, however, lasted barely three generations—less time than many of today's ranching and farming families have spent in that seductive, difficult country.

The Cheyennes' steep rise and rapid fall raise an intriguing question. Given the many players and the Indians' successes, how were the Americans able to bring three centuries of struggle to such a quick and emphatic end? Part of the answer is obvious: the proximity of a restless society, its yeasty growth, its land hunger and economic ambitions, its purposeful imperialism, including a war of aggression against its southern neighbor. Less obvious was the power of mass imagination, specifically as the chance discoveries of precious metals from the Rocky Mountains to the Sierra Nevada recast the very meaning of the continental center in the popular mind. That is the subject of "Golden Dreams: Colorado, California, and the Reimagining of America."

Americans had other advantages, too, unsought and unintended. Their great leap westward in the 1840s happened to coincide with a global revolution in how things moved. One new technology, the railroad, has long been recognized for its historical clout. Another, considered in "Wired to the World: The Telegraph and the Making of the West," is much less appreciated. This most important breakthrough in the history of human communication happened to be perfectly suited to the demands of western geography. First formally tested only months before we began acquiring the Far West, the telegraph played a role equal to the railroad in subduing the new country and then knitting it together into a national region. Here is yet another reminder of how conquest was always contingent, partly a matter of timing and fortune.

Conquest had to do with more than grabbing land. It also involved how the conquerors treated the people on that land. When we move into that terrain, the lessons again get messier the closer we look. Take, for instance, the question of race. A prominent part of the "new" historians' retake on expansion was the role of racism. Specifically they highlighted nineteenth-century beliefs in the superiority of Anglo-Saxons and in the inevitability, indeed the moral requirement, that the white race (whatever that meant) dominate the lesser peoples living in the West. This was an especially useful point, for the historical discussion of race had always concerned the East, specifically the South and the tortured relations there between blacks and whites. The "new" history insisted that racial issues have always been continental and, if we use the color coding of racial discourse, multichromatic. (For that matter, colors changed with location. In the later nineteenth century, the Irish were "black" on the East Coast and "white" in the West, and in parts of the West, African Americans, because they were neither Hispanic nor Chinese, and thus not "colored," were considered "white" or even "Anglo." The California Supreme Court in 1854 ruled that Chinese were both Asian and American Indian, which in the parlance of the day made them both "yellow" and "red," which in turn meant, logically, that Chinese were "orange.") Conquest made the United States quite the rainbow, although not at all in the modern benign sense.

The "new" history thus shifted discussion of race and racism into the West, which needed the attention, and away from the South, which had hogged it for so long. Redirecting the focus from one section to another, however, missed a fascinating point that is startlingly obvious when we bring the two perspectives together and look at race nationally, all of a piece. "Reconstructing Race" addresses that point. As racial ideas were helping push the nation westward, they were inspiring abolitionists and fueling the sectional tension that led finally to war and emancipation. Put a bit differently, the same basic thinking that out west encouraged the aggression against Mexico; the defeat, dispossession, and sometimes slaughter of Indian peoples; and the mistreatment and eventually the exclusion of Chinese—that thinking back east worked to liberate more than four million persons and to admit them (admittedly with limits) to citizenship. When the same impulses were giving freedom to slaves and taking it away from Indians, something very interesting was going on. The moral tone of those years gets a lot murkier. Emancipation, our nation's moral high point, was partnered with some of its most appalling actions. That very muddiness, however, strikes me as more faithful to what followed, the mixed racial history of the new America born of civil war and expansion.

So conquest can teach us a great deal, and not only about why and how the West emerged. It illuminates as well the full national narrative: its contingent nature, how it fits into global history, the broader forces transforming American life, and the moral crosscurrents running through an era of rapid and volatile change. The invitation prompts us to take as wide a perspective as possible, setting western history within the histories of the nation and the world over many generations. But history is also personal, a matter of individuals playing out their lives, typically inside a tight radius of home and neighborhood. Western history has to be approached on that level, too, and when it is, again asking new questions and looking back from new angles of vision, the results are equally rewarding.

For that kind of history, there is no better access than the second section's subject, the family. I have always been especially intrigued by how people of the past have managed to do what most of us do: how they muddled through their days, meeting basic responsibilities, coping with irritations and disasters, enjoying simple pleasures, loving and despising—in short, living out the ordinary lives that always have formed the stratum beneath those grand events unfolding in the textbooks. Families, besides being the prime setting for such historical dailiness, have something to commend them. Everybody has one, or at least has at some point. Definitions vary enormously—a family might be the staff and other occupants of an orphanage—but everyone grows up shaped fundamentally by a core of persons bound to them more intimately than anyone else, and for as far back as we can see, the family has been the irreducible cell of every society ever studied. Those two points make of the family a unique area of historical interest. The density of its ordinary experience in its particular place allows us maybe the best chance we have to glimpse the on-the-ground history of the West's many parts. At the same time, because the family is a cultural universal, we have the chance to place that history in the contexts of other places and other times.

Families, for instance, can be the means to explore, through gritty particulars, one of the points raised in the first section. Conquest involved many parties grappling for control over a long stretch of time, and when the contenders came together, whether trading, allying, or trying to kill each other, they invariably connected through the intimate bond of family. "The West before Lewis and Clark: Three Lives" traces some of those linkages among the French, Spanish, Americans, Karankawas, Pueblos, Pawnees, Comanches, Osages, Missourias, and others. The stories range from the Rio Grande to the rue des Boucheries in Paris, and with only a few degrees of separation they relate a murdered explorer, Pawnee celestial deities, the alcalde of Santa Fe, and the king of France, all of it unfolding during the century and a quarter before the event commonly seen as setting western history in motion in 1804, the expedition of the Corps of Discovery.

As the "new western history" emphasized, the family was also an institution of distinct members with their own roles and perspectives. The vigorous work in women's history highlighted the roles and experiences of wives and mothers and how they differed from those of husbands and fathers. In conversations over coffee or beer, a common remark at the time was that this new attention was, at last, opening up the western narrative to fully half of the participants, mostly ignored until then. But in much of the West, women were not half the actors in the story. Nor were the men. In fact, lump the women and men together, and they were still a minority. Because much of the West was settled by families that, for practical reasons, produced children at a clip greater than anywhere on earth today, parents typically were much outnumbered by their offspring, and so girls and boys, not women and men, made up the majority. And it has been largely a silent majority. Children have been western history's most unvoiced figures.

Any parent will agree that children simply look at the world differently from us grownups. It follows that the point of view of the young offers a fresh prospect even on those episodes already told and retold many times. Nowhere was this clearer than in how children amused themselves. "Child's Play: Tradition and Adaptation on the Frontier" looks into the lives of boys and girls on the familiar historical turf of overland trails, homesteads, and mining towns, and it uses their games and playtime to revive an old question. From Frederick Jackson Turner on, western historians have studied how those moving into new country tried to implant past ways of life, then adjusted those hopes to realities, and with that, created hybrid lives reflective of particular places. Children acted out that process as they turned work into play, found fun in exploring their immediate worlds, and bore westward an old culture of games and playtime. Children's lives also remind us that westering was not one but many stories, some starkly different from the rest. "Becoming Mormon" considers the odyssey of the Latter-day Saints—their midwestern trials, their exodus, and their resettlement in the Great Basin—as it was known by their youngest members. Parts of the experience were disturbing, some of it was heartbreaking, and all of it suggested the distinctive identities that emerged during that first generation of Saints who grew into their own in Deseret. That in turn raises intriguing questions about how that generation, once in power, negotiated the Mormons' reconciliation with the nation they had tried to escape.

In a way the family, as an entryway into the ordinary lives of westerners, is a healthy reminder of the elusiveness of any historical lesson. To me the sheer variety of experiences, impressions, and exchanges, the range of mood and tone and personality in the voices speaking to us from the scores of thousands of documents are both a caution and a profound pleasure. "Listen Up: Hearing the Unheard in Western History" does suggest some patterns in and insights into how westerners passed their time, including their tribulations and joys, but in the end what I hear is an insistence that people not be corralled into the meanings that historians rightfully believe they are called to search for. Instead people offer the satisfaction of sharing the human condition in its wondrous unpredictability. Just listen, and enjoy.

In fact, western history, more so than other subfields of the national narrative, can be approached as something akin to literature. The final section has to do with our unique blessing and, some would say, curse—that many millions of persons have been drawn to the West as a playground of the mass imagination. Other regions obviously have their place in popular culture, but none remotely approaches the West as a stylized setting for novels, films, songs, television series, and art. We speak of Westerns but not of Southerns and, Lord knows, not of Midwesterns. This has its frustrations, starting with the Sisyphean job of correcting popular clichés of the West and trying to convince readers and students that what really happened is so much more interesting than what they have grown up thinking. But there are advantages, too. The mythic West has been something like a screen on which the public has projected images and stories that express evolving values, beliefs, anxieties, hopes, and conceits. This fantasized West is worth studying exactly because it is so revealingly at odds with the real one.

"Bison R Us: The Buffalo as Cultural Icon" takes what is arguably the most distinctive western animal and follows it, not on any actual movements across the plains, but as it took on one meaning after another among an American people concocting their own identity and adapting it to the wild changes of their first century. Of those changes, none had greater consequences than expansion to the Pacific and the Civil War, and just as the two events resonated with one another in the matter of race, so they did as reflections of popular culture. I've long been puzzled why so many in my vicinity consider Jesse James a great hero despite all the evidence that shows him to have been a common (if uncommonly successful) thug. "Jesse James, Borderman" argues that James straddled two eras and two mythic traditions of the underdog. He was first portrayed as the oppressed southerner battling for the Lost Cause, then after his death he became one of the first of many western outlaw-heroes who stood against institutions, notably railroads and banks, vilified in the emerging industrial age.

Something a bit less obvious than bison and outlaws—trails, the seemingly simple lines across the land taken by those heading west—can also tell us something about Americans' evolving attitudes. "American

Pathways" looks at trails as mythic expressions, starting with the history of the word itself, and looks as well at how they can be exceptionally revealing of the historical West in all the old and tangled complexity I try to suggest in the first section. Their mythic weight has made trails and trailing an irresistible motif in hundreds of pulp Westerns. That's the case, too, in a recent and highly acclaimed case of a familiar western plot elevated to mass and critical success: the Pulitzer Prize winner by Larry McMurtry that is the focus of "On the Trail with Gus and Call: *Lonesome Dove* and the Western Myth." *Lonesome Dove,* however, is not simply a more nuanced telling of a traditional Western. Especially when read against the background of McMurtry's upbringing on a West Texas ranch, it is a richly mixed take on the western myth. Its power and emotional pang come from an affection for the pioneer dream and an admiration for the freedom and courage of frontier life mingled with an understanding that the dream and the life led all too often to pointless obsessions and an emotional deadening.

That hardened look at the mythic West of cattle drives, Texas Rangers, outlaws, Indian renegades, and good-hearted prostitutes leads to the final essay, "Stories." It's an encouragement to think about its topic as something more than things we tell and listen to for amusement. Some stories become historical forces. These are the ones that play out inside our heads and tell us who we are, where we have come from, how we fit among what is around us, and, through all of that, how we ought to act in the world. These are collective stories—myths in the word's most respectable meaning—and among Americans, the Western has been one of the most powerful. The Western's relation to the West of history, however, is complicated and in many ways both troubling and trouble-making. Fortunately, it has by no means been alone in shaping the West. There are other stories waiting to be heard, and as the West of the years touched on by these essays—that of French explorers and globe-trotting Osages, Indian empires and Indian wars, epidemics and the telegraph, iconic beasts and heroized killers—has evolved into the West of McMurtry and other children of the pioneers, those are the stories that can more fruitfully guide those of us who love the West for what it is and has been.

Conquest, families, myth: there has been so much to learn in and around these broad notions since I stumbled, blinking, out of graduate school forty years ago. Looking ahead, we can take heart that there will be plenty more to come. The Bancroft Prize is among the most prestigious in American history. Columbia University awards three each year to works of special quality and originality. Of the nine given from 2008 to 2010, five were in western history. More remarkable, four of the five were by younger scholars, and three of those were first books. The same years saw one of three Francis Parkman Prizes go to a western historian, again for a first book. The vitality of the field today is as undeniable as the excitement of its past quarter century. I envy those who will see the harvest of the generation ahead.

PART ONE
Conquest

Lewis and Park

Or, Why It Matters That the West's Most Famous Explorers Didn't Get Sick (or at Least Not *Really* Sick)

The Lewis and Clark expedition is one of the most overrated events in American history—and one of the most revealing. Meriwether Lewis and William Clark failed in their main assignment, to find a serviceable route to the Pacific. For most of the journey they simply followed rivers, which required no particular talent at exploration, and the one time they left them, they nearly starved. They did bring back a fine map, and they managed mostly good relations with Indian peoples, but anyone would be hard-pressed to argue that the expedition had the slightest immediate impact on much of anything, save for some fur trapping and trading. For a full century after its return the Corps of Discovery dropped out of our national awareness, partly because Lewis chalked up yet another failure. It was his job to compose an account of the great adventure, but in 1809 he committed suicide. Besides alcoholism, a failed romance, and possibly syphilis, one conjectured reason is terminal writer's block. Three years after his return to St. Louis, Lewis apparently had not put one word on paper.

Nonetheless, the expedition offers extraordinary insights into those years when our youthful nation was, paradoxically, both changing rapidly and coming into focus. Its story is a primer in imperial geopolitics. It takes us into the mind of the remarkable president who was curious in two senses of the word—hungry to learn about the unseen West, and driven by an odd mix of idealism, canny calculation, and voracious ambition. The captains' Indian encounters are revelations of Native life, and their misreadings of Native cultures anticipate the botched relations just ahead. The Lewis and Clark expedition might not have amounted to much when it happened, but as a wide window back onto its time, few

episodes can match it. Quite rightly, historians have given it as much attention as any event in western history.

One angle, however, has been mostly neglected. Its cue is what seems
an odd question: What problems did Lewis and Clark *not* face? Plenty
of answers (samurai warriors, king cobras) need no attention. One absent
danger, however, is worth a close look—disease. With one exception, the
men of the Corps survived their long journey without suffering much
more than fatigue and stomachaches. Partly that was a tribute to the captains as seat-of-their-pants doctors, but there is much more to learn than
that.[1] The Corps's freedom from diseases is especially revealing when the
expedition is set in its widest context, that of global discovery, exploration,
and colonization.

Among other things, that global context introduces a striking coincidence. As Lewis and Clark were moving to and from the Pacific, another
explorer on another continent was leading another expedition. Mungo
Park was a Scot physician, an accomplished naturalist, and an adventurer
already experienced in probing new lands. In 1795–97 he had captained an
expedition into the West African interior.[2] Malaria had nearly killed him
then, but when the British government asked him to return in 1805, he
agreed. His instructions were startlingly similar to Lewis's from Jefferson.
He too was to puzzle out the course of a great river and its relation to its
continent. The Niger is the third longest river in Africa (and almost exactly the same length as the Missouri, 2,590 versus 2,540 miles).[3] It passes
through what today is Senegal, Mali, Niger, and Nigeria, but although
Park had spent time on its upper reaches, no one in the West knew where
it went from there, nor even where it emerged into the Atlantic, so while
Lewis and Clark were told to find the Missouri's headwaters and the
easiest route from there to the Pacific, Park's order was to march back to
the upper Niger and follow it to its mouth. His other instructions were
virtually the same as those for the Corps. He was to observe the region's
resources. He was to open relations with the peoples he met and explore
the chance of trade with them and of English settlement.[4]

For the journey, Park assembled a crew of forty-four, eleven more than
Lewis and Clark's. Like the Corps, they were mostly soldiers, including
Park's surgeon brother-in-law, a few artisans, and a guide—like Saca-

gawea, a native to the area. On the last day of January 1805, while Lewis and Clark and their men were wintering at the Mandan and Hidatsa villages in present North Dakota, Park set sail from England for an island off the coast of Senegal. From there he was to strike out overland to the upper Niger and follow it back to the Atlantic. In one more parallel to Lewis and Clark, Park kept a journal, his from April to November 1805. For those seven months we can lay the accounts of the two expeditions side-by-side and follow the journeys, their trials, surprises, victories, and troubles day-by-day. Merely as serendipity, the parallel stories are a precious stroke of historian's luck. As insight into how empires were made, especially their shaping forces beyond human control, the paired journals are a revelation.

At the start the parallels continued, almost exact. On April 7, 1805, the Corps set off up the Missouri River from the Mandan villages. Lewis wrote that his men were "in excellent health and sperits [*sic*] . . . and anxious to proceed."[5] One day earlier Park had written the same of his crew as they departed their island garrison to start their own journey: "They jumped into the boats in the highest spirits, and bade adieu . . . with repeated huzzahs."[6] As the Corps paddled their canoes up the Missouri, Park and his crew made their landfall and began beating their way through dense jungle toward the Niger. That was when the two stories, so alike in so many other ways, began radically to diverge.

How they did, and why, can teach us plenty about the making of empires around the earth, including America's rise as a world power. More particularly, the twinned stories of Lewis and Park are reminders that the nation's prodigious growth in size, strength, and wealth came in part through outrageous strokes of luck. Those lessons hinge on the seemingly strange question of the threats unencountered by the West's most famous explorers, specifically infirmities beyond the aches and disorders peppered through accounts of the journey. Seeing the connection in turn calls for another sort of trip, a lengthy digression into how diseases have influenced the course of empires in the era of modern exploration.

Getting sick is a natural part of living, but when unusual numbers of persons fall ill in unusual ways, it can be a historical force. Epidemics have played roles in the shifting of civilizations from as far back as the record goes.[7] In the last thirty years historians have come to appreciate the crucial and awful part diseases played in the history of imperialism after 1492.[8] Their numbers thinned, their economies battered, their psyches shaken, New World natives put up far less resistance than they would have otherwise, easing the way of European expansion.[9] But this grim scenario, now part of any legitimate history of the world since Columbus, is oddly imbalanced. Some of history's most voracious killers have never gotten their historical due. This would have puzzled the empire builders at the time, including those who sent Lewis and Clark to the Pacific. They knew those devouring contagions, sometimes from afar, sometimes firsthand in their cities, their neighborhoods, their homes. All were properly impressed. Some were haunted.

Diseases of empire can be roughly divided into two types. Contact, or "crowd," diseases pass directly from person to person, usually via human bodily fluids, most commonly feces that contaminate water sources or tiny droplets of moisture coughed or sneezed out by one person and taken in by another. Contact diseases range from smallpox and cholera to HIV-AIDS and the common cold. The second sort, vector diseases, spread not directly but by mediators, usually insects, that carry a virus or parasite from one human or animal host to another. Examples are bubonic plague, Lyme disease, and West Nile virus, passed respectively by fleas, ticks, and mosquitoes. Vector diseases flourish especially well close to the equator where their insect carriers swarm year-round. Contact diseases are all over the place.

If vector diseases can be said to have a home turf, it would be Africa south of the Sahara Desert. Tropical Africa is humanity's birthplace. There humans and their hominid ancestors have spent the great majority of their time on earth, so it is there that the complicated relations among microbes, insects, and animals, including people, have had the scores of millennia needed to coevolve into their modern arrangements. Some vector diseases have remained at home. Trypanosomiasis, or sleeping sickness, transmitted via the tsetse fly, is found only in Africa south of the Sahara and north of South Africa. Others have made the jump to colonize other parts of the world.

Two of those have shaped profoundly the history of imperialism. Malaria, caused by a parasite of the genus *Plasmodium,* invades red blood cells and periodically bursts out, causing the famous bouts of high fever and bone-rattling chills. Of the four species of malaria, the two most common are *Plasmodium vivax* and *Plasmodium falciparum.* The first is debilitating but rarely fatal, but *P. falciparum,* which can obstruct the flow of blood to the brain, often kills its host. Its toll is especially high among infants. The vectors for malaria are mosquitoes, specifically about sixty of the nearly four hundred species of the genus *Anopheles.*[10]

The other vector disease important to the history of imperialism is yellow fever. Caused by a virus of the family Flaviviridae, it is also transmitted through mosquitoes, though only by one species, *Aedes egypti.* The virus attacks various organs but especially the liver, with the resulting jaundice giving the disease its common name. As the liver shuts down, its flow of blood is diverted elsewhere, much of it into the stomach, and when that organ's overtaxed vessels rupture, the victim regurgitates the blood—the source of another name for the disease, the "black vomit." Some victims feel only vague flulike symptoms, but mortality rates can range from 50 to 80 percent of those infected.[11]

For us humans, contact and vector diseases offer both bad news and good. Because we are the native homes of their pathogens, contact diseases go wherever we do, but because they can live *only* in us, we gain an advantage, too. Once a contact disease is gone from our bodies and from those of our neighbors, we have a safety zone around us. No one in a crowded auditorium need worry about getting the flu as long as nobody there has the flu. But not so with vector diseases. They get along fine without us, and consequently a person living alone, far from any other person, is still vulnerable. The next mosquito buzzing by might carry in its gut and saliva a yellow fever virus or malaria's parasite. But that problem is also an advantage. That third actor, the vector, is the only means the diseases have to make the jump to us. So even if someone in that crowded auditorium is dying from yellow fever, no one else has anything to worry about—as long as no *Aedes egypti* mosquitoes are flying through the crowd.

In thinking about empires, a couple of implications are obvious. Any contact disease among an empire-building people will go anywhere they go. Vector diseases, however, can colonize only where its vector can too. With yellow fever and malaria, that means only where the *Aedes egypti* and *Anopheles* mosquitoes can live and play their parts. There is a finer distinction. Mosquitoes, and therefore malaria and yellow fever, really get down to business only when the temperature rises above seventy degrees Fahrenheit and the humidity stays above 50 to 60 percent, and when the temperature drops below fifty degrees, they die or go dormant. So yellow fever and malaria can be endemic—always present, lurking, ready to strike—only in the tropics, earth's hot and muggy belt reaching twenty-three or so degrees of latitude on either side of the equator. In temperate regions, where temperatures swing with the seasons, the diseases can flare up, but only during the warmer months.

On the eve of modern empire making, there was another crucial distinction as to where diseases were and were not. As Columbus set sail from Spain, smallpox, cholera, influenza, malaria, yellow fever, and many other familiar modern maladies were exclusively in the Eastern Hemisphere. Because many contact diseases are variants of animal illnesses, they appeared only after people began living in close quarters with cattle, horses, chickens, and the rest of the modern barnyard—essentially during the most recent five to seven thousand years—and because New World peoples had very few domesticates, they had none of those spinoff illnesses. Vector diseases had appeared in Africa much earlier—the prototype of *vivax* malaria, for instance, may have appeared as early as three million years ago and its contemporary form two to three hundred thousand years ago—but they thinned out steadily to the north and never made it to the Arctic.[12] When the first immigrants to the Western Hemisphere crossed from Siberia to Alaska fifteen to eighteen thousand years ago, they left those insect-borne diseases behind.

Being free of the scourges on the other side of the Atlantic was a grand plus for residents of the Western Hemisphere—as long, that is, as the two hemispheres were not in contact. Meanwhile peoples of the Eastern Hemisphere were gaining a vital, painfully won advantage. Living with diseases can lead to two sorts of protections—acquired and innate immunities. By the first, anyone surviving a virus, such as measles or chickenpox or yellow fever, will not get it again, and because so many persons in the Old World had taken on such viruses as children, much of the adult population stayed well when diseases came around again. Surviving other maladies does not grant immunity, but with some, notably the malaria parasite, repeated bouts, especially when young, gives a person some resistance and weakens the impact of later doses.

Innate immunities are ingrained genetic defenses that evolve in a population over long spans of time. Once in place, they are part of each generation's biological equipment. Such protections are most apparent where people and diseases have coevolved the longest, in the tropics. Nearly all Africans below the Sahara, for instance, lack the "Duffy antigen," something found elsewhere in the walls of red blood cells. Its absence bars entrance to the *P. vivax* parasite, thus protecting "Duffy-negative" persons from one form of malaria. In tropical Africa and parts of Asia red blood cells evolved into the sickle cell, which blocks invasion of all forms of the malarial parasite in a considerable portion of the population. (Unfortunately, inheriting the sickle cell gene from both parents means a child will probably die before maturity due to anemia.) And although the evidence is hotly debated, sub-Saharan Africans also may have evolved some genetic resistance to yellow fever.[13]

So in 1492 one hemisphere was relatively free of contagions, while the other teemed with them, but exactly because the Old World had suffered so much for so long, its peoples, hardened veterans of the germ wars, had gained some protections, while the millions in the other half of the planet had none. Again, however, there was a distinction. People in the temperate Old World had less exposure than those in the tropics to the vector killers that had long plagued the steamy regions around the equator. Malaria's less malignant form, *P. vivax,* had spread its chills and fevers well to the north, including to the British Isles and northern Europe, but its much deadlier cousin, *P. falciparum,* had remained mostly in Africa. Yellow fever still has never appeared in Asia, and it had struck only occasionally in southernmost Europe.[14]

Think of zones. One, in temperate Europe, crawled with contact diseases. The other, in Africa between the Sahara and the Tropic of Capricorn, had plenty of those and was also rife with insect-borne vector diseases. Europeans and Africans had developed defenses against what was in their respective zones, but not necessarily against what was in the other, and consequently, when lines were crossed, bad things could happen.

The Portuguese made the earliest sustained European contact with sub-Saharan Africa, probing its western coast for possibilities in the mid-fifteenth century from what is today Senegal to the Bight of Benin on the coast of Togo, Benin, and Nigeria. They made overtures to African leaders and looked for openings for trade and colonies, but whatever promising futures they imagined, one fact offset everything else. If they tried even the slightest move into the interior, mysterious and relentless fevers would attack, gnawing at their numbers.[15] During the next four centuries European occupation was possible only along the coast, and even there the losses were appalling. Among British troops in Sierra Leone in the early nineteenth century, the annual death rate from malaria and yellow fever was 40 percent. Yellow fever outbreaks in 1825 and 1826 killed 86 and 73 percent of the British garrison. The mortality rate for Africans in the same area was less than 3 percent.[16] West Africa's reputation became that of "the white man's grave." A bit of soldier's doggerel summed it up:

> Beware and take care
> Of the Bight of Benin.
> One man comes out
> Where twenty goes in.

Tropical Africa, among the first potential candidates for European colonization, would be the last conquered.

Elsewhere conquest and colonization would come far more easily. Soon after the first Portuguese caravels skirted the West African coast, other voyagers crossed the Atlantic, and in less than a century Europeans had seated their empires in much of the Americas. There followed a massive migration from the Old World to the New, the greatest shuffling of human population in history. Nor were people the only things in movement. Voyages after 1492 brought together two hemispheres that might as well have been different planets, and once the connection was made, all sort of organisms moved back and forth across the Atlantic— horses and cattle, turkeys and tomatoes, rice, tobacco, earthworms, goats, and crabgrass. Some migration was microscopic—and deadly. As people moved, so did their maladies. The imbalance of global diseases, with so many more congregating in the Eastern Hemisphere, righted itself after the two worlds merged, with terrible consequences.

The story, however, was not simply one of a bunch of different germs moving east to west. Each of the two zones of Old World diseases, the temperate and the tropical, had its own history as it made the crossing. Together they shaped profoundly the course of empires, but they shaped different empires in different ways. Just how profoundly is suggested by following the Corps of Discovery as it poled its way up the Missouri River and into our national mythology. Just how differently is shown by following that other explorer, Mungo Park, as he moved down another river toward another fate.

Part of what happened when Old World diseases crossed the Atlantic is now well known, and it's not pretty. The Western Hemisphere held perhaps around fifty million people in 1492, isolated for thousands of years from the microbial killers that had spread across the other half of the world.[17] Then Columbus and other early explorers abruptly ended that isolation, as if puncturing a sterile protective sheath. Diseases poured in, colonizing native bodies and, as they had when they had first invaded Europeans, killing appalling portions of each group they met. Now, however, the diseases did not appear one at a time over millennia but roared in within decades. Mortality rates of each epidemic were as high as one in three persons. Invading pathogens were not the only cause of the disaster—their awful impact has to be understood as part of a complicated interaction with physical displacement, social and economic disruptions, and direct assaults by Europeans—but that they played a key role is unquestionable.[18] Estimates of the overall decline of the New World population vary from 50 or 60 to 95 percent between 1500 and 1900. If the lower rates are correct, the losses rivaled the worst horrors of the Old World. If the higher are true, it was the worst thing ever to happen in recorded human history.

Microbial invaders eased the way for their human counterparts. This happened everywhere in the Western Hemisphere, but historians tracking the epidemics have looked mostly at what Alfred Crosby calls "Neo-Europes"—North America, lower South America, and, in the colonized Eastern Hemisphere, South Africa and Australia—where European ethnic stocks, institutions, and economies would come to dominate. These historians focus there mostly on European contact diseases, among them measles, whooping cough, influenza, mumps, and worst of all, smallpox. As those epidemics did their awful work, biologically favored newcomers quickly took over. The country visited by Lewis and Clark, for instance, had been swept in 1780–81 by a smallpox epidemic that killed perhaps twenty-five thousand in the Pacific Northwest. Another hammered through in 1800. Yet another in 1837–38 nearly annihilated the Mandans and Hidatsas, who had hosted the Corps during its first winter, and broke the power of the Blackfeet, the only Indians the expedition fought during its journey.[19]

The usual story, that is, follows Europeans and their diseases as they left the temperate Old World, outward into empire. That is natural enough, since Europeans were the big players in the big picture. Theirs is not the whole story, however. The other disease zone, the tropical, also expanded. It played its own powerful role in empire making, including the creation of Neo-Europes. On North America's Atlantic Coast, for instance, malaria rooted with the first colonies, then made its way across the continent, eventually into the country visited by the Corps. A British ship visiting the Northwest Coast twenty-five years after Lewis and Clark brought what local Indians called the "cold sick." The epidemic killed many thousands from British Columbia south to California's Central Valley.[20]

Both disease zones have to be in the picture if we are to understand how empires emerged. More to the point, we have to consider both zones *together*. They interacted as they spread. They played off one another, both in the environments they invaded and in the minds of those who lived there. As empires spread across the globe, that interplay shaped them in unpredictable and, for all the story's grisliness, in highly interesting ways.

It happened from the start, in the hot regions where Europe first touched the New World. Contact diseases from the temperate zone first ravaged Caribbean peoples. Hispaniola was home to perhaps half a million Taino Indians when Columbus made landfall on his first voyage. By the 1530s smallpox, measles, and other epidemics, as well as economic disruption, overwork in goldfields, and outright slaughter, had virtually annihilated them.[21] It was the same throughout the West Indies. The Caribbean then might have become another Neo-Europe, as in temperate climates, but for an economic twist. Tropical America was found to be one of the best places anywhere to grow what became the world's most profitable crop—sugarcane.

Called by a seventeenth-century writer that "pleasant and profitable reed," sugarcane spread from India to much of Asia, the Middle East, and parts of Africa by the eighth century, and by the fourteenth century, sugar, the cane's crystallized and refined juices, had made it to Europe. Used at first as medicine and even a cosmetic, sugar soon assumed its obvious role as a sweetener, yet its limited production kept it beyond the reach of all but the uppermost European market. That changed when Europe bridged the Atlantic. In the West Indies, write two culinary historians, sugarcane "found . . . its climate of election and bloomed like a happy woman."[22] The first six loaves of Caribbean sugar arrived in Europe in 1516, brought by one of Spain's inspectors of gold mines—appropriately enough, given that its imperial income would rival that of precious metals.[23] Production sputtered until the mid-seventeenth century. Then innovations in cultivation and processing sent it soaring. The Portuguese, Dutch, French, and English converted the northeastern Brazilian coastal lowlands, coastal Suriname, and the islands of St. Domingue, Martinique, Barbados, and Jamaica into plantations. As its market price dropped, sugar became a common—and an insistently demanded—part of the European diet.[24]

The sugar industry's most nagging problem was labor. Work in the cane fields was brutal. British and European indentured servants met the need early on, but the trying conditions and the erratic availability of new workers led plantation owners to look elsewhere. Indians had been taken off the economic table by mistreatment and the devouring waves of contact diseases.[25] The obvious answer was to import African slaves, already impressed into sugar production on the other side of the Atlantic. Between 1676 and 1800 at least 426,000 Africans came to Barbados,

909,000 to Jamaica, 783,000 to St. Domingue. From the late sixteenth century to 1820, between 60 and 70 percent of all Africans brought in bondage to the New World were sent to work in the cane fields. The essential cause of the Atlantic slave trade, writes a leading historian of the topic, "was Europe's sweet tooth."[26]

Slaves brought more than their labor, however. In the blood they would shed in the New World they carried the ancient killers of sub-Saharan Africa.[27] Malaria arrived first. Once the malaria parasite is in someone's blood, it will stay there indefinitely, and because West and Central Africans had typically survived many bouts by adulthood, they carried the disease wherever they were taken. The New World also had plenty of anopheline mosquitoes to move the parasite around. As sugar cultivation spread, the deadly *P. falciparum* moved with it, eventually to virtually all the Caribbean world.[28]

Yellow fever doesn't travel so easily. A person can pass it to someone else only during its first three to five days in the bloodstream, before it attacks the liver and other organs, and because it is not a parasite but a virus, any survivor acquires immunity and is forever done with yellow fever—can't get it, can't give it away. The virus also requires as its vector that single mosquito species, the *Aedes egypti,* which was only in the Old World at the time of the Columbian contact. Thus three conditions were required for the fever to cross the Atlantic. Somebody boarding a ship had to have just taken it on. On board, there had to be enough uninfected persons for the virus to jump around and sustain itself during the voyage. And there had to be enough *A. egypti* mosquitoes on the ship and in America to pass the fever along.

We know when those conditions converged—in 1647 on a voyage to Barbados, the sugar island closest to the tropical disease zone.[29] At the end of that voyage someone, the active virus swimming through his veins, stepped ashore. *Aedes* mosquitoes were waiting—they had earlier crossed the Atlantic and spread through the Caribbean, doubtless by laying eggs and hatching in the water casks that every ship carried. Now one of them lit on the infected newcomer, sunk its proboscis into his flesh, and drank. Nine or ten days later (the virus has to incubate that long in a mosquito's gut) it did the same to some local. Like tumblers in a lock, the factors fell into place and the New World opened to one of history's most lethal organisms.

Outbreaks quickly began popping across the Caribbean—in Guadalupe, St. Kitts, and the Yucatan in 1648; in Cuba the next year; and perhaps in Jamaica in 1655. But who was dying? Very few Africans, who arrived with acquired immunity and perhaps with evolved resistance. Victims were overwhelmingly European whites—nearly six thousand in Guadalupe in 1648, a third of the white population, with the same proportion taken in Cuba the next year.[30] More than a dozen major epidemics occurred by the end of the century, every one with the same seemingly racial selection.[31] As yellow fever and *falciparum* swept away Europeans, the fearful news pinched off the flow of white immigrants.

The Caribbean's human makeup shifted again, nearly as sharply as after 1492. The white population of Antigua increased by only a quarter during the few generations after yellow fever appeared, and that of Jamaica shrank. Meanwhile Africans were arriving by the hundreds of thousands—from 1700 to 1810 nearly a million to Jamaica and Barbados alone. Even with the awful mortality rate in the cane fields, by the late eighteenth century the ratio of blacks to whites was often six or ten to one. In St. Domingue in 1789 it was fifteen to one.[32] Demographically, America's sugar colonies became Neo-Africas.

Tropical diseases were further encouraged by other involuntary arrivals—European soldiers and sailors sent to fight for what was now some of the most valuable real estate on earth. Besides offering new blood for the *falciparum* parasite, the military ranks were especially vital for yellow fever. Because it moves person to person through such a tiny window of time, it needs lots of fresh bodies to make an epidemic. After its initial Caribbean ravages, yellow fever often retreated for long stretches until some island acquired enough uninfected persons to set it off again. A European army was a sudden abundance, thousands of corporal colonies waiting to be invaded. In an early instance yellow fever reduced a British squadron occupying St. Lucia in 1665 from fifteen hundred to eighty-nine men.[33] The pattern was repeated over and over in the next century. In failed assaults on Cuba in 1741 and 1762 the British lost 40 to 50 percent of their troops to disease, and the military's annual mortality rate in Jamaica twenty years later was reportedly 25 percent.[34] Early on, Europeans had devastated New World populations by introducing their temperate contact diseases to the "virgin soil" of indigenous peoples. Now similar epidemics raged through the Caribbean, but instead of bringing their own diseases into new terrain, Europe gathered up its own virgin soil, the bodies of its own fighting men, and sent it to the diseases.

That irony was part of a larger one. Kept out of Africa by its fevers (and often by fierce resistance), Europeans conquered and colonized the New World. Then, needing workers to replace Indians killed off by their contagions, they brought in slaves, thereby importing the same killing fevers that denied them an African foothold. Moved by the sweet seduction of the sugar trade, European imperialists themselves carried their great global enemy, the tropical disease zone, into the New World. They made of some of their most valued conquests another "white man's grave."

From Caribbean epidemics to Lewis and Clark—it seems quite a stretch, but it's not. For one thing, that other expedition, faraway and deep in the tropical zone, offers an illuminating perspective on the famous American odyssey. There was also a more immediate link between tropical diseases and the journey of the Corps. Recall the state of the Atlantic world and its leaders' state of mind. The political map on both sides of the ocean was as fluid as it ever would be, and of the many questions, none was more unsettled than who would command the North American West. Jefferson and those around him looked toward that West, and in Lewis and Clark they would put in their bid. But they looked southward too, not with ambition but with unease. They were well aware of Caribbean invasions and rebellions, the social churn, and the death scything, and they wondered how that turmoil might spill into their own world. Displaced Africans might bring dangerous ideas to American slaves, for instance.

And what of infections to the south, the tropical fevers? Their killing did not stop with the tens of thousands in the Caribbean. They struck often along the southern and middle Atlantic coast, the Gulf Coast, and the great river that was the nation's western border. Yellow fever arose in Mobile and Pensacola in 1765. It may have arrived in New Orleans as early as 1739, probably was there in the 1760s, and was definitely the epidemic that killed about 6 percent of the city and as many as one in four non-Creole whites in 1796.[35] It would ravage the Mississippi Valley during the next century. Its devastating visit to Memphis in 1878 would be the worst epidemic in American history. No one knew where these scourges had come from or how they spread. No one knew the extent of where they were or where they might still go. Everybody, however, knew how they could turn the course of empires this way or that.

So tropical epidemics were part of Lewis and Clark's expedition—if nothing else, as they played on the thoughts of the men who sent them out. Even before the captains left, in fact, Africa's invisible killers had given the journey a new meaning. When Congress authorized the expedition in 1803, the United States stopped at the Mississippi River. The country beyond had passed from France to Spain in 1763, then back to Napoleonic France in 1800. Two months after Thomas Jefferson asked Congress to fund his expedition to the Pacific, his agents in Paris signed the treaty for the Louisiana Purchase, defined essentially as the Mississippi's western watershed. A year later, barely two months before the captains started up the Missouri in May 1805, France officially transferred Louisiana to the United States. Instead of a trip onto foreign turf, the expedition now was to map and describe an enormous portion of the republic that no citizen had ever seen. Napoleon's decision to sell Louisiana turned the expedition into an act of national definition.

He decided to sell in part for the cash he would need in a looming war with England, but just as compelling was the collapse of his dream of a new American empire. Around 1800 Napoleon had hatched an audacious plan to reestablish a French presence rivaling what had been lost in 1763. That was why he reacquired Louisiana from Spain, but the heart of his dream was St. Domingue, today the nation of Haiti. By the 1780s it was the world's leading producer of sugar—and a classic Neo-Africa, with half a million blacks and barely thirty thousand whites. Louisiana's role was to be subsidiary to St. Domingue's, growing food to feed the workers on the "Pearl of the Antilles."[36]

First, however, Napoleon had to deal with a familiar problem—labor. Plenty of workers were there, but they were free, and so not fully dependable. The revolutionary French Assembly had abolished slavery in 1794, but behind emancipation was a stubborn independence movement led by the extraordinary Toussaint L'Ouverture. Playing French, Spanish, and British forces against one another, he had led campaigns that eventually controlled both St. Domingue and its island neighbor, Spain's Santo Domingo. If Napoleon was to make of St. Domingue his envisioned cash cow, he would have to reestablish French command and (although he never used the term) reinstate slavery.

To that end he sent an army of more than thirty thousand prime troops under his brother-in-law, Charles LeClerc. It landed in early 1802, and by military thrusts and playing on opposition to L'Ouverture, LeClerc controlled St. Domingue within a few months. Then came the June rains. What followed was the same as if LeClerc's army had invaded Senegal or Nigeria. Yellow fever quickly began to hobble, then cripple, the reconquest. Fifteen thousand soldiers died in two months. An officer wrote of troops dying "by the hundreds daily, like dogs, like flies, they disappear unaccountably." By October 80 percent of the troops and 60 percent of their officers, including LeClerc, were dead.[37] Napoleon sent still more men and turned to a war of terror, but it was no use. Recognizing that the disaster had dashed his American dreams, strapped for funds and on the edge of war, Napoleon gave it all up and offered Jefferson's envoys all of Louisiana for pennies an acre.

It was a stunning moment. The master of Europe pulled out of the New World. The New World's newest nation, Haiti, indirectly compelled Napoleon to hand an unasked gift to the hemisphere's second-newest nation. Aided by Caribbean patriots and *aedes* mosquitoes, the United States doubled its size and gained who-knew-what. We know now that it was a crucial step in the decline of one empire and the rise of another.

We know this, however, only by looking back, which leaves us blinkered to the perspective at the time. For the new nation's leaders, the hopeful moment was also full of uncertainty, including fears of diseases that had played so prominently in the American story so far. Fevers in the hot zone had just handed them an incalculable opportunity. But what if those same plagues should turn on them in their own new country? The republic's leaders had watched an epidemic humble the seemingly invincible Napoleon. It was natural to wonder what was in store for them.

Chief wonderer was Benjamin Rush, a founding father and the republic's leading physician. At Jefferson's request Rush gave Lewis a crash
course as a field scientist and doctor, supplied practical health tips (wash
your feet, wear shoes without heels, lie down when tired), prepared questions the Corps should answer about the new country, and assembled a
medicine chest to cope with dangers he thought might await.[38] Tropical
fevers in the West were clearly in his thinking. No American, in fact,
was more likely to have an eye cocked for the scourges that had dropped
Louisiana into his country's lap. By the time he met with Lewis, Rush
had become a well-published authority on medical theory, on tropical
diseases generally, and on yellow fever in particular.[39]

Rush's interest extended well beyond the academic. He lived in the
nation's largest city and its former capital, Philadelphia. Yellow fever had
struck there in 1793, carried in by refugees from the war of independence
in Santo Domingo—one more reminder of how the two disease zones
could overlap. Most of the city's fifty-five thousand residents had fled.
Five thousand of the rest had died.[40] Rush had stayed. He treated up
to a hundred and fifty persons between each dawn and midnight with
methods that included wrapping victims in vinegar-soaked blankets and
dashing them with buckets of ice water.[41] Between visits he had worked
with city fathers to control the epidemic, but it had raged unabated from
mid-August until early November, often devouring more than a hundred a day. Rush's wife and sons were away, but his sister was with him.
She died. So did three of his five assistants and many close friends and
their families. Rush was devastated. In wrenching letters to his wife and
friends he poured out his frustrations and confessed to "the gloom which
now oppresses every power of my soul."[42] The next year he published a
memoir of the plague, followed by annual accounts of lesser recurrences
through 1804. For the rest of his life he would wrestle with what he might
have done to blunt the horrors of those three months in 1793.[43]

In 1805, the year Lewis and Clark reached the Pacific, Rush published
his fullest word on yellow fever and on fevers generally.[44] Three conclusions are crucial. The fevers were not imported, he wrote, but home-grown
from local sources. Second, they were not contagious. They were not, that
is, what later would be called contact diseases. Rush did not guess that

they were transmitted through insects—nobody would argue that for generations—but rather that they were acquired from local conditions like miasmas, the "bad air" that gave the name to malaria (*mal aria*). Finally, fevers were best treated by bleeding and by intestinal purging with laxatives. That treatment followed from a new theory of disease. It argued that a body threatened by any malevolence, whether extreme cold or heat, or miasma, or even some moral deviance, responded with a "morbid excitement" of veins and arteries. A doctor's job was to calm that agitation by aggressive bleeding and, because the circulatory and digestive systems were thought to be directly related, by thoroughly flushing the victim, input to output.[45]

Already leaning toward that new approach in 1793, Rush had fully embraced it during the grim autumn of Philadelphia's plague. On his dozens of daily rounds he drew off hundreds of gallons of blood—he once relieved a patient of seventy-five ounces in a day, nearly half the volume of an adult body—and sent untold effluvia into the city's waste.[46] He also earned the wrath of fellow physicians who took a minimalist approach of broths, baths, and rest. One called Rush's regimen "one of those great discoveries that are made from time to time for the depopulation of the earth."[47]

The critics were right. Bleeding and purging an overstressed victim made as much sense as opening portholes on a foundering ship. But while nobody struck today by yellow fever should follow Rush's advice, his ideas still have a lot to teach us. They are the backdrop to the way he prepared the Corps for their journey, and provide the code to deciphering the doctor's thoughts and fears—about what had just fallen to the republic and what might be out there, waiting to pounce.

Since he believed the ferocious fevers were domestic, not imported, Rush would have suspected them in any place where local conditions inspired them, which seemed just about anywhere. Besides marsh gasses and stagnant water, he thought yellow fever could spring from straw, duck ponds, old tent canvas, rawhide, locusts, coffee, mint, wet paper money, or cabbage.[48] Because he believed fevers were not contagious, he would not have worried about the Corps passing them among themselves, but each man still would be independently vulnerable to multiple threats (sleeping in an old tent? wading with money in rawhide boots?) bound to crop up while crossing the continent. Rush must have figured the odds were strong that the explorers would meet some malignance like what had upended his life at home.

Rush sent them off well armed. In the medicine chest were a tourniquet and three of the "best lancets" for his favored remedy of bleeding. Among the several curatives, the most expensive item—at thirty dollars, a third of the entire cost—was fifteen pounds of "Peruvian bark." This was the powdered bark of the cinchona tree, found in the seventeenth century to be a near-magical antidote to both *vivax* and *falciparum* malaria. In the 1830s chemists would isolate quinine, the most powerful of cinchona's four curative alkaloids, but in Rush's day the powdered bark was the drug at hand wherever malaria thrived, as in the middle Mississippi and lower Missouri Valleys where Lewis and Clark began their journey.[49] How far west from there malaria reached—that nobody knew. Rush was guarding against the worst. Among the other items the Corps carried, including salves and eyewash, most were dedicated to purging. There was ipecac and tartar emetic to induce vomiting and mercury for salivating, but the main components were the powerful laxatives calomel, jalap, sodium sulfate, and magnesia, and just in case those didn't do the trick, an enema syringe.[50]

The prime weapon, however, was a stash of six hundred "Bilious Pills of Dr. Rush." Each was about four times the size of one of today's aspirin. Each contained ten grains of calomel and ten to fifteen of jalap. Calomel is mercury chloride, jalap a concoction from the root of a Mexican plant. Each alone is a powerful laxative, and when taken together in the pills' hefty dose, the spectacular result earned them the nickname "Rush's Thunderclappers." Given the large number—at five dollars for the six hundred, they were literally a dime a dozen—Rush surely meant the pills as something of a cure-all, and on the trip west the captains doled out these depth charges of the food tube for any intestinal distress.[51]

The pills' history, however, shows they were born with a particular focus. Early in the 1793 epidemic, Rush had come across a paper on yellow fever arguing that purging was "more necessary in this than in most other fevers." Immediately he began experimenting with laxative combinations, and on September 13 he published the results in *Dunbar's American Daily Advertiser.* He advised, at the onset of symptoms, a periodic dose of what, eleven years later, would be packed, fifty-dozen strong, for Lewis and Clark—a powder "consisting of ten grains of Calomel and fifteen grains of Jalap." Thus the Thunderclapper debuted under the headline "Dr. Rush's Directions for Curing and Preventing the YELLOW FEVER."[52]

Rush and others feared any number of diseases out west, of course, including smallpox. The captains were given lymphatic material from cowpox to treat any Indians suffering from it.[53] Rush made no distinction, however, between the scourges all too common in the temperate world and those of the tropics, and he sometimes seemed near-obsessed with the fevers that burned through the turbulent colonies to the south, that struck the republic's semitropical borderlands, and that reached as far north as his beloved Philadelphia. At one point he was quite specific. Jefferson had asked Rush what they most needed to know about the unseen West, that "of which it is most desirable [Lewis] should bring us information." Rush came up with twenty-two questions. The first ten were on health and medicine. Heading the list was this one, ending with a reference to yellow fever's notorious final symptom: "What are the acute diseases of the Indians? Is the bilious fever ever attended with a black vomit?"[54]

The answer was "no." Rush had no reason to fear that Lewis and Clark would be laid low by yellow fever or anything else tropical. But in a wider sense he was right on the mark. Out of his confused nightmare Rush understood what too many historians do not—that Old World diseases all flooded the New World together, all in a jumble, and even when they stayed physically apart, they still bled into each other through their influences and in the minds of men in power.

Diseases were the first true agents of globalization, the first grand unifiers. They scrambled outward from their nests, riding along with and ahead of explorers and the ever-greater, ever-swifter movement of peoples, creating what the French historian Emmanuel Le Roy Ladurie called "a 'common market' of microbes."[55] They connected Parisian sugar bowls with wars of liberation, blistering death on the Puget Sound with pock-marked Londoners, the Bight of Benin with Lewis and Clark's laxatives. But while they could tangle the history of any part of the world with any other—Napoleon's unloading of Louisiana, projecting the United States toward the Pacific, and changing the meaning of the Corps of Discovery may be colonial history's starkest example—diseases also treated each place differently. They left different prints across the world; they shaped each empire in a particular way; and in its rise as a continental empire, the United States was grimly blessed. Contact diseases, allies of the invaders from the beginning, kept at it all the way to the Pacific, easing the path of conquest, while the tropical fevers, contagions that were as likely to kill white conquerors as Indians, fell away. Most of the West was malaria free, and yellow fever rarely if ever struck west of Arkansas.[56] The nation, that is, expanded alongside its microbial best friends, while its worst enemies, even as they were crippling the competition to the south, gave it a free pass. To a cold imperial eye, the country Lewis and Clark were entering was the best of all worlds.

Which brings us at last, at the end of the digressive trip among global epidemics, back to the other expedition unfolding coincident with the famous journey of the Corps of Discovery. We last saw Mungo Park and his crew of forty-four as they set off with "repeated huzzahs" into the West African interior, slashing their way toward the upper Niger River. Their story, so stunningly like that of Lewis and Clark's in its origins, purposes, and early unfolding, here veered sharply away. While Lewis and Clark saw not a single Indian from April until mid-August, Park's route was well populated with Africans who stole whatever they could—donkeys, cattle, supplies, and, once, all the clothes off an ill soldier. Lewis and Clark had their thirty-eight grizzlies, but Park faced countless crocodiles, one of which attacked and nearly ate his guide, and scores of "wolves" (probably jackals). Three lions once came at Park, hissing like giant tabbies, and at night his men fended off others with swords. While the Corps complained often of gnats and mosquitoes, on May 26 a vast swarm of bees attacked Park's camp, driving everyone into the underbrush, stinging two asses to death, and nearly "put[ting] an end to our journey."[57]

The greatest difference was what no one could see—the microbes threatening each expedition. Besides one death from either a ruptured appendix or blood poisoning, the Corps suffered bellyaches and diarrhea, occasional fevers, boils, skin infections, and other ailments expected from exposure and a long, stressful journey.[58] Park and his men faced something more as they moved into the jungle, deeper every day, at the onset of the rainy season. On June 18 near the Missouri's Great Falls Lewis reported that Sacagawea was slightly ill but was improving. Half a world away Park was boiling a kettle full of cinchona (Peruvian bark) for his men, half of them already down with fever. The first fever death had come ten days earlier, another would occur ten days later. Clark complained on July 6 of a pounding by hail the size of musket balls, while Park wrote of his guide recovering from the crocodile attack and every man but one being either sick or weakened to the point of collapse.[59] By now his men, often delirious, were falling behind, wandering off into the torrential rains or simply lying down and refusing to rise. Some would eventually turn up in the evening's camp. Others did not. On July 27, on the upper reaches of the Jefferson River, Clark suffered his worst bout of illness, with high fever and aches. He took five of Rush's pills (one can only imagine the claps of thunder) and a few days later was much better. On the 27th, four of Park's men dropped away. He never saw them again.[60]

By the time Park reached the Niger, on August 19, his party had dwindled from forty-four to eleven. As they moved downstream, the expedition unraveled. On October 2, when Clark had "nothing to eate but roots" in Nez Perce country, two of Park's men died in a village on the Niger, and that night jackals dragged one of the bodies into the brush and ate it.[61] By the time Park reached the town of Sansanding, not yet a third of the way down the Niger, only four men besides himself remained. One was insane. Park lashed canoes together into a boat with a sail, christened it the *Joliba* (the local name for the river), and set off for the Atlantic on November 19. Before leaving, he handed his homeward-bound guide his journal and letters to his wife and patron. To the latter he noted the "horror" of the rainy season, "extremely fatal to Europeans," but, using a phrase identical to Clark's the previous June as he had looked uncertainly ahead from the Great Falls, Park swore to discover the mouth of the Niger "or perish in the attempt." About a thousand miles later, probably about the time the Corps were beginning their return from Fort Clatsop, the *Joliba* hung up on some rocks as locals rained spears and arrows from shore. Park and the others hesitated briefly, then stepped off into the rapids and were swept away and drowned.[62]

The classic medical history of Lewis and Clark's expedition is Eldon Chinaud's *Only One Man Died*.[63] A comparable book about Park's might be titled *Nobody Made It*. The different endings were not a matter of leadership. Park was seasoned, savvy, determined, intelligent, and brave. He was equally able and more experienced than Lewis and Clark. Support was not his problem. His men were amply provisioned and well armed and backed by a government that, to put it mildly, knew something about expanding an empire. The difference was not in the leaders or what they had or what they did. It was in where they went and what was there. Lewis and Clark departed from St. Louis. That was on the 40th parallel, as far north as the worst of the tropical disease zone normally reached, and the farther they went, the farther behind they left the murderous afflictions so feared by Rush. Mungo Park left the temperate safety of England and sailed thirty-five degrees southward, deep into the zone the captains were escaping; then he marched right into its fevered heart.

Without venturing too far into "what if" history—a journey that for historians can be as treacherous as Park's—it is worth reflecting on how differently things would have gone in western and national history if Lewis and Clark had found themselves facing the kind of menace that finally left the remarkable Scot stepping off the *Joliba* into the churning Niger. The fur trade, gold and silver rushes, the overland migration, the building of transcontinental railroads, the rise and spread of ranching, the flood of farmers, and the vigorous sprout of towns and all those events sometimes trumpeted as evidence of America's unique go-get-'em spirit and thus of its rightful claim to the continent—something like that might have happened eventually, but maybe not, and if so, it would have been at a tortuous pace and at an incalculably greater human cost, and much of the West might well have been populated by slaves and others of African descent. The rise of the American empire, when we see it together with the stumbling and falling of others, has less to do with destiny than with biology and bugs.

In no way, of course, should this lessen our respect for the abilities, persistence, and courage of the captains and their men. It does, however, matter that none of the Corps, save one, got really sick. Asking "why not" is an invitation into a larger perspective. Answering is a reminder of why the expedition continues to enthrall us. It may have shifted only slightly the nation's course, but it can teach us so much about its time. The more we pull away to a wider view—in this case including Lewis and Park as well as Lewis and Clark—the more this great American story pushes outward our understanding of an extraordinary time in national and global history.

Notes

1. Two works consider the medical aspects of the expedition: Eldon G. Chuinard, *Only One Man Died: The Medical Aspects of the Lewis and Clark Expedition* (Glendale, Calif.: Arthur H. Clark Company, 1979), and David J. Peck, *Or Perish in the Attempt: Wilderness Medicine in the Lewis and Clark Expedition* (Helena, Mont.: Farcountry Press, 2002).

2. Park wrote a commercially successful account of those years. A recent edition is Mungo Park, *Travels in the Interior Districts of Africa,* ed. Kate Ferguson Marsters (Durham, N.C.: Duke University Press, 2000).

3. Kenneth Lupton, *Mungo Park, the African Traveler* (New York: Oxford University Press, 1979); Stephen Gwynn, *Mungo Park and the Quest of the Niger* (New York: G. P. Putnam's Sons, 1935).

4. Mungo Park, *The Journal of a Mission to the Interior of Africa, In the Year 1805* (Philadelphia: Edward Earle, 1815), 37–38, 51–52.

5. Gary E. Moulton, ed., *The Definitive Journals of Lewis and Clark: From Fort Mandan to Three Forks* (Lincoln: University of Nebraska Press, 2002), 4:10.

6. Park, *Journal of a Mission to the Interior of Africa,* 57.

7. The early classic study is William H. McNeill, *Plagues and Peoples* (Garden City, N.Y.: Anchor Press, 1976).

8. One remarkable essay was most influential in encouraging the effort: Henry F. Dobyns, "Estimating Aboriginal American Population: An Appraisal of Techniques with a New Hemispheric Estimate," *Current Anthropology* 7 (1966): 395–416, 425–49.

9. A few of the many useful works synthesizing the enormous literature on the topic: Noble David Cook, *Born to Die: Disease and New World Conquest, 1492–1650*

(Cambridge: Cambridge University Press, 1998); Ann F. Ramenofsky, Alicia K. Wilbur, and Anne C. Stone, "Native American Disease History: Past, Present and Future," *World Archeology,* 35:2 (October 2003): 258–75; Michael R. Haines and Richard S. Steckel, eds., *A Population History of North America* (Cambridge: Cambridge University Press, 2000). For a critique of the methods some have used to calculate the losses, see David P. Henige, *Numbers from Nowhere: The American Indian Population Debate* (Norman: University of Oklahoma Press, 1998).

10. A fine, accessible recent work on malaria is James L. A. Webb, *Humanity's Burden: A Global History of Malaria* (Cambridge: Cambridge University Press, 2009). See also Margaret Humphreys, *Malaria: Poverty, Race, and Public Health in the United States* (Baltimore: Johns Hopkins University Press, 2001), esp. chapter 1.

11. George K. Strobe, ed., *Yellow Fever* (New York: McGraw-Hill, 1951); James L. Dickerson, *Yellow Fever: A Deadly Disease Poised to Kill Again* (Amherst, N.Y.: Prometheus Books, 2006); Margaret Humphreys, *Yellow Fever and the South* (Baltimore: Johns Hopkins University Press, 1992); John R. Pierce and Jim Writer, *Yellow Jack: How Yellow Fever Ravaged America and Walter Reed Discovered Its Deadly Secrets* (Hoboken, N.J.: John Wiley & Sons, 2005).

12. Webb, *Humanity's Burden,* 20–21.

13. R. Carter and K. N. Mendis, "Evolutionary and Historical Aspects of the Burden of Malaria," *Clinical Microbiology Review* 15 (2002): 564–94; Webb, *Humanity's Burden,* 21–27. For an exchange of views on possible innate immunity to yellow fever, see Sheldon Watts, "Yellow Fever Immunities in West Africa and the Americas in the Age of Slavery and Beyond: A Reappraisal"; Kenneth F. Kiple, "Response to Sheldon Watts, 'Yellow Fever Immunities in West Africa and the Americas in the Age of Slavery and Beyond: A Reappraisal'; and Sheldon Watts, "Response to Kenneth Kiple," *Journal of Social History* 34:4 (2001): 955–67, 969–74, 975–76.

14. William Coleman, *Yellow Fever in the North: The Methods of Early Epidemiology* (Madison: University of Wisconsin Press, 1987). In Europe the fever struck in southern France and Spain and once, remarkably but briefly, in Wales.

15. Two Portuguese voyages, 1454–58, by Alvise Cadamosto and Diogo Gomez, make the point. Each made forays up the Gambia River, but each was forced quickly to withdraw when his men soon sickened from fevers and many died. Richard Henry Major, *The Discoveries of Prince Henry the Navigator and Their Results; Being the Narrative of the Discovery by Sea, Within One Century, of More than Half the World* (London: Sampson Low, Marston, Searle, and Rivington, 1877), 160–77.

16. Philip D. Curtin, *Disease and Empire: The Health of European Troops in the Conquest of Africa* (Cambridge: Cambridge University Press, 1998), 8, 15. See also Philip D. Curtin, *Death by Migration: Europe's Encounter with the Tropical World in the Nineteenth Century* (Cambridge: Cambridge University Press, 1989);

Philip D. Curtin, "'The White Man's Grave': Image and Reality, 1780–1850," *Journal of British Studies* 1:1 (November 1961): 94–110.

17. For an excellent treatment of the continuing vigorous argument over the New World population at the time of the Columbian landfall, see Suzanne Austin Alchon, *A Pest in the Land: New World Epidemics in a Global Perspective* (Albuquerque: University of New Mexico Press, 2003), 147–72. Her own conclusion puts the number at between 46,800,000 and 53,800,000.

18. Recent work has begun to complicate nicely earlier views that attributed the population collapse almost wholly to "virgin soil" epidemics. See especially Alchon, *Pest in the Land,* and David S. Jones, "Virgin Soils Revisited," *William and Mary Quarterly,* 3rd Series, 60:4 (October 2003): 703–42, and David S. Jones, *Rationalizing Epidemics: Meanings and Uses of American Indian Mortality since 1600* (Cambridge, Mass.: Harvard University Press, 2004). For a promising application of these new approaches to one area, see Paul Kelton, *Epidemics and Enslavement: Biological Catastrophe in the Native Southeast, 1492–1715* (Lincoln: University of Nebraska Press, 2007).

19. Elizabeth A. Fenn, *Pox Americana: The Great Smallpox Epidemic of 1775–82* (New York: Hill & Wang, 2001), 200–23; Robert Boyd, *The Coming of the Spirit of Pestilence: Introduced Infectious Diseases and Population Decline among the Northwest Coast Indians, 1774–1874* (Seattle: University of Washington Press, 1999), chapters 2, 4, and 9; Robert Boyd, "Smallpox in the Pacific Northwest: The First Epidemics," *BC Studies* 101:1 (Spring 1994): 5–40; Clyde D. Dollar, "The High Plains Smallpox Epidemic of 1837–38," *Western Historical Quarterly* 8:1 (January 1977): 15–38.

20. Boyd, *Coming of the Spirit of Pestilence,* 84–115, 242–44. Boyd's estimate of a death rate of 88 percent in four years seems unlikely, but the toll was clearly horrifyingly high.

21. Irving Rouse, *The Tainos: Rise and Decline of the People Who Greeted Columbus* (New Haven: Yale University Press, 1992); Samuel M. Wilson, *Hispaniola: Caribbean Chiefdoms in the Age of Columbus* (Tuscaloosa: University of Alabama Press, 1990), esp. 94–110.

22. Georges and Germaine Blond, quoted in Waverly Root, *Food: An Authoritative, Visual History and Dictionary of the Foods of the World* (New York: Simon & Schuster, 1980), 490.

23. W. R. Aykroyd, *Sweet Malefactor: Sugar, Slavery and Human Society* (London: Heinemann, 1967), 15. Columbus himself, whose father-in-law owned a sugar plantation in Madeira, tried unsuccessfully to establish one on Hispaniola.

24. Among the several recent works on the history of sugar and the sugar trade, see, especially, Peter Macinnis, *Bittersweet: The Story of Sugar* (London: Orion, 2002); Ulbe Bosma, *Sugarlandia Revisited: Sugar and Colonialism in Asia and the Americas, 1800 to 1940* (New York: Berghahn Books, 2007); Sidney W. Mintz, *Sweetness and Power: The Place of Sugar in Modern History* (New York: Pen-

guin, 1986); Richard B. Sheridan, *Sugar and Slavery: An Economic History of the British West Indies, 1623–1775* (Baltimore: Johns Hopkins University Press, 1974).

25. Russell R. Menard, *Sweet Negotiations: Sugar, Slavery, and Plantation Agriculture in Early Barbados* (Charlottesville: University of Virginia Press, 2006), 29–48.

26. David Eltis, "The Volume and Structure of the Transatlantic Slave Trade: A Reassessment," *William and Mary Quarterly,* 3rd Series, 58:1 (January 2001): 44–45; Robert William Fogel, *Without Consent or Contract: The Rise and Fall of American Slavery* (New York: W. W. Norton, 1989), 18. African slaves first arrived in the Caribbean with the earlier attempts at sugar production on Hispaniola. By 1524 they outnumbered Indians there, and sixteen years later they had all but replaced them. Rouse, *The Tainos,* 158. This first try at sugar cultivation did not prosper.

27. For a recent, superb study of the transfer of African diseases to the Caribbean and their role in the imperial struggle there, see John Robert McNeill, *Mosquito Empires: Ecology and War in the Greater Caribbean, 1620–1914* (Cambridge: Cambridge University Press, 2010). Because contact diseases were common in the tropical zone as well, African slaves brought them, too, including the worst of them, smallpox. Slaves apparently were the primary means of the pox's transmission to Brazil. Dauril Alden and Joseph C. Miller, "Out of Africa: The Slave Trade and the Transmission of Smallpox to Brazil, 1560–1831," in Robert I. Rotberg, ed., *Health and Disease in Human History: A* Journal of Interdisciplinary History *Reader* (Cambridge, Mass.: MIT Press, 2000), 203–30.

28. Webb, *Humanity's Burden,* 69–79. Oddly, Barbados had no anopheline mosquitoes, and so no malaria, until well into the nineteenth century.

29. Yellow fever possibly appeared before 1647, but the evidence is unclear. See McNeill, *Mosquito Empires,* 61n.

30. Kenneth F. Kiple and Brian T. Higgins, "Yellow Fever and the Africanization of the Caribbean," in John W. Verano and Douglas H. Ubelaker, eds., *Disease and Demography in the Americas* (Washington, D.C.: Smithsonian Institution Press, 1992), 241.

31. The selection was not truly racial. The Africans who did not come down with yellow fever were spared not by any racial component but by prior exposure and perhaps by some genetic protection that other Africans lacked.

32. Karen Ordahl Kupperman, "Fear of Hot Climates in the Anglo-American Experience," *William and Mary Quarterly,* 3rd Series, 41:2 (April 1984): 213–40; Kiple and Higgins, "Yellow Fever and the Africanization of the Caribbean," 241; J. H. Galloway, *The Sugar Cane Industry: An Historical Geography from Its Origins to 1914* (Cambridge: Cambridge University Press, 1989), 114; Kenneth F. Kiple and Kriemhild Contee Ornelas, "Race, War and Tropical Medicine in the Eighteenth-Century Caribbean," in David Arnold, ed., *Warm Climates and Western Medicine: The Emergence of Tropical Medicine, 1500–1900* (Amsterdam: Rodopi, 1996), 68.

33. John R. Pierce and Jim Writer, *Yellow Jack: How Yellow Fever Ravaged America and Walter Reed Discovered Its Deadly Secrets* (Hoboken, N.J.: John Wiley & Sons, 2005), 14.

34. Kiple and Ornelas, "Race, War and Tropical Medicine," 68–69.

35. Jo Ann Carrigan, *The Saffron Scourge: A History of Yellow Fever in Louisiana, 1796–1905* (Lafayette: University of Southwestern Louisiana, 1994), 18, 26.

36. E. Wilson Lyon, *Louisiana in French Diplomacy* (Norman: University of Oklahoma Press, 1934), 112–18.

37. C. L. R. James, *The Black Jacobins: Toussaint Louverture and the San Domingo Revolution* (New York: Dial Press, 1938), 294. On these events, see also Laurent Dubois, *Avengers of the New World: The Story of the Haitian Revolution* (Cambridge, Mass.: Belknap Press of Harvard University Press, 2004), and Thomas O. Ott, *The Haitian Revolution, 1789–1804* (Knoxville: University of Tennessee Press, 1973).

38. George W. Corner, ed., *The Autobiography of Benjamin Rush: His "Travels Through Life," Together with His* Commonplace Book *for 1789–1813* (Princeton: Princeton University Press, for the American Philosophical Society, 1948), 267.

39. A. Balfour, "Some British and American Pioneers in Tropical Medicine and Hygiene," *Translations of the Royal Society of Tropical Medicine and Hygiene* 19 (1925): 189–229.

40. The standard history remains J. H. Powell, *Bring Out Your Dead: The Great Plague of Yellow Fever in Philadelphia in 1793* (Philadelphia: University of Pennsylvania Press, 1949).

41. Nathan G. Goodman, *Benjamin Rush, Physician and Citizen: 1746–1813* (Philadelphia: University of Pennsylvania Press, 1934), 175–76.

42. L. H. Butterfield, ed., *Letters of Benjamin Rush,* Vol. 2: *1793–1813* (Princeton: Princeton University Press, for the American Philosophical Society, 1951), 685. Rush's almost daily letters are reproduced on 637–745.

43. Benjamin Rush, *An Account of the Bilious Remitting Yellow Fever, As It Appeared in the City of Philadelphia, In the Year 1793* (Philadelphia: Thomas Dobson, 1794). A more accessible recent reprint is Benjamin Rush, *An Account of the Bilious Remitting Yellow Fever, As It Appeared in the City of Philadelphia, In the Year 1793* (New York: Classics of Medicine Library, 1997).

44. Rush's 1805 essay was republished four years later in a four-volume collection of his medical works: "An Inquiry into the Various Sources of the Usual Forms of Summer and Autumnal Disease," in Benjamin Rush, *Medical Inquiries and Observations* (Philadelphia: Hopkins and Earle, 1809), 4:171–231. This volume also contains (233–84) his "Facts Intended to Prove the Yellow Fever Not to be Contagious," as well as his accounts of yellow fever in Philadelphia between 1794 and 1804.

45. Richard Harrison Shryock, *Medicine and Society in America: 1660–1860* (Ithaca, N.Y.: Cornell University Press, 1960), 69–70.

46. Goodman, *Benjamin Rush,* 179.

47. Shryock, *Medicine and Society in America,* 70.

48. Rush, "Inquiry into the Various Sources," 173–80. Rush traced the source of Philadelphia's 1793 epidemic to a mound of rotting coffee in the wharf district. Butterfield, *Letters of Benjamin Rush,* 637.

49. See Webb, *Humanity's Burden,* 94–105, for an excellent summary of the discovery and spread of cinchona and quinine.

50. Peck, *Or Perish in the Attempt,* 49–52; Chuinard, *Only One Man Died,* 153–61.

51. Lewis also took the pills, and thought they did some good, when he had a bout of malaria on the Ohio River. Chuinard, *Only One Man Died,* 157.

52. *Dunlap's American Daily Advertiser* (Philadelphia), September 13, 1793.

53. Jefferson and, as of 1802, Rush were enthusiastic proponents of vaccination and played prominent roles in introducing Edward Jenner's revolutionary methods to the nation. Chuinard, *Only One Man Died,* 101–105.

54. Corner, *Autobiography of Benjamin Rush,* 265–66.

55. Emmanuel Le Roy Ladurie, "A Concept: The Unification of the Globe by Disease (Fourteenth to Seventeenth Centuries)," in *The Mind and Method of the Historian,* trans. Sian Reynolds and Ben Reynolds (Chicago: University of Chicago Press, 1981), 28–83; the quoted term is on 30.

56. Malaria, at least *vivax* and probably some *falciparum,* would creep onto the plains with the farming frontier, but it would recede after a couple of generations. It would be endemic only in California's Central Valley. Webb, *Humanity's Burden,* 88–90, 146–48.

57. Miller, *Mungo Park's Travels,* 301, 317–18, 324–26, 331, 348.

58. Chuinard agrees with the usual conclusion, that Sergeant Charles Floyd died of a ruptured appendix, while Peck suggests other possibilities: an ulcer or runaway infection. Chuinard, *Only One Man Died,* 228–39; Peck, *Or Perish in the Attempt,* 106–109.

59. Miller, *Mungo Park's Travels,* 307, 322, 327; Moulton, *Definitive Journals,* 4:306, 364.

60. Miller, *Mungo Park's Travels,* 338–39; Moulton, *Definitive Journals,* 4:348.

61. Miller, *Mungo Park's Travels,* 360; Moulton, *Definitive Journals,* 4:244.

62. Park's letter is in Park, *Journal of a Mission to the Interior of* Africa, 75–76. Particulars of Park's death emerged when his guide, Isaaco, was sent to investigate in 1810. He found one African who had been with the Englishmen and had survived the encounter at the rapids. Captain Hugh Clapperson (in 1822–24) and Park's son Thomas (in 1827) entered the region in search of more details. Both died.

63. Chuinard, *Only One Man Died.*

2

Golden Dreams

Colorado, California, and the
Reimagining of America

On the eve of the Civil War the United States had a hole right in the middle of it. It was not an actual pit, of course; no one riding west from Kansas City would have tripped and fallen into an abyss. The hole was in America as it existed in millions of minds. People in the eastern and far-western United States pictured the country between them as detached, physically and historically. Plains and mountains seemed to have no part in what America was and would be.

That hole began suddenly to fill on July 6, 1858, the day a party of thirteen prospectors found gold dust in a small creek flowing from the Front Range of the Rocky Mountains. The next spring a stampede to the diggings had an economic and environmental impact that was enormous and obvious. Another change was easier to miss. The Colorado gold rush was a key moment in American mental geography. With its sister episode, the discovery of California gold, it reshaped the nation's perception of itself. During the middle years of the nineteenth century, as the republic changed in size, purpose, and values, the two gold rushes helped knit its parts into a newly imagined union, one sure in its blessings, imperial in vision, blindly arrogant, naïvely confident of a future of untarnishable luster.

The momentous shift in America's self-image began during the tumultuous 1840s. The decade opened with the nation two-thirds the present size of the lower forty-eight states. Its western border lay against Texas and along the crest of the Rocky Mountains, on the far-western edges of the Great Plains. The image of that borderland was vague and unpromising. Occasionally it was called the "Great American Desert," but more often the "prairies" and the "plains." The public understood those terms to mean great grasslands, windswept and rolling. It was well known that this country hosted lots of wild game, but the image was of open and exposed landscape, mostly treeless and covered with short, wispy vegetation. It was interesting, but in a Mongolian sort of way.[1]

Such a place had little significance in the nation's ideas of future greatness. By the 1840s the early republican dream of agrarian abundance had merged with two others: hopes for a modest but vibrant industry and for a vigorous commerce sending the fruits of garden and factory out to the world. In those terms the plains and the mountain fringe were next to useless. At best this country was a possible pasture, but as a future domain of full harvests, bustling market towns, and the occasional metropolis, it seemed a bum bet.

In 1840 that was no great problem. The plains were out there on the farthest edge of things. In fact, some thought the border's unpromising strangeness would serve us well. Zebulon Pike, the first agent of the United States to describe the region as desert and steppes, thought that overly restless Americans, "so prone to rambling and extending themselves on frontiers," would finally stop their wasteful ways and live by proper husbandry once they faced this vast expanse fit only for herds of game and tribes of "wandering and uncivilized aborigines."[2] The plains and mountain front, then, were the republic's outer edge in a double sense. Geographically, this was our western boundary; mentally, it was the place where the vision of abundance and purpose weakened and faded toward nothing.

Then suddenly the national map was dramatically redrawn. In three great gulps—the annexation of Texas, the granting of the Far Northwest from England, and the seizure of California and the Southwest in the Mexican War—more land was acquired than in any other previous act, including the Louisiana Purchase. Almost overnight, America became a transcontinental, dual-oceanic nation. In 1844 our size was impressive. In 1848 it was imperial.

Next came arguably the most stunning coincidence in American history. At almost exactly the moment of the last act of expansion, just nine days before the treaty was initialed ending the Mexican War, James

Marshall found those famous glittering flecks in the American River in northern California. "Boys, I believe I have found a gold mine," he announced.[3] He was right, and within a few years tens of thousands more came looking for theirs, first from other parts of the Pacific Coast, then from South America, the Sandwich Islands, Canton, and Australia, then from Europe and elsewhere in the United States. It was history on fast-forward. Dozens of towns sprouted within a few months, San Francisco emerged as a port rivaling most in the mercantile world, and a rapidly diversifying economy began to transform the Pacific Coast.

These two developments—expansion to the Pacific and the discovery of gold—reshaped fundamentally the nation's image of itself and its future. The ballyhoo and chest puffing that followed was as much about what would be done with these western possessions as about their size and expanse. This new territory, many said, brimmed with the raw stuff of our old agricultural vision. "Shall this garden of beauty . . . lie dormant in its wild and useless luxuriance?" asked an Illinois editor. The question was rhetorical, but many answered anyway that California's broad valleys and the wide embrace of Texas held fabulous fresh potential for America as a prolific garden, "not [only] for our own use," New York Democrats assured their supporters, "but for the use of man."[4]

The coincidence of gold, however, brought out and amplified the newer motifs of the national vision. Gold summoned images of bustling, productive cities and far-reaching commerce. The spirit of gold seeking—its plunging optimism and mix of labor and luck—fit the values of an urban speculative culture far better than the earlier rural faith in thrift, steady sweat, and plod. Gold was "the motive power which will put in operation the already-prepared vast machinery of American enterprise," a memorial of California citizens declared early in 1849. It was "but a means of accelerating the march to national supremacy." Congressman John McClernand (D-Illinois) predicted that the new country's resources, "trophies of a just and brilliant war," would soon birth a great city beside San Francisco Bay, bind Europe to Asia with thriving commerce, and inspire a railroad linking the Atlantic and Pacific. The *American Review* added soon afterward that gold "contains the elements, the principles, the forces" to establish "a great American epoch in the history of the world. . . .

The acquisition of these territories on the Pacific, seems destined to make our country the world's historical center."[5]

Coast would be bound to coast, trade to mines and factories. Cities and farms, east and west, would be woven into a grand continental enterprise. A strong racist undertone ran through this vision. Current residents of the western empire, Native American "primitives" and Hispanics sunk in "voluptuous pride" and "inglorious ease," had neither the eyes to see the land's promise nor the will to fulfill it, according to the new prophets. An Illinois editor wrote that these lesser peoples were "reptiles [who must] either crawl [away] or be crushed."[6] First conquest, then the earth's sudden gift of its most precious resource: the way was open for the full flower of national destiny. America would be the golden land in truth as well as metaphor.

But there was a problem. The grand vision of farms, manufacturing, and trade had been applied to the country east of the Missouri, and now it was projected westward to the Pacific Coast. But what about the country in between? It remained apparently useless, as it had seemed for decades, but now the plains and Rockies were no longer our western fringe. They were the American center. The vision of national destiny reached out *over* the continent, but it did not yet *cover* the continent. To the contrary, the heart of the expanded nation seemed to have nothing much to do with anything. As the former mountain man and present Indian agent Thomas Fitzpatrick put it, there was "a great disconnecting wilderness" at the nation's center.[7] America, that is, had a hole right in the middle of it.

Travelers crossing from the well-populated East to the imagined land of plenty on the Pacific called the plains "a dreary waste as far as the eye can reach," a "barren, trackless waste . . . an expanse of hot, bare sand," a bleak landscape that "equals any other scene on our continent for desolation." An overlander in the late 1850s thought the plains had only one useful function—erosion: "It looks as if the great Creator has made this vast desert as a sort of storehouse of materials from which he is day-by-day transporting them to other regions, where they can be made more available for the use and to the benefit of man."[8]

True, there were occasional wild and exotic sights—bison and antelope, spectacular storms, mirages, and the Plains Indians, who, travelers believed, always threatened to attack or rob them. Mostly, however, travelers were oppressed by what one called "so much sameness." The rolling, unbroken openness reminded many immigrants of the high seas. The plains were "an ocean of land, the same day in and day out," Tom Sanders remembered. An army unit traveled four days through a treeless stretch of eastern Colorado. When a line of streamside cottonwoods finally appeared on the horizon, an Irish private called out: "Be Jesus! We're in sight of land again!"[9]

The comparison went beyond appearance. On the plains, as at sea, people might find high adventure, or see schools of playful bison frolicking in the grassy waves, or meet those colorful but threatening land pirates, the Pawnees and Sioux. But for anyone hoping to move west, the Great Plains and Rockies comprised alien space. As somewhere to stop, start a farm, or plant a town, the plains had no more promise than the middle of an ocean. Like the sea, this country was something to get across.

Once again, however, mental geography was about to change. Only a generation into the future the American center would be pictured as the heartland of national hope, a region of bursting fields and prospering communities offering all we needed to confirm our destiny as a great and powerful people. The shift, one of the most sweeping in our history, was a startling reprise of the recent transformation of the Pacific Coast. As in California, the central moment came as a flash of light in a mountain stream.

The change began, however, in that straggling line of Missouri River towns along the eastern edge of the plains—Kansas City and Westport, Leavenworth, Atchison, St. Joseph, and a few others. In 1850 these communities considered themselves ports o' call where overland travelers could outfit themselves for the long voyages across the inland sea of land to the Pacific settlements. But as farmers moved into eastern Kansas, the towns also became market centers for those lovely prairies in the first thirty or so miles beyond the Missouri. In a classic promotional impulse, civic leaders soon pushed outward the imagined zone of cultivation. If corn was harvested thirty miles west of Leavenworth, why not fifty? If the land had been cropped around Lawrence, why not around Topeka, and fifty, eighty, a hundred miles farther on?

By 1855 this creeping boosterism had pushed the agrarian dream well past the middle of present-day Kansas. Flattering military reports of the far eastern plains were projected onto a much wider region, so land considerably west of the 98th meridian was pictured as well watered and nicely timbered.[10] Everyone understood that living well on the plains depended on rivers, the larger and more reliable the better. Now one booster wrote that the Arkansas River rose in Utah, cut all the way through the Rockies, and flowed vigorously across the plains, "watering and fertilizing the valleys through which it meanders." The Smoky Hill and Republican Rivers, which in fact rose on the plains near the present Kansas-Colorado border, more than a hundred miles east of the Front Range, also were said to begin "far up among the Rocky Mountains" and tumble to the Missouri through banks thick with timber: oaks six feet through the trunk, elms, sycamores, walnut, cherry, and beech.[11]

Farmers tilling the "rich, black vegetable mould" would send their bounty to market via steamboats that would ascend these rivers for hundreds of miles, according to promoters. One provided a map predicting regular steamboat traffic from the Atlantic Coast to the base of the Rockies, near what is today Denver. Railroad companies joined the chorus. As they built toward the Missouri Valley, they looked ahead hungrily to an inland empire full of farmers shipping their crops back east. A pamphlet for the Hannibal and St. Joseph Railroad, first to reach the Missouri, crowed about the grand possibilities of western Kansas: "As the whale remarked to Jonah, 'I deem it a good opening for a young man.'"[12] By the late 1850s, dream chasers could stand in the Missouri Valley and imagine the great American garden reaching out to some indefinite point to the west. Nonetheless, the process was almost all puff and blow. Or, as one writer admitted, no "foot-prints of Civilization" were yet imprinted on most of the plains.[13]

Then came the moment that sent this change rocketing forward. In summer 1858 William Green Russell, a Georgian with experience in the California diggings, led a party to pursue long-standing rumors of gold in the eastern Rockies. Word of their modest find on July 6 filtered out to Kansas City and arrived on the East Coast ten years almost to the day after the first astounding reports from California in September 1848. The United States was mired in one of the worst depressions of the century, and over the winter a shabby army of men, shaken loose by the hard times, gravitated to the Missouri Valley. "Hoosiers, Suckers, Corn crackers, Buckeyes, Red-horses, Arabs and Egyptians," said the *Missouri Republican*, "some with ox wagons, some with mules, but the greatest number on foot, with their knapsacks and old-fashioned rifles and shotguns. . . . Many have sold out all their homes, all their valuables, to furnish themselves with an outfit for Pike's Peak mines. . . . [They] blindly rush headlong into the wild delusion of glittering sands full of golden eggs."[14]

In spring 1859 more than a hundred thousand persons, twice the number that had crossed to California ten years earlier, flooded across the central plains to the Front Range. They walked, pushed wheelbarrows, pulled handcarts, and rode in farm wagons, ambulances, carriages, and phaetons drawn by oxen, mules, horses, milch cows, and, in one case, four hunting dogs. There was a "wind wagon" fitted with sails—a comic failure, but testimony of the gold seekers' imagination and naïve hopes. One group afoot planned to sleep in the barns they thought Indians had built for their buffaloes.[15]

The diggings that had sparked the rush soon played out, but in early summer, genuine strikes were confirmed in the mountains, and as miners flocked to Central City, Idaho Springs, and other camps, a cluster of supply towns blossomed along the base of the Front Range, Denver the most prominent. Within another year a rough political structure was in place. A critical core of Anglo-American society had appeared in what had been pictured as the republic's empty center.

In reshaping the mental map, the Colorado gold rush obviously had its most immediate impact on the Rocky Mountains. The Front Range was now seen as a place of vibrant towns populated by hard-muscled young Americans pulling wealth from the ground, the newest evidence of God's blessing on His chosen people. The mental force of the gold strikes, however, was felt almost as powerfully on the plains that stretched out six hundred miles to the east. Until now the push for reimagining this country had come from its eastern border. Now a new vision was projected from its western edge, from the Rockies. Correspondents wrote that the area's valleys were already being planted: "That the Platte and Arkansas bottoms will yield abundantly to the industrious farmer, there can be no doubt, [and] neither can they be excelled for cattle." Others added that High Plains winters were so mild that domestic herds could graze all winter with hardly a shiver as gardeners tilled happy rows of vegetables virtually year-round.[16]

Back on the eastern side of the plains, Missouri Valley boosters also moved into high gear. Leaders in each town worked to portray their jumping-off place as the true gateway to the gold mines. The trick lay in convincing the crowds that the overland route closest to a particular town was the easiest and fastest way west. There were three such routes—the northern road up the main valley of the Platte River, the southern path up the Arkansas River, and the central route up the Kansas River. Local boosters tried to raise one road over the others with glowing descriptions of its lovely terrain, its rich grasses and stands of timber, its sure sources of water. Thus urban promotion translated directly into a remaking of the image of the plains. As one critic wrote, town boosters "have changed the course of rivers, removed mountains, lengthened streams and made bleak hills and barren sand wastes smooth and even highways."[17]

More than fifty guidebooks appeared in 1859, most of them linked to one town and one route.[18] Champions of the northern and southern roads reported lush pastures, plenty of water, and easy travel all the way to the mines. The central route ascended the Kansas and Republican Rivers through country known to only a few non-Indians. Advocates of this route, undeterred by mere ignorance, described the region in the sunniest terms. Repeating earlier booster fictions, they said the two rivers flowed all the way from the Rockies (rather than rising far out on the plains). One book's map showed a large Kansas Lake on what was in fact the arid high plains. Another, answering immigrants' concern for protection, simply moved two forts northward from the Arkansas River to the central route it described as lush and flat—and now safe as well.[19]

To pump traffic westward through their stores, hotels, and liveries, Missouri Valley promoters also puffed up the land awaiting travelers at the far end of the trails. The Rockies were littered with fifty-dollar nuggets and dusted with "the purest gold that has ever been discovered." But that was only the start. Farmland of the high plains, according to one guidebook, "recalls the luxuriance of the tropics, or the magnificence of the ideal world of old navigators." Rumors of drought were dismissed, and in any case, wrote a promoter, there was "a peculiarity in the soil that enables it to withstand the absence of rain." Ranchers too would find magnificent pasturelands of natural grasses that could sustain "millions of cattle" year-round.[20]

Precisely ten years after the reimagining of the Pacific Coast, the same process was transforming the continental center. Gold again worked its magic. Once the precious metal was found, all else was assumed to follow: the original dream of flowering gardens, the newer vision of instant cities, budding industry, and speculative fever, and with those, a robust trade. The new Eldorado, an editor stated, would be "the evangel of a new commerce." The sleeping possibilities of mountain and plain would awaken, and "the buffalo path will turn into highways for hurrying merchandise."[21]

Wish fed reality. Within months mercantile outposts were popping up beside the Platte road. Freight cattle wintering along the Front Range became the seed herds for ranchers; farmers planted crops beside every likely tributary of the South Platte and upper Arkansas; Denver and other piedmont towns funneled goods in and out of mountain settlements. Over the following decade the Missouri Valley was bound by trade and interest to the western plains and Rockies, and both regions were woven into the rest of America by the rhetoric of national ascendance. The gold that poured from the mountains was called the fuel of greatness. It would build eastern factories, which in turn would heft us to our proper place. Growing cities would be fed by the generous toil of the heartland. The great pasture of the center, "boundless, endless, gateless," would fatten the cattle that every great nation must have, "vegetable food alone degenerating people to the condition of the Macaroni Eaters of Italy."[22]

Carnivore dreams are a good reminder of how mass imagination helps determine what we do with the places we inhabit, and thus shapes the history we make. Imagined America changed more between 1845 and 1876 than at any time in our history. The vital events are well known—

with two conspicuous exceptions. Gold rushes, one on the far-western edge of the expanded nation and the other in the middle, redrew the mental contours of the nation far more than we have recognized.

Events of 1845–48 left America thinking continentally, but by deepening the strains between North and South, they came close to fatally fracturing the expanded nation. The Civil War insured that the Union would remain; it allowed the survival of a vague image of an ocean-to-ocean nation. But what exactly would that nation be? The redrawing of America, begun fifteen years before the war, continued for a dozen years after it. This was our larger, more significant reconstruction. It involved far more than pulling the South back into the Union. The entire nation was being reperceived, with the role and image of each region rethought.

Gold reconstructed the West and America, physically and mythically. The strikes in California and Colorado drew floods of new population and spawned centers of Anglo-American power where none had been before. They also gave a shape to the new territory's vague promise of instant cities, humming trade, bountiful fields. Unlike images of earlier Wests, fitting a slower, steadier rural life and virtues, those of the gold rushes caught a new intoxicating spirit of plunge and grab. Mining camps, chugging locomotives, and throbbing smelters—they were fitting symbols of the new national vision.

That vision was as flawed as ever. Anyone who got in the way, notably Indian peoples and Hispanics, were at worst assaulted as lower life-forms and at best patronized as anachronisms who were, as the commissioner of Indian Affairs told a delegation of Plains tribes in 1867, "by the law of God, and the great law of nature, passing away."[23] In unstoppable numbers the newcomers rolled over everything before them, then paid their own price for the overblown rhetoric. Droughts and blizzards devastated plains settlers in 1860 and 1861, again later in the decade, and then again in 1872. Thousands were driven back east. Mining camps busted by the dozen. Denver, Queen City of the Plains, often languished in depression.

But as usual with Americans, and almost always with the West, belief shouted down the facts. "An erroneous impression has gone forth that Kansas is subject to drought," the Kansas Board of Immigration wrote in 1861, astonished at the rumors.[24] Boosters assured everyone that the mines were bottomless, cattle would have plenty to eat, and farmers had nothing to fear. Doubts dissolved. The lovely dream spread and colored nicely.

By 1876, as the republic marked its hundredth birthday and the formal reconstruction of the South drew to a close, the West was also in its final stages of re-vision. The theme of gold bound it to the Union and expressed its larger meaning. California sat "in the circle of sister States," as a Napa orator put it on the centennial day, "her veins throbbing with gold and silver and precious metals, her heart sending out its pulsations to all lands and climes, her lap full of all good things for the healing of the nations."[25] The rhetorical starburst was at least as great in Colorado, born and confirmed in gold and admitted that year as the Centennial State.

The two coasts now were linked by the technology of a new age, the final connection marked appropriately with the hammering of a golden spike and the telegraphed word "Done." The hole in the center had been filled. This geographical alchemy transformed the popular image of other parts of the region as well—Montana and Idaho in the 1860s, parts of the Southwest in the 1870s and 1880s. In fact and fancy, the West was integrated into an America looking toward its second century, one that would show the terrible contradictions and self-deceptions, as well as the true possibilities, of dreams born from the rush for gold.

Notes

An earlier version of this chapter appeared as "Golden Dreams: Colorado, California, and the Reimagining of America," *Montana The Magazine of Western History* 49, no. 3 (Autumn 1999): 2–11.

1. For a survey of impressions of the region, see Martin J. Bowden, "The Great American Desert and the American Frontier, 1800–1882: Popular Images of the Plains," in *Anonymous Americans: Explorations in Nineteenth-Century Social History,* ed. Tamara K. Hareven (Englewood Cliffs, N.J.: Prentice-Hall, 1971), 48–79.

2. Elliott Coues, ed., *The Expeditions of Zebulon Montgomery Pike . . . during the Years 1805–6–7,* 3 vols. (New York: F. P. Harper, 1895), 2:525.

3. Quoted in Rodman Wilson Paul, *Mining Frontiers of the Far West* (New York: Holt, Rinehart, & Winston, 1963), 13.

4. Albert K. Weinberg, *Manifest Destiny: A Study of Nationalist Expansionism in American History* (Baltimore: Walter Hines Page School of International Relations, Johns Hopkins University, 1935), 168, 89–90.

5. "Californian Gold," *United States Magazine and Democratic Review* 24:127 (January 1849): 3; *Congressional Globe,* 30th Cong., 2d sess., February 27, 1849; *American Review* 9 (April 1849): 331–38.

6. "Californian Gold," 3; Weinberg, *Manifest Destiny,* 168.

7. Thomas Fitzpatrick to A. Cumming, November 19, 1853, in *Report of the Commissioner of Indian Affairs, 1853* (Washington, D.C.: Government Printing Office, 1853), 370.

8. Perry Kline Reminiscence, 61, Colorado State Historical Society, Denver (hereafter CSHS); Francis Parkman, Jr., *The Oregon Trail* (New York: Penguin Books, 1982), 106; "Diary of E. H. N. Patterson," in *Overland Routes to the Gold Fields, 1859, from Contemporary Diaries,* ed. LeRoy R. Hafen (Glendale, Calif.: Arthur H. Clark, 1942), 129–30.

9. Rose Bell Diary, May 30, 1862, CSHS; Thomas Sanders Reminiscence, 27–28, Western History Collections, Denver Public Library; Merrill J. Mattes, ed., "Capt. L. C. Easton's Report: Fort Laramie to Fort Leavenworth via Republican River in 1849," *Kansas Historical Quarterly* 20 (May 1953), 404.

10. The reports most often quoted (or rather misquoted) were John Charles Frémont, "A Report of the Exploring Expedition to Oregon and North California, in the Years 1843–44," in Donald Jackson and Mary Lee Spence, eds., *The Expeditions of John Charles Frémont,* vol. 1: *Travels from 1838 to 1844* (Urbana: University of Illinois Press, 1970), e.g., 42–43, 721–24; and Lieutenant Francis Bryan, "Report of Lt. Francis T. Bryan," 35th Cong., 1st sess., 1857, House Exec. Doc. No. 2, Appendix H, serial 943, pp. 455–520.

11. An excellent example is Walter B. Sloan, *History and Map of Kansas and Nebraska: Describing Soil, Climate, Rivers, Prairies, Mounds, Forest, Minerals, Roads, Cities, Villages, Inhabitants, and Such Other Subjects as Relates to This Region—Politics Excepted* (Chicago: R. Fergus, 1855).

12. Hannibal, Missouri, *Messenger,* September 30, 1858.

13. Sloan, *History and Map of Kansas and Nebraska,* 27.

14. *Missouri Republican,* March 27, 1859, in LeRoy R. Hafen, ed., *Colorado Gold Rush: Contemporary Letters and Reports, 1858–1859* (Glendale, Calif.: Arthur H. Clark, 1941), 17.

15. Elliott West, *The Contested Plains: Indians, Goldseekers, and the Rush to Colorado* (Lawrence: University of Kansas Press, 1998), 147–51.

16. Hafen, ed., *Colorado Gold Rush,* 207, 225, 231.

17. Kansas City, Missouri, *Western Journal of Commerce,* March 12, 1859.

18. For a list of all known guidebooks, see West, *Contested Plains,* 387–89.

19. William N. Byers and John H. Kellom, *A Hand Book of the Gold Fields of Nebraska and Kansas* (Chicago: D. B. Cooke, 1859); *Toledo, Wabash and Great Western Railroad Co. Direct Route to Pikes Peak and the Gold Regions* (New York: Robertson, Seibert & Sherman, 1859).

20. Pratt and Hunt, *Guide to the Gold Mines of Kansas: Containing an Accurate and Reliable Map* (Chicago: Print. Office of C. Scott & Co., 1859), 14; LeRoy R. Hafen, ed., *Pikes Peak Gold Rush Guide Books of 1859* (Glendale, Calif.: Arthur H. Clark, 1941), 285; *Report and Map of the Superintendent and Engineer of the Smoky Hill Expedition, Together with a Table of Distances* (Leavenworth, Kans.: "Times" Book and Job Establishment, 1861); Parker & Huyett, *The Illustrated Miners' Hand-Book and Guide to Pike's Peak* (St. Louis, 1859), 16.

21. St. Louis *Daily Missouri Democrat,* November 24, 1858.

22. Dr. Hiram Latham, *Trans-Missouri Stock Raising: The Pasture Lands of North America: Winter Grazing* (Omaha: Daily Herald Steam Printing House, 1871), 6, 23.

23. U.S. Office of Indian Affairs, "Report in Full of an Interview Between Indian Tribes of the State of Kansas and the Commissioner of Indian Affairs (Mr. Bogy); Reported by C. H. Emerson, January 30, 1867," Kansas Collection, Spencer Research Library, University of Kansas, Lawrence.

24. Kansas Bureau of Immigration, *The State of Kansas: A Home for Immigrants; Agricultural, Mineral, and Commercial Resources of the State . . .* (Topeka, Kans., 1865), 5–7.

25. Napa, California, *Register,* July 8, 1876.

3

Called-Out People

The Cheyennes and the Central Plains

During the century after 1750, the Great Plains were transformed by an imaginative and material revolution, one wrought especially by Indian peoples. The Cheyennes, Comanches, Kiowas, Lakotas, and others looked at the grasslands and saw an open, inviting path to wealth and power. Within a few generations they followed that road into a time they considered the pinnacle of their modern story.

Western history traditionally celebrates the ability to exploit new challenges. The praise is usually reserved for white pioneers, but if we rethink the frontier as a general turbulence set loose by Euro-Americans, and if we bring all participants fully into the action, the Indians emerge not only as frontier peoples but as the champions of imaginative courage. Their stunning achievement was a masterpiece of adaptive fluency. Like every frontier people, however, Plains Indians brought along their own problems and contradictions. Those problems were compounded by natural and human forces beyond their view or control. They failed to grasp a fundamental ecological principal. In 1840, just as the Cheyennes were settling firmly onto the plains, a German scientist proposed what has been called Liebig's law, or the "law of 'the minimum.'"[1] It is deceptively simple: An organism's limits are set, not by the maximum profusion of necessary things, but by those things' minimum availability. To know how large something will grow, that is, or how successful a people ultimately will be, do not measure their essential resources at their most abundant. Look instead for how much is available when vital supplies are the tightest, lowest, and stingiest.

The rule sounds absurdly obvious, like telling a friend planning a long trip to pack for the worst weather as well as the best. But over and over in western history, people have ignored what seems unignorable and have paid the price. For the Cheyennes that key measure was of pasture, wood, shelter, and water during the deepest winter, under the heaviest use, and when the droughts were most vicious. By the 1850s, after accomplishments as impressive as any on the unfolding frontier, Plains Indians were feeling Liebig's law at its sternest. History and the weather were catching up with them.

Around 1680, as the Comanches began their odyssey toward the southern plains, the Cheyennes left their homes on the upper Mississippi River and moved westward to the Minnesota River. Soon they moved to the James River in eastern North Dakota and then, by the 1770s, to the upper Missouri Valley in central North Dakota. They had abandoned their wigwams for the earthen houses typical of villages along the Missouri, but continued to live by their traditional economy of horticulture, hunting, and trade.

The Cheyennes settled in three villages near others of the Mandans, Hidatsas, and Chippewas. Their neighbors were not entirely happy with the intrusion, and within a few years tensions were increasing. Two events around 1780 forced the Cheyennes to make a critical decision. The Chippewas struck one of the Cheyenne villages with a devastating raid, and a series of terrible epidemics, probably smallpox and measles, ravaged their whole population. In the wake of these twin disasters, bands of Cheyennes began moving westward again, this time away from the Missouri and toward the plains.[2]

Emigration to the plains would demand a far greater adjustment in economy and lifestyle than any previous move had, but the Cheyennes were drawn westward by two new and powerful inducements. Both offered unprecedented power, but both were very risky. The Cheyennes were drawn first by an older resident of the plains—the bison. Bison had long been hunted by virtually all Indian peoples living between the 85th and 115th meridians. By 1800 the animal's population east of the Mississippi was shrinking drastically, but bison still lived in astonishing numbers where they were best adapted—on the Great Plains. Tribes living in the Missouri Basin, including the Cheyennes during their sojourn there, made long forays onto the plains to harvest from the herds. No animal was more useful and widely revered. It walked prominently through Native American cosmologies. Various parts of the bison were eaten, worn, fought with, slept on, traded, played with, and worshiped.

River villagers nonetheless complemented their bison hunting with other activities—gathering wild plants, trading, and hunting other animals, and above all the gardening of maize, squash, sunflowers, beans, and other foods. Their economies were reasonably balanced and therefore somewhat protected from full-scale disaster. Their collective energy was widely and shrewdly invested in activities that were fairly independent of one another and thus not too vulnerable to one another's failures. Bison were very important in such economies, but not preeminently so. The acquisition of horses in the mid-eighteenth century upset that balance by expanding the possibilities of hunting bison. Mounted hunters could range much farther in search of their prey, kill far more efficiently when they found it, and transport the results more easily. It appeared now that hunters could concentrate mainly on this one resource and bring in enough to supply most of what their people required, plus a surplus with which to trade for whatever else was needed and more.

It was tempting. Abandoning villages for a seminomadic life would mean living year-round on the plains, but the rewards appeared to be worth it. Besides, the opportunity to hunt bison on horseback meshed with the second powerful reason to take that leap of faith into a new homeland—commerce.

On the plains the Cheyennes had the chance to play a vital role in an old but expanding economic system.[3] The plains had long been central to a vigorous and extensive trade spanning the continent. European contact invigorated this old system, just as the Cheyennes' horses expanded the power to hunt bison. New products appeared, and new peoples to trade for them. New trading centers sprang up. The changes presented opportunities for peoples willing to take advantage of the rapidly evolving situation.

The main axis of this new trading arrangement ran eight hundred miles, from the middle Missouri Valley in North Dakota to northern

New Mexico. Villagers along the middle Missouri had long traded surplus maize, pumpkins, melons, and tobacco to plainsmen, who provided bison meat and robes, pemmican, flour from grinding and pounding prairie turnips, tents, dressed robes and skins, moccasins, and clothing of deer and antelope skin ornamented with beads and quillwork. With the coming of Europeans, Missouri villagers now could offer manufactured goods from French and English traders—axes, kettles, awls, mirrors, knives, scrapers, and more—along with the food products. Plains hunters also brought silver, sugar, and other articles from Hispanic settlements in New Mexico and the Far Southwest.

Two items, firearms and horses, the pair of European imports that inspired the greatest bursts of power, affected trade more than any others. Firearms came mainly from the East. The Spanish, fearing that Indians might ally with their French and English rivals, were always extremely reluctant to provide weapons to plains Natives. English and French traders, by contrast, were happy to offer guns, powder, balls, and bullets at trade fairs and in commercial forays conducted from the middle Missouri Valley to central Texas. Horses and mules came from the opposite direction, from their original source in the Southwest and from the southern plains. A line running roughly along the 40th parallel separated two climatic zones of relative hospitality for horses. Above the line fierce weather took a heavy toll on the animals. The northern herds were especially depleted in the spring, at the end of the murderous cold. Below the parallel, winters were not so vicious; the cured winter short grasses were also more accessible, and the midgrasses greened earlier in the spring along the streams to replenish the hungry herds.[4]

This irregularity—guns to the north and east, horses to the south and west—created a forceful dynamic. By a kind of commercial gravity, firearms were pulled from the area of their greater concentration toward the lesser, from the east to the south and west. The same was true of other manufactured goods more easily obtained from the English and French. The trade in horses meanwhile flowed from the great southwestern herds toward the horse-poor country north of the 40th parallel, out of New Mexico, the Staked Plains, and the Arkansas Valley northward across the Platte and into the Dakotas and to the middle Missouri.

This dynamic imbalance called for someone to play the middleman. Whoever facilitated the movement of goods back and forth might ride the flow to a new level of power and affluence. The Cheyennes answered the call. Doing so, however, required them to move with a full commitment away from the Missouri and into the main channel of trade on the plains. That move, in turn, demanded that they depend far more heavily on horses. Those animals were not merely a key item of commerce; they were the Cheyennes' essential tool in carrying out that trade and in pursuing and defending their new way of life.

Across America, from Philadelphia to Astoria, swiftly changing economies were offering unprecedented chances for the people who could see and act on them. One of the most promising was squarely in the continental center, on the Great Plains. The Cheyennes responded. After taking several steps westward over the previous hundred years, they then took another that was more consequential than any before it.

The next twenty years are among the fuzziest in tribal history, at least to outsiders. The Cheyennes' course ran west and sharply southward through the center of North and South Dakota. They returned often to trade on the Missouri but remained on the plains proper most of the year. They acquired many more horses. To take the crucial step away from villages to a nomadic life, Native peoples needed a critical mass of about six horses for every man, woman, and child, with considerably more, as many as a dozen per person, for a secure life.[5] The first credible estimates from a few decades later show the Cheyennes with ten or more horses per person. In the years after 1780 they must have steadily acquired these essential elements of their new existence.[6]

The country's gifts must have seemed irresistible and nearly limitless. By chance the grasslands of the early nineteenth century were watered by a stretch of unusually high rainfall, so the Cheyennes saw the country much greener and lusher than usual. Grazing there were bison in herds that sometimes covered two hundred or three hundred square miles during the mating congregations of high summer. Cheyennes found the profusion of deer, pronghorn antelope, elk, and grizzlies that had fed earlier tribes, only now they had vastly better means of hunting them. Like all jobbers, Cheyenne traders could increase their own share from the marketplace, in this case in both horses and trade goods. They began to flaunt their wealth. An Englishman on the Missouri about 1810 described a Cheyenne man draped in a magnificent robe, acquired from Arapahos, that was worked with red and yellow split quills and bordered entirely with hooves of young fawns. As the man walked, he whirred like a rattlesnake.[7]

Like the Comanches, Kiowas, Lakotas, and others, the Cheyennes quickly put these resources to the service of their vision. They adopted skin lodges (tipis), much larger variations of those first seen by Coronado, and learned to transport them and other possessions by horse travois. They ferreted out the parts of the High Plains that best met their varied needs for water, pasture, shelter, and fuel. They sharpened hunting techniques and honed skills that later impressed visitors to the plains. Racing after bison on carefully chosen ponies, hunters brought down their galloping quarry with rapid volleys from powerful shortbows that could send arrows entirely through the dense muscle of the mighty animals. They learned the fine distinctions among their main prey. Cheyennes had twenty-seven words for bison in their varieties of age, sex, and condition. A newborn or "yellow" calf was *heovoksa*, a two-year-old heifer, *moncess*. *Ookoenemehe* referred to a late-bearing cow. *Hotoxpeoeva* was a young, scabby bull.[8]

Other skills were less obvious. Although an elderly informant recalled planting corn as a child in the Black Hills, the Cheyennes gradually abandoned gardening, but they continued to use a remarkable range of native plants.[9] Some of this knowledge they brought with them; some they learned in their new homes.

As they moved into the plains, the Cheyennes named its parts according to how they saw and used them. Rivers were especially telling. Nebraska's Niobrara was the Sudden or Unexpected River. The Platte was the Moonshell or Musselshell, the Arkansas was the Flint Arrowpoint, and the South Platte was the Fat or Tallow River. They named the Solomon by its prolific game bird—the Turkeys Creek. The Smoky Hill went by its most welcoming feature: the Bunch of Timber River.[10]

The basis for this remarkable adjustment was laid during the first couple of generations after 1780. New leaders emerged during that time.

North West Company trader Charles Mackenzie told of accompanying a Gros Ventre delegation to a Cheyenne plains encampment. Six miles from the camp they were met by a chief who galloped up on a large milk-white horse, accepted their offer of a pipe, then stripped himself and clothed the Gros Ventre delegate in his war dress before seating the man on his horse and leading the column to his camp, chanting and singing all the way. Soon afterward fellow trader Alexander Henry visited a camp on the Knife River. He was met by a friendly and outgoing chief dressed in a blue Spanish coat and wrapped in a striped Spanish blanket. The man rode skillfully a great black stallion. With him were many warriors on horses with heads painted to resemble bison and antelope and with nostrils trimmed in red cloth.[11]

Such isolated encounters suggest a quickening contact with distant trade centers, a blossoming self-assurance, and a deepening sense of possession of the country. Meanwhile the Cheyennes continued to drift to the southwest. Then, in the early 1800s, there was a new coalescence in the area of South Dakota's Black Hills. Just northeast of the Black Hills was a lovely, steep-sided mountain that whites later called Bear Butte. To the Cheyennes it was Noaha-vose. Its significance can hardly be exaggerated. At Noaha-vose occurred the defining episode of modern Cheyenne history.[12]

By Cheyenne tradition their guide and prophet on their trek onto the plains was Sweet Medicine, also called Sweet Root Standing. As the people approached Noaha-vose, a great door opened in the mountain and Sweet Medicine was called inside by Maheo, the All Being, whose lodge was within. The prophet remained there for four years. With the help of the four sacred powers and the four sacred persons, Maheo instructed Sweet Medicine in codes of law and behavior. In the end he gave him four sacred arrows that conveyed power over enemies and the bison in the country surrounding Noaha-vose.[13]

From this point to the present, Noaha-vose has been the holiest site in the Cheyenne world. It is the lodge of the All Being. The generous essence of Maheo, the people's spiritual sustenance, pours forth from the sacred mountain. A Cheyenne political and spiritual map would have Noaha-vose at the center, with its edges roughly at the Rockies and at the Missouri, Arkansas, and Yellowstone Rivers. The defining direction at the top of this map would not be north, as in European cartography, but southeast. The greatest of the four sacred persons, Esseneta'he, lived in that direction. Creator of light and life, Esseneta'he sent the sun into the Cheyennes' world each morning and reaffirmed his blessing of the earth. Lodge entrances among the Cheyennes faced the southeast, toward Esseneta'he and the origin of life.[14]

That map is a reminder that the Cheyennes' move to the plains was more than an emigration. It was a fundamental reorientation of identity and reality. Taken literally or not, the story of Sweet Medicine tells that at some point in their journey the Cheyennes were changed so radically that they became a people apart from those who had lived before. The All Being granted the prophet's people true possession of the country around Noaha-vose. As in other spiritual traditions, Judeo-Christian among many others, this defining benediction was accompanied by another gift—a new name. This was proper and necessary. Maheo was proclaiming that the passage had transformed his chosen children. Their world's center had shifted; its horizons lay on a new pivot. They were now the Tsistsistas, the Called-Out People.

Unfortunately, the move to the plains brought plenty of problems, too. The Cheyennes' vision had implications they did not fully appreciate until the costs began to mount. For one thing, others had the same ideas they had. The Cheyennes fought ferociously with other tribes drawn into the country by the new possibilities, especially by the wonder of the horse. Around Noaha-vose and the Black Hills they struggled with the Kiowas and drove them southward. Soon, however, they were pushed in the same direction by the expanding Lakotas, with whom they continued to fight intermittently for years. They formed a close and lasting alliance with the Arapahos, but as they were pressed south, they came into increasingly bitter conflict with the Comanches, the Kiowas, and the Plains Apaches. The three groups lived mostly below the Arkansas River but ranged north to hunt on the central plains. Especially after about 1825, as the Cheyennes rode more often below the Platte River, they clashed fiercely with these three formidable tribes.

The spilled blood finally encouraged both sides toward accommodation. Each side needed to occupy the upper Arkansas without being threatened by the other.[15] The result was the great peace of 1840. Prominent leaders from all groups pledged friendship with an elaborate exchange of gifts at a crossing of the Arkansas that the Cheyennes still call Giving Presents to One Another across the River. By then Cheyennes had forged an alliance with the Lakotas as well. The peace of 1840 led to a lasting amity on the high plains among the Cheyennes, Arapahos, Lakotas, Comanches, Kiowas, and Plains Apaches. For twenty years Colorado east of the Rockies had been a country that several groups wanted but none could fully control. In 1840 it became the common hunting and camping terrain of a broad alliance of former enemies.[16]

East of the 100th meridian, however, was still a bloody ground. All High Plains tribes fought there with Pawnees, Osages, Potawatomis, Omahas, and others who lived on the low plains and ranged westward for bison, as villagers had for centuries before the horse frontier. Western Kansas would be wracked by almost continual conflict for another twenty-five years. For the Tsistsistas, fighting and dying there became part of their annual cycle. Late each spring and in early summer warriors rode against their low-plains enemies in revenge for past losses and to expand and protect vital hunting territory that eastern tribes also desperately needed. In the fall they raided again, this time mainly to increase their horse herds before the killing winter.[17]

Warfare became a natural extension of the plainsmen's feeling of expanded power. As had been true among most horseback societies, the cult of the warrior and the celebration of courageous killing took a central place among peoples on the hotly contested plains. War's importance was expressed in the names of leaders. A man born at the turn of the century was known variously as Eager To Be First (in a fight), Brave, Impetuous, and Shot By A Ree (an Arikara).[18] Cheyenne traditions were filled with men of legendary prowess and heart.

The costs of heroism, however, were enormous. From the 1820s to the 1860s, the central plains were probably the most viciously contested terrain of North America. Intertribal conflict took at least as heavy a toll, and probably a much higher one, as later battles with whites. Behind the inspiring memories and moments of transcendent daring were immense suffering and accumulated mourning. Raids and counterraids chewed at populations, ripped apart families, and upset crazily the balance of men and women. Cheyennes learned the truth behind the ancient tradition of many Old World cultures: Death rode a horse.

The bloody wars were only the start of their problems. Trade, and the lure of its wealth, carried the Tsistsistas in directions they could never have foreseen. Although they gained far greater power over the bison herds, for instance, the Cheyennes also became dangerously reliant on this one wild ungulate. Their way of life was inextricably bound to the bison's well-being—a shaky situation, as it turned out. Their great reliance on the bison trade, and on the hunting and military life generally, was especially unsettling for women. Before, in the riverine villages, women had controlled the produce of the gardens and the considerable income those foods brought through trade, and that control had given them substantial economic, social, and spiritual authority. In the seminomadic plains life, however, the most valuable assets, horses and bison carcasses, were acquired and controlled by men. Power within the tribes shifted steadily toward males and away from females. Rather than producers, women became processors, in this case supplying the backbreaking labor of skinning bison and scraping, rubbing, and kneading the hides into pliable, saleable robes.

Everyone, of both sexes and all ages, soon faced some of the trade's other implications. The plainsmen's greater affluence, for instance, was possible only by immersing themselves in an economic system subject to all sorts of forces beyond their control or understanding. Anyone who relies on trade is putting himself somewhat at the mercy of people and situations far beyond his edge of sight, but the Cheyennes' situation was different on two counts. They and their neighbors depended considerably more on trade goods and imported technologies than earlier plainsmen had. And although they might acquire those goods through other Indians, the source of those products was a distant society unlike any that Natives had ever encountered. By trading with whites, even indirectly, the Tsistsistas were locking themselves into an economic order changing more rapidly and less predictably than any that plains peoples had ever dreamed of, much less experienced.

The Cheyennes were caught in unanticipated irony. To chase their dream of independence and power, they found themselves dancing to others' tunes. The lesson came home dramatically a couple of generations later as the fundamental structure of plains trade shifted under their feet. When they had first moved to the plains, the Cheyennes had transferred British trade goods, garden produce, bison products, and horses back and forth between Indian villages on the middle Missouri and tribes on the southern plains. By the 1820s, however, the river villages were in steep decline, and the Tsistsistas faced the loss of one end of the profitable shuttle. But just then alternatives appeared. White trading companies established substantial posts or temporary entrepôts at several locations on the northern and central plains. Quickly the Cheyennes reoriented toward these new outlets, and soon they were trading primarily for goods channeled through those posts.

That switch, in turn, demanded two other adjustments. Although they continued to deal in some of the old goods, especially horses, the Cheyennes had to concentrate increasingly on what white traders wanted most—bison robes—which in turn heightened the stress on that crucial animal. More important, this trade was no longer with other Indians. The Tsistsistas now dealt directly and almost exclusively with whites. Their vital exchanges were with a society more alien, far larger, and more powerful than any Native people. This change placed a high premium on secure, predictable lines of communication and exchange between two very different cultures.

The Cheyennes responded with a momentous adaptation. Its immediate focus was the family, but its true relation was between societies. Its key figure was the white trader, and its central institution was marriage. Cheyenne hunters transacted some business at posts or fairs, but much was conducted through white men who moved back and forth between trading entrepôts and scattered villages, their horses and mules loaded with blankets, knives, muslin, coffee, foodstuffs, and other items. To ensure a reliable flow of goods, Cheyennes and other Indians married some of their women to these white men well connected within the trading network.

They could draw from a deep pool of possible husbands. Since the early 1820s white trappers, "mountain men," had worked the plains and mountains, earning considerable knowledge of the region and its peoples. They had dealt directly with white merchants. They themselves had caught their prime prey, beavers, and had prepared and swapped the pelts with firms operating out of New Mexico and Missouri. Some had taken Indian wives as helpmates and as a hedge against problems with the tribes, but Native Americans had relatively little direct role in the main business of trapping and exchange.

That changed around 1840. In that year, coinciding exactly with the great peace among the Cheyennes, Comanches, and Kiowas and the full occupation of the high plains, the beaver trade nose-dived, the victim of overtrapping and collapsing prices. Mountain men shifted toward trade in a variety of animal products but especially in bison robes. Switching products also meant a change in production. The out-of-work beaver-killers found it far more efficient to rely on Indian men to kill bison and Indian women to turn skins into robes. Indian camps, that is, became the new production centers of the regional fur trade. To acquire those robes, the former trappers thus became traders who carried goods from white outposts to Indian camps. Mountain men became middlemen. This new arrangement obviously required dependable, secure lines of exchange among the plains bands.

The match seemed perfect. Precisely when Cheyennes and others were looking for reliable links to trade goods, former trappers needed sure access to what were suddenly the essential products of their business. The common ground of this mutual adjustment was the trade marriage. With amazing speed a marital network laced over the high plains and bridged Native and white societies.

But as with their leap to horseback, this change left the Cheyennes open to other dangers. Not only had they linked themselves to a society that was immeasurably more powerful, wildly different, and not especially sympathetic to their own, but by relying on intermarriage as their connective mechanism, they were also handing over a key to security to men who, despite their beaded buckskins and braided hair, were products of that other, potentially threatening culture. If the floor of the plains economy should again collapse, the Cheyennes would have to count on their white in-laws to speak for them and fashion some viable place for Indian peoples in whatever social order followed. Whether they were up to the job, or whether they had any interest in it, remained to be seen.

These problems—the vicious competition from other tribes, the specter of shrinking herds, the shifting economy, and vulnerability to outside power and further change—were external. The people would need to face them together. But by Cheyenne tradition, the gravest peril of these years had nothing to do with assaults from other tribes or pressures from whites. This threat came from within their own ranks. The same passage that gave them a new identity and a new name also ate away at their unity and common perception of themselves.

Part of the cause lay in the new economy. Trade at first pulled the Cheyennes southward to a more central position between the poles of trade in New Mexico and the middle Missouri. About 1815 or 1816, for example, they were reportedly the primary figures at a great trading council on Cherry Creek, near the future site of Denver. There was a price, however. Their move toward a better trading position took them farther away from Noaha-vose, their spiritual base. The Tsistsistas literally were drawn off center. The aggressive Lakotas, who saw the Black Hills as their own blessed homeland, also pushed them southward. By the 1820s this problem was compounded by the decline of the Missouri villages and the appearance on the plains of white trading posts. The various bands looked for dependable connections wherever they could find them. Several gravitated toward American Fur Company posts on the North Platte.

Then, in the late 1820s, a portentous arrangement was struck with William and Charles Bent, two brothers from a prominent St. Louis family. The pair were operating a small post near the base of Pike's Peak when an emerging Cheyenne leader, Yellow Wolf, suggested that if the brothers would move their operations to a more favorable spot farther down the Arkansas River, his followers would stay close and trade with the Bents and their partner, Ceran St. Vrain. By about 1830 Bent,

St. Vrain and Company had built an imposing adobe fort near present-day La Junta, Colorado. Bent's Fort became the preeminent trading entrepôt of the central plains. Many Cheyennes began to depend on it as a market for horses and robes and for access to outside trade. The move had the added advantage of a climate friendlier to people and horses.[19]

Not all leaders agreed with Yellow Wolf, however. Those who followed him became the Hairy Rope band (Hevhaitaneos), named probably for the rope halters used with the main items of their trade, horses. Later they were joined by the Southern Eaters (Wotapio) and the Scabbies (Oivimana), their name reportedly a caustic comment on the other basic trade good, bison robes. Other bands, including the Aorta (Heviksnipahis), Northern Eaters (Omisis), Bashful (Totoimana), and Pipestem (Hisiometanneo), kept their home ranges farther north, along the North Platte and in the Powder River country of Wyoming. They traded at Fort Laramie and at smaller posts opening in the region.[20]

This was an unprecedented fracture. The opportunities of trade, part of their dream of new life, were pulling the Tsistsistas apart. After 1830 those remaining close to entrepôts along and above the North Platte were known as the Northern Cheyennes. Those drawn by Bent's Fort and the lodestone of the southern horse herds became the Southern Cheyennes, committed to a home range along the Arkansas, on the far edge of the map centered on Noaha-vose.

The Cheyennes were fragmented still more by another force. The plains environment splintered them at a more fundamental level and kept them broken into far smaller units. Earlier, in the river villages to the east, large numbers of persons could live closely together throughout the year, and in fact plenty were needed to defend the sprawling gardens and permanent dwellings. Nomadic life, by contrast, had a shattering effect. It was yet another paradox of the more promising life. Hunting from horseback offered greater affluence and power, but those greater resources could only support people who lived in much smaller groups.

The problem (another paradox) was also the nomads' chief asset—their horses. With several horses for every person, the size of herds mounted quickly. A gathering of only forty people might have three or four hundred animals grazing nearby. Each of those animals needed considerable forage, so even a small camp required a great arc of pasture around it. The addition of just a few more people brought a considerable increase in the number of horses, the living tools essential to their new way of life, which meant a far greater demand for what those tools needed. Defense against horse thieves also became more difficult as the herds grew. The implications were obvious: the need *for* horses and the needs *of* horses put a practical limit on the size of nomadic groups. And that limit was reached fairly quickly.[21]

Weather compounded this difficulty. Summer, given adequate rainfall, brought out the plains' generosity. The giant pastures of buffalo and grama grasses permitted huge gatherings of horses and therefore of people. Herds of tens of thousands were sometimes reported. During winter, however, forage became much scarcer at the very time that the horses' energy needs increased. Especially during storms Indians had to keep their herds close to them, frequently in small, tight places along streams protected by bluffs and timber groves. During the cold months, when weather could change almost instantly for the worse, congregating in any significant numbers was impractical. From November to April, plains peoples had no choice but to break up into small groups that the country could support.

The environment, in short, demanded a social fission. On the Missouri the Cheyennes had lived in villages of about eight hundred to one thousand persons each. Within and among villages were smaller units, bands united by kinship and other groups bound by common functions. Pressures on the plains led to a hiving off and the creation of several new bands, and to some shuffling and realignment as people changed their allegiances from one group to another. At the head of each matrilineal band was a man, a "chief," considered its spokesman for trade and other matters. Increasingly the band became the focus of an individual's identity. Week to week, however, Cheyennes often lived in a still-smaller group, a camp, or *vestoz* (literally, "that which has tipis"), a collection of a couple of dozen or so related persons.[22] A camp was the maximum number of persons and horses supportable when the plains were at their stingiest.

Living in these small groups, year after year, naturally ate away at any sense of common spirit. Heroic efforts were made to nurture an identity as a single people. Because military societies drew from all the bands, they helped stitch the bands together. There was also one common institution, the Council of Forty-Four. These highly respected chiefs were selected for their sagacity, courage, generosity, and self-control. Their traditional purpose was to resolve disputes and promote peace among the bands, and beyond that they provided some central authority and sense of unifying character. Once a year it was still possible for Cheyennes to act out their seamless collective identity. In highest summer, with the highlands an enormous banquet of grasses, their new home briefly allowed gatherings even larger than in the old villages. The various bands of the Northern and Southern Cheyennes converged. They performed their various unifying rituals, including their sun dance, appropriately honoring the ultimate source of new power and reaffirming the Called-Out People's communion under the All Being. In those weeks their vision was most real.

Nonetheless, the stresses and fissures became increasingly apparent. The pattern was inexorable and devilishly perverse. Everything good about the plains had a way also of limiting or threatening the Cheyennes' new life. With the power of grass came grinding warfare. Economic opportunity laid them open to events far beyond their influence. The inspirations of a new identity, trade, and an environment swelling with unimaginable energy ate steadily at their cohesion and sense of kinship. As they acted out their vision of the plains, the Tsistsistas were losing sight of who they were.

It got worse. Not only did the Cheyennes have to face unforeseen implications of the best of their new world, but they also miscalculated badly how well the plains could support their newly imagined lives. Their brilliant adaptations were undermined by three forces. The first was their own misunderstanding. Their prime error was a failure to see how fully their life was bound to the demands of the very objects that opened the country's possibilities—their horses. Their leaders asked the All Being for animals of their own. Maheo answered:

> You may have horses.... You may even go with the Comanches to take them. But remember this: If you have horses everything will be changed for you forever. You will have to move around a lot to find pasture for

your horses. You will have to give up gardening and live by hunting and gathering, like the Comanches. And you will have to come out of your earth houses and live in tents. I will tell your women how to make them, and how to decorate them. And there will be other changes. You will have to have fights with other tribes, who will want your pasture land or the places where you hunt. You will have to have real soldiers, who can protect the people. Think, before you decide.[23]

The leaders chose horses, of course, and their decision brought all that Maheo predicted—and more. By becoming people of the horse, the Cheyennes were stepping into an ecological arrangement, a relationship among land, climate, and resources, that was more complex and precarious than they could have guessed.[24]

A second problem, a historical event far beyond their control, compounded the effects of the first. In the 1840s white pioneers began an emigration across the plains toward the Pacific Coast. They followed the main valley of the Platte River and the river's north branch to the Continental Divide and beyond. At first this movement of people and animals was barely noticeable, but it gradually grew and then exploded with the California gold rush of 1849. The cross-plains traffic added to freighting on the Santa Fe Trail that had run along the Arkansas River between Missouri and New Mexico since the early 1820s. Great numbers of draft animals and huge herds of cattle and sheep accompanied the overlanders and freighters. The total of the two-legged and four-legged travelers was staggering. Between 1841 and 1859, more than 300,000 persons and at least 1.5 million oxen, cattle, horses, and sheep moved up the Platte road.

The thousands of outsiders brought an upsurge in one of the frontier's prime influences, epidemics. Other devastation, slower but in its way just as terrible, came from the streams of animals that moved annually up the roads. Every summer tens of thousands of oxen and other cattle ate voraciously at the grasses along the river trails. Iron-rimmed wagon wheels tore and crushed the earth, and emigrants and freighters felled and burned trees throughout the great Platte Valley and along the Arkansas. This abrasion of resources was calamitous for Plains Indians. In the autumn, after the last wagon trains had passed through, the

Cheyennes and other nomads left the highlands and headed for the river valleys. Now, however, they found many of those sanctuaries stripped of the timber and forage they needed to survive the winter.[25]

A third force came not from human actions but from a return of an old natural cycle. Beginning in the late 1840s, just as the overland migration was really cranking up, a series of droughts hit the central plains. One blistered the Arkansas Valley in 1849, another struck the entire region in 1855, and in the early 1860s two more, worse than the others, cooked the country from Nebraska to Indian Territory. The blows seemed even harsher because they followed a quarter century of generous rainfall that had brought out the best the plains could offer.[26] The normally rich pastures took on a singed, balding look. The largest streams slowed, sometimes to a trickle, and the hundreds of seeps and ponds on the uplands shrank or disappeared.

Dry spells compounded the effects of the first two forces. As the highland grasses and ponds shriveled away, Indians stayed closer to the rivers and their forage, the same places they were overusing in the winter and that the white travelers and their animals were chewing, cutting, and burning between April and August. Making matters even worse, the bison—the Cheyennes' prime source of food, shelter, and trade goods and another great inducement for their shift to the plains—were disappearing. The reasons are cloudy. In part, however, the Indians' own prodigious hunting was surely to blame, and possibly diseases imported by overland animals. Certainly the degeneration of river habitats played a role; bison relied on those places as much as Indians and horses, and for much the same reason.[27]

A lifeway that had seemed pure allurement was turning out to be something more complicated. The Cheyennes were caught up in an old theme of gain and cost. As they broadened their command over valuable resources, they became absolutely reliant on the essentials they were helping to destroy. They found the dream of a people chosen for greatness, and with it an unstoppable cultural fracturing. They became some of the continent's finest warriors—and watched their men fall away in almost continuous battling. They expanded their grasp over the land's energy and wealth; they became subjects of events they were powerless to affect. "Everything will be changed for you forever," the All Being had cautioned the Cheyennes when they asked for horses. Maheo's children were seeing the full truth of God's word.

Notes

An earlier version of this chapter appeared as "Called-Out People: The Cheyennes and the Central Plains," *Montana The Magazine of Western History* 48, no. 2 (Summer 1998): 2–15.

1. Justus von Liebig, *Die organische Chemie in ihrer Anwendung auf Agrikultur und Physiologie* (Braunschweig, Germany, 1840). The first edition in English was *Organic Chemistry and Its Applications to Agriculture and Physiology* (London, 1840).

2. E. Adamson Hoebel, *The Cheyennes: Indians of the Great Plains* (1960; repr., Fort Worth: Harcourt Brace Jovanovich College, 1988), 3–9; George E. Hyde, *Indians of the High Plains: From the Prehistoric Period to the Coming of the Europeans* (Norman: University of Oklahoma Press, 1959), 47; John H. Moore, *The Cheyenne Nation: A Social and Demographic History* (Lincoln: University of Nebraska Press, 1987), 129–38.

3. Still the best single source on the role of Cheyennes in this evolving trade is Joseph Jablow, *The Cheyenne in Plains Indian Trade Relations, 1795–1840*, Monographs of the American Ethnological Society, vol. 19 (New York: J. J. Augustin, 1950).

4. Ibid., 10–18.

5. The best discussion, based on the Blackfeet of the northern plains but bringing in other tribes as well, is in John C. Ewers, *The Horse in Blackfoot Culture: With Comparative Material from Other Western Tribes*, Bulletin 159 (Washington, D.C.: Smithsonian Institution, Bureau of American Ethnology, 1955), 129–47.

6. Jürgen Döring's *Kulturwandel bei den Nordamerikanischen Plainsindianern: Zur Rolle des Pferdes bei den Comanchen und den Cheyenne* (Berlin: Reimer, 1984) contains a useful summary of estimates of horses per capita over time among the Cheyennes.

7. John Bradbury, *Travels in the Interior of America in the Years 1809, 1810, and 1811* (2nd ed., London, 1819), Vol. 5 of *Early Western Travels, 1748–1846*, ed. Reuben Gold Thwaites (Cleveland, Ohio: Arthur H. Clark, 1904), 139.

8. Rudolphe C. Petter, *English-Cheyenne Dictionary* (Kettle Falls, Wash.: Waldo Petter, ca. 1915), 193.

9. Iron Teeth died in 1928 at the age of about ninety-three. Living until the year of President Herbert Hoover's election, she could recall the great peace of 1840 as well as gardening in the Black Hills. See "Iron Teeth, a Cheyenne Old Woman," in Thomas B. Marquis, *The Cheyennes of Montana* (Algonac, Mich.: Reference Publications, 1978), 53–55.

10. Father John Peter Powell, *People of the Sacred Mountain: A History of the Northern Cheyenne Chiefs and Warrior Societies, 1769–1974,* 2 vols. (San Francisco: Harper & Row, 1981), l:xxxix.

11. Stan Hoig, *The Peace Chiefs of the Cheyennes* (Norman: University of Oklahoma Press, 1980), 16–20.

12. There are many sources for this episode and others of the Cheyenne sacred traditions. See Powell, *People of the Sacred Mountain;* George Bird Grinnell, *By Cheyenne Campfires* (New Haven: Yale University Press, 1962); Grinnell, *The Cheyenne Indians: Their History and Ways of Life,* 2 vols. (Lincoln: University of Nebraska Press, 1972); George A. Dorsey, *The Cheyenne,* Vol. 1, *Ceremonial Organization* (Chicago: Field Columbian Museum, 1905).

13. A recent reinterpretation of Cheyenne history places this episode much earlier. By this tradition the Cheyennes' ancestors had come onto the northeastern plains from the far north about 500 B.C. Sometime during the next two centuries the *maiyun,* or powerful spirits, instructed and guided them to the region stretching in four directions from Noaha-vose. Centuries later the Cheyennes moved eastward into the woodlands near the Great Lakes, then migrated back to the plains around 1800. By this tradition, then, this recent journey was a return and reclamation of the homeland granted by the maiyun more than two millennia earlier. See Karl H. Schlesier, *The Wolves of Heaven: Cheyenne Shamanism, Ceremonies, and Prehistoric Origins* (Norman: University of Oklahoma Press, 1987).

14. For an example of such a map, see Father John Peter Powell, *The Cheyennes, Maheo's People: A Critical Bibliography* (Bloomington: Indiana University Press, 1980), xxviii–xxxi.

15. Powell, *People of the Sacred Mountain,* 1:38–46, 51–66.

16. For various accounts, see George Bird Grinnell, *The Fighting Cheyennes* (Norman: University of Oklahoma Press, 1955), 63–69; Donald J. Berthrong, *The Southern Cheyennes* (Norman: University of Oklahoma Press, 1963), 82–84; Jablow, *The Cheyenne in Plains Indian Trade Relations,* 72–77; James Mooney, *Calendar History of the Kiowa Indians* (1898; repr., Washington, D.C.: Smithsonian Institution Press, 1979), 275–76; Powell, *People of the Sacred Mountain,* 1:67–73; George Bent to George Hyde, January 23, 1905, George Bent Papers, Western History Collections, Denver Public Library.

17. The best discussion of the evolution of this pattern and its significance is in John H. Moore, "Cheyenne Political History, 1820–1894," in *Ethnohistory* 21 (Fall 1974): 329–59. The standard sources on the consequences of horses for Indian military culture and the way the two of them influenced social developments and the quest for rank are Frank Raymond Secoy, *Changing Military Patterns on the Great Plains,* Monographs of the American Ethnological Society no. 21 (1953; repr., Seattle: University of Washington Press, 1966); and Bernard Mishkin, *Rank and Warfare among the Plains Indians,* Monographs of the American Ethnological Society no. 3 (1940; repr., Seattle: University of Washington Press, 1966).

18. Powell, *People of the Sacred Mountain*, 1:626n.

19. David Lavender, *Bent's Fort* (Lincoln: University of Nebraska Press, 1972), 130–47; Jablow, *The Cheyenne in Plains Indian Trade Relations*, 63–66.

20. The division into northern and southern branches is treated in every history of the Cheyennes. One article in particular places it within the context of continuing stresses within the people. Moore, "Cheyenne Political History, 1820–1894."

21. For a schematic illustration of the spatial demands of keeping horses on the plains, see Moore, *The Cheyenne Nation*, 165–67.

22. Ibid., 178–80.

23. Alice Marriott and Carol K. Rachlin, *Plains Indian Mythology* (New York: Crowell, 1975), 96–97.

24. In addition to sources cited in the following discussion, see the opening chapter of a fine study: James Earl Sherow, "Discord in the 'Valley of Content': Strife over Natural Resources in a Changing Environment on the Arkansas River Valley of the High Plains" (Ph.D. diss., University of Colorado, 1987), 9–35.

25. For an extended discussion of this important development, see Elliott West, *The Way to the West: Essays on the Central Plains* (Albuquerque: University of New Mexico Press, 1995), 18–19, 27–33.

26. Merlin Paul Lawson, *The Climate of the Great American Desert: Reconstruction of the Climate of Western Interior United States, 1800–1850* (Lincoln: University of Nebraska Press, 1974). A more localized tree-ring study was conducted around North Platte, Nebraska, near the forks of the Platte, an area traversed by the Pacific trails and especially popular as a hunting and camping area for the newly arrived Native groups. This study showed an eighteen-year stretch free from drought after the opening of the nineteenth century (1804–1821), followed by eleven dry years (1822–32), and then, coinciding with the great overland migration and movement of larger numbers of Indians into the area, a quarter century without drought (1833–57), and after that, at the time of the Colorado gold rush and Indian wars, another very dry period, this time nine years long (1858–66). See Harry Weakly, "A Tree Ring Record of Precipitation in Western Nebraska," *Journal of Forestry* 41 (January 1943): 816–19. Yet another investigation, correlating sunspot occurrence with drought cycles as indicated through tree-ring analysis, finds conclusive evidence of severe drought from 1859 to 1861 and suggestions of a major dry spell from 1846 to 1851. See Frederick E. Clements, "Drought Periods and Climatic Cycles," *Ecology* 2 (July 1921): 181–88. See also Edmund Schulman, *Dendroclimatic Changes in Semiarid America* (Tucson: University of Arizona Press, 1956), esp. 85–89.

27. The question of the extent, and especially the causes, of the decline in bison population is extraordinarily complicated. For a discussion and suggestion of some of the causes, see West, *The Way to the West*, 51–83.

4

Wired to the World

The Telegraph and the Making of the West

Consider this oddly neglected fact: the West was acquired, conquered, and largely consolidated into the nation coincident with the greatest breakthrough in the history of human communication. The breakthrough was the telegraph. The great advances that followed it, the telephone, radio, television, and the Internet, were all elaborations on its essential contribution. The telegraph separated the person from the message. Before it, with a few exceptions such as semaphore and carrier pigeons, information moved only as fast as people did. By the nineteenth century, people were certainly moving a lot faster, and indeed a second revolution, that of transportation, was equally critical in creating the West, but before the telegraph a message still had to move with a person, either as a document or in somebody's head. The telegraph liberated information. Now it could travel at virtually the speed of light. The railroad carried people and things, including letters, ten to fifteen times faster than the next most rapid means of movement. The telegraph accelerated communication more than forty million times. A single dot of Morse code traveled from Kansas City to Denver faster than the click it produced moved from the receiver to the telegrapher's eardrum.

This revolutionary development began simultaneously with the birth of the West as a national region. The Morse-Vail telegraph was formally tested on May 24, 1844. Roughly six months later the expansionist James K. Polk was elected president, and over the next four years the United States acquired the Far West in three enormous gulps—the annexation of Texas (1845), the Oregon Treaty covering the Pacific Northwest (1846), and the Mexican War and Treaty of Guadalupe Hidalgo (1846–48), which added California, Arizona, Nevada, Utah, and parts of New Mexico and Colorado. As the federal government began to organize its new country politically and to bring it under its sway, thousands of miles of wire were being strung every year across the East. In 1861 the first line was run to California. By 1870 the nation was enmeshed in nearly 120,000 miles of telegraphic wire. Europe had about the same, and in 1866, as Washington shifted from saving the Union to bringing the West under its full control, the American and European systems were connected by a transatlantic cable. Soon other cables were laid under other oceans, and that in turn inspired a steadily denser copper web across the globe.

Meanwhile western territories matured into states, the last Indian resistance was suppressed, and rails and roads bound the West ever more tightly into the nation. Conquest and consolidation were roughly finished around 1880. By then the number of telegraphic messages in the country had increased from one ("What hath God wrought?") to nearly thirty-two million a year, and a vast grid bound the nation and much of the earth into a single system of informational exchange. London and New York were in electronic contact with Berlin, Tokyo, and Calcutta, which meant Calcutta, Tokyo, and Berlin were also in touch with San Francisco, Boise, Tombstone, and scores of other western towns. The West and the telegraph grew up together. They were historical twins, and like many twins, they profoundly shaped one another. Ultimately neither can be truly understood alone.

The idea of sending messages electronically through wires had been around quite a while, and several prospects had appeared before 1844. All had problems. Sustaining a current over long distances was a puzzle, and receiving devices were complicated and clumsy—armatures pointing to letters in the alphabet, rolling marbles, bubbles generated in watery solutions. What turned out to be the answer began with a painter. Samuel Finlay Breece Morse was a Yale-educated artist whose landscapes and portraits had drawn critical praise and earned him appointment as the first president of the National Academy of Design, but in 1832 his career was faltering. While he was sailing home that fall from Europe, the dinner conversation turned to electromagnetism. At some point, as he recalled later, it struck him that "it would not be difficult to construct a

SYSTEM OF SIGNS by which intelligence could be instantaneously transmitted" over great distances.[1]

Over the next several years he collaborated with Albert Vail (who has received far less acclaim than deserved) and drew on the brilliant Joseph Henry's work on generating and projecting electrical transmissions. Morse and Vail designed an elegantly simple receiver based on the insight that information was best sent in code. The electrical transmission need not use some other device to interpret it. The impulses could *be* the message. The sender could arrange them into a system of dots and dashes, caused when the transmitter interrupted the electrical flow, that represented letters. Morse and Vail devised a simple code, with the commonest letters the quickest to send. The letter *e* is a single dot, for instance; an *x* is a dash, then two dots and another dash. At first a stylus marked each dot and dash, but experience soon showed that a practiced operator could take down messages as he heard them. Eventually telegraphers communicated almost as rapidly as if they were speaking, and in time each grew to know each other's styles as if they were hearing accents and inflections.

After several years spent developing the fundamentals, Morse needed money to build a prototype to demonstrate how messages might be sent over long distances. In 1843 Congress gave him thirty thousand dollars to string a line from the Supreme Court chamber in Washington, D.C., to a rail depot in Baltimore, Maryland. It was over that thirty-seven miles that Morse sent to Vail those words schoolchildren would memorize over the following many generations.

As the nation acquired the Far West over the next four years, some immediately saw how the new technology might be applied. In 1848 the *New Era* of St. Louis predicted that the telegraph, a "streak of lightning," soon would provide "instantaneous and continuous communication" with the just-acquired Pacific Coast. A government report noted that many people doubted whether the communication essential to a "common representative republic" would be possible within the "immense bounds" of the expanded nation, but all concern had been "put an end to forever" by Morse's invention.[2] The West and the telegraph indeed were beautifully in complement. The one was characterized by yawning distances and diverse topography. The other was well suited to spanning them both. Construction was relatively cheap and essentially simple, a matter of stringing wire between large sticks. As the web grew ever thicker in the East, it began to extend to the west. In the early 1850s the first lines were run out of San Francisco as far as Marysville in the mountains, and from those trunks others bled off to smaller settlements. Wires snaked between trees and through bushes and over thousands of crossbarred poles that some Californios reportedly believed were crucifixes raised to forestall Satan. In 1858 the Placerville, Humboldt, and Salt Lake Telegraph Company crossed the Sierra Nevada just in time for the great strike at the Comstock Lode. Two years later it reached 150 miles eastward to Fort Churchill. Logically, the next step would seem to have connected California's network with that in the East, but the assumed cost and technical challenges (both, as it turned out, exaggerated) scared away even the wealthiest investors.

The Civil War changed that. The need for fast communication with the far coast was obvious, starting with fears of Confederate designs on California goldfields. In June 1860 Congress passed the Pacific Telegraph Act. The federal government would give its support to offset the reluctance of private capital. In its basics the law was strikingly similar to the one passed almost exactly a year later to support a railway to the Pacific. The government would provide public land for a right of way and repair stations. It would offer financial support—not massive loans like those to railroads but a guarantee of forty thousand dollars a year in business for ten years. A contract was given to Western Union Telegraph Company, whose kingpin, Henry Sibley, had long advocated a transcontinental line, and in turn Western Union arranged with allies in California to form a company to build eastward. Again anticipating the transcontinental railroad, the two companies hired two separate firms, which they controlled, to do the building. One would build westward from Omaha, the other eastward from Carson City, Nevada. They would meet in Salt Lake City.

The first pole was set in Omaha on July 4, 1861, the day Congress authorized President Abraham Lincoln to raise an army of half a million men to preserve the Union. With the law requiring the link be finished by July 31, 1862, construction from both ends was frantic. Few of the predicted difficulties—Indian resistance, bison herds knocking down poles—materialized. Finding enough trees in the Great Basin and parts

of the plains took some doing, and especially on the western side, transporting giant spools of wire into the interior was a challenge, but as crews
of surveyors, hole diggers, pole placers, and wire stringers settled into a
rhythm, the process smoothed out and the pace quickened. The two lines
were joined at Salt Lake City on October 24, 1861, an astounding nine
months ahead of schedule. In the first message sent across the continent,
Stephen Field, California's chief justice and future justice of the nation's
High Court, assured Lincoln of his state's loyalty to the Union.

Controlling sole telegraphic access to the Pacific Coast gave Western
Union an unbeatable edge over its competition. At the close of the Civil
War, one historian writes, its position was "impregnable, its influence immense," and once it merged with the American Telegraph Company, its
chief rival and owner of the transatlantic cable, it was effectively a national monopoly. By 1880, 90 percent of all messages sent throughout the
country were through its wires.[3] In yet another parallel to the first transcontinental railroad, Sibley and other principals in the company milked
their position to amass enormous wealth. The company they created to
build the line was capitalized at a million dollars, seven times the actual
cost of construction, and by various manipulations they multiplied that
many times over. Referring to what was paid out to run the line to the
Pacific, one of the investors later testified that "an original expenditure
of $147,000 (and a part of that not honestly spent) came to represent
$6,000,000 in Western Union Telegraph stock."[4] Outlandish rates were
needed to support that bloated paper value. Customers at first paid six
dollars for seven words and forty-five cents for each additional word—
twice the maximum allowed by the Pacific Telegraph Act. Facing the
equivalent rate today, a person would pay about $150 to send "All us cus-
tomers are being badly overcharged."

As the transcontinental line was completed, efforts to lay a transatlantic cable had been repeatedly frustrated, and in 1866 Western Union
hatched an audacious scheme to link America to Europe via the long
way around. They would extend their system northward from California, across the Pacific Northwest and western Canada, through Russian
America (the future Alaska), under the Bering Strait, then across eastern
Siberia to the mouth of the Amur River. The Russian government prom-

ised to connect this terminus to St. Petersburg, seven thousand miles farther west, which in turn would link the system to Europe and England.
The newly wired American West would then be the middle link in a
global circuitry. The work was well under way, with crews setting poles
and stringing wire through Siberia, when a second cable was successively
laid across the Atlantic, and in March 1867 Western Union abandoned
the Russian project. Copper wire was sold as snare work to Siberian trappers, and glass insulators were marketed as uniquely American teacups.

In the emerging West, on the other hand, the telegraphic system grew
steadily. Any town that showed hints of surviving usually set out to provide itself a connection that was both a practical advantage and a badge of
status, a prerequisite of respectability. Locals raised funds—typically not
much was needed—often by forming a small company and floating stock,
and unless obstacles were especially daunting, a team with little expertise
could set a line in place. A new settlement, especially one of any promise,
was wired in sooner than later. Leadville, ten thousand feet up in the
Colorado Rockies, was linked over Mosquito Pass (13,185 feet) only a year
after the first silver discovery.[5] In time, scores of smaller companies tied
into the grid. In 1880 the Cheyenne and Black Hills Telegraph Company,
with 225 miles of line, had nine employees at eight stations; the Montana
Central sent fifty-seven hundred messages over its eighty-three miles.[6]
Some such businesses operated for years. Those showing any real promise
usually were bought out. Together they were like capillaries feeding into
ever-larger veins and arteries that moved information into, out of, and
around the West. As the mesh of wire expanded, less and less of the region could truly be called isolated.

The West was bound into a global system that had grown up alongside
it. That simple point is key to understanding how the young West worked,
in two senses of the word—in how it functioned as a newborn region,
and in how westerners labored. The most obvious example was railroads.
Networks of track, like those of wire, knit the West together within itself
and to the outside, and from the start it was assumed that the two would
operate in tandem. What is usually called the Pacific Railway Act in fact
was formally titled "An act to aid in the Construction of a Railroad and
Telegraph Line from the Missouri River to the Pacific Ocean . . . ," and

as rails were laid from east and west toward their junction at Promontory Summit, poles sprouted right along with them. The reason was obvious. The faster and farther things moved, the greater the need for coordination in their coming and going. Before a merchant in Nevada ordered goods from Pennsylvania, he needed to know roughly when he would get them, and getting them there involved a series of timed relays across an increasingly complex arrangement of carriers. It is a cliché among western historians that the railroad allowed just about everything else to happen—settlement, town building, victory in the field, the rise and flourish of enterprises from family farms to the Comstock Lode. Far less recognized is that the telegraph allowed the railroads to do what they did. None of it would have worked without news moving ahead of lumber, plows, cable, and soldiers. More exactly, all the parts—the railroads, the telegraphs, a western economy, and its workers—emerged inextricably together, allowing and feeding each other.

Ranching was a prime example. It is often seen as historically exotic. Cowpokes sing to sleeping herds in between stampedes, while posses of ranchers are stringing up rustlers. In fact, post–Civil War ranching was a splendid example of a process transforming the nation at large. From coast to coast, businesses that had always been local were morphing into integrated continental enterprises. Just as Americans had always made their own clothes or bought them nearby, so they had raised, hunted, slaughtered, and dressed their meat or had gotten it from a local butcher. Many continued to do so, but after 1865 a wholly new arrangement developed. Cattle for market were raised in one part of the nation and slaughtered elsewhere in industrial workplaces, then the beef was distributed through a harmonized system of transport. New technologies were applied, paid for with capital concentrated in corporations. Regions specialized in what each could do best. The plains and much of the semiarid West offered a pastureland second in size only to that of central Asia; the Midwest applied its innovative methods of manufacture; the Northeast provided a hungry market and a reservoir of investment funds.

Railroads tied the parts into a whole. Cattle at first were driven north from Texas to railheads on the central plains, and as railroads built into other parts of the western grasslands, ranching spread with them. When ready for market, cattle bawled their way in railcars to slaughterhouses in Kansas City, Chicago, and Cincinnati. Once disassembled, they traveled by rail to dinner tables, first in cans ("embalmed beef," some called it) and later in refrigerated cars. Easier movement, however, was not enough. Everything relied on coordination, and the telegraph literally strung this system together. In making decisions, parties hundreds of miles apart had to be privy to common information that could change day-to-day. The telegraph told the pertinent people what they needed to know when they needed to know it. The day's quoted prices and conditions of markets in Kansas City, St. Louis, Chicago, New York, and San Francisco became part of the daily browse of newspapers across the nation, the West included. A dealer in Galveston, Texas, on July 23, 1874, would find the price of corn-fed Texas steers in Kansas City at a respectable $3.50 to $4.00 per hundredweight, but he would open his paper two weeks later to find a slump to $3.25 or $3.00. In Denver, meanwhile, cattle sold locally at the opening of August for what they had in Kansas City a week earlier.[7] Anyone interested would find the options laid out, the risks there to be weighed, and if risks were already taken, there was good news or bad.

Ranching meanwhile was spreading across much of the West—out of Texas into the plains and northern Rockies and into Canada, out of California into the Great Basin and Columbia Plateau, out of the Midwest onto the northern plains and beyond. Cattle were placed near other emerging economies, mining in particular, and as soldiers and hide hunters cleared more and more of the West of Indians and bison, ranchers took over the most promising pastures. It was less an expansion than an explosion. At twenty years old, the unfortunately nicknamed R. G. "Dick" Head helped drive one of the first herds to Abilene in 1867. Over the next seven years he drove others not only to Wichita, Ellsworth, Great Bend, and Dodge City in Kansas but also to Cheyenne, Salt Lake City, Nevada's Humboldt River ranges, and California and to Indian agencies on the upper Missouri River and in the Black Hills. Head was taking part in what one authority calls "the largest short-term geographical shift of domestic herd animals in the history of the world."[8]

Wires, as much as rails, allowed it to happen. Owners dispatching herds across the region, as much as agents marketing them back east, needed distant information close at hand, sometimes to shift strategies and directions on the fly. In 1868 the twenty-four-year-old W. A. Peril hired on to drive a herd from Gillespie County in central Texas to Montana goldfields, but after wintering at Brown's Hole on the Green River, he heard from the owners that he was to proceed to better prospects in Nevada. There he got word to put the fattest of the herd on a train to San Francisco, then to drive the rest up to Oregon, fifteen hundred crow-flying miles from where he started. There he sold them. After nearly two years on the trail, he took the train through Cheyenne and Denver to St. Louis, where he boarded a steamboat for New Orleans, took ship to Galveston, moved on to San Antonio by train and stage, bought a horse, and road home to Gillespie County.[9]

Farming, the oldest American enterprise of all, was undergoing the same expansion and integration. Start with a remarkable statistic: more land was brought under cultivation in the United States between 1870 and 1900 (225 million acres) than between the founding of Jamestown in 1607 and 1870 (189 million acres). Most of this was in the West, partly because that was where most unplowed land was and partly through vigorous federal encouragement. The Homestead Act (1862) made unclaimed land easier to acquire than ever before. Railroads were doubly influential. For farmers looking to markets, the richest western lands were worthless until rail connections gave them the means to send crops out and bring goods in. Railroads were also the most aggressive land promoters in American history. The Pacific Railway Act, passed within a month of the Homestead Act, and all but one subsequent law supporting transcontinental construction gave railroads enormous amounts of land to sell to help pay off their equally massive government loans. Besides recruiting farmers from the East, corporations sent hundreds of agents to Europe to offer cheap or free transportation, alluring land prices, free seed, and other inducements to potential emigrants. This confluence of forces brought a powerful tide of family farmers onto the Great Plains and elsewhere in the interior West. During the twenty years after 1860 the number of farms in Kansas grew from around 10,000 to about 239,000.

So impressive was this wave, and so strong is our collective fondness for images of sturdy pioneer yeomen, that it is easy to miss another, especially portentous side of the agrarian West. Not long after the gold rush transformed it into one of the world's great seaports, San Francisco became one of the nation's major exporters of wheat. Grain raised in California's Central Valley soon satisfied local markets, and by the early 1850s merchants of the Bay City were looking outward. Wheat first was shipped around the Pacific, to Australia, Peru, Chile, Hawaii, and China, but its most common destination turned out to be, remarkably, Great Britain. By 1860 nearly half of the wheat and flour leaving San Francisco was headed for England. Eight years later more than a third of all U.S. wheat exports left through the Golden Gate, and of that 80 percent went to the British Isles. Part of the explanation lies in the low cost of production. Developed from scratch (and obliterating long-established Native uses), much of the Central Valley farming was in large mechanized units worked by cheap temporary labor. The low cost per bushel helped offset the expense of distant marketing. Meanwhile, covering those distances also grew easier and cheaper. A new type of clipper ship, the "Down Easter," first launched by New England shipbuilders in 1869, could carry larger, bulkier cargoes faster than the earlier, sleeker clippers. Travel time from California to Liverpool dropped from four or five months to as little as a hundred days. English grain production plummeted in competition with the Pacific Coast as well as India and the Black Sea region. Rapid rail construction meanwhile let San Francisco tap ever deeper into the Sacramento, San Joaquin, and Salinas Valleys.[10]

Equally important was the other side of the revolution in movement—communication. In this the key figure in California was a towering (six feet, seven inches) German Jewish immigrant, Isaac Friedlander, soon known as the Grain King of San Francisco. Friedlander's essential insight was to see that an intermeshed global transportation system was useless unless information also could be coordinated over great spaces. Liverpool merchants were not going to send their ships fourteen thousand miles to California unless they were reasonably sure there was something there to carry away. California growers would not keep producing more wheat without the reasonable expectation that somebody would buy it at a good price. Friedlander devised a sophisticated system of gathering forecasts of valley wheat production. Using the continental telegraph and undersea cables, he determined which commercial ships were available across much of the planet. Then he found the credit to put it all together, connected the various parties, and set the scheme in motion. Scarcely a decade after the gold rush, wheat grown in the San Joaquin Valley rolled by rail and sailed down inland rivers to San Francisco, where it was loaded on New England Down Easters, which carried it around Cape Horn and across the Atlantic, there to be joined along the way by cargoes from Bombay and Odessa bound for bakeries and kitchens of Londoners and Liverpudlians.

San Francisco, similarly, quickly emerged as a major manufacturing center. Looking inland, it produced slaughtered beef, clothing, glassware, books, coffins, crackers, paper, vinegar, and macaroni. Looking outward, it provided steel, ships, whale oil, and lumber. Mining equipment was the city's forte. South of Market Street factories made pumps for deep mines and stamps for mills; boilers, retorts, and amalgamation pans for processing; hoses and nozzles for hydraulicking. Rails and wires allowed it all to be marketed and sent over an enormous radius. Soon, in fact, industrial San Francisco was supplying an area second only to Chicago's.[11] Western mining itself was a variation on the Bay City's boom. The Comstock Lode, like the sites of most gold and silver strikes, was isolated in the western high country, yet within only two years of its strike, Virginia City, plugged into the revolutionary network of movement, was humming with forty-six mills processing ore from more than fifty miles of tunnels beneath them. Many other boomtowns across the Mountain West were, almost immediately, industrial cities more fully developed than many eastern manufacturing centers.

The rise and blossom of places like Virginia City and San Francisco, as well as experiences like those of W. A. Peril and Isaac Friedlander, tell us something fundamental about the new West. Because it grew up alongside those revolutionary leaps in communication and transport, this West emerged by a pattern exactly opposite the one of westward expansion before it. That traditional pattern was famously summed up by Frederick Jackson Turner in 1893. Settlers of those earlier Wests, Turner wrote, had to revert to earlier, simpler ways of living—more basic means of subsistence, less elaborate social organization, elemental political structures. He argued that it was in building new lives out of those simpler beginnings that a distinctive American culture evolved. Turner's thesis has drawn many justified criticisms, but his point about new settlements reverting to earlier forms was valid. Moving westward in space in a sense meant moving backward in time.

The basic reason behind that time traveling was isolation. Because settlers in the new country were relatively cut off from markets, support from home folks, and sources of many needful things, they had to rely mostly on what was right around them. They built homes from what was at hand. They did their work with what little they brought with them and what they could produce locally. They ate their own crops or sold them inside a tight radius. Then came the railroad and telegraph. As they and the new West grew up together, the new country enjoyed an accessibility unimaginable in earlier regions newly opened. General stores had bags of flour and barrels of pickles; saloons had billiard tables and elaborate mirrors behind the bars; sodbusters had steel-tipped plows and pianos. Before long, westerners were ordering all types of things out of catalogs, from prefabricated houses to corsets and pump organs. Settlers and storekeepers bought it all with drafts and loans wired from family members and distant creditors. One consequence is immediately clear in early photos of towns and interiors of businesses and homes: soon after its first settlers arrived, a new area might look strikingly like another back east.

Being plugged into national and global networks of trade thus meant that new westerners could bring with them much more, and much more easily. Less obvious, they could also more readily send out into those same markets more of what they could offer. As rails let them bring in the necessary machines and equipment, and as the telegraph let them choreograph production and demand, they could put into place from the outset the latest systems of production.

Turner's insight—that frontier settlements had to build a new life from scratch—had a corollary not often recognized. In the second half of the nineteenth century, as the nation shifted rapidly and dramatically toward a modern economy, having to start from nothing suddenly could be an advantage. Well settled areas of the East might be slow to turn to new means of production, because their older, now outmoded ways first had to be done away with, an expensive and laborious process. New westerners, using the revolution in the movement of things and information, could put into place new technologies without the costs of doing away with the old.

The pattern Turner had seen on earlier frontiers was reversed. Those moving westward were no longer moving backward in time. They were moving forward. The expansive ranching system of W. A. Peril's odyssey emerged more rapidly than any Gilded Age industry and rivaled any in its sophisticated connections among raw materials, their processing, and the transport and final distribution of finished goods. It took Isaac Friedlander, the "Grain King," only a few years to organize an enterprise that linked the latest mechanized large-scale agriculture into a newly coordinated system of global trade. Elsewhere western farming sprouted in strikingly modern forms. A map in the 1870 census ranked agricultural areas by their "*relative* power" to produce the most bushels of wheat on the least amount of improved acreage and with the fewest workers. It coded each place's efficiency on a scale of I to IV. In the Midwest, which produced by far the most wheat, a few spots rose to III and a slice of Minnesota earned a IV, but most of the nation's established breadbasket ranked only I or II. Out West, where wheat production had barely begun, four areas scored a III—Montana's Yellowstone and Gallatin River Valleys, the South Platte River near Denver, Oregon's Willamette Valley, and part of the country around the Great Salt Lake—while California's Central Valley earned the highest grade of IV.[12]

The key to this turnabout in western development was connectedness, and of the connections that made the difference, wires deserve as much credit as rails. Not only did the telegraph allow railroads to do what they did, directing their traffic and permitting the ordering, the transfer of capital, and the rest that set it all in motion; but, in one instance, it eliminated the need for railroads altogether. The telegraph was essential to creating arguably the purest expression of the new western economy, one that distilled the frontiering impulse to its essence—the western stock exchange.

A typical frontier boom began when some new potential was found in some place not yet widely settled by people from more populous parts of the nation. The news made its way to those more populous areas. When it arrived, usually exaggerated, some responded by heading to the place reported, confident and expectant of wringing gain from the new possibilities. A boom, that is, happened when a burst of local knowledge traveled to persons waiting for a chance to act on the belief that they could work that knowledge to their own betterment, and could do it better than most. In the 1820s and 1830s southern farmers heard about great farmland in Texas, and they went there. Word arrived back east in late 1848 of gold along the American River, and people rushed to California. The same impulse had been followed from the beginning of what Walter Prescott Webb called "The Great Frontier," in the fifteenth and sixteenth centuries when Europeans sought out newfound possibilities in Asia and the subcontinent.[13]

As Webb also noted, from the start some pursued another variation of a boom. They acted out the same response, but long-distance. Early-modern world frontiers coincided with the emergence of modern commercial life. With that came prototypes of the corporation, and through them people could invest in distant booms. In a sense they were taking the frontier plunge, just like those who rode or walked or sailed to some faraway place, but instead of actually going there, they stayed home and plunged vicariously, by putting down their money. These long-distance frontiersmen sought, not the richest claim or the best land, but the most exploitable intelligence about such things. The resource they were after was lucrative information. They were prospectors and cultivators of distant knowledge.

By essentially eliminating distance, the telegraph revolutionized this vicarious frontier. It brought information and impulse immediately together. News no longer traveled at the excruciatingly slow pace of ships, horses, feet, or trains. It now moved at 670 million miles per hour, so anyone inside the telegraphic grid had nearly immediate access to knowledge from some remote locality. Before, investors could take part in a frontier boom without actually going there. Now they could take the plunge as if they *were* there.

Seen in that light, an urban stock exchange was as emblematic of the emerging West and its meanings as a placer claim or a homesteader's soddie. The San Francisco Mining and Stock Exchange offers the best example. It opened in 1862 with a handful of members paying fifty dollars each for a seat. Within a year it was trading the stock of more than thirteen hundred companies. As an ever-wider public became caught up in the speculative experience, the result was a frenzied electronic marketplace. The number of a company's shares traded in a single day sometimes was twice the number in circulation. The capital produced, on paper at least, was astonishing. When news arrived of Virginia City, Nevada's "Big Bonanza" in 1874, the value of Comstock mining shares rose in two weeks from $93 million to more than $300 million, half again the assessed value of all San Francisco real estate. The orders, a founder of the exchange wrote years later, came from all classes in the city and surrounding region, but the sources went far beyond that: "Wherever the telegraph wire extended, our orders would roll in on us. The Eastern cities also, New York in particular. . . . London, Paris, Berlin and Frankfort sent us orders."[14]

Returns, of course, were hardly equal. Robert Louis Stevenson, in the Bay City courting his future wife, called the stock exchange "the heart of San Francisco." This "great pump" sucked money from the masses and funneled it into the pockets of men with talents that generated the greatest profits in the emerging West—manipulating information and riding the soar and dive of stock prices.[15] They were masters of a new variation on the frontier boom. Its raw stuff was wealth wired from around the earth, but in a sense the true commodity was public hope and naïveté expressed as bets on the western future. In essence this boom was invisible, units of capital and abstract commitments riding electricity, an economy of the ether. Its material consequences, however, were enormous. The money pumped from the public to a small club of millionaires helped pay for hydraulic mining (including its gargantuan water delivery systems), manufacturing, ranching, real estate, shipping, and not least, more railroads and telegraph lines. The twin revolutions fed each other. The collapse of distance in the movement of information generated capital. That capital was used to construct economies now possible because of new systems of moving physical things. Moving those things, whether machinery or wheat or cattle, made sense and made profits only if information was always moving ahead of them, bringing far-distant impulses into harmony.

The telegraphic web was a "network of iron nerves," wrote Oliver Wendell Holmes, "which flash sensation and volition backward and forward to and from towns and provinces as if they were organs and limbs of a single living body." Railroads, in turn, were "a vast system of iron muscles which . . . move the limbs of the mighty organism one upon another." Writing in 1861, Holmes referred to the body at war. A regiment ordered by wire to ride southward by rail was "a contraction and extension of the arm of Massachusetts with a clenched fist full of bayonets at the end of it."[16] Once the Civil War was over and the Union preserved, that body military turned westward to confirm the Union's full command of the recently acquired Far West. In the Indian wars troops were ferried by rail to where they were needed, sometimes from across the continent, while commanders positioned those soldiers according to what they learned of their quarry's whereabouts from information clicked to them over the expanding copper net.

Holmes's metaphor, of a nation bound into one body by a vast neural network, played out through millions of ordinary lives. In 1876 William Storey, a telegrapher in Camp Grant, Arizona, was in love with Clara Choate of San Diego. Unfortunately, his commander would not let him go to California to marry, and Camp Grant had no minister. So Clara traveled to Arizona, and once the southwestern lines were cleared after working hours on April 24, the two exchanged vows administered by the Reverend Jonathan Mann, 650 miles to the west in San Diego. For years Storey heard from colleagues that they had been present at his wedding.[17]

And in a sense, of course, they had been. Space and time, if far from irrelevant, were redefined in what they meant to life's dailiness and, for William and Clara, its fundamental choices.

One result was a striking shift in the human composition of far-western frontiers. Settlers of previous generations, leaving for new lives in Kentucky, Illinois, Mississippi, or Texas, rightly assumed that they might never again see families left behind. They presumed that any exchange of news, including the happiest and most dire, would be slow and chancy. By contrast, their descendants could move into and out of the new West as easily as longhorns and carloads of corn. Once there, they could count on the emotional sustenance of letters carried via railroads, stage lines, and ships. By the 1860s the postal service delivered two million letters a year to the Pacific Coast via the sea lanes and twenty tons a month overland, while through the wires the most pressing news could pass among relatives within hours, albeit for a hefty price.[18] Suddenly moving west was no longer necessarily a lifetime commitment. Now men—not only bachelors but also husbands and fathers—could head for the new country intending to stay only a year or three, even as economies like mining and ranching placed a premium on adult male labor. While families had dominated earlier frontiers, in the Far West, except in Mormon country, males were overwhelmingly the majority. For every hundred females in 1850, 1870, and 1890, there were, respectively, 278.9, 147.0, and 142.3 males. The West's accessibility pulled in a foreign flood. Eight western states and territories had a higher portion of foreign-born persons than New York in 1870. As late as 1880 San Francisco still had more foreigners than females.[19]

In its human makeup, as well as in the way its people worked, in its relations with the wider world, and in its basic structures of power and wealth, the West was shaped profoundly by the twin revolutions of communication and transportation, and of those the former, driven by the telegraph and its transcendence of past limits, had an influence both enormous and underrecognized by historians. It is worth wondering, in fact, whether it would have been possible to think of "the West" as a single region at all without the changes the telegraph brought to popular perception. Depending on where its boundaries are set, the West comprises as much as half the territory of the lower forty-eight. It is also by far the most varied of our regions, embracing Death Valley and Glacier National Park, the Grand Canyon and the rain forests of the Olympic Peninsula. Perhaps it was only after people grew used to such vastness being knit practically together, allowing a couple in Arizona to be married by a minister in California, that it became conceivable to call such far-flung diversity by one name.

One point is certain: we cannot understand the Far West without recognizing that, compared to other regions, it was born connected, within
itself and to the world beyond. In turn, that meant that, compared to
all frontiers before it, the Far West was also born modern. It took its
shape as a projection of forces remaking a nation. First came the explosive
expansion to the Pacific, then the speedy rise and spread of new enterprises, with cattle raised in Texas and slaughtered in Cincinnati, California wheat ending up as English biscuits, massive machines bought with
fantasies sold in the form of stocks, raw wealth pulled out of western
mountains to help pay for retooling distant industries. If previous Wests
had stood for individual opportunity in country thrown back into simpler
times, this one was a confident boast of collective greatness in a rapidly
changing world. There was, too, the promise of a nation reaching farther
still, as caught in a scene connected to that emblematic moment of western power, the driving of the final spike at the completion of the first
transcontinental railroad. On that day, May 29, 1869, as Leland Stanford
famously swung the sledge to drive home the spike, wires were wound
around the spike and sledge and run to a telegraphic key, so that when
metal touched metal, a single impulse let the world know, instantaneously,
that the job was done. Meanwhile in San Francisco an inventive young
army officer had laid his own wire from a receiver to the firing mechanism
of a fifteen-inch artillery piece pointed across the city's bay. Thus the same
blow that symbolically bound coast to coast also sent a shell through the
Golden Gate toward the next rim of American ambition.

A sense of destiny and conquest in fact had been there from the start,
embedded in another famous moment in the technological binding of
the nation, the first official telegraphic transmission sent from Morse to
Vail in May 1844: "What hath God wrought." The standard story behind
those words has it that on the night Congress gave Morse the money to
build that first line from Washington, D.C., to Baltimore, he was too ner-
vous to stay at the Capitol for the vote, so he heard the good news from
a young friend, Annie Ellsworth, who came to his home late that night.
In a burst of relief and gratitude, Morse supposedly gave her the honor
of choosing the first message. It's a great story, and it might be true, but

whether Morse approved Ellsworth's words or picked them himself, they have an intriguing resonance when set in the context of the man's origins and upbringing. Morse had a father who was famous on two counts. A staunchly orthodox Congregationalist minister, Jedidiah Morse was a leading opponent of new religious ideas expressed most prominently in the Unitarian movement. Morse's father also earned the reputation of the "father of American geography." First composing primers for schoolchildren, he eventually produced the monumental *American Universal Geography*. In these first attempts to describe the young nation and its landforms, he occasionally played the prophet. The tide of American expansion was unstoppable, he wrote, and although the Far West, country currently beyond our borders, was then "in a state of nature, wild and uncultivated," white settlement would inevitably cover it. Native peoples must either give way and join the new order, or they would spend a few miserable generations in decline before vanishing forever.[20]

Samuel Morse thus grew up steeped in both biblical orthodoxy and the conviction of a superior people's rightful, destined expansion. The famous message of May 24, 1844, came from the first and expressed the second. It is found in the Book of Numbers, the account of the Israelites long desert sojourn after escaping Egypt. The passage comes as they are approaching the promised land. They have vanquished any who have stood in their way and now are drawing close to the Moabites. Fearing that the newcomers will destroy his people next, "as the ox licketh up the grass of the field," the Moabite king, Balak, asks a nearby prophet and holy man, Balaam, to call on God to curse the invaders. In a series of semicomic scenes Balaam reports that he can do nothing, that in fact God favors the Israelites and turns attempted curses into blessings. Try harder, a frustrated Balak tells Balaam. Finally Balaam puts his foot down. God is no human who might change his mind, he says. God means what God means, and having blessed the Israelites with great strength ("the shout of a king is among them"), God means them to fulfill their destiny. The world will stand in wonder: "It shall be said of Jacob and Israel, What hath God wrought!" (Numbers 23:23). And woe to any who oppose them. God's chosen people will be like a great lion, Balaam says, who rises up and "shall not lie down until he eat of the prey, and drink the blood of the slain."

The phrase that Morse tapped to Vail, usually taken to mean a marveling at the telegraph's godlike accomplishment, in fact expressed a certain horrified wonder at the terrible destruction bound to come to anyone resisting God's chosen people. Morse surely knew the original point of the words, and given the lessons from his father, he might well have heard in them God's blessing of the marriage of his own nation's destiny to the new technologies he had help set loose. Others certainly saw the connection. "Steam and electricity," plus the American spirit, had created "the greatest, the most original, the most wonderful [country] the sun has ever shone upon," wrote a New York editorialist musing on the telegraph and its meaning. With such powers America's sweep to continental dominance was unstoppable, he added, and any who stood in the way and failed "to mix with this movement . . . will be crushed into . . . impalpable powder."[21] We can cringe at the arrogance and question whether it was a divine hand that was smiting the Indians, but the telegraph's significance in winning and shaping the Far West is undeniable. The region was born of forces creating a modern nation, and none was more influential than the revolution in the movement of word and thought. From the start the West was wired to the world.

Notes

1. Morse's recollection is in a letter written in September 1837 to Secretary of the Treasury Levi Woodbury, reprinted in Alfred Vail, *The American Electro Magnetic Telegraph: With the Reports of Congress, and a Description of All Telegraphs Known, Employing Electricity or Galvanism* (Philadelphia: Lea & Blanchard, 1847), 152.

2. Kenneth Silverman, *Lightning Man: The Accursed Life of Samuel F. B. Morse* (New York: Alfred A. Knopf, 2003), 241.

3. James D. Reid, *The Telegraph in America: Its Founders, Promoters, and Noted Men* (New York: Derby Brothers, 1879), 496. Armin E. Shuman, "Report on the Statistics of Telegraphs and Telephones in the United States," in U.S. Census Bureau, *Report on the Agencies of Transportation in the United States, Including the Statistics of Railroads, Steam Navigation, Canals, Telegraphs, and Telephones,* 10th Census, 1880, vol. 4, 784–85.

4. *Report of the Committee on Post-Offices and Post-Roads, United States Senate, on Postal Telegraph,* Senate Report 577, 48th Cong., 1st sess., 4–5.

5. Eugene Floyd Irey, "A Social History of Leadville, Colorado During the Boom Days, 1877–1881" (Ph.D. diss., University of Minnesota, 1951), 278.

6. Shuman, "Report on the Statistics of Telegraphs and Telephones in the United States." These companies were hardly financial behemoths. Nebraska's Beatrice Electric Company, chartered in 1880 with two thousand dollars in stock sold among eighteen persons, provided local telegraph and eventually telephone connections for two years until it was bought out. Its final balance sheet showed income of $1,269.12 against expenses of $1,279.34, leaving it $10.22 in the hole. Beatrice Electric Company Records, Nebraska State Historical Society, Lincoln.

7. *Galveston Daily News,* July 23, August 8, 1874; Denver *Daily Rocky Mountain News,* August 1, 1874.

8. Terry G. Jordan, *North American Cattle-Ranching Frontiers: Origins, Diffusion, and Differentiation* (Albuquerque: University of New Mexico Press, 1993), 222.

9. J. Marvin Hunter, *The Trail Drivers of Texas: Interesting Sketches of Early Cowboys and Their Experiences on the Range and on the Trail During the Days That Tried Men's Souls—True Narratives Related by Real Cowpunchers and Men Who Fathered the Cattle Industry in Texas* (Austin: University of Texas Press, 1985), 411–13, 734–35.

10. On the California wheat trade during these years, see Rodman W. Paul, "The Wheat Trade between California and the United Kingdom," *Mississippi Valley Historical Review* 45:3 (December 1958): 391–412.

11. Richard Walker, "Industry Builds the City: The Suburbanization of Manufacturing in the San Francisco Bay Area, 1850–1940," *Journal of Historical Geography* 27:1 (2001): 37–38.

12. U.S. Bureau of the Census, *Ninth Census, Volume III: The Statistics of the Wealth and Industry of the United States . . .* (Washington, D.C.: Government Printing Office, 1872), 80–81, 367.

13. Walter Prescott Webb, *The Great Frontier* (Boston: Houghton Mifflin, 1952).

14. Jos[eph] L. King, *History of the San Francisco Stock Exchange Board* (New York: Arno Press, 1975), 9–10, 78.

15. Robert Louis Stevenson, "The Old and New Pacific Capitals," in *The Works of Robert Louis Stevenson,* South Seas Edition, vol. 4 (New York: Charles Scribner's Sons, 1925), 173.

16. Oliver Wendell Holmes, "Bread and the Newspaper," *Atlantic Monthly* 8:45 (July 1861): 348.

17. Tom Standage, *The Victorian Internet: The Remarkable Story of the Telegraph and the Nineteenth Century's On-line Pioneers* (New York: Walker & Co., 1998), 137–38.

18. Report of the Postmaster General is in *Message from the President of the United States to the two Houses of Congress at the commencement of the first session of the Thirty-sixth Congress; December 27, 1859,* Sen. Exec. Doc. 2, part 3, 36th Cong. 1st sess., Serial Set 1025, vol. 3, 1408–11, 1484; LeRoy R. Hafen, *The Overland Mail,*

1849–1869: Promoter of Settlement, Precursor of Railroads (Cleveland, Ohio: Arthur H. Clark, 1926), 45–46.

19. Warren S. Thompson and P. K. Whelpton, *Population Trends in the United States* (New York: McGraw-Hill, 1933), 183; U.S. Bureau of the Census, *Report on the Social Statistics of Cities, Compiled by George E. Waring, Jr., Expert and Special Agent* (Washington, D.C.: Government Printing Office, 1887), 800.

20. Jedidiah Morse and Sidney Edwards Morse, *A New System of Geography, or a View of the Present State of the World* (Boston: Richardson & Lord, 1822), 56. Morse expressed the same views in a report to the secretary of war following a tour of Indian peoples in New York and the Great Lakes. Jedediah Morse, *A Report to the Secretary of War of the United States on Indian Affairs* (New Haven: S. Converse, 1822), esp. 65–66. Reprinted as *A Report to the Secretary of War of the United States on Indian Affairs* (New York: Augustus M. Kelley, 1970).

21. Silverman, *Lightning Man,* 243.

5

Reconstructing Race

I live in a town that doesn't know where it is. Fayetteville is in northwestern Arkansas—that's clear enough—but when somebody asks us locals to explain just where in this wide republic that is, things get dicey. The architecture and the lovely fall colors suggest the Midwest. The pace of life, people's accents, and the studied eccentricities all speak of the South. Some put us elsewhere. At a party soon after I arrived, I told a colleague's wife my field of study. "Oh, the West is a wonderful place to live!" she said in her soft Carolinian rhythm. I asked when she had lived there. She looked at me, as if at a slow nephew, and answered: "Why, now."

Living and working along the seams of national regions is a fine encouragement to wonder about the differences and continuities among them—in appearance, in habits and points of view, and beneath all that, in their histories. Two things I know for sure: the South thinks it is different from the rest of the country, and it is race that southerners use most often to explain their separateness. The tortured relations of black and white, slavery and its rage and guilt, the war that ended slavery and the tormented generations that followed, the centuries-long embrace, intimate and awful on so many levels—all that, we're told, has set southerners apart and has made the South the central stage of America's racial drama.

Yet from my office on the cusp of regions, I have questions. I have no doubt that the South and southerners are peculiar, and I am sure that race helps explain how and why. My problem lies in how we have allowed the South to dominate the story of race in America. From my perch, three hundred miles west of Memphis and east of the 98th meridian, it looks as if the South, with a Jeb Stuart audacity, has surrounded and confined how we think, talk, and write about this essential part of our history. And with a few recent exceptions, we have mostly gone along with it.[1]

It is high time to look again at race in America during the crucial middle years of the nineteenth century and to wonder what that story might look like if expanded to a continental perspective. Specifically, we need to bring the West more into the picture. The acquisition of the Far West in the 1840s influenced, much more than we have admitted, our racial history—how people have thought about race, how racial minorities have fared, and which policies our government adopted. Because race is always a bellwether of larger forces, we ought to consider also that the great gulping of land in the 1840s had as much to do with shaping the course of our history as did any event of that century, including the Civil War, which dominates the story as told today.

Taken together, the acquisitions of 1845–48 constituted our greatest expansion. The annexations of Texas and Oregon and the Mexican Cession made the United States much larger, much richer, and far more ethnically mixed. Languages are one crude measure of the last-named aspect. While the United States grew in area by about 66 percent, the number of languages spoken within it increased by more than 100 percent. That number would grow still greater during the next few years as tens of thousands flooded into the California goldfields. In the 1850s no nation on earth had a region with so rich an ethnic stew as the American West.

Expansion triggered an American racial crisis. We have always taught that to our students, of course, but we have missed at least half the point. The connection we make is between expansion and slavery. We say that new western lands, full of opportunity, made the question of black slavery dangerously concrete outside the South. That, in turn, set loose disputes that by 1861 would tip us over the edge of catastrophe.

This sequence seems to give the West a prominent role in America's racial history, but the effect is ironic.[2] Because race remains strictly a matter of black and white, and because its prime issue is African American slavery and its central event is the Civil War, western expansion is important only on eastern terms. Once the Mexican War does its mischief, the focus quickly swings back east and stays there. The West has its consequential moment, then remains at the edge of the action.

That is nothing close to the whole story. Expansion was double trouble. Not only did it speed up the old conflict between North and South, but by complicating so hugely America's ethnic character, it raised new questions about the relation between race and nation. These questions centered on the West. The best introduction to them is through the rhetoric surrounding expansion. In that rhetoric the acquisition of the West was both explained and justified in terms of the inferiority of its nonwhite native peoples. Mexicans were called inherently debased, unable to govern themselves, and too slothful and torpid to realize the West's potential. In a minor masterpiece of circular reasoning, Thomas Jefferson Farnham declared southern California's darker peoples indolent, then cited as evidence their "lazy color."[3] Indians were said to be mostly incapable of settling down to the useful arts of farming and industry, and they were inherently violent to boot. Anglo-Americans, by contrast, were described as so naturally superior that they could hardly help but expand into neighboring territory so unsuitably held by lesser peoples.[4]

The racial rationale for conquest was one more expression of the Romantic spirit coloring all aspects of the westward movement. The world of the Romantics was made up of distinct groups—the terms "races," "nations," and "peoples" were used interchangeably. Every race had its own virtues and vices.[5] Only a generation or so earlier, in Jefferson's America, such traits were said to be pliable. Eastern Indians, the Jeffersonians argued, had only to be immersed in white culture in order to evolve in abilities and manners, finally reaching something like parity and merging into full citizenship. By the 1840s, however, the Jeffersonian view had given way to the Romantic, which drew a far harder line. Now the character of each race was said to be as innate and unchanging as fur to a cat and hoots to an owl. One writer went so far as to give Mexicans a category separate from humanity, "Mexicanity." Anglo-Saxons (or Caucasians, or Teutons, or Anglo-Normans), on the other hand, were humankind's finest, but their superior traits were just as unchangeable as the inferior ones of western natives. Whites and nonwhites were separated from each other by what Francis Parkman called in *The Oregon Trail* the "impassable gap" between his own kind and Indians.[6]

Romantic racism pervaded American culture in the 1840s. Even many abolitionists and opponents of the Mexican War, like Ralph Waldo Emerson and Theodore Parker, embraced Romantic racial thinking.[7] It found its sharpest focus, however, where we would expect, in the nation's two racial hotspots, the South and West. We can hear it in southerners' defenses of slavery and in the histories and essays about inevitable expansion, in high literature like the southern fiction of William Gilmore Simms, and in the dozens of popular western novels portraying "Mexican monkeys" and bloodthirsty Indians.[8] The western racial crisis was in a dynamic relationship with that of the South. The new questions raised by expansion were distinctively western—they took their shape from the West's own conditions—but they also played on, and were played on by, older issues rooted in the South and in black slavery. What emerged was a dialogue between regions that tells us a lot about America's genuinely continental racial preoccupations.

Some Americans focused on the racial similarities of two regions inhabited by darker peoples. What, they wondered, might happen if southern blacks should move west and mix with other races? The Mississippian Robert Walker argued cleverly to northerners who disliked both slavery and blacks that Texas annexation would actually reduce the nation's black population. Freedmen and slaves would flow naturally toward the Southwest and eventually into Mexico, attracted by the concentration of duskier peoples. This ingenious notion of Texas-as-siphon was picked up by several prominent figures, including James Buchanan and John O'Sullivan, coiner of the phrase "manifest destiny."[9] Others were deeply disturbed by the mingling of nonwhite peoples of the South and West. When Senator Thomas Hart Benton looked at Florida's Seminole conflict, then looked westward, he saw the prospect of a continental race war—an alliance of blacks and Indians that would set loose "the ravages of the colored races upon the white!"[10]

Others feared not conflict, but intimate union. Romantic racists held that sex across the racial divide dragged the superior partner down toward the inferior. They explained Mexico's defeat by its mixing of European blood with Indian—the term of the day was "mongrelization"—and pointed at what they considered the sorry state of southern mulattos to warn what might happen as triumphant Anglos mingled with the West's motley of peoples.[11] What may be the two earliest applications of the word "hybrid" to people rather than plants and animals were by the Alabama physician Josiah Nott, whose racial theories were a major prop of slavery, and by Washington Irving. In *The Adventures of Captain Bonneville*, Irving warned that out West the amalgamation of Indians and whites would produce hybrid races, the mongrel peoples he described in Astoria as being "like new formations in geology, . . . [made from] the 'debris' and abrasions' of former races, civilized and savage."[12]

Other commentators concentrated on the obvious differences between West and South. These contrasts, like the parallels, tell us a lot about the thinking of the day. In particular, they bring out a crucial theme otherwise easily missed—the relation between race and distance. At the heart of the southern dilemma was the fact that blacks were enmeshed in white society. They were considered always a threat, yet they were economically essential, from cotton fields to kitchens, and so had to be kept close. From the white perspective, the problem with blacks was that, metaphorically and literally, they were inside the house. The problem with Mexicans and Indians was the opposite. They might have been technically inside the nation's borders in 1848, but they were far removed from white control. Just as troubling, they were close by to others of their own kind. The 49th and 33rd parallels cut arbitrarily across nearly two thousand miles of the West's cultural grain, and as for the Rio Grande, it did not divide the land and peoples on either side of it any more than a zipper divides a pair of pants. The fear was that cultural kinsmen just over these meaningless borders would reinforce every deviant tendency of western peoples. The possibility of overcoming these problems of distance, and bringing the new country fully under control, raised a further problem. We had justified conquest by calling western natives cultural simpletons, political knuckle-walkers, and violent drifters hopelessly incompatible with our way of life. How then would they ever fit in once the West was made truly part of the republic?

This conversation between West and South suggests the full racial crisis triggered by expansion. It was partly about Free Soil, the question of whether southern slavery, with its nonwhite peoples as essential insiders, would spread to the West. But equally pressing were questions about nonwhite peoples already there, racial outsiders beyond the government's reach and with no obvious part to play in national life. Should they—could they—be brought inside? And if they should, how? And if not, what should we do with them? The quick and facile answer, commonly heard at the time of the Mexican War, was that Indians and Mexicans would simply melt away before the expansion of superior white society. What exactly melting meant, how it would happen, and where the residue would go—all that was vague. In any case, this notion of ethnic evaporation kept the potentially explosive issues comfortably out of focus.[13] White America could tell itself that as time passed, the problems would solve themselves. As Anglos took possession of the West, they would never need to live in any numbers for very long as close neighbors with nonwhites.

And then, within roughly two hundred hours of the signing of the Treaty of Guadalupe Hidalgo, that glib expectation vanished. Gold was found in California. What melted away was not Mexicans and Indians but the easy conceit that whites and nonwhites would never have to face each other. Anyone looking for the regionally lopsided treatment of race in these years need only look at California's story, starting with the name given to those who supposedly first found and dug the gold: forty-niners. The rush, of course, began the year before. By the time easterners showed up, the diggings had some whites from California, Oregon, and Australia, but mostly Indians, Californios, Sonorans, Chileans, Peruvians, and Hawaiians. These first gold diggers, the forty-eighters, blasted the easy comforts of racial supremacy. Far from twiddling away their time, these crowds of lazy-colored people were energetically and efficiently pulling money from the ground—wealth that white Americans presumed was theirs. Then, only a few years later, came the Chinese, more alien in appearance and custom than any other voluntary immigrants in American history. Now they too worked, and worked well, this field of dreams.[14]

In California, the racial crisis sparked by expansion was suddenly taken to a new level. The 1850s saw two violent episodes in the West. Both arose from the prospect of white settlement, and both concerned the role of race in controlling natural resources. One episode has gotten plenty of attention; the other has been virtually ignored. The first was in Kansas. Its question was whether southern slavery, that system involving nonwhite insiders, would have a part in the new agricultural economy of the plains. Every survey text covers in detail the Free Soil fight, its characters and events. The second episode was in California. The question there concerned nonwhite outsiders and their place in the new economy of mineral wealth. This episode was just as revealing and a lot uglier. First Chileans, Sonorans, and others from South and Central America and Mexico were forcibly expelled or confined to marginal diggings. Then much the same was done to Chinese through physical and economic harassment. And throughout this period and the decade that followed, white Californians waged a brutal campaign against Indians.[15] The term "genocide" is tossed around far too easily in discussions of Indian policy, but this was the genuine article—roundups, assaults, destruction of families (including child-stealing), and organized hunts of extermination. This second conquest of California took a human toll hundreds of times that of the Kansas raids and bushwhacking, yet it gets at most a line or two in our texts and rarely a sentence in our lectures.[16]

These twin episodes, Bleeding Kansas and Bloodier California, were fitting preludes to the 1860s, years of unmatched violence rooted in our racial dilemmas. The toll of those years, of course, was incomparably greater in the East, but the level of carnage there should not obscure the fact that the Civil War's racial consequences, like its preliminaries, were truly continent-wide. While the war resolved part of the southern question by ending African American slavery, it made western issues more pressing than ever. The war accelerated developments that drew the West into the nation more quickly and fully than anyone had predicted. That, in turn, made it impossible to avoid the West's racial questions. Put another way, the Civil War did for much of the West what the gold rush had done in California. It destroyed the illusion that whites somehow would never have to answer the question of how they planned to live with free people of color. More generally, the war shattered or shook institutions regulating race from coast to coast. It jumbled identities and began a time of unprecedented racial disarray.

Anybody back then who was curious about the shiftiness of race relations and categories should have visited the area where I live now, called at the time "the border," a southwesterly arc of a thousand miles from western Missouri and eastern Kansas down to what is called the border today, the Rio Grande Valley. Here, where South touched West, was a grand display of the seemingly limitless combinations of racial arrangements and identities. Imagine a tour of the border during the fifteen years after the war. We would start in Kansas with a new look at the Exodusters, whose move from South to West was, paradoxically, both a rejection of and an aggressive claim to a traditional racial order. We might listen to the freedman J. H. Williamson praising former slaves as the rightful inheritors of manifest destiny. In cultural terms, he was saying, blacks were whites, and out West they would fulfill the promise of Jamestown and Plymouth, saving the wilderness from those who would never do it justice. "The Indians are savage and will not work," he argued. "We, the negro race, are a working people" who would, he implied, subdue the land and build towns, churches, and schools.[17] Frederick Douglass also reminded white America of the freedman's privileged status as an insider. The only reason the African American had not been hunted down like the Indian, he told the American Anti-Slavery Society in 1869, was that "he is so close under your arm, that you cannot get at him." This closeness, however, had made "the Negro . . . more like the white man than the Indian, in his tastes and tendencies, and disposition to accept civilization. . . . You do not see him wearing a blanket, but coats cut in the latest European fashion."[18]

From Kansas we would move southward into Indian Territory among the Creek freedmen. These former slaves argued, to the contrary, that they *were* Indians, or at least so mixed in blood and history that distinctions were meaningless. The point was worth making, since being Indian meant keeping the political power and an economic stake that mixed-blood leaders were trying to take away. Here we might listen to the ex-slave Warrior Rentie ridiculing his mixed-blood opponents, those "Indians, or

rather would be Indians, . . . who have the strong vein of Negro blood . . .
[men] who hardly know whether [they are] black, red or white."[19]

Next we would travel to central Texas into a variation of what historian
Albert L. Hurtado calls, in a California context, an "intimate frontier" full
of households of whites, Indians, blacks, Hispanics, and mixes of all four.
We would see this familial snarl helping create new social and legal forms
on this segment of the border.[20] This troubled region was the temporary
home of Buffalo Soldiers, black and Seminole cavalrymen who fought
Plains Indians and who also patrolled southward along our final stop, the
national boundary with Mexico. Here we would see these blacks and Indians and black Indians clash with Hispanics moving as always back and
forth across this porous border.[21] If we paid our visit in 1875, we would see
the racial ambiguities mixing with changing politics, with bewildering
results. When black troops clashed with Mexican Americans not far from
Brownsville, Texas, authorities—Redeemer Democrats hardly known for
their Hispanic sympathies—suddenly embraced these locals as noble
white citizens most dreadfully abused by degraded black invaders sent by
foul Republicans. Philip Sheridan shook his head at the confused identities along the stream that itself was always shifting restlessly in its bed.
"It is hard to tell who is who, and what is what, on that border," he wrote
William Tecumseh Sherman. "The state of affairs is about as mixed as the
river is indefinite as a boundary line."[22]

Sheridan's confusion should be ours. In the years after the Civil War,
all America was a kind of borderland where racial edges and meanings
were shifty and blurred. First, expansion had vastly complicated our human composition, then more aliens had arrived out West by the tens of
thousands. Old issues and new were compounded by unprecedented distances and unimagined wealth. Then war dismantled the nation's most
elaborate racial institution and brought western questions to a boil. Never
had Americans been so uncertain of how the nation's racial parts fit together, or even what those parts were.

Small wonder, then, that many looked hard for unconfused racial
boundaries, and how predictable it is that they found answers in the area
they trusted more and more to understand the present and predict the

future—the field of science. One of the most startling points that pops up when we look at race continentally, bringing the West into the story, is this: our moment of highest idealism, as we ended slavery and as some talked genuinely of racial equality, was also the moment when we gave the gravest credit to the most rigid racial divisions imaginable.

Race science had long overlapped with Romantic racism. Now it came to the fore. While Romantics defined races intuitively through gauzy notions of tribal and national spirits, scientific racists said they could puzzle it all out by carefully describing, physically measuring, and comparing this group and that. The implications were the same, however. Races were distinct. Some were better than others. And mixing them was risky business, especially for those at the high end of the scale. The most radical race scientists were the polygenecists, who argued that races had separate origins—that, in effect, Africans, Asians, Europeans, and Indians were different biological species.[23] As with the Romantics, their discussions always pointed toward public policies, and always these discussions were a dialogue between West and South.

Before 1861, not surprisingly, race scientists focused on slavery and differences between blacks and whites. Slavery apologists like Josiah Nott said that science made clear that African Americans would forever be intellectually and morally inferior and so must remain slaves. He argued that races were physically, measurably distinct and, just as important, had been so since creation, with no apparent changes. Physical differences reflected different natures and qualities, so it followed that some races had been superior to others from the start. And so they always would be.[24] This argument depended ultimately on showing physical distinctions among living peoples and those long gone, especially among skulls, the subject of the new field of craniometry, the measurement of angles, slopes, and above all brain capacity. When African Americans ended up last in the skull rankings, Nott and others concluded that science declared slavery to be the natural order of things.

To make their case, however, scientific racists relied far less on Africans than on Indians. Their principal authority, and the nation's leading polygenecist, was Samuel Morton, the founding father of American anthropology, whose masterwork, *Crania Americana,* was a collective study of hundreds of Native American skulls. Morton's work was buttressed by what many consider the first work of modern American archaeology, Ephraim Squier's *Ancient Monuments of the Mississippi Valley.*[25] Squier, backed by Morton, wrote that skulls dug from Mississippian mounds were thousands of years old (in fact it was hundreds) and yet were identical to modern Indians. So the links of the argument ran as follows: Indians were separate, always had been and always would be; the same was true of blacks; both were inferior to whites. Blacks, although inferior, were economically necessary, inside the house, and so had to be controlled by whatever means possible. Science and common sense demanded it. Thus, scientific racists held up Indian skulls and pronounced them proof that black slavery was good and proper.[26]

By the Civil War, the focus of race science was shifting dramatically westward. Scientific racists addressed the perplexing issue of the Chinese. As long as Asia had been a distant abstraction, persons as varied as Thomas Hart Benton and Bishop (later Cardinal) John Newman said that by reaching the Pacific, we were fulfilling a global destiny; in the Far West the noblest traits of European and Asian cultures would magically merge to become the finest flowering of civilization.[27] But then large numbers of Chinese actually showed up. Here were people at least as alien in appearance and custom as Africans, yet free to move through society, and unlike Mexicans, they were impossible to picture as lazy. They were frighteningly industrious. As their numbers grew, so did the anxieties of white Americans. Verbal attacks on Chinese, in a sense, were the oldest form of race-baiting—Asians were ascribed dangerous and incompatible traits sure to wreck our future if they took root—but the rhetoric was up-to-date. It was staunchly scientific. Besides the usual cranial measurements, much was made of the immigrants' smaller stature, relative hairlessness, and delicate features, all suggesting an innate femininity that would dilute America's vaunted Anglo-Saxon manliness.[28]

Most striking was how scientific authority was applied to customs and cultural traits. Their apparently ancient, unchanging lifeways meant Asians were biologically unable to rise to Western civilization and join our political process. In this golden age of the study of disease, the racial rhetoric also leaned sharply toward the medical. In 1862 a California physician, Dr. Arthur Stout, published *Chinese Immigration and the Physiological Causes of the Decay of a Nation*. Chinese, he wrote, would seed America with various diseases, including consumption, scrofula, syphilis, and the vaguely defined "mental alienation." Interestingly, Stout considered these diseases both inherited, part of the Asian's racial makeup, and communicable. Chinese, that is, apparently could not get rid of these diseases, but they could give them away.[29] The most infamous Chinese custom, opium smoking, was called a kind of infectious disease. Not only could hearty Caucasian lads who picked up the pipe become listless addicts, but, some medical writers claimed, anyone who smoked would develop Chinese coloring, attitudes, and behavior—which in turn became a transmittable condition: "Orientalness."[30]

Chinese immigration helped make the West a prime focus of scientific racism, yet the fresh notions and the bizarre theories always spoke to older, broader questions. As Americans reshaped their institutions after the Civil War, all those Asians were simply one more proof of white superiority; they reminded us how vital it was to keep racial rankings uppermost in our thinking. How could anyone expect Chinese to blend into American society, asked an essayist in *Popular Science Monthly*, if neither Indians nor blacks could? Science insisted that the only healthy society was one that was racially homogenous. Mixing races—any races—led to cultural decline. This essayist pointed to current and ancient examples of what were, in his opinion, the seediest mongrelization: Mexicans and Romans.[31] Or, as Dr. Stout put it, moving from a discussion of specific diseases to medical metaphor, welcoming either Chinese or black freedmen into American society would create "a cancer" in the nation's "biological, social, religious and political systems."[32]

Race science shifted westward in its fieldwork. America's prime material for racial measurement were Indian remains, and the lands acquired in the 1840s offered bounteous opportunities for bone hunters. This strange variation of westward expansion is hinted in the career of one of the most ardent scientific racists, Louis Agassiz. Swiss émigré, naturalist, and geologist, founder of Harvard's Museum of Comparative Zoology, opponent of Darwin, and arguably America's best-known scientist, Agassiz was an enthusiastic convert to polygenesis.[33]

He befriended and collaborated with both Nott and Morton and considered the latter's skull studies one of the great accomplishments of the age. The outbreak of the Civil War shocked him, not because of its promised bloodshed, but because he predicted it would free the slaves and thus mongrelize white America. When news of Fort Sumter arrived at Harvard, a friend found Agassiz walking the streets, sobbing and exclaiming: "They [the abolitionists] will Mexicanize the country!"[34] At the end of the war, with his wife, Elizabeth, and a young William James, he toured Brazil, ostensibly to gather specimens and study geology, but also to observe, photograph, and criticize the human results of that country's long history of racial amalgamation.[35] By then he was also looking westward into his adopted nation's ethnic stewpot. He acquired for his new museum at least one Native American head, bottled in alcohol, and in January 1865, he wrote a reminder to Secretary of War Edwin Stanton: "Now that the temperature is low enough . . . permit me to recall to your memory your promise to let me have the bodies of some Indians. . . . All that would be necessary . . . would be to forward the body express in a box. . . . I should like one or two handsome fellows entire and the heads of two or three more."[36]

After the war thousands of bodily remains, particularly skulls, were taken from graves, battlefields, and hospitals. A small army of amateur and professional collectors packed them off to Harvard and to the Field Museum, the Smithsonian, and the American Museum of Natural History. Franz Boas financed his research in the Pacific Northwest partly through this grisly trade. "It is most unpleasant work to steal bones from a grave," he wrote his wife, "but what is the use, someone has to do it."[37] The most aggressive collector by far was the federal government. The Army Medical Museum began gathering remains soon after its founding in 1862, and in 1868 it formally asked its field officers to acquire large numbers of "adult crania," past and present, to provide "accurate average measurements."[38] Over the next quarter century more than two thousand skulls arrived in Washington.

The head-hunting frenzy was partly a macabre competition for all Native artifacts, especially among private museums, but the government kept its eyes fixed on the goals of race science. The purpose of anthropometry, the measurement of living and dead bodies to document racial divisions, was to describe a statistically average specimen for every category. All then could be set within a descriptive schematic that showed relations of races to one another and, through that, an intellectual and moral hierarchy of peoples—sort of a racial flow chart. There were some setbacks—the brain capacity of the Apache leader Mangas Coloradas turned out to be greater than that of that legendary pumpkinhead Daniel Webster—but the quest continued. The burst of activity made the American West the envy of international anthropology. Continental researchers clambered for data from American graverobbing.[39]

This vigorous government bone-gathering—this three decades of publicly funded skull-duggery—is remarkable by itself. It is also revealing, especially when we bring its western perspective together with that of the South. Its very luridness makes it impossible to miss how thoroughly conflicted Americans were, not just about their ideas of race but also about their basic moral stance toward it. At the moment we took the most dramatic step in our history toward racial justice, freeing one nonwhite people from slavery, we were gathering up skulls of another, and doing it on the premise that this nation was composed of starkly defined races that scientists could tabulate into an obvious hierarchy from best to worst. As some white Americans were considering how and how much African Americans might be integrated into public life, others (and sometimes the same ones) were thanking the fates that hopelessly unfit Hispanic Americans would soon melt away to nothing, were hunting to annihilation Native Americans in the hills of California, and were warning that Asian Americans were a human pestilence—were literally an intrusive disease in the body politic.

That racial attitudes in these years were uncertain is not news. But when we pull back to a truly continental viewpoint, "uncertain" seems a pale word to use. Never had this nation been so mixed and multicolored in its human makeup. Never had our presumptions about race been so jangled and divergent. And never had we faced such fundamental decisions about the arrangement of our racial parts—their standing and social prerogatives, the reach and limits of their political due, whether indeed they should be here at all.

The term for this era, "Reconstruction," has always thrummed with racial implications, but when broadened to apply seriously from coast to coast, the term strengthens and its implications deepen. In the twenty years of tumult after 1846, attitudes and institutions of race were in fact being reconstructed, and more thoroughly than we have recognized. Listening to the clatter of opinions, not merely about black-white relations but also, in the color code of the day, about red, brown, and yellow, the range of possible outcomes seems a lot wider than we have allowed. When I shift my attention from the idealism of Reconstruction's radicals toward what was being said and done out west, and when I remember how rapidly that idealism would wither by the late 1870s, I wonder whether this nation flirted more seriously than we have admitted with a racial order far more rigid than the one we finally got. I wonder what kind of America we might have seen if the headhunters and racial purists had carried the day. To use a boyhood phrase, it gives me the shivers.

But of course something else happened. We turned away from the western tendency toward absolute racial divides, even as we compromised an eastern ideal of a fuller racial equality for former slaves. Among the theorists, the hard lines of scientific racism softened. Polygenesis, the teaching that races were born separate and could never merge, fell from favor. Racial distinctions were as strong as ever, and so was the trust in sorting them out by skull volume and the length of fingers, but now everyone once again was called part of one humanity. Races were unequal at the moment, but they were all moving along the same path of development. We seemed to be back to around 1800, back to the Jeffersonian faith in turning Indians into whites. But there were two big differences. The new ideas about race were full of pretensions from the new science, especially evolutionary notions of social Darwinism.[40] And now the government was expected to take charge of racial development as it never had before. The federal government, newly muscular after the Civil War, would act within its borders much as other imperial powers did in their distant colonies of Africa and Asia. Washington would claim the jurisdiction and the know-how to be a kind of racial master—part policeman, part doctor, part professor.[41]

The key to understanding this last twist is the powerful drive toward national consolidation. This theme—the integration of a divided America into a whole—is the one our textbooks tell us ruled the late nineteenth century. And so it did. Those texts, however, usually tell us that the sectional crisis and Civil War were the prime causes behind that drive, whereas, in fact, consolidation took its energy at least as much from the expansion of the 1840s. Acquiring the West stretched our distances, enriched our variety, and uncovered enormous wealth on our farthest edge. That, as much as secession, compelled us to think in terms of pulling it all together and keeping it that way. Making a firmer, tighter union also meant resolving questions about differences within this nation, and close to the top of the list were questions about race. Westward expansion, as much as the conflict of North and South, had churned up matters and pushed us toward some resolution. If we want to understand what happened—in national consolidation, in American race, and in how the two wove together—we need to keep our eyes moving in both directions, toward both West and South.

Consolidation, racial or any other kind, meant finding common ground. There had to be standards to measure the parts of the nation and to decide what fit where. In bringing West and South and their peoples more tightly into the union, two standards were most important. The first was economic. From Virginia plantations to Nevada mines and Nebraska homesteads, the nation would be pulled together under the ideals of free labor and yeoman agriculture and through the realities of corporate capitalism. The second standard was a union of mores—custom, religion, language, and the rest of what we call, inadequately, "culture," nurtured from Boston to Charleston to Tombstone. A national economy and a national culture together would provide the common ground of the new America, and America's racial parts would have to find their place, if they had a place to find, on that ground and inside its boundaries. Watching the results, West and South, is a revelation, not just about our racial drama but also about the entire process of expansion and the remaking of a nation.

The case of the Chinese was the most extreme. They were America's most anomalous people. In language, dress, foodways, religion, and customs they seemed beyond the pale, and with their vast predominance of men, they lacked what all other groups, however different, had in common: the family as their central social unit. Culturally, then, the Chinese were uniquely vulnerable. Economically, their potential was much more promising, but ironically that made them a special threat. From early in the 1850s, some had compared Chinese work gangs to black slavery and had suggested them as a solution to the Far West's chronic labor shortage. An editor predicted (and he meant it positively) that the Chinese will "be to California what the African has been to the South."[42] After the Civil War, some raised the possibility of Chinese playing the African in the South itself. In 1869, businessmen met in Memphis to consider importing Asia's rural workers into their cotton fields and factories. They heard that the Chinese, "industrious, docile, and competent," could be shipped in five hundred at a time at $44.70 per head.[43] Bitter opposition, however, came from opponents of slavery and, more effectively, from champions of free white labor. Close to the heart of the Chinese image as hopelessly alien was the notion that they were sheeplike, easily controlled, and utterly without the individual gumption to stand up to their bosses. This made them free labor's ultimate nightmare: a race of automatons used by monopolists and labor bashers to undercut wages or cast out honest workers altogether. The most vicious assaults on Asians came from spokesmen for white workingmen like Henry George and in political movements like California's Workingmen's Party. In the end, the Chinese found themselves without either a cultural or an economic base in the new nation and with virtually no natural constituency. They suffered the most excessive response to America's racial question: as of 1882, they were excluded.[44]

The case of Hispanics was the oddest. Their numbers were greatest in relation to whites in the Southwest, our least populous region with resources that were, for the moment, the least exploitable. This corner of the nation consequently was the last to be brought close and consolidated, which in turn lessened somewhat the pressure to resolve its racial issues. Mexican Americans still carried the burden of the old rhetoric, the images of listless, unenlightened people, but they were not as alien as the Chinese. After all they were Christian, albeit Roman Catholic, and were family-oriented farmers. And they fit the emerging economy. They did the grunt labor in mines, and they worked the land in a system of debt peonage strikingly similar to southern sharecropping. Hispanics, that is, posed little cultural threat and played useful economic roles. The upshot was partly to ignore the racial issues raised by expansion and partly to turn vices into virtues. Mexican Americans either were rendered invisible, segregated in cities and countryside, or were reimagined as a bit of American exotica in a region we could afford to fantasize as an escape from fast-paced modern life. In the land of *poco tiempo,* these people of color became what was much tamer: people of local color.[45]

That left African Americans and Native Americans. Their case was most revealing of all. Since the 1840s, southern blacks and western Indians had been counterpoised in our racial thinking: insiders and outsiders, enslaved and free-roaming, the essences of South and West. Now they converged. They were brought together as events of the 1860s shattered older arrangements and assumptions. Emancipated blacks still were insiders—they were, in the fine phrase of Frederick Douglass, close under the arm of white America—but they were no longer controlled through slavery. While not as free-roaming as Indians, they were definitely on the loose. Indians, meanwhile, contrary to the claims of the 1840s and 1850s, were obviously not vanishing. In fact, their lands were being pulled into the national embrace far more quickly than anyone had guessed possible. Indians were not as enmeshed in white society as the freedmen, but they were being brought inside the house. Blacks and Indians found themselves suddenly moving from opposite directions into the national mainstream. Paradoxically, liberation and conquest were carrying them to the same place.

Figuring out where exactly they would end up, and how they would get there, would be the self-appointed job of the newly centralized government, and nothing in the history of Reconstruction is more illuminating than the programs that resulted. As usual, we have treated events in the West and South as if they rolled along utterly independent of each other, while in fact, Washington's treatment of blacks and Indians ran as a stunning parallel. Official strategies were virtually the same. Economic integration for freedmen was to come through forty acres and a mule, or at least some measure of agrarian self-sufficiency; for Indians, the answer was to be allotment in severalty. For cultural integration, ex-slaves would be educated under the Freedmen's Bureau; for Indians, it would be agency and boarding schools. (And sometimes, most famously in the Hampton Institute, the two were schooled in the same places.) For both, Christian service and evangelism directed and suffused the entire enterprise, mixing religious verities with the virtues of free enterprise, patriotism, and Anglo-American civilization.

The differences were not in the government's goals and methods but in the responses to them. Freedmen, as insiders, had worked within private agriculture for generations and had been sustained by their own Christian worship. They found the government's stated goals perfectly suitable. The Sioux, Apaches, Nez Perces, and others, as outsiders, had their own traditions and cosmologies and relations with the land. They replied differently. Some accepted the new order, but for others the government finally had to turn to its strong arm to impose what former slaves wanted all along.

It takes a little effort, I will admit, to see freedmen's schools and the Little Bighorn as two sides of the same process, but blink a few times and it makes perfect sense, once you look at Reconstruction's racial policies—not on strictly southern terms, narrowly, as an outgrowth of Civil War—but rather as a culmination of a development that began in the 1840s. Its first stage began with the expansion of the nation: with that physical enlargement, we were unsettled profoundly in our sense of who we were and might be. This stage raised a series of new racial questions and aggravated older ones. The second stage, the Civil War, brought those questions to the sticking place. By ending slavery and bringing the West closer into the Union, the war left the nation as mixed and uncertain in its racial identity as it ever had been or would be. By revolutionizing relations of power, the war also opened the way for a settlement of a sort. In the third stage, from 1865 to the early 1880s, the government used its confirmed authority to flesh out the particulars of a new racial arrangement. Some peoples it excluded, some it left on the edges, and some it integrated on the terms and by the means of its choosing, including in some cases by conquest and coercion.

This Greater Reconstruction was even more morally ambiguous than the lesser one. It included not one war but three—the Mexican War, Civil War, and war against Indian America—and while it saw the emancipation of one nonwhite people, it was equally concerned with dominating others. It included the Civil Rights Acts and the Thirteenth, Fourteenth, and Fifteenth Amendments, but it began with U.S. soldiers clashing with a Mexican patrol on disputed terrain along the Rio Grande in 1846. It closed practically with the Chinese Exclusion Act of 1882 and symbolically in 1877, with Oliver O. Howard, the former head of the Freedmen's Bureau who had risked his life and given his arm for emancipation, running to ground Chief Joseph and the Nez Perces along our northern border, forty miles shy of freedom. Always the Greater Reconstruction was as much about control as liberation, as much about unity and power as about equality.

Indians were given roles they mostly didn't want, and freedmen were offered roles they mostly did, but both were being told that these were the roles they would play, like it or not. There has always been a darker side to *e pluribus unum,* and when we look at the parallel policies toward Indians and blacks, we can see it in its full breathtaking arrogance. When the Lake Mohonk Conference of Friends of the Indians turned from its usual concerns to devote two annual meetings to answering the so-called "Negro Question," one of its members, Lyman Abbott, was asked why no African Americans would be attending. He answered: "A patient is not invited to the consultation of the doctors in his case."[46]

Bringing the West more fully into the history of race should in no way lessen the enormity of southern slavery in our history or devalue in the slightest its human costs. My southern friends, especially, might argue that the way I am telling the story neglects the sheer weight of black-white relations in our national consciousness and the scale of the calamities spun off by slavery. They might tell me also that my version misses the genuine idealism generated from abolition and the Civil War. They might say all that and more, and if they do, I will admit that they might be right.

But there are a few things I know. I know we should put our foot down and not allow the Civil War to continue behaving as it does now in our texts and histories, sitting there like a gravity field, drawing to itself everything around it and bending all meanings to fit its own shape. While we call the mid-nineteenth century the Civil War Era, I am certain that acquiring the West had at least as much to do with remaking America as the conflict between North and South. I know that race is essential to understanding what happened during those years, and I know that the conquest and integration of the West is essential to understanding race. I am sure that we will never grasp the racial ideas of that time without recognizing that they took their twisting shapes partly from exchanges between West and South, a vigorous, strange dialogue that included not only slavery apologists and the familiar tropes about black inferiority but also rhetorical flights on opium smoking, color-coded zeitgeists, and headhunters and body snatchers in caps and gowns. And I am confident that when we bring the West more into the story, when we end the isolation of episodes like the California gold rush and the Indian wars and make them part of a genuinely coast-to-coast history of race in America, we will have learned a lot.

The lessons will have taught us again how western history has plenty to say about America today. In the 1960s, movements for the rights of black Americans encouraged us to look back with new care at slavery, emancipation, and Reconstruction. The situation today—when Hispanic Americans are our largest minority and Asian Americans are arriving in unprecedented numbers, when some public officials are fanning fears about brown and yellow hordes, when the fastest-growing minority in southern cities is American Indians, and when I read in my local newspaper about rallies by an Arkansas anti-Hispanic group with the unintentionally ironic acronym of AIM (Americans for Immigration Moratorium)—these circumstances should encourage us to look yet again at those middle years of the nineteenth century, this time in search of the roots of racial thinking that goes beyond the simpler divisions of black and white.

The larger point, of course, is a broader awareness of the most troubling theme of our past. For many of us that awareness has a more intimate implication, especially if we live outside the South, or like me along its edges. Race is not the burden of southern history. Race is the burden of American history. Its questions speak to all of us, whichever region we call home, and press us all to ask where and how far we have fallen short in keeping promises we have made to ourselves. In 1869, near the end of the Greater Reconstruction, the reformer and spiritualist Cora Tappan took this continental perspective when she offered her audience an observation that, in its essence, is still worth making today:

> A government that has for nearly a century enslaved one race (African), that proscribes another (Chinese), proposes to exterminate another (Indians), and persistently refuses to recognize the rights of one-half of its citizens (women), cannot justly be called perfect.[47]

Notes

An earlier version of this chapter appeared as "Reconstructing Race," *Western Historical Quarterly* 34 (Spring 2003): 6–26.

1. For two studies of race in America that go beyond consideration of black and white, see Scott L. Malcomson, *One Drop of Blood: The American Misadventure of Race* (New York: Farrar, Straus & Giroux, 2000), and Ronald T. Takaki, *Iron Cages: Race and Culture in Nineteenth-Century America* (New York: Alfred A. Knopf, 1979). A recent approach complicates the issue nicely through study of evolving notions of whiteness and what has distinguished it. See David R. Roediger, *The Wages of Whiteness: Race and the Making of the American Working Class* (London: Verso, 1991); Matthew Frye Jacobson, *Whiteness of a Different Color: European Immigrants and the Alchemy of Race* (Cambridge, Mass.: Harvard University Press, 1998); Noel Ignatiev, *How the Irish Became White* (New York: Routledge, 1995); and for a survey of the literature, Peter Kolchin, "Whiteness Studies: The New History of Race in America," *Journal of American History* 89 (June 2002): 154–73.

2. My admittedly crude generality is based on an estimate of non-Indian languages, plus the relative numbers of Native languages spoken in the United States before and after the annexations of the 1840s, as compiled by Ives Goddard in "Native Languages and Language Families of North America," to accompany William C. Sturtevant, gen. ed., *Handbook of North American Indians*, vol. 17 (Washington, D.C.: Smithsonian Institution Press, 1996). The area of the United States increased from roughly 1.77 million to 3 million square miles.

3. Farnham is quoted in David J. Weber, "'Scarce More Than Apes': Historical Roots of Anglo-American Stereotypes of Mexicans," in *New Spain's Far Northern*

Frontier: Essays on Spain in the American West, 1540–1821, ed. David J. Weber (Albuquerque: University of New Mexico Press, 1979), 302.

4. On racial justifications for expansion, see Reginald Horsman, *Race and Manifest Destiny: The Origins of American Racial Anglo-Saxonism* (Cambridge, Mass.: Harvard University Press, 1981), 208–48; Robert W. Johannsen, *To the Halls of the Montezumas: The Mexican War in the American Imagination* (New York: Oxford University Press, 1985), 270–301; Thomas R. Hietala, *Manifest Design: Anxious Aggrandizement in Late Jacksonian America* (Ithaca, N.Y.: Cornell University Press, 1985), 132–72; Albert K. Weinberg, *Manifest Destiny: A Study of Nationalist Expansion in American History* (Baltimore: Walter Hines Page School of International Relations, Johns Hopkins University, 1935), 162–89.

5. George M. Fredrickson, *The Black Image in the White Mind: The Debate on Afro-American Character and Destiny, 1817–1914* (New York: Harper & Row, 1971), 97–129; Horsman, *Race and Manifest Destiny,* 158–86.

6. Richard L. Wilson, *Short Ravelings from a Long Yarn, or Camp March Sketches of the Santa Fe Trail,* ed. Benjamin F. Taylor (1847; repr., Santa Ana, Calif.: Fine Arts Press, 1936), 120; Parkman quoted in Brian W. Dippie, *The Vanishing American: White Attitudes and U.S. Indian Policy* (Middletown, Conn.: Wesleyan University Press, 1982), 85.

7. Emerson opposed the Mexican War, in part because it was an unnecessarily violent means to do what was already ordained—to bring about the domination of the continent by "the strong British race," part of the Teutonic tribes that "[had] a national singleness of heart, which contrast[ed] with the Latin races." Parker, an ardent abolitionist, nonetheless believed in rankings of civilization: Africans were on the bottom, and Indians only slightly higher, whereas Anglo-Saxon America was destined to rule North America—"we are the involuntary instruments of God." Emerson and Parker quoted in Horsman, *Race and Manifest Destiny,* 177–80.

8. For an excellent analysis of these themes in popular literature set in the West, see Robert Charles Cottrell, "A Study of Western and Southwestern Popular Fiction of the 1835–1860 Period" (master's thesis, University of Texas at Arlington, 1977).

9. James P. Shenton, *Robert John Walker: A Politician from Jackson to Lincoln* (New York: Columbia University Press, 1961), 38–39.

10. *Congressional Globe,* 25th Congress, 3d sess., February 5, 1839, Appendix, 162.

11. To Thomas Jefferson Farnham the same "law of Nature" that left the southern mulatto inferior to either of the races that produced him cursed the mingling of white and Indian races in California and Mexico. Weber, "'Scarce More Than Apes,'" 295.

12. Washington Irving, *The Adventures of Captain Bonneville,* ed. Robert A. Rees and Alan Sandy (Boston: Twayne, 1977), 269–70; Washington Irving, *Astoria, or Anecdotes of an Enterprise Beyond the Rocky Mountains,* ed. Richard Dilworth Rust (Boston: Twayne, 1976), 152. Robert J. C. Young attributes to Nott the

first use of "hybrid" as applied to humans. See Young's *Colonial Desire: Hybridity in Theory, Culture, and Race* (New York: Routledge, 1995), 6. He refers to Nott's "The Mulatto a Hybrid—Extermination of the Two Races if the Whites and Blacks are Allowed to Intermarry," *American Journal of the Medical Sciences*, n.s., 6 (1843): 252–56.

13. Dippie, *Vanishing American*, 12–31; Hietala, *Manifest Design*, 155; Horsman, *Race and Manifest Destiny*, 210, 230, 243–44.

14. Rodman Wilson Paul, *Mining Frontiers of the Far West, 1848–1880*, rev. and expanded ed. by Elliott West (Albuquerque: University of New Mexico Press, 2001), 226–52.

15. For an excellent work that has gotten too little attention from historians of race during this period, see Tomás Almaguer, *Racial Fault Lines: The Historical Origins of White Supremacy in California* (Berkeley: University of California Press, 1994). Almaguer's is by far the best work we have thus far on the impact of California on the shaping of American racial thinking. On ethnic and racial conflict spawned by the gold rush, see Malcolm J. Rohrbough, *Days of Gold: The California Gold Rush and the American Nation* (Berkeley: University of California Press, 1997), 220–29; Paul and West, *Mining Frontiers of the Far West*, 204–206, 228–30, 239–42, 244–47; James J. Rawls, *Indians of California: The Changing Image* (Norman: University of Oklahoma Press, 1984), 171–201; Clifford E. Trafzer and Joel R. Hyer, eds., *Exterminate Them! Written Accounts of the Murder, Rape, and Enslavement of Native Americans during the California Gold Rush, 1848–1868* (East Lansing: Michigan State University Press, 1999); Robert F. Heizer, ed., *The Destruction of California Indians* (Lincoln: University of Nebraska Press, 1993); Albert L. Hurtado, *Indian Survival on the California Frontier* (New Haven: Yale University Press, 1988), 100–192.

16. Dale E. Watts, "How Bloody Was Bleeding Kansas? Political Killings in Kansas Territory, 1854–1861," *Kansas History* 18 (Summer 1995): 116–29. Watts tallies fifty-six killed in politically motivated violence in Kansas.

17. Williamson quoted in *Report and Testimony of the Select Committee of the United States Senate to Investigate the Causes of the Removal of the Negroes from the Southern States to the Northern States*, Part II, 46th Cong., 2d Sess., Report 693 (Washington, D.C.: Government Printing Office, 1880), 305.

18. Douglass quoted in Linda K. Kerber, "The Abolitionist Perception of the Indian," *Journal of American History* 62 (September 1975): 294.

19. Muskogee, Indian Territory, *Phoenix*, November 7, 1892. My thanks to Gary Zellar for pointing out this article.

20. Albert L. Hurtado, *Intimate Frontiers: Sex, Gender, and Culture in Old California* (Albuquerque: University of New Mexico Press, 1999); Mark M. Carroll, *Homesteads Ungovernable: Families, Sex, Race, and the Law in Frontier Texas, 1823–1860* (Austin: University of Texas Press, 2001).

21. See James N. Leiker, *Racial Borders: Black Soldiers along the Rio Grande* (College Station: Texas A&M University Press, 2002).

22. P. H. Sheridan to General W. T. Sherman, 6 July 1875, Special File of Letters Received, War Department, Military Division of the Missouri, 1866–91, M1495, reel 11 (in author's possession; acquired from the National Archives and Records Administration, Washington, D.C.). My thanks to my colleague Patrick Williams for pointing out Sheridan's remark.

23. For examples of work on racial science, see William Stanton, *The Leopard's Spots: Scientific Attitudes toward Race in America, 1815–59* (Chicago: University of Chicago Press, 1960); Thomas F. Gossett, *Race: The History of an Idea in America* (Dallas: Southern Methodist University Press, 1963), 54–83; Robert E. Bieder, *Science Encounters the Indian, 1820–1880: The Early Years of American Ethnology* (Norman: University of Oklahoma Press, 1986); David Hurst Thomas, *Skull Wars: Kennewick Man, Archaeology, and the Battle for Native American Identity* (New York: Basic Books, 2000), 36–43; Horsman, *Race and Manifest Destiny*, 116–57; Gustav Jahoda, *Images of Savages: Ancients* [sic] *Roots of Modern Prejudice in Western Culture* (London: Routledge, 1999), 63–96; Joseph L. Graves, Jr., *The Emperor's New Clothes: Biological Theories of Race at the Millennium* (New Brunswick, N.J.: Rutgers University Press, 2001), 86–104; Stephen Jay Gould, *The Mismeasure of Man* (New York: W. W. Norton, 1981), 30–72.

24. For a succinct statement by Nott, see Josiah C. Nott, *An Essay on the Natural History of Mankind, Viewed in Connection with Negro Slavery* (Mobile, Ala.: Dade, Thompson, 1851).

25. Samuel George Morton, *Crania Americana; Or, a Comparative View of the Skulls of Various Aboriginal Nations of North and South America . . .* (Philadelphia: J. Dobson, 1839); E. G. Squier and Edwin H. Davis, *Ancient Monuments of the Mississippi Valley; Comprising the Results of Extensive Original Surveys and Explorations* (New York: Bartlett & Welford, 1848).

26. Stanton, *Leopard's Spots*, 22–44, 82–89.

27. William M. Meigs, *The Life of Thomas Hart Benton* (Philadelphia: J. B. Lippincott Co., 1904), 308–10; Newman is quoted in W. H. Hickman, "The Coeducation of Races," in *Mohonk Conference on the Negro Question*, reported and edited by Isabel G. Barrows (1890; repr., New York: Negro Universities Press, 1969), 63.

28. A western editorial, for instance, advised that "the Chinese are half-made men. . . . As the strong races fall back before their hordes, there is, of course, a weakening of the State, for they have none of the elements of the men who make formidable soldiers." (Virginia City, Nevada, *Territorial Enterprise* June 23, 1877).

29. Arthur B. Stout, *Chinese Immigration and the Physiological Causes of the Decay of a Nation* (San Francisco: Agnew & Deffebach, 1862), 20–23.

30. Diana Ahmad, "Opium Smoking, Anti-Chinese Attitudes, and the American Medical Community, 1850–1890," *American Nineteenth Century History* 1 (Summer 2000): 57.

31. Gerrit L. Lansing, "Chinese Immigration: A Sociological Study," *Popular Science Monthly* 20 (April 1882): 724–26, 734.

32. Stout, *Chinese Immigration and the Physiological Causes of the Decay of a Nation*, 7–10.

33. Edward Lurie, "Louis Agassiz and the Races of Man," *Isis* 45 (September 1954): 227–42.

34. Quoted in Louis Menand, *The Metaphysical Club* (New York: Farrar, Straus & Giroux, 2001), 102.

35. Louis Agassiz and Elizabeth Agassiz, *A Journey in Brazil* (Boston: Ticknor & Fields, 1868), 298–99. Agassiz used his observations of the population around Manaos to comment that the "natural result" of interbreeding among races and the further mixing of "halfbreeds with one another" was to create "a mongrel crowd as repulsive as the mongrel dogs." With obvious implications for social policy in his adopted home of the United States, he went on to write that "boundaries of species" of all kinds were "precise and unvarying," a truth applying to "the different species of the human family . . . or so-called races," and that the mixing of these species/races would result in irreversible degeneration of the original stock.

36. Edward Lurie, *Louis Agassiz: A Life in Science* (Chicago: University of Chicago Press, 1960), 338.

37. Quoted in Robert E. Bieder, *A Brief Historical Survey of the Expropriation of American Indian Remains* (Bloomington, Ind.: Native American Rights Fund, 1990), 30.

38. Ibid, 36–37.

39. Ibid, 40.

40. Dippie, *Vanishing American*, 95–138; Gossett, *Race*, 144–75.

41. For an interesting comparative study that places the United States in the context of contemporary modern states' campaigns to absorb indigenous peoples by subduing them, transforming their cultures, and integrating them economically, see John H. Bodley, *Victims of Progress* (1975; repr., Mountain View, Calif.: Mayfield, 1990). My thanks to John Mack Faragher for introducing me to this book.

42. Quoted in Earl Pomeroy, *The Pacific Slope: A History of California, Oregon, Washington, Idaho, Utah, and Nevada* (1965; repr., Lincoln: University of Nebraska Press, 1991), 266.

43. Stuart Creighton Miller, *The Unwelcome Immigrant: The American Image of the Chinese, 1785–1882* (Berkeley: University of California Press, 1969), 173; John R. Commons et al., *A Documentary History of American Industrial Society*, vol. 9 (Cleveland, Ohio: Arthur H. Clark, 1910), 80–83.

44. Elmer Clarence Sandmeyer, *The Anti-Chinese Movement in California*, Illinois Studies in the Social Sciences Series, 24:3 (Urbana: University of Illinois Press, 1939; reissued in 1973 with a new introduction by Roger Daniels, and in 1991 in paperback).

45. David G. Gutiérrez, "Significant to Whom? Mexican Americans and the History of the American West," in *A New Significance: Re-envisioning the History of the American West*, ed. Clyde A. Milner II (New York: Oxford University Press, 1996), 68–71; George I. Sánchez, *Forgotten People: A Study of New Mexicans* (Albuquerque: University of New Mexico Press, 1967).

46. Abbott quoted in *The Booker T. Washington Papers*, ed. Louis R. Harlan, vol. 3 (Urbana: University of Illinois Press, 1974), 70n.1.

47. Boston *Standard*, May 29, 1869, quoted in Kerber, "Abolitionist Perception of the Indian," 29.

PART TWO

Families

6

The West before Lewis and Clark

Three Lives

The Gateway Arch, elegant and silvery, lifts magnificently over the St. Louis riverfront. More than four million visitors a year ride gimballed cars to an observation room at the top, and from there they can look from one side over the Mississippi River and from the other, to the west, over downtown and to Forest Park farther out. One of the great American monuments, the arch invites us into Missouri's largest city, but its meaning goes well beyond that. It is a soaring emblem for a particular perspective on the land and its history. Any ordinary gate opens two ways, but few would think of passing through Gateway Arch any way but westward, and in that way it reminds us that our national story traditionally unfolds from east to west. Looking at the map, we have been taught to read American history from right to left, like Hebrew or Chinese, so that true history in any particular place really begins only when the westward-moving narrative arrives and passes through. Where the arch is concerned, that moment is clear. It was when Lewis and Clark arrived in 1803 and with the Corps of Discovery began their ascent of the Missouri River the next spring.

From that perspective, Lewis and Clark were not just setting off on a long trip. They were setting in motion western history itself. The displays in the visitor center beneath the arch make the point. They bow to Thomas Jefferson, the expedition's godfather, and they follow the Corps westward with a grand semicircle of photographs paired with excerpts from the captains' journals. The images and words leave us with familiar impressions of the land the expedition entered—a wild world of exotic peoples, country essentially untouched by change, beyond the rim of history. In the often-quoted words Lewis wrote as the Corps left their winter camp among the Mandans at the end of their first winter, this West was one "on which the foot of civilized man had never trod."

As a national myth, that imagined narrative has quite an appeal. It is our version of stories people have told from Borneo to Siberia to explain how they have come into their country and how, by ordeals survived, they have earned for their descendants a new identity. Outside of myth, however, the narrative has problems. Lewis and Clark were not entering an unhistoried country. If history is the account of how people have acted in the world, the West in 1804 was layered with it at least twelve millennia deep, and even if we start the clock only when Europeans showed up, the West was no more a timeless, static place than Philadelphia or London. For more than two centuries new arrivals had been stirring things up, and as they did, western Indians were engaging in new ways with one another and with a far wider world. Lewis and Clark came into the West during an era of convulsive change, and they showed up pretty late in the game.

Just how late can be shown by following the lives of three westerners. The three are not much remembered. No image of them has survived, and for one the record lacks even a name. Their stories do, however, cover a great deal of history and plenty of territory in the West during the century and a quarter before Jefferson's famous expedition. If nothing else, the stories bring out the changes set loose by the first touch of Europeans in the 1540s. The breadth of those changes, and their sheer dynamism, also put the lie to the notion that Lewis and Clark determined what would follow their twenty months in the West. Tracing the three lives, it is hard not to wonder how, with only a twist or two of chance, the course of our continental history might have gone quite differently.

Jean L'Archevêque

At the age of twelve Jean L'Archevêque joined the expedition of one of the era's most famous explorers. L'Archevêque had been born in France in 1672 and had come with his parents to the port of Petit Goave in the French West Indies. There René-Robert Cavalier, Sieur de La Salle, stopped in 1684 for supplies on his way to what was hoped to be a tri-

umph for the empire of Louis XIV. Two years before, La Salle had led
the first European expedition to trace the Mississippi River from its upper reaches to its mouth on the Gulf of Mexico. By international law
this feat established for his king a claim to the entire watershed of the
great river—all land drained by it and by all of its tributaries, a vast domain stretching from the crest of the Appalachians to the spine of the
Rocky Mountains. La Salle's 1682 voyage would shape profoundly North
American history, including that of the young nation born a century later.
The "Louisiana" that Jefferson purchased in 1803 would be the western
watershed of La Salle's claim, and when Lewis and Clark set off the next
year up the Mississippi's greatest tributary, one of their jobs was to begin
defining just what that claim was.

When La Salle stopped at Petit Goave, however, that was 120 years
in the future. His charge in 1684 was to follow up on earlier success. He
was first to establish a post at the mouth of the Mississippi as an anchor
to Louis's interior empire. To the west and south were France's greatest
rivals in the region, the Spanish, but although they were well entrenched
in central Mexico, on their northeastern frontier, in what would become
Texas, their presence was shadowy at best. If the French could insinuate
themselves there, they would be in position to move against the Spanish and their fabulous silver mines around Zacatecas, in what is today
northern Mexico. That seems to have been the larger goal when La Salle
set out from France in July with more than three hundred persons in four
ships. Petit Goave was his final stop before heading for the Mississippi,
and there the young L'Archevêque joined the enterprise.

From the start La Salle's second expedition was ill-starred. Spanish
privateers captured one ship in the Indies, and through a combination
of ignorance, flawed maps, and botched navigation, La Salle could not
find the mouth of the Mississippi. In early 1685 he disembarked instead
on what is today the Texas coast at Matagorda Bay. There one ship sank
after grounding on a sand bar, and another sailed home. With just one
ship remaining, much of his supplies lost, and many of the expedition
returned to France, La Salle chose a spot on a nearby creek to build Fort
St. Louis, but by the time it was completed, hostile Indians, disease, hunger, and sheer exhaustion had reduced the colony to fewer than a hundred

persons, L'Archevêque included. Nonetheless, in early 1686 La Salle led a large party in search, he said, of the elusive Mississippi. That river was about four hundred miles to the east, but La Salle did not head that way. He marched instead to the west. How far he went is uncertain, but he claimed to have crossed thirty streams before finally reaching, he said, the Mississippi. Obviously the river was something else, and the best guess is the Rio Grande; some speculation puts the site as far west as what would be the town of Langtry, Texas.

Could La Salle have been *that* poor an explorer, claiming to locate the Father of Waters near present Big Bend National Park, close to the spot later famous for the courtroom of Judge Roy Bean? Part of the answer lay in sheer ignorance. Because of miscalculations on his first voyage and from what he had heard from others, La Salle placed the Mississippi much farther west than it was, although later, when he set off for the great river in a desperate bid to save his colony, he went in the correct direction, eastward. More to the point, La Salle's second expedition had always aimed to feel out the contested country between Louisiana and northern New Spain. His westward foray probably was a reconnoiter before a more serious move against the silver prize of northern Mexico. The Spanish thought as much. As La Salle was claiming to look for the Mississippi River in West Texas, Spanish commands were looking for him. Equally malinformed and confused, they stumbled around in a futile grope for their imperial adversary.[1] La Salle's behavior, that is, appears less odd when it is remembered that in the last quarter of the seventeenth century this part of the West was a cockpit where two of Europe's three dominant empire builders jockeyed for position from the swamps of the Gulf Coast to the deserts around the Rio Bravo. The diplomatic consequences would persist for more than a century. On acquiring Louisiana in 1803, Thomas Jefferson argued that the purchase extended to the Rio Grande. He based that claim, astonishingly, on La Salle's calamitous sojourn in Texas.[2]

Whatever his motives, La Salle knew he was in serious trouble when he returned to Fort St. Louis, especially when he learned that his last ship had foundered and sunk in a storm. His supplies dwindling, his shrinking command increasingly surly and with no way to escape by sea, he chose to take sixteen men, about half of those who were left, and walk eastward to the Mississippi in hopes of reaching French posts in the Illinois country. Young Jean was one of the sixteen, as was Pierre Duhaut, a Petit Goave merchant and family friend who had brought L'Archevêque onto the expedition. Duhaut's relations with La Salle had become, to put it mildly, strained, and near present Navasota, Texas, they snapped. After La Salle's nephew and two others were slain in their sleep, axed in their heads in a quarrel over the marrow in some bison bones, Duhaut shot La Salle as he approached the camp to investigate. The ambush required someone to lure the commander into the open to be killed. That was Jean L'Archevêque. Of the remaining party, six eventually made it to Illinois and safety. L'Archevêque and a few others chose to stay with nearby Caddo Indians. Back at Fort St. Louis, Karankawa Indians soon killed about a dozen remaining adults and adopted the few surviving children. Thus ended one bid by France to press its empire against Spain's. It would not be the last, however.

Meanwhile the Spanish had sent several expeditions by land and sea to meet that rumored thrust out of Louisiana. None succeeded until April 1689 when Alonso de León found the ruins of Fort St. Louis and, soon after, L'Archevêque and two other survivors. The French trio were pleased. Earlier, in fact, they had sent a letter with some Indian traders pleading to be arrested and spared a life among the Caddos, "beasts . . . who believe neither in God nor in anything."[3] De León obliged and took the three to Mexico City, and after several months in confinement they were sent to Spain, "provided with suitable clothes" but kept under arrest.[4] But what to do with them? Execution might cause problems with France, but release would give Spain's rivals precious intelligence about country still much up for grabs. The answer came when L'Archevêque and a companion, Jacques Grollet, swore allegiance to Spain and returned to Mexico in 1692 as soldiers. Two years later the pair marched north to Santa Fe to help garrison the northern frontier recently reconquered after the Pueblo insurrection of 1680. Having survived an imperial disaster, conspired in a murder, lived with Indians, languished in prison for three years on two continents, and switched nationalities, Jean L'Archevêque, now known as Juan Archebeque, entered a dramatically new life. He was twenty-two years old.

In New Mexico he prospered.[5] After several years as a soldier he became a merchant, married, and began a family. The family's numbers would grow prodigiously as its members spread out to establish farms up and down the Rio Grande. The Spanish meanwhile were forging new relationships with Indians during these years, and as someone experienced in cultural brokerage, Juan proved useful, particularly in dealing with Indians to the east in Texas. Whatever taint remained from his French origins was lost, and Archebeque rose steadily into the upper levels of society on New Spain's northern frontier. He purchased an estate and with his son did business southward in Sonora and Mexico City. In 1719 he was remarried—his first wife had died—this time to the daughter of the alcalde of Santa Fe. The territorial governor, Antonio Valverde y Cossío, was witness to the union.

For Spanish authorities, however, all was not well. Once again the French were making a move. The initiative this time was not from the Gulf Coast toward their Mexican mines but out of the Mississippi and Missouri River Valleys toward the central Great Plains, and the lure was not silver but the essential wealth of French America—animal pelts, especially beaver. The fur trade was big business. From sources as distant as western Russia and the Pacific Coast, European merchants sought out the skins of animals to process and sell in various forms but especially beaver hats, stylish to those shopping for them and lucrative for whoever made and sold them. The French fur trade had been centered from eastern Canada to the western Great Lakes, but lately its directors had worked to expand it down the Mississippi and up the Missouri. From the start the trade had relied on Indians as providers of both furs and protection, so French envoys now were courting peoples where they hoped to expand. Among the most important to them were the Otoes and the powerful and numerous Pawnees of the eastern plains. Based on Coronado's expedition in the 1540s, the Spanish considered that country theirs, and rumors of the French overtures came as a shock, particularly the news that the French were supplying tribes with firearms. In 1720 Governor

Valverde ordered his lieutenant governor, Pedro de Villasur, to lead an expedition to feel out the French presence and, he hoped, to forge alliances with the Indians of the central plains.

It was quite an undertaking.[6] Besides sixty Pueblo and Apache Indians, Villasur gathered forty-two experienced soldiers, an experienced guide, and a Pawnee slave. Also along was Juan Archebeque, whose knowledge of French and Frenchmen was thought an obvious asset. In June 1720 the expedition set out from Santa Fe, and although their route is uncertain, they probably crossed through what is today eastern Colorado and into Nebraska, where they followed the Platte River downstream farther east than any Spaniards had ever ventured. By the time they approached the juncture of the Platte and Loup Rivers, there were signs of a considerable Native presence and, alarmingly, hints of hostility. In mid-August they found a large Pawnee village. Villasur tried to make friendly contact, but there was no response until dawn on August 20, when several hundred Pawnees, perhaps with some French allies, fell on the Spanish camp and killed most of the soldiers, several Indians, Villasur, and Archebeque.

Thus Juan Archebeque, née Jean L'Archevêque, died at the indirect hand of his original countrymen, eighty-four years before Lewis and Clark entered the American West. To follow his life is to get some sense of the new currents of power at play in the West, their vigor, and the range of the maneuvering. As he sat in Mexican and Spanish jails and later served in Santa Fe, Spain was responding to La Salle's calamitous move against Mexico by founding missions in Texas and the military outpost of Pensacola in Florida. The French weathered the setback, gathered their strength, and dug in with their own towns and posts along the Gulf and the Mississippi. By 1720 they were pushing back in yet another offensive, the one that indirectly ended L'Archevêque/Archebeque's remarkable odyssey.[7]

Europeans, however, were not the only ones caught up in the vibrant changes of those decades. In Texas L'Archevêque was threatened by Karankawas and saved by Caddos; in New Mexico Archebeque prospered among Pueblos; in Nebraska he was killed by Pawnees. Indian peoples were as active as any Europeans in responding to opportunities and

threats. As both natives and newcomers played their roles in the quickening pace of events, their lives were continually entwining. One result was
a journey at least as improbable as Archebeque's.

A Missouria Woman

We are not even sure of her name. For that matter "she" might have been
two persons. The lives of individual Indians from her time are largely hidden to us, and those of Indian women even more obscured. This much of
her story, however, is clear: she saw more of the world than did most of
Europe's highborn women, and in her way she played a vital role in the
diplomacy that strove to bridge two continents.

She was born probably around 1700, likely in a village where the
Grand River joins the Missouri, today in the north-central part of the
state of that name. Her people, the Missourias (or Missouris), and their
close relatives the Otoes had migrated to the region from north of the
Great Lakes.[8] They were closely related to the Iowas—like them, speakers
of a Siouan language—and were allies of the Caddoan-speaking Pawnees.
The Missourias lived in permanent riverside villages of circular lodges,
each about forty feet in diameter with a floor sunk three feet and a sodded
roof supported by twenty-foot poles. They relied on gardening large plots
of corn, pumpkins, squash, and beans; on gathering wild plants; and on
hunting bison on the plains, work they would pursue more enthusiastically after they acquired horses around 1730. They were patrilineal (tracing
families through males) and organized into clans, but the focus of anyone's identity was his or her extended family, and in that system the Missouria woman was highly placed, the daughter of a prominent leader.

At birth she would have been rubbed with tallow and wrapped in a
blanket and soon after had her ears pierced. Whatever her name was, she
got it then; it was chosen carefully to bless her with a long life. If she were
the first or second of her father's children, that name would have been
sacred to the clan and would have carried with it a song that became her
official property. As she matured, she was tattooed, and if she were her
father's eldest daughter, a highly regarded tattooist would have inscribed
her breasts, forehead, and the backs of her hands. By then she would have

been taught women's responsibilities, especially the care of gardens, and women's prerogatives: everything harvested from the gardens was theirs, and wives owned everything in the household except their husbands' few personal possessions. Growing up, the woman would have heard stories of Missouria and Oto history and of the origin of her clan and would have absorbed a cosmology that bestowed particular meanings to each cardinal direction. The east stood for the life force and birth, the south for adolescence, the west for middle age and danger, and the north for old age and pleasure. The circle they formed together symbolized Wakanda, the sacred power suffusing all life.

At some point during her childhood a new influence had walked into this woman's world. He was Étienne Véniard de Bourgmont, and he arrived with a checkered past. As a young man he had fled France as a convicted poacher. In Canada he had worked for a tannery before entering the military and being tapped to command Fort Pontchartrain at Detroit, but in 1706 after botching a clash with Ottawas he had deserted, first running off with a colleague's wife and then taking up life as a coureur de bois ("runner of the woods"), the French term for a trader and trapper. At some point in the next few years Bourgmont began living with the Missourias in their Grand River village, and there he began a relationship with a Missouria woman, apparently well placed in her society. In the usual accounts, their connection gets a romantic gloss, with Bourgmont smitten by a Native beauty. Perhaps it was a love match, but whatever the emotions, he was following the standard script of a trader, finding security and useful relations inside the net of an influential family. In terms of that day and ours, "marriage" does not truly apply to their union, but it was certainly more than a dalliance. Its diplomatic weight grew all the greater about 1714 when she bore a son, later called Little Missouri, solidifying Bourgmont's position in the tribe. By then he was earning exceptional regard within his new society, and as his status rose, his woman's likely did as well.

Like other coureurs de bois, however, Bourgmont worried French officials. They saw a man of mounting influence who was beyond their control, and outraged Catholic priests, too, huffed at this prominent man living outside Christian wedlock. At one point there was a warrant issued for his arrest. Nonetheless any efforts to reel him in were feeble at best, for like other independent operators among the Indians, Bourgmont was also potentially of great use. Clearly, he knew this. He seems in fact to have set out to work his way upward in both cultures, and as his status rose among the Missourias, he moved as well to reposition himself among the French. In 1712, when the Fox Indians threatened Fort Pontchartrain, site of Bourgmont's earlier disgrace, he returned with Missourias and Osages to fight in the post's defense. Seven years later he helped in capturing Pensacola, the Florida outpost Spain had planted in response to LaSalle. Far more to his benefit, he explored. From his adopted home on the Grand he pushed up the Missouri River farther than any white before him, at least as far as the mouth of the Platte River and perhaps beyond, and wrote two accounts of what he saw, *The Exact Description of Louisiana* (1713) and *The Route to be Taken to Ascend the Missouri River* (1714). The latter became the basis of the first European map of the lower and middle Missouri.

Bourgmont's timing was perfect. The French had a heightened interest in the region. The Scot economist John Law, directing French economic policy, was boosting outrageously the prospects of Louisiana as part of a scheme to stabilize the empire's shuddery foundation. The French were also maneuvering once again against New Spain. After the Spanish had blocked LaSalle's thrust along the Gulf Coast, they had made their own moves into Texas and Florida. Now the French counterpunched. They felt for openings. For a while the Red and Arkansas Rivers looked like invasive pathways, but neither was, and by the time Bourgmont wrote of the route up the Missouri, that river had become the new hope. It ran through the lands of several Indian peoples anxious for trade, but that was just the start. Presumably it rose somewhere between the French and Spanish, in country that was virtually unknown to either and thus was full of grand possibilities. Out there, according to one report, a rich and large-eyed people lived around a great lake. They had lots of rubies and wore gold-plated boots. Some thought they were Chinese. There were also the usual dreams of mountains rich in silver and gold, another Mexico. As a final allure, the Missouri headwaters were believed to be a short march from those of some other river, yet to be found, that flowed into Spanish lands.[9] This vision, of the Missouri as the gateway to New Spain, would persist and help inspire the Lewis and Clark expedition more than eighty years later.[10] Bourgmont, then, could claim unique knowledge of the river thought to be a key to empire, and to that qualification he could add a rare authority among the strategically placed Missourias, a position cemented by his "marriage" to the wellborn woman.

From being a renegade and a rogue, Bourgmont was suddenly transformed into "a man of incomparable value," according to a French journal, one admired by all natives of the region: "If he were at their head, he would be able too undertake everything." Bourgmont did not disagree. "For me, with the Indians nothing is impossible," he would boast.[11] On the crest of his rising position he sailed to France in 1719 and was greeted with great enthusiasm. While he was there, word arrived of Villasur's disaster. Governor Valverde had sent Villasur on that fatal march in response to the fresh pulsing of French activity that Bourgmont, more than anyone, had provoked, and it had been the Pawnees, allies of Bourgmont's Missourias, who had handed Spain that crushing defeat. Bourgmont's star rose even higher. He was granted letters of nobility and named commandant of the Missouri River.

Moving back into the French orbit naturally meant moving out of the Missourias', which meant cutting, or at least severely straining, familial ties. The mother of his son did not go to France, but Bourgmont did take the five-year-old "Little Missouri," who reportedly was quite a novelty in his new society. The forty-one-year-old Bourgmont now was something of a catch, and he married a wealthy widow, twenty-nine, who soon bore him a daughter. He might have stayed there, rich and landed and pursuing gout, but French officials hoped to press their new advantage, or at least to stiffen defenses against New Spain, so in 1722 Bourgmont was sent back. The Missourias, his former bedmate among them, greeted him joyfully and welcomed Little Missouri home to the Grand River village. There Bourgmont built a timbered post he named Fort d'Orleans.

In 1724 Bourgmont first marched with a large party of Missourias and Osages to the Kansa Indians, who pledged their loyalty after receiving bountiful gifts and promises of royal support. In a scene that probably was reminiscent of an earlier one among the Missourias, a Kansa chief proposed to seal the deal by offering Bourgmont his daughter of thirteen or fourteen. He declined, but the girl was promised to Little Missouri in a few more years. Bourgmont then kept going, father west than any Frenchman had before, and somewhere in present-day central Kansas he met with a powerful horseback people called the Padoucas, probably plains Apaches, traditional enemies of Bourgmont's allies to the east. At a large encampment he lavished the Padoucas with muskets, powder, and ammunition, hawks' bells and scissors, red and blue cloth, Flemish knives, kettles, brass wire, sabers, axes, and much else. Make peace with the Osages, Otoes, and the others, he said, and be our allies, and there will be more where this came from. The astonished Padouca spokesman ("Is it true that you are really men?") pledged his fealty and stood ready to provide two thousand warriors against New Spain whenever needed. The visit lasted two days. Each French soldier was feasted and offered a young woman for the night. Near the end of the visit the Padouca leader picked up a handful of earth and raised it high. "Now I regard the Spaniards as I do this dirt," he shouted. Then to Bourgmont: "And you, you I regard you as the sun."

Bourgmont's final assignment was to invite delegates from several tribes to sail with him to France as a demonstration of amity—and of course to be suitably impressed with French power and majesty. Fifteen persons signed on. After weeks in steamy, fetid New Orleans, allotted only sailors' rations, then having their ship sink under them when they were barely underway, nine of the delegation backed out. Of the remaining six, five were chiefs of the Otoes, Osages, Missourias, Illinois, and Mitchigameas.

The sixth was our Missouria woman. A later report in Paris provides the only name for her in the record: Ignon Ouaconisen. Given the article's eccentric spelling of other names of individuals and tribes, it is uncertain how accurate hers was, or whether the name was genuine at all. The leader who sent her off said she was "the daughter of the head chief of our tribe."[12] The article in France said she "passed as [Bourgmont's] mistress" ("*passait pour sa maîtresse*").[13] Together the two references suggest she could well have been the wellborn paramour of his early years with the Missourias, the mother of Little Missouri, now following her son's path into Paris society. Or she could have been a more recent bed-mate.[14] That she had some personal connection to Bourgmont, however, seems highly likely, given that tribal leaders would not have sent a woman to represent them.

Nothing in the record mentions what the Indians thought of the transatlantic crossing, although one did wonder how ships of such size, built on land, could be moved to water (could "arms enough . . . be found for this purpose?").[15] Surely much more must have startled them—the ocean's extent, the men climbing in the rigging, the forest of masts in the harbor at La Havre on arrival. The only impression of the ride to Paris is a memory of "moving cabins of leather." More is known of the rest of the visit. Paris was a marvel—multistoried buildings ("five cabins, one on top of the other") and streets thronged with more people than blades of grass on the prairie or "mosquitoes in the woods."[16] Parisians seemed freed of some of life's elemental pressures. At the Hôtel des Invalides the men were astonished both by the surgeons' skills—lose an eye, an arm, or a breast, a chief told his people, and the French can give you another so natural "that it will not be noticed"—and by the large copper vats and roasting spits in the kitchen. When one was asked later what he found most beautiful, he said the rue des Boucheries. Why? "Because of the quantity of meat he had seen there." They chiefs laughed and clapped and jabbed each other in delight at an opera performance; they found the grand gallery of Versailles so astounding that they asked whether mere human beings could have had built it.[17] Not all impressions were positive. An Illinois chief would speak scornfully of men who seemed half-women, mincing coquettes with curled hair and corsages. They were rouged. They "smelled like alligators."[18]

Those at the French court in turn were naturally curious. At Fontainebleau lords and ladies crowded close for a look at the delegation and soon found the chiefs "as full of spirit and good sense as ordinary men." There the men visited for more than an hour with Louis XV. In the official report they removed their headdresses and set down their war clubs as an act of homage, while the young king admired their goodwill, plied them with questions about customs and religion, and pledged to see to their peoples' needs. Two days later he rode with them on a rabbit hunt.[19]

At receptions in Paris and at Fontainebleau some of the men spoke formally through a Jesuit translator, beginning with the humility common
in Indian rhetoric ("I am nothing" and "I am ashamed to be so mea-
ger") and proceeding with praise and commitment ("I love prayer and the
French" and, to Louis, "You are like a beautiful rising star"). Then came
particulars—the request for protection, support, preference among other
tribes, and aid in warring on such common enemies as the Fox.[20]

The visit from Missouri to France fascinates us as a snapping together
of distant worlds, but as those speeches attest, this was as well a diplomatic mission. The Indians doubtless were genuinely awed by what they
saw, and they spoke in terms of fealty and deference, calling themselves
children and the king their Great Father, but behind it all was the solid
fact that these were men of substance. The allusion to children and parents was traditional rhetoric. It assumed not subservience but reciprocal
obligations between mutually respectful parties, with the parent taking
the role of provider in troublesome times. The French in turn played the
benevolent overlords, but they understood well that the friendship of the
Missourias, Otoes, Illinois, and others was crucial to any ambitions they
might have on the river courses and plains more than five thousand miles
away. The point of the visit to Paris and Fontainebleau, that is, is less one
of Native rubes all a-gawk in the big city than an exchange between centers of power on two continents. Two groups of leaders were positioning
for advantage, and as they did so, they found in each other something to
work with.

That was men's work, and accounts mention the Missouria woman
hardly at all. When the delegation was outfitted in the French style, each
man received red knee breeches and a silver-trimmed red dress coat, another dress coat, a plumed hat, and "elaborate shirts," while the "Sava-
gesse" was given blouses with puffed sleeves, a flowered "flame-colored
linen dress," a petticoat, a pair of corsets, and gold and silver ribbons. She
got no ornaments, however, "because she always went bare-headed."[21]
What might be read into that—designation of status? a tender scalp?
just her style?—is only one of many puzzles about the Missouria woman
in France. Most frustrating is the silence about what *she* thought—of
the city, the court, the men, the women on the streets and in salons and

how they lived and what was expected of them, the gap and any parallels between her world and this one.

Two especially intriguing facts are known. Just before leaving for home, she was baptized in Notre Dame, and soon after that she was married to a sergeant named Dubois, who had served Bourgmont during his time on the plains and then on the trip to France. If nothing else, the union presumably severed any of Bourgmont's obligations. It also seems to have been a shift in the woman's diplomatic role. Dubois was promoted to captain and assigned to command Fort d'Orleans. By marriage into a prominent Missouria family he would insinuate himself into that society, much as coureurs de bois had done for decades, but now as an official presence. If his new wife had been Bourgmont's early mistress, she was now reprising that role, this time formally blessed by French authority and the Catholic fathers who had fumed at her previous unchurched liaison.

After two months on the continent the travelers—one had died during the visit—sailed for America. The tales they told back home seemed so outlandish that the hearers presumed the chiefs had been bewitched. They had some evidence of the wondrous world they had seen, however. Besides their French finery, each had been given gifts—a rifle, a gold chain, a painting of their royal audience, and finally a jeweled chiming watch, a precious item of the day that testified to the weight their friendship carried.[22] Nonetheless French interest in the region was cooling, especially since John Law's schemes for Louisiana had collapsed. Officials did not follow up on Bourgmont's initiative up the Missouri and onto the plains, and without the institutional support they had fashioned in the Great Lakes area, their position was weak.[23] Fort d'Orleans was abandoned. The Missouria woman's new relationship was also short-lived. Dubois was killed not long after his return, though how and why is not known. Although his widow inspired several apocryphal stories and eventually a mural in the Missouri state capitol, she apparently did not remain long with her people, gravitating instead to Kaskaskia in the Illinois country. There she married again, this time to a French agent named Marin.[24]

Her story, like L'Archevêque's, not only speaks of how intricately enmeshed the West was in imperial maneuvering but reminds us as well of the fluidity of power and the unpredictability of western history. When Oto and Osage chiefs were marveling at the steaming vats in the Hôtel des Invalides and hunting rabbits in the royal woods, those who in time would dominate the continent had barely begun to feel their way off the Atlantic. In 1716 Alexander Spotswood, governor of Virginia, had led an expedition to land he considered deep in the American interior. In this distant country beyond the mountains he found a splendid valley watered by a river he named the Euphrates. Today it is called the Shenandoah. Spotswood's brave foray was to a spot a hundred miles west of Richmond and more than a thousand miles east of Bourgmont's meeting with the Padoucas.

We can speculate that as Spotswood was later regaling friends with stories of his "far West" (central Virginia), Kansa Indians were reminiscing about Parisian evenings and a woman in Illinois was listening to the chimes of a watch given her by the king of France. Connections between the continents had bridged 120 meridians. Peoples on the Great Plains and the court at Fontainebleau were feeling a common cultural pulse. And it was still more than four decades before either Lewis or Clark was born.

María Rosa Villalpando

A third life, one more journey across time, space, and cultures, shows again just how tangled the West's history was before Jefferson's Corps of Discovery.[25] It begins on the far side of the plains from the Missouria woman, in northern New Mexico. When Jean L'Archevêque (now Juan Archebeque) was soldiering around Santa Fe, he almost surely knew Juan de la Villa el Pando, another enlistee who had marched up from central Mexico and who stayed and began his own extended family. His son Pablo (his surname contracted to Villalpando) moved north and began ranching south of Taos. Interwoven with the sprawling Romero clan, the family grew with each generation, the children born in and out of wedlock. María Rosa Villalpando was born about 1739, daughter to the grandson of the original soldier-settler. Around the age of nineteen she married Juan José Xaques and bore a son, José.[26] The young mother seemed settled onto the course of many others who were rooting hybrid Spanish ways into *la frontera*. Her life was about to change, however, onto paths she could not have imagined.

By now the Villalpando-Romero community held scores of persons—relatives near and distant, workers, priests, and others. They clustered south of Taos around an adobe hacienda with high walls and four towers. It was essentially a fortress, and there was a reason: Comanches. By the early eighteenth century they had migrated from the Great Basin through New Mexico onto the southern plains, and especially after acquiring horses, they increased prodigiously both in numbers and power. By 1760 they were on their way to dominating a swath of middle America from present Oklahoma southward deep into Mexico, eastward to central Texas, and westward to the upper Rio Grande Valley where María Rosa and her family lived. A recent study depicts a remarkably sophisticated empire with diplomatic and economic strategies exercised through a decentralized system of bands, yet the enduring image of Comanches as merciless horseback warriors is grounded in fact.[27] Their influence and control relied much on a terrifying military ferocity. Like the Missourias, Otoes, and Osages, the Comanches were the dominant power in their world, and like the French on the far side of the plains, the Spanish in New Mexico dealt with them as best they could, now exchanging goods and captives in trade fairs, now fighting or hunkering down when warriors swept in out of the east. On August 4, 1760, a large body of Comanches attacked and overran the Villalpando hacienda, killed all its men, including Juan José Xaques, and carried away fifty-six women and children as captives, among them María Rosa. They spared her son, José, but left him behind.

Trade in human beings in the Southwest and on the plains long predated European arrival. In a raid men almost always were killed, but women and children were commonly taken, sometimes for ransom but usually to be kept or traded. They had a twofold value. They bolstered populations, both in their persons and through future children, and they provided labor. Women in fact did much of the work among both the region's nomadic and settled peoples—processing bison hides into robes, gathering plants and preparing meals, making and repairing clothes, making and breaking camps, and in the villages of peoples on the eastern plains, tending the great gardens that lined the rivers and streams. Nothing is known of María Rosa's life with the Comanches except that within a year or so they traded her to Pawnees in southern Nebraska. There she began the second phase of her extraordinary odyssey.

Pawnees lived in permanent streamside villages—her new home might have been the one where L'Archevêque had died when the Villasur expedition met its calamitous end more than forty years earlier—with large domed earth lodges similar to those that had sheltered the Missouria woman. Also like the Missourias, they maintained large plots of corn and vegetables and ventured periodically onto the plains to hunt. As did all Indian peoples, the Pawnees had a highly developed cosmology, part of a spiritual kaleidoscope of Native religions and calls to the divine splayed across North America. Pawnees considered owls and woodpeckers sacred messengers who flew between humans and heavenly creative beings. Those great creators were the stars. They had made the world and all that was in it, and they continued to enliven it all, by glorious singing. All of us, the Pawnees believed, are star song.[28]

María Rosa settled in as a Pawnee, taking on the roles and obligations typical of captives. Her new life must have given her a new name, but we don't know it. She was taken as a mate by a village man, and by him she had her second child, another son. The world she was drawn into could not have been more different from that in Taos: sacred woodpeckers, butchering bison, melon harvests. At first it must have been as alien as Paris had been to the Missouria woman, as strange as L'Archevêque had found his Caddo village, but in time she probably grew enough accustomed to her life that she began to find some days normal and to think of the next one in terms of the expected. Her future, however, was as unpredictable as ever.

Probably in 1764 or 1765 the village was visited by a young Frenchman. Jean Salé dit Lajoie had come from an outpost recently set where the Missouri River met the Mississippi. Its founders, Pierre de Laclede and Auguste Chouteau, named it St. Louis. This germ of today's great city was evidence that yet again the French were looking ambitiously at the great midcontinent watershed and the plains beyond. Specifically

Laclede and Chouteau were interested in furs, which meant they needed men to develop ties of the kind Bourgmont had cultivated so skillfully a half century earlier. Salé was ready. He had come to America as a boy, drifted westward, and become a voyageur in the Mississippi country.[29] His experience and knowledge of the area would have made him an obvious recruit. Numbered among St. Louis's founders, he was given the important job of opening trade with the nearer Plains tribes, including the Pawnees.

At some point in his visits to the village Jean Salé began an intimate relationship with María Rosa, and through him she bore her third child, yet another son they named Lambert. In 1770 Salé took her (she now went by Marie Rose), Lambert, and her half-Pawnee son, now called Antoine Xavier, to St. Louis. There they were married and set up housekeeping on the Rue des Granges, fittingly the westernmost street in the still-raw river port. Marie Rose bore three more children—a son, Pierre, in 1771 and, two years later, twin daughters, Marie Joséphe and Helene. Pierre and Marie Joséphe apparently died young. The family did well financially. The censuses of 1787 and 1791 show a household with several slaves and considerable stores of corn and wheat, with Jean and Lambert listed as merchants and Antoine as a trader. In 1792, for reasons unknown, Jean Salé sailed to France and never returned.[30] Marie remained, as did Lambert, Helene, and probably Antoine Xavier. Helene married a prominent French expatriate, Benjamin Leroux. Their grandson, Wilson Primm, became a prominent jurist and early historian of St. Louis.[31]

St. Louis would be the final stop in Marie Rose's remarkable life journey. She was there, at age sixty-three, when the United States acquired her city and the rest of the Louisiana Purchase (roughly defined by LaSalle's first voyage, though Jefferson would try to push its limits farther based on LaSalle's, and Jean L'Archevêque's, ruinous time along the Texas coast). Technically her identity had morphed once again, now into a citizen of the young republic. She was eighty-one when Missouri became a state in 1821. By then she likely knew characters pushing the American frontier beyond Missouri—Thomas Hart Benton, Moses Austin, Silas Bent and his sons Charles and William, and others. Marie Rose Salé dit Lajoie died at ninety-one at Helene's home, seventy years after being torn from her first family, a hundred and five years after the Missouria woman had donned her stylish blouses and walked the promenades at Fontainebleau, and nearly a century and a half after Jean L'Archevêque had lured LaSalle into a clearing to have his brains blown out.

There is a coda to her story. Some time in 1802 or 1803, Marie Rose received a visitor. The details of his arrival are unknown, of course, but we can imagine a rap on her door, and when she opened it, there stood José, the son she had last seen as an infant in New Mexico. Somehow he had heard that his mother had not only survived but had prospered among a foreign people on the far side of the plains. José, now in his mid-forties, was a farmer with a second wife and nine children. Apparently he had made the still-treacherous crossing through Comanche country to reconnect with and tap into what was now a considerable estate. Connect he did, but the payout was limited. Years earlier Salé had given Marie's second son, the half-Pawnee Antoine Xavier, his name and had agreed to raise him to manhood, but by their marriage contract all family wealth and possessions were to pass only to Salé's blood children. Marie Rose now honored that commitment. José formally surrendered to his half-sister Helene all claims to the estate, and in return he received two hundred pesos. José signed the document on August 3, 1803, one day shy of the forty-third anniversary of the Comanche raid that had killed his father and snatched him away from his mother.[32]

The timing of José's visit was serendipitous. If he had stayed with his mother only a few more months, he would have been in St. Louis when Lewis and Clark and their men arrived after a float down the Ohio River and set up winter camp a short way up the Mississippi. As the Corps of Discovery prepared to set off the following spring, José Xaques and Marie Rose might have been reminiscing their way through her western odyssey among five cultures (Spanish, Comanche, Pawnee, French, and Anglo-American). For his part, José likely would have told of his tenuous years after he was effectively orphaned. As he spoke of the persistence and spread of the Spanish along the Rio Grande, he might have mentioned the Archebeque family, like him farmers in the area, and he might even have mentioned their patriarch, Juan, the displaced Frenchman, and his death at the hands of Pawnees. If he did, Marie would have answered with the Pawnee side the Villasur disaster, a story she surely had heard during her years among them, and that in turn could well have sparked some mention of the Frenchman who soon afterward came into her country and took neighboring Indians to faraway France. Maybe she had seen something from their return, surviving treasures from another world. A gold chain? A painting of a king long dead?

It's all speculation, of course. Who knows how much Marie Rose and José talked, and about what? It's imagined eavesdropping, but it deepens and broadens the usual perspective on western history. The lives of Jean L'Archevêque, the Missouria woman, and Maria Rosa Villalpando show us that for a century and a quarter before the young United States gained the slightest toehold in the West, that country was rippling with changes— imperial tussling, shifts of power among Indian peoples, oceans and continents linked by influences ranging from ideas, languages, and horses to religions, children, and watches. Surely no one can follow those three lives and still look into the West with the usual perspective, the one that has us gazing out of the St. Louis of 1804 into a timeless, unhistoried land. The point is driven home by the spot where Marie and José would have spun out their tales. Marie's house, built for her by Jean Salé, was on what would become Third Street between Elm and Myrtle. Today it would sit virtually at the base of the Gateway Arch. When we look westward from Marie's parlor, then ride to the top of the arch, it's a different view. We look now into country that was already deep in history when Lewis and Clark stepped into it. This West is full of ghosts with much to tell us. Listening is the first step toward knowing the West as it truly is, tangled in old stories, a revelation of the fluid, evolving identity of America itself.

Notes

1. Robert S. Weddle, *The French Thorn: Rival Explorers in the Spanish Sea, 1682–1762* (College Station: Texas A&M University Press, 1991), 15–21; Donald E. Chipman, *Spanish Texas, 1519–1821* (Austin: University of Texas Press, 1992), 75–61.

2. Thomas Jefferson, *Documents Relating to the Purchase and Exploration of Louisiana* (Boston: Houghton, Mifflin & Company, 1904), 23–45. In "An Examination Into the Boundaries of Louisiana," Jefferson wrote that the United States had purchased from Napoleon land France had rightfully claimed based on La

Salle's first and second expeditions. The first expedition, he wrote, laid claim to all lands drained by the Mississippi. The second gave France "the possession [!] of the coast, & . . . all the depending waters," which apparently meant all rivers flowing into it. Louisiana, then, included "the sea-coast & islands from the river Perdido [in present Florida] to the Rio Norte or Bravo [the Rio Grande], then up the Rio Bravo to it's [sic] source; then to the highlands of the Mis*ipi [the continental divide], and along those highlands round the heads of the Missouri and Mis*ipi & their waters to where those highlands assume the name of the Alleganey or Apalachian [sic] mountains, then along those mountains, and the highlands encompassing the waters of the Mobile, to the source of the Perdido, & down that to the ocean." This would have given the nation what was later confirmed as the Louisiana Purchase, plus Texas, half of New Mexico, and part of southern Colorado. Spain, not surprisingly, disagreed.

3. Robert S. Weddle, *Wilderness Manhunt: The Spanish Search for La Salle* (College Station: Texas A&M University Press, 1999), 173.

4. Herbert Eugene Bolton, *Spanish Exploration in the Southwest, 1542–1706* (New York: Charles Scribner's Sons, 1916), 364.

5. The great anthropologist Alfred Bandalier discovered records in the pueblo of Santa Clara, New Mexico, that revealed L'Archevêque's story after he returned to Mexico as a Spanish citizen. A. F. Bandalier, *The Gilded Man (El Dorado) and Other Pictures of the Spanish Occupancy of America* (New York: Appleton & Co., 1893), 289–302.

6. Early histories located the expedition's disastrous end at the forks of the North and South Platte Rivers, but the current understanding places it at the entrance of the Loup into the Platte. A. B. Thomas, "The Massacre of the Villasur Expedition at the Forks of the Platte River, August 12, 1720," *Nebraska History* 7:3 (July–September 1924): 68–81; Thomas E. Chávez, "The Villasur Expedition and the Segesser Hide Paintings," in *Spain and the Plains: Myths and Realities of Spanish Exploration and Settlement on the Great Plains,* ed. Ralph H. Vigil, Frances W. Kaye, and John R. Wunder (Niwot: University Press of Colorado, 1994), 90–113; Gottfried Hotz, *Indian Skin Paintings from the American Southwest* (Norman: University of Oklahoma Press, 1970), 171–220.

7. William Edward Dunn, *Spanish and French Rivalry in the Gulf Region of the United States, 1678–1602: The Beginnings of Texas and Pensacola* (Austin: University of Texas, 1917), 108–109; Bolton, *Spanish Exploration,* 364–65.

8. For a historical and cultural sketch of the Missouria, see Marjorie M. Schweitzer, "Otoe and Missouria," in Raymond J. DeMallie, ed., *Handbook of North American Indians,* vol. 13, *The Plains,* part 1, William C. Sturtevant, gen. ed. (Washington, D.C.: Smithsonian Institution Press, 2001), 447–61.

9. A. P. Nasatir, ed., *Before Lewis and Clark: Documents Illustrating the History of the Missouri, 1785–1804,* vol. 1 (St. Louis: St. Louis Historical Documents Foundation, 1952), 12–13.

10. When Lewis and Clark were sent westward, it was not only to open trade with Indians and find a usable route to the Pacific. Jefferson believed (or rather hoped) the Missouri sprang from a great interior highland. Once there, the captains were told to ask about a river flowing southward, a waterway to the Spanish frontier, an easy path for American ambitions. Eight decades before Lewis and Clark would test Jefferson's hopes, Bourgmont was using the same notion to tantalize authorities in Paris. James Ronda, *Finding the West: Explorations with Lewis and Clark* (Albuquerque: University of New Mexico Press, 2001), 1–16.

11. Henri Folmer, "Etienne Veniard de Bourgmond in the Missouri Country," *Missouri Historical Review* 36:3 (April 1942): 284–85.

12. Frank Norall, *Bourgmont: Explorer of the Missouri, 1698–1725* (Lincoln: University of Nebraska Press, 1988), 81.

13. Marc de Villiers du Terrage, *La Découverte Du Missouri et l'Histoire de Fort d'Orleans (1673–1728)* (Paris: H. Champion, 1925), 112.

14. More often than not, the assumption has been that the woman on the trip to France was Bourgmont's original mistress among the Missourias. See, for instance, Margot Ford McMillen and Heather Robertson, *Called to Courage: Four Women in Missouri History* (Columbia: University of Missouri Press, 2002), 5–33. A biographer of Bourgmont, however, writes that she was probably "a new conquest," since if she were his earlier lover, she would not have been described in the Paris press as *"une jeune Sauvagesse."* Folmer, "Etienne Veniard de Bourgmond," 295. What "young" meant, on the other hand, might well have varied between the cultures. Women of the eastern plains often married at around thirteen—that was the age of the girl offered Bourgmont by the Otoes—and if Little Missouri's mother had been about fourteen at his birth, she was born around 1700. Thus she would have been twenty-five during her visit to France, which could well have passed for "young" there.

15. The account of the visit to France is taken from the following: Richard N. Ellis and Charlie R. Steen, eds., "An Indian Delegation in France, 1725," *Journal of the Illinois State Historical Society* 67:4 (September 1974): 385–405; "First Visit of Nebraska Indians to Paris in 1725," *Nebraska History* 6:1 (January–March 1923): 33–38; M. Bossu, *Travels in the Interior of North America, 1751–1762* (Norman: University of Oklahoma Press, 1962), 82–84; Reuben Gold Thwaites, ed., *The Jesuit Relations and Allied Documents,* Vol. 68 (Cleveland, Ohio: Burrows Brothers Co., 1900), 213–15 A reproduction of the original is available in *Mercure de France, Tome IX, Juillet-décembre 1725* (Geneva: Slatkine Reprints, 1968), 358–66. The account in *Nebraska History* originally appeared in the *London Postman* of January 27, 1726, and was first reprinted in the April 1890 issue of the *United States Catholic Historical Magazine.* The document edited by Ellis and Steen is translated from the December 1725 issue of *Mercure de France.*

16. Comments on the ship, coach, and buildings in Thwaites, *Jesuit Relations,* 213.

17. Bossu, *Travels,* 83; Thwaites, *Jesuit Relations,* 213; Ellis and Steen, "Indian Delegation," 391–92.

18. Bossu, *Travels,* 84.

19. Ellis and Steen, "Indian Delegation," 397, 401–402.

20. Ibid., 392–401.

21. Ibid., 394, 396.

22. Bossu, *Travels,* 83; Ellis and Steen, "Indian Delegation," 402.

23. Richard White, "Creative Misunderstandings and New Understandings," *William and Mary Quarterly* 63:1 (January 2006): 11–12.

24. Bossu, *Travels,* 82–83. A persistent myth about the woman claims that rather than Fort d'Orleans being abandoned from declining French interest, it was overrun and Dubois killed by Missourias and other Indians—this at the instigation of the woman, who supposedly chafed at civilized ways. An account of this story ends: "So much for the attempt to tame lions and tigers!" Charles Gayarré, *History of Louisiana,* Vol. 1: *The French Domination* (New Orleans: F. F. Hansell & Bro., 1903), 395–96. In a later version, even more fanciful, she was especially driven back to savagery by the discomforts of her French corset. Richardson Wright, *Forgotten Ladies: Nine Portraits from the American Family Album* (Philadelphia: J. B. Lippincott, 1928), 13–30. This tradition is effectively demolished in Villiers de Terrage, *La Découverte Du Missouri,* 115–24.

25. The most accessible summaries of this life are Jack B. Tykal, "Taos to St. Louis: The Journey of María Rosa Villalpando," *New Mexico Historical Review* 65 (April 1990): 162–74; James F. Brooks, *Captives and Cousins: Slavery, Kinship, and Community in the Southwest Borderlands* (Chapel Hill: University of North Carolina Press, 2002), 64, 66–67.

26. There is disagreement about her age. By some accounts she was born in 1726 or even 1723. This would have her bearing her first child quite late, in her early to mid-30s (and having him by a boy of 16), having her last children at around 50, and dying at 104 or 107. More likely she was born around 1739, became a mother at about 20, and died at 99. For a discussion, see Tykal, "Taos to St. Louis," 165–66, 173–74. Supporting the later birth date is the census of St. Louis of 1787, in which she is listed as forty-six years old. "General Census of the Towns of St. Louis and Ste. Genevieve, 1787," Census Collection, Missouri Historical Society, St. Louis.

27. The study is Pekka Hämäläinen, *The Comanche Empire* (New Haven: Yale University Press, 2008).

28. Patricia J. O'Brien, "Prehistoric Evidence for Pawnee Cosmology," *American Anthropologist* 88:4 (December 1986): 939–46; Patricia J. O'Brien, "Speculations about Bobwhite Quail and Pawnee Religion," *Plains Anthropologist,* 33:122 (November 1988): 489–504.

29. Frederic L. Billon, *Annals of St. Louis in Its Early Days* (St. Louis: G. I. Jones & Co., 1886), 426.

30. "General Census of the Town of St. Louis and Ste. Genevieve, 1787"; Louis Houck, *The Spanish Regime in Missouri,* vol. 2 (Chicago: R. R. Donnelly & Sons Co., 1909), 374. For an excellent genealogical study of this complex family tree, see Carmalee Gallegos Owen, "The Jaquez Family," *New Mexico Genealogist* 44:1 (March 2005): 1–7.

31. William Clark Breckenridge, "Biographical Sketch of Judge Wilson Primm," Missouri Historical Society *Collections* 4:2 (1913): 127–59.

32. Tykal, "Taos to St. Louis," 70–71.

7

Child's Play

Tradition and Adaptation on the Frontier

In *The Laws,* Plato wondered about the best and purest form of child's play. His answer—leaping—let children joyfully test their abilities, he decided, while also learning something of life's possibilities and limits. Like all good play, leaping blended education, growth, and fun.[1] The Greek philosopher might have been pleased had he jumped twenty-two centuries into the future to witness what was likely the West's first ox-bouncing competition. Along the Platte River in 1841 a group of boys in a company bound for Oregon came across a dead ox, its paunch swollen tight by gasses of decay. Quickly they found that if they jumped against the animal's bloat, it would vigorously fling them back. A contest soon began. Champions rose and fell as boys ran faster, jumped harder, and bounced farther. Finally, a long-necked redhead backed off a great distance as his friends took up a cry: "Give her goss, Andy!" Andy did. Lowering his head, he sprinted and jumped like a pile driver—and plunged deep into the rotting carcass. Only with some difficulty did his friends pull the wriggling boy out. The contestants then went on their way, the observers with a good story, Andy with a deeply entrenched memory.[2]

The slightly bizarre episode belongs to a part of western history that deserves far more attention than it has gotten so far. Children in much of the newly settled West made up more than half of the population. They shaped significantly their emerging societies, if in no other way than by the many responsibilities they shouldered and in the remarkable range of tasks they performed. Children's lives also say something about the making of western character, for the world that girls and boys were helping to shape was also shaping them. They found their values, their sense of reality, and their understanding of the possible in large part through growing up in places evolving as rapidly and as profoundly as they were themselves. No part of children's lives was more revealing than their play. It was part of their most practical concerns. In it they found an encouragement in their difficulties, a help in understanding, and a wondrously flexible tool in adapting to the special world of the far-western frontier.

Child's play in the newly settled West can be grouped roughly into four categories: exploration, playful work, organized games, and amusements directed or encouraged by adults. Psychologists consider playful exploration especially important. During an infant's first few years, play and the discovery of the immediate world are virtually one and the same. As babies instinctively test their surroundings, they practice physical coordination and learn to form concepts, to discriminate among objects, and to remember things. This exploration continues in increasingly elaborate forms throughout childhood and into adolescence. With its help the young mold their mentalities and come to identify with the world in which they find themselves.[3]

Exploring play was especially significant on the frontier. The country was new to pioneers of all ages, but there was a difference between younger and older. Adults arrived with their ways of thinking already well formed, with preconceptions that they would test and modify. Their sons and daughters were engaged in a more basic discovery. Especially for the very youngest, this was no "frontier" at all; there was no disconnect between a well-remembered past and an unfamiliar present. This was their first and only reality. Those slightly older were still forming their likes and dislikes, their fears and aspirations, their definitions of the expected and the marvelous. Children were establishing a frame of reference for the rest of their lives, and that frame would necessarily be different from that of mothers and fathers who had come of age in other places and times. Exploring play naturally drew children apart from their parents and helped shape a distinctive generation.

The process began immediately. On the trip west, crawlers and toddlers tumbled from their wagons at day's end and fanned out to enter the scenes they had gawked at for hours. Tired and harried adults wrote only that "all [is] well, and young ones in high glee" or "the children is grumbling and crying and laughing and hollowing and playing all around."[4] It was a passionate investigation. Lucy Fosdick recalled that older travelers soon tired of the trip, while she and her friends never did. There was so much to see, so many new experiences, such an array of new tasks to learn. One mother panicked when she could not see her two-year-old an hour after setting him in the dirt to play. Digging curiously, pulling up small rocks, and shaping the sand, he had burrowed himself out of sight. Some parents leashed their infants or strapped them into chairs, but given the chance, these youngest pioneers hunted wildflowers, chased prairie dogs, and in hundreds of other ways tried to touch the details of a new life.[5]

The urge continued after families reached their destinations. Some of what the youngsters found on their homesteads and in the mining camps left them frightened and anxious, but much also drew them out. "A happier set of children I think I never saw," a mother, newly arrived in Kansas, wrote her relatives. "Johnny [two] goes 'yout' [out] to his hearts content."[6] The children were everywhere—gathering bright pebbles, fossils, pottery shards, snakeskins, bottles, and animal dung. One boy preferred playing with the bones and horses' hooves he found near his West Texas dugout. Some found more than they bargained for. An Arizona mother hanging out her clothes heard her three-year-old daughter's scream simultaneously with the whirring of a rattlesnake. The horrified mother kicked away the rattler, snatched up her daughter, and asked in terror if the snake had bitten her. "No," the girl answered through her tears, "but it said it would."[7]

As older children roamed outward in expanding circles, they gathered knowledge with a growing confidence and developed a deepening affection for their surroundings. The memories of a woman growing up in Montana's Deer Lodge Valley were dominated by "fields of wild hay . . . or gathering, with my brother, bright colored stones in the dry gulches for playthings. . . . From early March, when the snow was disappearing and the first flowers beginning to bloom, until October, when the hardiest fall flowers and the autumn leaves covered the mountain sides with treasures, I with my brothers and sisters roamed the mountains and hills and explored the streams for miles in every direction."[8] Mining town children explored both an urban wilderness and the countryside beyond. "We spent our leisure playing in the back streets or learning the haunts and names of the wildflowers," Mary Ronan said of Alder Gulch. Boys prowled the mines and backstreets and then headed for the hills to try to sight a bear or puma. To Carolyn Palmer, "our real books were the sagebrush plains" around Boise, yet she and her friends also loved the streets where they were scared by free-roaming bulls and charmed by Indians, miners, and soldiers: "What a picturesque tableau it all made."[9]

While adults felt affection for the country, they tended to focus on how it differed from the lands of their own upbringing and how it might be changed and made to pay. Some, like author Mary Hallock Foote, dwelt on its unchangeable deficiencies. The high country of the Rockies was unnatural, she thought: "Grass could not grow there, and cats could not live."[10] Children, by contrast, often grew up believing they had a deeper fondness and appreciation for their surroundings than their elders did. "There was something about it that a kid loved," West Texan Owen McWhorter remembered of the "beautiful, beautiful" sweep of grassland around his dugout. A rich sensuality in children's words suggests that their feelings for the country were based on an intimate physical contact, one occurring as their perceptions were still evolving. During the winter's worst, for instance, one girl of the California camps would sit under a fir and scrape away the snow so she could feel and look at the earth. An Arizona man would later remember that he had loved "the familiar damp, the blasted rock smell" in the mine tunnels where he played as a boy.[11]

Parents set down their children in a new environment at just that stage of life when immediate sensations meant more than they ever would again. As they scattered into this new world, children were not escaping but seeking, testing their own potential, and defining their particular reality. Many would look back on their childhood explorations as "some virgin chance conquered," as Erik Erikson has defined play at its best.[12] The result was a claim of emotional possession, a unique bond with the country.

Not long past their infancy, most frontier children were put to work, and some of this labor they turned into a second category of play. Children were working everywhere in America, of course, but those on the frontier toiled at a greater variety of jobs, many of which drew them into the new country to test their abilities, alone or with other children. This burden of labor could be heavy, its pace grueling, and it might be argued that western youngsters were exploited more than children were elsewhere. The children themselves, however, found a great deal of fun. Working play helped them develop skills they would need a few years ahead; and, like their explorations, it contributed to an independence and a sense of distinct identity.

Hunting was a job assigned almost entirely to the children in many families. In stalking the abundant small game, boys and girls new to the frontier found an excitement they had never known. During his first year in western Kansas, fourteen-year-old John Norton peppered his diary with word of him and his younger brother killing jackrabbits, ducks, and various varmints, some of them eaten but many not. Soon he was ready for larger prey, and his friends' tales of a foray to the Canadian River inspired wonder tinged with jealousy: "Game! Buffalo! 2 antelope and a deer!"[13] Sunday rabbit hunting was "about the only good time that we ever had," Dora Bryant remembered of her Oklahoma girlhood. For others, it was snake chasing. One daughter of the plains bagged a dozen victims still-early in the 1872 summer season. Game birds on ponds and buffalo wallows, raccoons, deer and occasionally bears in the mountains, squirrels in the woodlands, rabbits and coyotes everywhere—children found enjoyment in bringing them all down. "Hunting seemed to me the greatest sport in all creation," one remembered. "Compared with [it,] everything else was as dust in the cyclone."[14]

Gathering wild greens and berries, another important children's chore, also was turned to their enjoyment. Hunting raspberries was the one job she never had to be goaded to do, a Colorado girl recalled. It was a chance to search out secret spots in the meadows and hills and to fantasize about future adventures. For a plains daughter, the burning of a firebreak around her farm was "one of the joys of our childhood." In mountain towns, boys and girls loved to search the streams for traces of gold dust overlooked by prospectors.[15] In playful work, children were often aided by one of their most essential tools—the horse. Many frontier children were on horseback, herding and delivering messages, by their fourth or fifth year, and in the more arid and sparsely populated regions they rarely left the saddle. As a general rule, Agnes Cleaveland wrote, "one must never be seen afoot except in the business of looking for a horse." An acquaintance claimed to have dismounted only during a two-week bout of measles. A newcomer's introduction could be swift. A mother fresh to Utah wrote home that her young son's love for riding came almost instantly: "He says you could not hire him to go back."[16]

Children on horseback had a freedom of movement and a sense of power comparable only to a modern teenager in an automobile, and their work atop their ponies is most difficult to separate from their play. To break the monotony of watching over cattle and sheep, they raced, practiced stunts, and chased (but rarely caught) coyotes and antelopes. Given a break from chores, they still loved to gallop after that swift prey.[17] "Wasn't it fun though!" the young teenager Luna Warner gushed to her diary about racing across the Kansas grasslands. But that adventure paled beside her several days on a bison hunt with her father. There were so many new sights and sounds, and when the shaggies were found and her father shot at one, things got tense: "Pa fired and then the buffalo came right for me. My horse sprang and snorted and whirled around me but I kept fast hold and talked to her and she arched her neck. Patty [a friend] had just come up and she went for him and worried him until Pa had shot four times. Then he [the bison, not Pa] fell dead in the ravine."[18] No wonder Hamlin Garland could write of his youthful friends on the Iowa frontier: "They lived in the saddle when no other duties called them, . . . and the world seemed a very good place for a boy."[19]

Horses were just one part of a menagerie moving through the child's world of play. Youngsters adjusted to their isolation by seizing upon animals as surrogate playmates. A woman newly arrived in Arizona wrinkled her nose at the "chickens, children, and dogs . . . promiscuously mixed together," but the sight was a common one. A mother in that territory rounded up a puppy, two lambs, a fawn, two kittens, and a calf to entertain her baby on the family's remote claim. Youngsters romped and ran with bear cubs, antelopes, and coyote pups (one girl named hers Dart and Whizz). A young Kansan found baby badgers particularly intelligent. Others sat for hours handling ground squirrels, prairie dogs, owls, and pigeons. When traveler and essayist Bayard Taylor found a girl frolicking with prairie dogs in the corner of a stage station, he speculated that she was learning to cope with the loneliness she would likely know as an adult. Then she told him that she actually preferred animals as companions. He was impressed: "What a western woman she will make!"[20]

Children sometimes made play of the work in households and the fields. Martha Collins of Oregon learned to make even threshing fun:

> When the wheat was harvested we put the shocks in a corral and turned the calves and young stock in on it to tramp it out. I greatly enjoyed the process of threshing out the grain. I would go in and catch a young heifer by the tail and hang on like grim death while she would fairly sail around the corral trying to get away. I would take steps about ten feet long as she ran around the corral. This would start all the calves running and the grain got well tramped."

Children felt their deepest affection, however, for the country beyond the fields and homes. Of that, we have testimony from an unlikely source: Fiorello LaGuardia, reformist mayor of New York City, who spent his youth in South Dakota and Arizona. Adults called that country the badlands, but to the Little Flower and his chums it was "a paradise. . . . Our playground was not measured in acres, or city blocks, but in miles and miles."[21] Play as exploration, play as work—the two meshed as children grew, developing useful skills, learning of their surroundings, finding confidence and self-reliance.

Sooner or later, all boys and girls met with others their ages, and then they turned to a third category of play—the more formal games that have been so much a part of childhood culture throughout history. Such amusements usually become an important part of children's lives at about the age of five or six, as the young begin to assume new roles and responsibilities that take them beyond their families into an ever-widening circle of peers and adults. As a child's world embraces more people and situations, his or her play adjusts to include them. Games are, among other things, social exercises. Through them, a boy or girl can grapple with complex questions, the how and why of getting along with others and of surviving in society.[22]

The range of games was enormous. There were games played in circles and in lines, with sticks and cans and balls and bones, some with boys against girls and others not, chanting, singing, and dancing. Just as striking, the same games were played in all of the West's many settings. Children passed time with Anti-I-Over in emigrant camps on the Truckee River and on the Llano Estacado. They played Blackman and Shinny from southern Arizona to the Montana mountains and told the same riddles in Silver City, New Mexico, and Silver City, Idaho. Of all institutions brought westward by persons of all ages, children's games were some of the most pervasive and consistent.[23]

Childhood games are both ancient and remarkably similar across cultures. In their games, songs, and chants, children have created their own language and lore to express their peculiar view of the world. Because many joys and fears of the young change slowly over the generations, the games that reflect these feelings persevere, sometimes for centuries.[24] Boys and girls of the Cross Timbers region of Texas amused themselves with How Many Miles to Miley Bright, a game with rules and rhymes dating back to medieval English pilgrimages.[25] Children implanted in a new setting a rich inheritance that they in turn would pass on to younger siblings and acquaintances. They were "tradition's warmest friends, . . . respecters, even venerators, of custom."[26] Child's play was an important facet of the pioneers' conservative impulse.

Games helped solve some of childhood's thorniest problems, among them one especially pressing on the frontier—the disorientation that came with settlers' extraordinary mobility. Demographers have shown that these pioneers were probably the most footloose citizens of a very restless nation, forever arriving in unfamiliar places, starting over among people who likely had arrived only recently themselves. A sense of community was hard to come by. Adults attacked this problem with the West's legendary hospitality toward strangers and by quickly establishing

public institutions—churches, saloons, fraternal lodges—with traditions
and settings that offered an instant sense of belonging. Pioneer children
felt a similar longing for community, yet they had no Masonic halls or
grogshops. They did, however, have games.

Consider how it worked. It is lunchtime, first day of the term, in a
schoolyard in the Niobrara sandhill country, or in Hangtown, or in the
Cherokee Strip. The children gather, as usual with some unfamiliar faces
among them. A call goes up for a game. Sides form for Wolf Over the
River. The splayfooted girl in the gingham dress, recently arrived from
Caribou, knows the rules. She takes her place in one of the two lines
that face each another, holding the hands of her teammates and taunting
the other side with the usual jibes. With feelings running properly high,
the two lines run full tilt at each other, each child yelling and squealing,
fighting to cross the field of battle, grabbing at the enemy while trying to
avoid their clutches, for anyone taken captive thereby joins the opposition. The melee is fairly rough. In the second charge the new girl grabs a
towheaded boy and wrestles him into submission, but the tide is against
her side and at the next round she is carried away. Soon the few surviving stalwarts are subdued. It is over. Thoughts turn to Pop the Whip and
Shinny in the Hole.

The newcomer thus took part in two processes: she shared a group experience, and she competed. In the first process, the established patterns
of play allowed children to merge quickly and easily into a group. The
particulars were unimportant; participation was the thing, the fact that all
players knew what to do. A game was a ritual, like Holy Communion or
treating in a barroom, and in a ritual there are no strangers. Every child
also competed as an individual, putting herself or himself on display, and
thus began to establish a public identity. In outdoor games, there was a
chance for a bit of bravado and a show of strength, speed, agility, and
strategy. Word games stressed quick thinking and experience. In all of
them the youngster from Caribou could introduce herself, physically and
mentally, and learn something about each of the other children.

Considered in this way, games were among the most impressive of
those institutions the pioneers relied on to help balance the fragmenting,
centrifugal force of the settlement process. They were crucial as well to the

children's search for their own community. Certainly no tools were easier
to carry westward. Wherever children came together, these games were
in place and ready to do their work. From another perspective, however,
it was the differences among frontier games and those elsewhere that
are significant. In games, children acquaint themselves with the specific
values, goals, and tensions of the adult societies they will soon enter as
full members. Because these societies change over time, so does this kind
of play.[27] Children therefore could be rather choosy in the games they
brought westward. As pioneers of all ages rummaged through their institutions and customs, keeping those that best fit their needs, the young
sifted through their games and chose the ones that suited the frontier's
peculiar demands.

According to one authority, for instance, an "achievement game culture" was emerging throughout the United States toward the end of the
nineteenth century. While games of the colonies and the early republic
had taught children to accept traditional roles and to respect authority,
the new ones emphasized aggression, competition, and imagination. They
told of a rapidly changing society that celebrated individualism and social mobility.[28] Frontier children turned to these games with special enthusiasm. Eastern boys and girls seemingly preferred particular types of
competition—board and parlor games, for instance, and above all highly
organized sports, especially baseball. Well down their list of preferences
were the games that were far and away the most popular in the developing West—games like Prisoner's Base (or Dare-base), Blackman (or Black
Tom or Wolf Over the River), Flying Dutchman, Pom-Pom-Pullaway,
Shinny, Anti-I-Over, and Old Two Cat.[29] The highly physical frontier
favorites fit a vigorous life spent mostly out-of-doors, required no special
equipment, and were easily organized, even among strangers. Other reasons might also have been at work. A sport like baseball, played by rather
rigorous rules and complex strategies, rewarded players who worked together smoothly and who sometimes sacrificed individual glory. Here was
a cooperative individualism that mirrored the increasingly urban, inter-
dependent, industrialized culture of the East. By contrast, most frontier
games began with contestants on two teams, but the play quickly turned
into individual displays of strength, skill, and spontaneous maneuvering.

Western games worked by a kind of democratic scramble in which a boy or girl, shining or failing in the full glare of the group's attention, trained for a society that applauded individual aggressiveness kept within broad rules. Pioneer America was an achievement culture writ large, and so were the games of its young.

The young often amused themselves by imitating adults in much more specific ways. Some of this they did in miniature, as if reducing the baffling to a manageable scale. In mimic of those awesome figures, the freighters, boys and girls crafted tiny wagon outfits out of pillboxes, bottles, spools, buttons, and twine. A Kansas brother and sister harnessed large locusts to their rigs and drove them mercilessly. Had they carried their goods north to Nebraska, they could have sold them in two entire counties laid out to scale by a pair of sisters. The girls had created two families of corncob dolls, the Cobs and the Bocs, who worked and visited amid wee dugouts, roads, fences, ditches, and fields. The larger the children, the bigger the mockups. A reporter in Virginia City, Nevada, ran across a company of "juvenile firemen" pulling around a ten-foot outfit, complete with diminutive hooks and ladders. "A large crowd of boys were running 'wid de machine,' and we didn't see but that they made as much noise and enjoyed the fun quite as much as firemen of more mature age," he wrote. "They were a gallus lot."[30]

Theorists call this "rehearsal." Some was vicarious adventuring, but children also were making of these games an opportunity to think through the roles they would live as adults, now in this situation, now in that. It was another kind of exploration, in this case not of the land but of social relationships.[31] Most revealing were those spontaneously invented games that abstracted some fundamental aspect of the adult world the children had observed. The same boys who developed the sport of ox-bouncing provided an excellent illustration. Somewhere along the trail they turned their evening chore of gathering fuel into a competition. At day's end they formed teams, each with its own district, and began piling up buffalo chips. The pace quickened. Certain piles rose faster than others. Soon youthful footpads were trespassing to raid neighboring dung stacks, and with that came retaliation, chips hurled at rustlers and claim

jumpers. Eventually blood was shed, but not much. As they acted out and
nurtured the impulses that had driven their parents westward—the passion for property and the fight for the main chance—they also learned
how those desires could have violent implications.[32]

The young similarly create games reflecting tensions and fears in their
own lives and in those of their elders. As they play them out, they live
through the anxieties and begin to gain mastery over them. Children in
an isolated camp in Arizona's Huachuca Mountains invented one game
they called All the Tigers Are Gone. It was always played at night. One
child, the Tiger, would slip away among the trees and boulders. The rest
would remain at home base for a time, then disperse cautiously into the
dark, each calling "All the tigers are gone." Alerted by these shouts, the
tiger would stalk and pounce, and anyone caught became in turn a tiger
who began prowling for victims.[33] There was a delicious tension. No one
wanted to be among the first caught, but to be the last, creeping among
the deep shadows with no one but enemies around, was even less envi-
able. Here was a variation of chase and tag with some peculiar twists
suggestive of the frontier. The "it" player did not wait and count while the
others ran and hid, but rather went into the dark, a menacing cat of the
night. Home base became like the frontier cabin, a sanctuary surrounded
by danger. Still, the children had to leave it, calling out their reassuring
lie ("All the tigers are gone") as they ventured Out There to meet an
accumulating dread. It was a child's nightmare of the new country in
microcosm.

Some of the children's fears arose from the distinctive frontier institutions of their elders. The volatile style of religion, with its stress on
the imminent agonies of damnation and its tumultuous meetings full of
shouting and wailing, provided a release of tension among adults struggling with a precarious way of life, but for literal-minded children the
fearsome messages of itinerant preachers could be terrifying. Some of
them took their parents' search for catharsis one step further, exorcising
their own anxiety by turning religion into play. From Kansas in the 1870s
comes an example. Youngsters there invented the game of Heaven and
Hell. Two boys, appointed God and Gabriel, climbed atop a haystack in

a barn. Satan descended into the lower regions—a shed dug beneath the floor to store broom corn. The divine drama then began:

> People were married and were given in marriage, stole horses, murdered and jumped claims. To be realistic, because "straight is the gate and narrow is the way and few there be that find it," and since each was anxious to experience what Hell was like, there were more fit subjects for Hell than Heaven. When the earth was full enough of violence, Gabriel blew his trumpet, a buffalo horn, and the dead came to life (all who had been buried in the hay)—there had been many violent deaths and sad funerals. . . .
>
> God pronounced judgement by telling each sinner of his evil deeds and with "Depart from me, ye workers of iniquity," or "No liar or drunkard shall inherit the kingdom," chucked the offending children of men through a hole where they slid down into the shed (Hell) and were burned by Guy, the Devil, who threw broom corn chaff all over them, as the substance nearest to fire. If it wasn't eternal, it at least lasted until we changed our clothes.[34]

Children came to this play instinctively, or they learned it from others their ages, or they invented it, but in each case it was theirs. The fourth category of play was fundamentally different. It included amusements that adults encouraged among their children. This play, too, became part of how the young learned about frontier life and their place in it, but it occurred partly as an exchange between older and younger.

All such play is partly manipulation. Parents and children realize early that with play they can influence each another. Like so many important things, it begins with a smile. When an infant a few weeks old makes what looks like a grin, its mother or father smiles back, stroking lightly and cooing. The child likes that and soon learns that a gurgling laugh, then other small performances, brings affection and comfort. Parent and child both assume they are controlling each other, and both are correct. It is part love, part (quite literally) power play. Usually it continues throughout their relationship.[35]

A century ago, parents and social engineers looked more and more to play for help in molding the young and, through them, the future. Child-rearing manuals recommended certain games and warned against improper toys and amusements, and urban reformers preached the need for playgrounds and wholesome amusements to elevate the characters of street children.[36] Frontier parents joined in this manipulation. In that early stage of their societies' development, their vision of a proper future hinged partly on their sons and daughters learning and accepting cultural norms, yet the demands of their new lives left parents with little time to direct their children's leisure hours. In the end, most mothers and fathers did what they could, selecting and pressing on their children amusements that encouraged values that these adults considered most important.

Like parents in all parts of the country, those in the West tried to define and reinforce the boundary between the sexes. Adrietta Applegate, heading for Oregon with her family in 1851, was given a reticule, a small bag filled with scraps of quilt, thread, and a thimble, and told to amuse herself along the way by learning to sew. A three-year-old boy headed for the same country a few years earlier got a toy with a different message when his mother converted her sewing basket into an imaginary emigrant wagon, harnessed wooden blocks as oxen, and fashioned whips out of small sticks and string. As the father drove this family's wagon westward, the son sat inside driving his.[37]

These not-so-subtle lessons were repeated everywhere on the frontier. Parents gave boys wooden horses, guns, tiny wagons, and lassos to fling at posts, dogs, chickens, and sisters.[38] Sons, in fact, typically received few toys at all. They were encouraged to find their amusement in the hills, fields, and streets in the "real world" of men. Their sisters' toys hinted of an indoor future of domestic tasks. The more affluent got delicate, hand-painted porcelain dolls with large wardrobes, small sewing sets, cradles, miniature pewter dishes, and china cups. Poorer girls had dolls of wood and rags and corn shucks. Most girls responded warmly to the gifts. When given her first doll, a young Californian seemed enchanted with her maternal role, her mother thought: "She danced about and her tongue went like a millrace. 'It looks at me! It's glad to see me!'"[39] Yet girls enjoyed taking these domestic portents outdoors, there to set up their imaginary households with the bits and pieces of the world they knew so well through their other play. A gold-camp girl used chunks of wood for extra children, and called formally at bushes she had named after neighboring houses. A young West Texan furnished her improvised dollhouse with rocks and broken pottery. The piano was a cow chip. One daughter of the Kansas flint hills gathered her dolls into a dwelling she had carefully constructed of buffalo bones. These girls were fitting their parents' lessons into their own experiences and fondnesses, despite intrinsic difficulties. "I was an only child," wrote a daughter of northern California, "so there were no children to play with at home, only myself and the cows and the dogs and the chickens. Mother bought me dolls, tried to get me to play with them. 'Pretend you're keeping house,' mother said. So I took the dolls out to the shed and sat them down in chairs and tried to talk to them, but they didn't talk back. The chickens were lots more fun."[40]

When parents did find leisure time in their busy lives, they invited their sons and daughters to be entertained on adult terms. Young and old passed evenings and wintry days playing cards or the board games then gaining a wide popularity. Often these pastimes were specifically aimed at shaping children's values. "Authors," a particular favorite, allowed players to impress others with their literary heritage. Girls and mothers in a Pacific-bound wagon eased their boredom with "Mansion of Happiness," a board game celebrating the familial bliss supposedly awaiting women reared by the standards of true womanhood.[41]

This sort of play overlapped, often in a single evening, with entertainments that introduced children to the society of adults. Spelling contests and group readings took place within families and among larger neighborhood gatherings. At lyceums, literary societies, and debating clubs children heard lectures on ancient religions and learned of moral and political issues. Music, another traditional amusement full of cultural meanings, was also easily carried westward. Boys and girls were taught songs that celebrated regional and ethnic identities and historical high points— "The Irish Immigrant," "John Brown's Body," "Annie Lisle," and "Captain Jenks of the Horse Marines." Hymns helped teach and preserve religious beliefs. There was little in their musical heritage that could not be heard. Some overlanders along the Arkansas River were soothed by the lighter airs of Mozart played by campfire musicians; another party awoke to the strains from *The Barber of Seville* performed by nearby soldiers.[42]

All these adult-directed amusements were meant to educate the young while reinforcing certain basic values. At a dance, boys and girls learned what their elders thought were normal relationships and proper lines of authority and deference. The most common form of adult leisure activity, visiting neighbors, taught such lessons while combining various amusements with the conversational arts. "We made up a fine log fire and with ox yokes for seats, had a fine singing, talking and telling of storys," wrote a man on the Oregon Trail with a company that included sixteen children; a woman on the same road told of "some fiddling & dancing, washing, baking, knitting, reading old compositions."[43] The pattern continued when the emigrants settled in. Affection, pleasure, and cultural education were assumed to be in harmony. As a mother on a Kansas homestead told her diary after a few relaxing hours with her husband and children, "We have been spelling and laughing this evening. It is a good thing to do both."[44]

Children's laughter was a familiar sound on the frontier. Boys and girls spent thousands of hours at play, in spelling matches and coyote chasing, playing games of Darebase, and roaming the countryside. As Plato probably would have understood, the amusements of "Give her goss" Andy and his friends added up to an important part of their upbringing and a rich, revealing aspect of western social life. Much of this play fits cozily into familiar themes of western history—the honing of essential skills, the defense of tradition, the quest for community, and the search for understanding in a puzzling land. In a deeper sense, however, the children's experiences were theirs alone. In their play, they were fashioning their own relationship with the western country.

One result was some intriguing contradictions in growing up western. A daughter was given dolls and dishes to prepare for her coming role as a traditional mother, yet, from her first crawling away, much of her play (and work) encouraged her to stretch her strengths in ways that had little to do with domesticity. Boys were pushed to be independent and aggressive; then they saw their parents wring their hands when the sons took these traits further than they were told.

Play in fact seemed always to pull the children in different directions. Parents encouraged fun that taught traditional values and prepared boys and girls for adult society as their elders meant it to be, yet for every hour spent at this type of play, youngsters enjoyed many more at the other three—the play of exploration, turning work into fun, and the inherited and invented games of youthful society—that drew them away from their parents. Through exploration, children's identities were shaped by surroundings different from those that had molded their mothers and fathers. This and the playful work of hunting, gathering, and herding bred an independence and a taste for unfettered rambling. Through their own games, children created communities distinct from those of their elders. Children were not so much rejecting wholesale their parents' way of life as finding their own answers to the challenges of pioneering. They did this while also struggling with those turbulent and creative times peculiar to the young, learning basic mental processes and interpreting for themselves their surroundings and the complicated truths of family and society. This twofold challenge, learning to live in the new country while mastering what one anthropologist has called the "art of becoming," gave frontier childhood its special complexity.[45]

It is from the crosscurrents of growing up with the country that children have the most to say. Historians have long studied the West both as frontier and as region—as an evolving area of new settlement and a mixing of cultures and as a part of the continent with its own geography, human makeup, and social and cultural traits. They have been especially curious about how one experience became the other, how from conquest and settlement a distinctive part of the country emerged with its own identity. In this work an obvious source of clues has been mostly overlooked—the youngest pioneers. Like children everywhere, they were shaped by their surroundings, and in that milieu they would grow into living artifacts of the West of their day, just as their cousins in Alabama and New Hampshire were reflections of their corners of the country.

Frontier children's lives, however, were in one way unique. They grew up on that historical cusp that has drawn much interest. They were shaped by both the pioneering experience and the country's enduring influence. They learned their parents' values and lived out the traditions and customs brought into the West from elsewhere, and as they did so, they were touching and naming the parts of the new country and making of them their own distinctive reality. The adults who came out of this blending were the first truly western generation. "I am a product of the American earth," wrote Wallace Stegner, who grew up playing on the wind-scoured prairie and willowed riverbanks just north of the Montana border, "and in nothing quite so much as in the contrast between what I knew through the pores and what I was officially taught."[46]

As their play showed so well, children in the developing West had far more command over their lives than their elders suspected. These boys and girls were not passive travelers on the journey from then until now. They helped shape their own world, and thus they had a hand in making ours. The story of the frontier and the West will not be fully told until we listen to them.

Notes

An earlier version of this chapter appeared as "Child's Play: Tradition and Adaptation on the Frontier," *Montana The Magazine of Western History* 38, no. 1 (March 1988): 2–15.

1. *The Laws of Plato*, trans. Thomas L. Pangle (New York: Basic Books, 1980).

2. Jesse Applegate, *Recollections of My Boyhood* (Roseburg, Ore.: Press of Review Publishing Co., 1914), 24–25.

3. Irene Athey, "Contribution of Play to Development," in Thomas D. Yawkey and Anthony D. Pelligrini, eds., *Child's Play: Developmental and Applied* (Hillsdale, N.J.: Lawrence Earlbaum Associates, 1984), 9–28; Roberta R. Collard, "Exploration and Play," in Brian Sutton-Smith, ed., *Play and Learning* (New York: Gardner Press, 1979), 45–68; C. Hutt, "Exploration and Play in Children," in Dietland Muller-Schwarze, ed., *Evolution of Play Behavior* (Stroudsburg, Penn.: Dowden, Hutchinson & Ross, 1978), 328–48.

4. Phillip Condit diary, May 26, 1854; Helen Stewart diary, June 16, 1853, Henry E. Huntington Library, San Marino, Calif. (hereinafter cited as HEH).

5. Lucy H. Fosdick, "Across the Plains in '61," reminiscence, Beinecke Library, Yale University, New Haven (hereinafter cited as BL); Mary L. Boatman

reminiscence, SC 444, Montana Historical Society Archives, Helena (hereinafter MHSA); Harriet P. Sanders reminiscence, SC 1254, MHSA; Harriet Wright reminiscence, Arizona Historical Society, Tucson (hereinafter AHS).

6. Josephine Moorman Reiley, "'I Think I Will Like Kansas': The Letters of Flora Moorman Heston, 1885–1886," *Kansas History* 6 (Summer 1983): 78.

7. Alice Carnow, "My Journey with Tom," reminiscence, 89–90, AHS.

8. Ella Irvine Mountjoy reminiscence, Wiley and Ella Mountjoy Collection, SC 545, MHSA.

9. Mary Ronan, *Frontier Woman: The Story of Mary Ronan As Told to Margaret Ronan*, ed. H. G. Merriam (Missoula: University of Montana Press, 1973), 18; Edwin Lewis Bennett, *Boom Town Boy* (Chicago: Sage Books, 1966), 17–18; Carolyn H. Palmer, "Reminiscences of Early Days in Boise," MS 224, Idaho Historical Society, Boise (hereinafter cited as IHS).

10. Rodman W. Paul, ed., *A Victorian Gentlewoman in the Far West: The Reminiscences of Mary Hallock Foote* (San Marino, Calif.: Huntington Library, 1972), 179.

11. Owen McWhorter interview, Southwest Collections, Texas Tech University, Lubbock (hereinafter SWC/TT); Mrs. John H. Smith reminiscence, 2, California Historical Society, San Francisco; Mrs. W. H. Hathaway reminiscence, AHS; Glen Berry interview, SWC/TT.

12. Erik H. Erikson, *Toys and Reasons: Stages in the Ritualization of Experience* (New York: W. W. Norton, 1977), 17.

13. John Norton diary, September–October 1877, January 26, 1878, Norton Family Diaries, Kansas State Historical Society, Topeka (hereinafter cited as KSHS).

14. Dora Bryant interview, 17/207–208, Indian-Pioneer Collection, Oklahoma State Historical Society, Oklahoma City (hereinafter IP/OSHS); Ben Wallicek interview, SWC/TT; Jack Stockbridge interview, no. 387, Pioneer Foundations Collection, University of New Mexico Library; Venola Lewis Bivens, ed., "The Diary of Luna E. Warner, a Kansas Teenager of the Early 1870s," *Kansas Historical Quarterly* 35 (Winter 1969): 416; Frank Albert Waugh, "Pioneering in Kansas," reminiscence, 68–69, 189, KSHS.

15. Anne Ellis, *The Life of an Ordinary Woman* (Lincoln: University of Nebraska Press, 1980), 99; Oello Ingraham Martin, "Father Came West," reminiscence, 19, KSHS; Emma Jane Davison reminiscence, IHS.

16. Agnes Morley Cleaveland, *No Life for a Lady* (Lincoln: University of Nebraska Press, 1977), 66, 68; Ursula Haskell to sister, August 4, 1848, Ursula B. H. Haskell Letters, BL.

17. John Ise, *Sod and Stubble: The Story of a Kansas Homestead* (Lincoln: University of Nebraska Press, 1970), 213; Katie Bell Crum interview, SWC/TT.

18. Bivens, "Diary of Luna Warner," 424, 436.

19. Hamlin Garland, *Boy Life on the Prairie* (Lincoln: University of Nebraska Press, 1961), 95.

20. Alice Barker reminiscence, 12, AHS; Irene A. Meyers reminiscence, HEH; George Cork reminiscence, Jessie K. Snell Collection, KSHS; Myrtel Smith reminiscence, 14, KSHS; Augusta Dodge Thomas, "Prairie Children: An Autobiography," MS, 47–48, KSHS; Frank T. Alkire, "Little Lady of Triangle T. Ranch," reminiscence, Appendix 1, AHS; Clayton Carter interview, SWC/TT; Cleaveland, *No Life for a Lady*, 68–69; Allie B. Wallace, *Frontier Life in Oklahoma* (Washington, D.C.: Public Affairs Press, 1964), 61; Bayard Taylor, *Colorado: A Summer Trip* (New York: G. P. Putnam & Sons, 1867), 21.

21. Fiorello H. LaGuardia, *The Making of an Insurgent: An Autobiography, 1882–1919* (New York: Capricorn Books, 1961), 19.

22. Jean Piaget, *Play, Dreams and Imitation in Childhood* (New York: W. W. Norton, 1951), 142–146; Frank and Theresa Caplan, *The Power of Play* (New York: Anchor Books, 1973), 61–85; Rivka R. Eifermann, "Social Play in Childhood," in R. E. Herron and Brian Sutton-Smith, eds., *Child's Play* (New York: John Wiley & Sons, 1971), 270–97; Susanna Millar, *The Psychology of Play* (New York: Jason Aronson, 1974), 188–90.

23. Of the scores of diaries and reminiscences that mention and discuss children's games, I have relied on the following for my impressions of how these games were played, their functions, and the relative popularity of some over others: Vera Tepe, Veta Harris, Lena Martin, and Katie Crump interviews and Lula M. Veale and Anna Wilkinson Reynolds reminiscences, SWC/TT; Fred C. Moore biographical sketch, Madison Loring Collection, AHS; Emma Teller Tyler reminiscence, Lynn Perrigo Collection, Western History Collections, University of Colorado Library, Boulder; Edna Hedges diary, MS 33, Box 11, MHSA; Robert E. Steiner, "Children in Early Alder Gulch," MS 268, Special Collections, Montana State University Library, Bozeman; Bennett, *Boom Town Boy*, 68; Samuel Evan Boys, *My Boyhood in the Flint Hills of Kansas, 1873–1893* (Plymouth, Ind.: n.p., 1958), 20; Fannie L. Eisele, "We Came to Live in Oklahoma Territory," *Chronicles of Oklahoma* 38 (Spring 1960): 62; Ellison Orr, "Reminiscences of a Pioneer Boy," *Annals of Iowa* 40 (Winter 1971): 543, and 40 (Spring 1971): 595; Glen R. Durrell, "Homesteading in Colorado," *Colorado Magazine* 51 (Spring 1974): 103.

24. Iona Opie and Peter Opie, *Children's Games in Street and Playground* (Oxford: Oxford University Press, 1969); and *The Lore and Language of Schoolchildren* (Oxford: Clarendon Press, 1960); Peter Opie, "The Tentacles of Tradition," *Advancement of Science* 20 (September 1963): 235–44.

25. Edward Everett Dale, *Cross Timbers: Memories of a North Texas Boyhood* (Austin: University of Texas Press, 1966), 90.

26. Opie and Opie, *Lore and Language of Schoolchildren*, 2.

27. May V. Seagoe, "Children's Play as an Indicator of Cultural and Intracultural Differences," *Journal of Educational Sociology* 35 (February 1962): 278–83. For an application of this approach, see David K. Wiggins, "The Play of Slave

Children in the Plantation Communities of the Old South, 1820–60," *Journal of Sport History* 7 (Summer 1980): 21–39.

28. Brian Sutton-Smith, "The Two Cultures of Games," in Sutton-Smith, *The Folkgames of Children* (Austin: University of Texas Press, 1972), 295–311.

29. Brian Sutton-Smith and B. G. Rosenberg, "Sixty Years of Historical Change in the Preferences of American Children," in Sutton-Smith, *Folkgames of Children,* 258–94.

30. Thomas, "Frontier Children," 41; Ben Wallicek interview, SWC/TT; Grace Snyder, *No Time on My Hands* (Caldwell, Ida.: Caxton Printers, 1963), 25; Dale, *Cross Timbers,* 82–83, 91; Virginia City, Nevada, *Territorial Enterprise,* April 5, 1865.

31. Miller, *Psychology of Play,* 136–57.

32. Applegate, *Recollections,* 19.

33. Mrs. W. H. Hathaway, reminiscence, AHS.

34. Thomas, "Prairie Children," 58–59.

35. Catherine Garvey, "The Natural History of the Smile," in Garvey, *Play* (Cambridge, Mass.: Harvard University Press, 1977), 17–24; Thomas R. Shultz, "Play as Arousal Modulation," in Sutton-Smith, *Play and Learning,* 7–22.

36. See, for instance, Bernard Wishy, *The Child and the Republic: The Dawn of Modern American Child Nurture* (Philadelphia: University of Pennsylvania Press, 1968); Dominick Cavallo, *Muscles and Morals: Organized Playgrounds and Urban Reform, 1880–1920* (Philadelphia: University of Pennsylvania Press, 1981).

37. Adrietta Applegate Hixon, *On to Oregon! A True Story of a Young Girl's Journey Into the West,* ed. Waldo Taylor (Weiser, Ida.: Signal-American Printers, 1947), 8; Glenda Riley, ed., "Family Life on the Frontier: The Diary of Kitturah Penton Belknap," *Annals of Iowa* 44 (Summer 1977): 49.

38. Lewis Carstairs Gunn, *Records of a California Family,* ed. Anna Lee Marston (San Diego: n.p., 1928), 162.

39. Thomas, "Prairie Children," 6–7; Wallace, *Frontier Life,* 64–65; Snyder, *No Time on My Hands,* 21; Minne Hodge interview, 62/162, Florence Woods interview, 50/394, IP/OSHS; Mrs. W. H. Hathaway reminiscence, AHS; Gunn, *California Family,* 169.

40. Abigail Emigh reminiscence, G. Donald Emigh Collection, MS 2/361, IHS; Martin, "Father Came West," 12; Maggie L. B. Holden reminiscence, SWC/TT; Craig Miner, *West of Wichita: Settling the High Plains of Kansas, 1865–1890* (Lawrence: University Press of Kansas, 1986), 51; Annette White Parks, "Children's Work and Play on the Northwest Frontier," *Henry Ford Museum and Greenfield Village Herald* 1:5 (November 1, 1986): 35–36.

41. Ward G. DeWitt and Florence S. DeWitt, *Prairie Schooner Lady: The Journal of Harriett Sherill Ward, 1853* (Los Angeles: Westernlore Press, 1959), 93; Fosdick, "Across the Plains," 4.

42. Waugh, "Pioneering in Kansas," 195–96; Anne Davies diary, February 1, 1887, KSHS; Durrell, "Homesteading," 105; Mary R. Powers diary, typescript, 11, BL; Hill, *Dangerous Crossing,* 28–29; Ellis, *Life of an Ordinary Woman,* 122–24; Perry Kline reminiscence, 54–55, Colorado State Historical Society, Denver; James Clyman journal, May 26, 1844, HEH; Susan Thompson Parrish reminiscence, 3, HEH; George McCowen diary, August 11, 1853, HEH; Benjamin F. Owen, *My Trip across the Plains* (Eugene: Lane County Pioneer-Historical Society, 1967), 24; James Bennett, *Overland Journey to California* (New Harmony, Ind.: Times Printing, 1906), 9; Ralph P. Bieber, ed., "Diary of a Journey to Pike's Peak Gold Mines in 1859," *Mississippi Valley Historical Review* 14 (December 1927): 366; Clarence W. Kellogg, "Early Day Life in California Mining Camps," reminiscence, 48–49, Bancroft Library, University of California, Berkeley.

43. John L. Johnson journal, April 26, 1851, BL; Mary Burrell diary, August 3, 1854, BL.

44. Mary Elizabeth Norton, in Norton Family Diaries, January 26, 1880, KSHS.

45. Colin M. Turnbull, *The Human Cycle* (New York: Simon & Schuster, 1983), chapter 1.

46. Wallace Stegner, *Wolf Willow: A History, a Story, and a Memory of the Last Plains Frontier* (Lincoln: University of Nebraska Press, 1980), 23.

8

Becoming Mormon

In the Mormon historical drama, children have always stood close to center stage. Joseph Smith was barely past childhood at the time of his first vision. Throughout his life he treated the young with special respect. The innocence of the child was an early, vital doctrine in Mormon theology, and Church fathers spent considerable energy setting standards for proper child rearing.[1] In the debates and ravings that swirled around this new religion, all sides used boys and girls as arguing points to press their cases. Critics warned that the crowds of unruly teenagers and "ragged, squalid, miserable looking children" in Mormon communities were living forecasts of the social disaster awaiting all who embraced the faith. Defenders answered that Latter-day Saint homes were islands of security and love—and then, when trying to shore up a flagging religious discipline, reversed course to claim that misbehaving youngsters were proof of a slippage of commitment.[2] And while observers fought long and hard about nearly everything else, all agreed on one point: nobody could match the Saints in at least one sort of production. A visitor to a Mormon rancher in 1863 wrote that the man "has been very successful in raising cattle and children. His cattle lie down peacefully in green pastures beside the still waters, and his [children] lie down peacefully all over the house, on beds and on the floor."[3]

All recognized the importance of children; however, few if any adults at the time apparently took the time to stop a few girls and boys to ask them what their lives were like, or how they saw their futures, or what they believed, or what they thought about what was going on around them.

And with some exceptions most historians have ignored the youngest Mormons as well.[4]

There is something to be learned by peeking into the lives of the youngest Saints during the Church's earliest years, from the early 1830s and the first conversions through the 1850s and the establishment of Mormon settlements in Utah. Peeking is not easy. Remarkably few documents from the hands of the boys and girls themselves have survived. There are, however, scores of reminiscences and memoirs written later, often much later, by men and women who lived through those years as children. Such evidence has its problems. Over time everyone rearranges memories, emphasizing some events and details and leaving others out, shifting things around and rephrasing conversations, embellishing here and inventing there.

These memories nonetheless certainly say something about what actually happened from the point of view of actors who have been mostly ignored until now—ones who have been seen but not heard. There is something to be learned as well from the very distortions of the stories. How those men and women altered their past, what they chose to alter and rearrange, can be just as revealing as the unvarnished truth. Anyone who thinks about his or her own experience with family tales will likely agree that memories do not change entirely at random. People revise their pasts according to how they have come to think about themselves. The stories they tell about their lives are a bit like movie scripts. Individual scenes, selected from a multitude of possibilities, build toward a conclusion— toward the people in the present who are doing the remembering. People revise this scene or that, adding and deleting action and dialogue to create a clean and understandable story about how they have come to be as they are. There is one obvious way the metaphor breaks down, however. While the end of a movie stays the same, people are constantly changing. Their values and views of the world change. They learn and evolve, and as they do, their understanding of themselves changes too. Consequently they keep revising their scripts. Each person is continually rewriting and rearranging scenes from the past, so that they form a story that, by the end of it, explains who he or she is at the moment, in the evolving present.

Once this human tendency is recognized—the process of reshaping continually a personal past to reflect a continually changing present—the very shifting of memory becomes a fertile field of study. Patterns in what people have chosen to stress, the stories and the words and the details they use, can reveal something about how they have come to see themselves and how they believe their early years have given meaning to their lives.[5]

In the stories of early Mormon children, that shifting and shaping is especially intriguing. The 1830s, 1840s, and 1850s were formative years as well for the Mormon religious and social community. Think of the terms often used to describe this period in LDS history. It saw the birth of the restored faith, then the youthful trials and self-exploration, a search for identity and a turbulent adolescence, a casting out by political and social parents, and finally a painful coming of age and the achievement of an independent character. The same language can be used to describe the children of those years and the communities they lived in, and the parallel is more than rhetorical. The memories of the youngest Saints of the early Church and those of the Church itself are tightly interwoven. The youngsters from those formative years in turn would grow into the generation that carried the maturing Church into a new era. Listening to what they had to say about growing up can shed light on views and values they would draw upon as they assumed their place as leaders of the faithful.

The Church's early years fall rather neatly into three periods—the time of conversion, as the first Mormons discovered their faith; the first gathering, when substantial numbers gravitated to Missouri and Illinois from the mid- 1830s to 1846; and the exodus, from 1846 to the late 1850s when the expelled Saints made the great trek and founded the new Zion. The memories of children and adults are in many ways much the same, but there are nuances and emphases that set them apart. Caroline West Larrabee was a young girl in London when her parents converted. She recalled meetings and prayers and problems with relatives unhappy with the family's new life. When she was ten and her sister six, her parents sent them ahead to America with an emigrant company. "We left London in the morning," she recalled. "I remember leaving Father, Mother, brother and sister. Did I cry? No, I was going to Zion."[6] The rest of the account of the long journey to Missouri, however, never mentions religion, or for that matter, much of anything outside of one topic: food. Caroline liked shipboard meals of beef and sea biscuit, and when she and her sister sang to the cook, he would give them sweetcakes, but on the train to Missouri, "oh, dear, how hungry we were.... We bought bread ... [but] it was like eating wind, there was nothing to it." On the steamboat, they suffered from hunger and from thirst, for the warm river water seemed half sand. The highlight of Caroline's trip came when a kind couple gave her and her sister candy, crackers, and cheese.[7]

Although the adult Caroline tells us that her religious commitment was foremost in her mind, in choosing her details, she betrays her real concern. When thrust into a frightening and uncertain situation like hers, a child will fix on primal needs, starting with the basic one of being fed. Caroline's concern was with a full belly, not a faithful heart, and it reminds us that conversion often brought with it a shattering of what had been a secure life. For her it was the temporary loss of parents and siblings. For others the break was far more traumatic. Lawrence Mariger of Denmark was one of many who watched their parents' marriages splinter, in his case in 1856 when his mother converted and his father did not. Under Danish law the father retained the children; but while Lawrence was visiting his mother, she had him baptized, secured false papers for him and his two siblings, and smuggled them out of the country with her. En route to Salt Lake City, his mother died, leaving twelve-year-old Lawrence and the others in the care of their new community.[8]

The thought of losing the protective net of kin and loved ones, "separation anxiety," is every child's deepest fear. Everyone can recall some twinge of it from early childhood, perhaps the brief terror of losing a parent in a store, but for Lawrence Mariger and many others, this nightmare was not briefly hinted at but made terribly real. In other memories we hear how losing faith in life's basics left children with fears that, years later, were raw and immediate. When five-year-old Carl Nielson's parents converted in Norway in 1860, all friends quickly turned against the family, and his father was fired. There was no other support. Gradually the food gave out, meals were missed, and finally the Nielsons went hungry for three days. Carl remembered a deep inner panic as he and his mother prayed and his father left on a desperate hunt for something for the table. The search ended with a prize that seemed heaven-sent: a sack of bread.[9]

For these children the choice of becoming Mormon triggered a frightful predicament. The struts that held life together suddenly fell away. Everything tottered as power shifted instantly into the hands of others who had nothing good on their minds when they looked down at children like Caroline and Lawrence and Carl. From that situation another theme emerges. As adults, these converts would look back and recall moments when, as children, they found within themselves what was needed to bring at least some control to their lives. Carl Nielson wrote:

> Several women came to our home, father being absent . . . , and they began to abuse my mother for being a Mormon, until my dear mother began to cry very bitterly at their abuse. Then little Carl got up on a chair and with doubled fist commanded the women to leave his mother alone and the women in astonishment at the five-year-old boy defending his mother, left the house.[10]

It is almost as if we are seeing someone new—the adult Nielson refers to himself in the third person—in the sense of Carl's character being turned sharply in a new direction. Years after the fact, men and women looked back on a troubled and unsettling time and recognized that from those troubles someone emerged strong enough to gain a grip on an unraveling life. These are stories of empowerment, and they are all the more intriguing because their setting is the emergence as well of a new faith facing its own rearing hostilities. Young people and the young religion mesh together in mutually painful memories.

This theme—the fear of separation, the desperation for needful things going or gone, then the discovery of some power and control—rises in pitch and intensity in memories of the gathering in Missouri and Illinois. One of the most disturbing documents from this time is the reminiscence of Mary Elizabeth Worth Peoples, written more than forty years after her time in Nauvoo, at age seven, during its bombardment and occupation in 1846. Her divorced mother, older sister, and younger brother joined her uncle, but by the time Nauvoo fell, he had already gone to Iowa. Authorities allowed her mother to stay the winter, but she fell ill and, with little food, weakened rapidly. The three children awoke one morning to find her dead:

> We sent to the neighbors to tell them. They came and performed the necessary duties and that night several young and giddy folks came and sit [sic] up with the corpse and the next day two men came with a wagon to take our Dear Mother away from us to bury her out of sight. We then more fully realized (perhaps they did not bury her at all) our condition. They would not let one of us go to see where they had laid her. No they took her away and left us alone.[11]

Mary's nine-year-old sister took them to the home of a doctor for whom she had done chores. "We was very cold and hungry. There we went in and saw the table spread with luxury [but] not one crust did [they] give my little brother, three years old, and myself but they said they would keep my sister."[12]

Mary was given to another family and her brother to yet another. Now isolated from anyone he knew, "my little brother so young cried to go home to mother and annoyed them so much they put him out of doors one evening. . . . He went to the old vacant lonely house and stayed all night alone, a cold frost night. They next morning [a woman] who lived a short distance away heard him crying and went and took him in and cared for him."[13] Soon afterwards, mercifully, the children's uncle came for them.

It would be hard to devise a waking nightmare worse than this: the gradual peeling away of family, the hunger, the loss of the final protector and denial even of knowing where to find her remains, then separation from each other, and that boy's heartbreaking night, crying in the darkness and looking for his mother in the cold, empty house. Benjamin Critchlow's reminiscence is almost as painful. When he was eleven, a mob forced his family out of their Missouri farm before harvest: "The latter part of the fall . . . I was hungry all the time. I went to bed hungry, and was hungry all day." His father punched holes in a piece of tin, nailed it to a board, and rubbed green corn across it to make a little meal for small cakes, "not half enough to satisfy . . . a hungry boy like myself."[14] Yet Benjamin was proud to have survived those hungry times, and in saying so, he pushes into the center of attention what he and others considered crucial in stories of the persecuted—healings, miracles, and moments of divine protection. Critchlow recalled the paralyzed made to walk and the instant curing of the near-dead. Some godly interventions are comically ordinary. William Moore Allred recalled as a boy knowing a Brother Harven whose mouth had an irritating way of drawing to the side when he laughed. After elders administered to him, he laughed out of the front of this face, just like everyone else.[15]

More suggestive were cases of children finding in themselves what was needed to shape their fate and that of others. An awareness of power could take institutional form, as with young boys volunteering for militia groups and the famous "whistling and whittling brigade," in which sons of Nauvoo surrounded suspected enemies of the Church, whistling loudly while whittling sticks with bowie knives.[16] Something similar was acted out by individual children calling up power from within. Samuel Gifford was twelve in 1836 when mobs of non-Mormon locals began harassing Saints who had recently fled Jackson County, Missouri, to settle in neighboring Clay County. He and friends were hiding in a corral when a crowd passed by on their way home from organizing a raid against his family and neighbors. Wishing harm to anyone, even an enemy, was shameful, he wrote later, "but nevertheless I said 'I hope they will all get drowned before they get across the river.'" Sure enough, the ferry sprang a leak midstream and sank. Among the lost was one of the two ringleaders. The other survived by stripping and swimming to shore far downstream. His fate was almost as satisfying: "He . . . was naked and far from home and had to pass through a large bottom of nettles that were densely thick."[17]

Sending your tormentor naked to a nettle field: it is a twelve-year-old's definition of empowerment, and variations run throughout memories of this time. Fantasizing power when nearly everyone is bigger and stronger and potentially threatening is a universal childhood impulse, of course, but two differences set these memories apart. These threats were not potential but real, and the power to stand up to them, the children's first germ of self-assurance, took its particular shape around the Mormon faith and the menace toward it. Occasionally this emerging child's puissance and the Church's trials fuse almost totally, then soar into flights of fancy. The result might be called the LDS Tall Tale, Juvenile division.

Mosiah Hancock was born in Kirtland and moved with his family to Far West when he was three. His dimmest early recollections were of a howling mob outside his house as his brother was being born, then of fleeing their farm with only what they could carry. He recalled his father as a man of exceptional powers who summoned out of thin air a new pair of shoes for his exhausted wife. In Nauvoo the future apostate Francis Higbee shot him in the breast with a rifle from twenty feet away, but the bullet fell harmlessly to the ground, and his father raised it to heaven as a thankful salute to God's protecting hand.[18] Mosiah must have inherited some of his father's powers. During a hungry stretch some pigs were bothering his father as he plowed. Mosiah prayed for their death, and his father promptly slew one with a thrown block of wood. There was meat on the table that night, with more to come:

> The rest of the shoats did not seem satisfied, so they came back again. The same boy made another prayer [note again the use of the third person describing a new person emerging], and the same arm threw the same piece of wood, another shoat died right there, and mother skinned [it]. We were all happy as long as the meat lasted. I always felt that god opened the way for us to get something to eat.[19]

Mosiah's powers were confirmed and blessed by none other than the Prophet himself. When the boy was eight, he recalled, Joseph Smith came to his father's carpenter shop in Nauvoo. He told Mosiah to fetch a map. Smith then predicted in detail the next twenty years of the Saints' story. He traced the move to Winter Quarters, the great trek to Salt Lake Valley, the rise of a prosperous society, its spread north and south, and the expanding sway of Deseret. He prophesied the nation's political course, including the rise of the Republican Party (by name) and the Civil War. All this he laid before young Mosiah. A few years later, Mosiah recalled, when the bodies of the martyred Prophet and his brother were returned to Nauvoo, his father brought him to the bodies after all the mourners had left: "[He] told me to place one hand on Joseph's breast and to raise my other arm and swear with hand uplifted that I would never make a compromise with any of the sorts of sons of Hell, which vow I took with a determination to fulfill to the very letter."[20]

However outrageous in tone and detail, Mosiah's story is merely an exaggeration of many others that recount growing up through those times. His story is both a history of the Saints' trials and a marking of authority and divine power passed from one generation of the Church's defenders to another. Stories like these relate that in far western Clay County and in Nauvoo these children found a direction for their lives, both in who they might become as individuals and in how their maturing selves were melding with a community of faith itself coming of age. The direction of both sides of the stories was westward along the path traced by the Prophet's finger across the map laid out in Mosiah's father's carpenter shop. In the third and final period of childhood memories, the themes of the first two are heightened still further. The exodus and regathering witnessed the ultimate separation through the journey into the wilderness; the harshest suffering, which culminated in an army marching against Deseret; and the final transcendence over both as the Saints survived and persevered in the new Zion. These recollections most often reveal as well the crystallization of the identities of the youngest Saints.

The exodus again shattered families and unsettled to the roots these children's earlier notions of who they were and where they belonged. Joseph Moesser's parents had joined the Church when he was nine, but when his father rejected it on the eve of emigration to Winter Quarters, his mother spirited her children across the Mississippi—all but the youngest daughter, who finally was delivered to the mother after she cried incessantly for weeks and would not sleep.[21] Edwin Pettit was eight when his newly converted parents died within two weeks of one another in 1842 near Nauvoo, and he was taken in by a non-Mormon family. When his older sister and her husband joined the exodus, he wanted to go, but his guardian refused, so Edwin stole away to the emigrant camp. There he fuzzed out his old identity still further to elude pursuers:

I borrowed a sunbonnet and a girl's dress and joined four or five girls in a line washing dishes when my brothers entered camp. They passed right in back of me but did not recognize me. Then the girls and I crossed the Des Moines river on a flatboat. . . . I had to ride sidesaddle behind my friend on a horse. Passing strangers, I would lower my head. Stangers would call out because they thought I was asleep, "Hey, old man, that girl will fall off; she's asleep." The old man would call back, "Mary Ann, wake up or you'll fall off and break your neck."[22]

Disease and hunger tore at other families. Within a matter of months ten-year-old Alma Hale saw his mother die in childbirth, his father of malaria, and his two sisters of scurvy, leaving him to head west from Winter Quarters with an older brother and sister and a younger brother. Fourteen-year-old Harrison Sperry and his three siblings also lost both parents and a brother during that awful winter. Martin Luther Ensign's father died there of scurvy on his forty-eighth birthday, leaving few provisions for his widow and six young children as they started west.[23] The most painful instances, and some of the most heart-wrenching documents in American history, are from the handcart disasters of 1856.[24] Heber McBride recalled, as a thirteen-year-old, slicing strips of rawhide from dead oxen, crisping them over a fire, and drawing them through his clenched teeth to scrape off a few charred bits. At day's end the wailing began: "Then was the time to hear children crying for something to eat[.] nearly all the children would cry themselves to sleep every night[.] my 2 little Brothers would get the sack that [used to have] flour in [it] and turn it wrong side out and suck and lick the flour off it[.] we would break the [ox] bones and make a little soup by boiling them."[25]

The first years in the Salt Lake Valley were not much better. "We only had bread once or twice a week," Joseph Moesser remembered: We "dug segoes and other roots in the spring and summer, eating every particle of an ox and cow killed, even to its hide."[26] George Washington Bean's family subsisted on thistle roots, greens, and thin milk. Barbara Bowen's parents, Scottish immigrants, had no firearms and were reduced to running down rabbits as their only meat. When the infant Barbara finally drew only blood from her famished mother's breasts, her mother traded some of their few clothes for eggs to wean her daughter. Decades later the feel of crisis remained vivid and raw.[27] For eight-year-old Franklin Young, the turning point came when his father returned from an unsuccessful hunt for a lost cow. "He looked pale, and careworn, as he said, 'Mother *I must have something to eat, or I can't keep up much longer,*' and I believe I felt the danger of starvation, as I never had done before or since. . . . I prayed in my heart as I had not prayed before. O Lord spare my Father to be a father and protector to us." Franklin's mother made broth from a cow's head that had been hanging on a post, and the slightly revived father found the lost animal the next day.[28]

In Franklin Young's answered prayer can be heard once again, now in the third phase, the reaching inward to discover a first touch of control, a foothold up the side of the abyss, and once more it is through the call and response of divine intervention. Virtually every childhood memoir features immigrants and settlers snatched miraculously from disaster. These stories are echoes by the dozen of more famous ones—flocks of quail miraculously appearing to feed starving Saints exiled from Nauvoo to the "poor camp" in Iowa; God-sent cricket-gobbling gulls saving the earliest crops in the Salt Lake Valley—spoken here in the vernacular of a child's primal fears. Margaret Ballard was ten when she was searching one night for a lost cow:

> I was not watching where I was going and was barefooted. All of a sudden I began to feel I was walking on something soft. I looked down to see what it could be and to my horror found that I was standing in a bed of snakes, large ones and small ones. . . . I could scarcely move; all I could think of was to pray, and in some way I jumped out of them. The Lord blessed and cared for me.[29]

Margaret's story is of one of the most frequent elements in these reminiscences—the Mormon childhood accident. Interestingly, accidents are far and away most common in the last phase, of settlement, and especially during the latter years when communities were firmly rooted and the worst dangers past. Four-year-old Aaron Johnson's family had begun its

farm when he fell into a creek and was fished out by a passing stranger; a
year later he fell into the same creek in the same place and was miraculously caught in an eddy; a few years later a wagon of fruit rolled over his
legs, and he was barely healed from that mishap when he fell through the
ice while skating and nearly drowned.[30] Typically it is God's protective
hand that saves these children, as when Horace Cummings arrived, apparently stillborn, in a Provo granary but began to breathe after his father
administered to him. An attack by a cat nine days later set the pattern
for a misadventurous childhood: he was thrown from a horse, toppled
off a fence, was in a wagon when the team bolted, and worst of all, fell
from a willow tree face-first onto a picket fence. Bedridden for weeks, he
was once thought dead but returned to life when his father once more
administered to him.[31]

Just why accidents and divine protection show up so often near the
end of this last phase is worth pondering. The world always has been
a chancy place for the young, of course, but unless Mormon parents,
once settled in Utah, suddenly began producing the clumsiest children
in North America, the bulking of accidents and divine rescue in those
final years would seem a matter of writers selecting those mishaps and
pushing them to the forefront. If nothing else, the recollections recognize
that surviving sudden disasters through godly help was close to the very
heart of being Mormon. After all, boys and girls had grown up hearing of
the assaults and terrors in Missouri and Illinois and how youngsters their
age had done their part in facing down a hostile world. Aaron Johnson
recalled the words to songs his mother sang about those terrible and courageous days: "The Mormons Never Tire" and "The Noble Brave Boys of
Nauvoo."[32] The mobbers might be hundreds of miles away and ten years
in the past, and the starving time replaced by full fields, but the traditions
were still fresh, and Mormons now had enough history to find a unifying
identity in a common experience of assaults, terrible blows of fate, and
godly deliverance.

Seen in that context, the better times, oddly, brought their own crisis
for the children. The very experiences that they knew had always defined
what it meant to be Mormon now had come to an end. Perhaps the children of these new circumstances were testifying in their own way to the

central importance of suffering and being saved. Perhaps they formed their own versions of these stories by sifting through their past to find their own transforming trials. Perhaps these accidents served as recapitulations of earlier, precarious times, when the Church in so many ways seemed always to be falling (or being pushed) out of trees and onto fences. In telling of their own survival, perhaps these men and women later were claiming their own places amongst the Saints in Clay County and Nauvoo, the men and women who had jumped out of their own beds of snakes and had been snatched so often from the torrent by a watchful God.

Perhaps. What is fully clear is that the memories together constitute a wider story critical to understanding early Mormon history. The story is one of dual emergence. The outward events of the conversion, the gathering and the exodus, show a religion and community taking shape. Within the details of those events, in what the authors choose to tell us and in how they put it together, men and women look back and tell how as children they discovered who they were and how they fit into the world. The pattern that ties the story together is clear and relentless and not very pretty. Adults had their property seized and their social standing destroyed. Children experienced their own dispossession—families shattered, friends turned into enemies, the wherewithal of life pulled away. Life before Mormonism had been a structure of safety and predictability; because of Mormonism that structure was torn down, and the children were left exposed, vulnerable, sometimes alone. The tearing down, however, brought with it a building up. Children found inside themselves what it took to gain some control over their lives and their future, and they built upon that discovery as they followed their own paths into adulthood.

The religious and individual identities of an entire generation merged. For the men and women looking back, the assaults and tearing down of their earlier lives as children were inseparable from the attack on their emerging church. Their discovery of strength, that vital step in the creation of an individual's character, they remembered as inextricably joined with saving the Saints and with ushering in the new Zion.

Except for the Civil War children of the invaded South, no other American generation experienced so radical a remaking through massive assaults from an outside force. As the young Saints matured, however, they would not spend their lives as their southern counterparts would, mournfully gazing into the past, identifying with a lost cause. They would live into a future bound intimately with a cause, an embattled new religion, that had won its struggle to establish itself and was, in fact, increasingly successful and secure.

That difference raises a final, particularly intriguing question. It is prompted by those psychologists who remind us how people select and shape childhood memories to form stories that reinforce and remind them of who they are. It is partly through those narratives, those personal scripts of their life-movies, that they respond to the countless choices they make as men and women. The stories constantly evolve as lives take their courses. Sometimes, however, something happens that demands a severe rupture in the narrative, a sudden break that changes the ending into one that just does not jibe with what has come before. The previously chosen scenes then build toward a finale that makes little or no sense.

Something of that sort happened to the generation that grew from the early years of the Church. Leonard Arrington isolated four great crises of identity during the first eighty years of LDS history.[33] During the first two—the devising of religious fundamentals amid rising persecution, and the search for new leadership after the death of Joseph Smith—the Church found its identity out of conflict with the nation's government and its dominant culture.[34] Those were the years that also shaped the young Saints considered here. The second pair of crises—the coming of the Union Pacific Railroad in 1869 and, in the 1890s, accommodation over the issue of polygamy—dramatically reversed course, away from hostility toward increasingly complete reconciliation.

The generation that led the way through the second two crises had come of age during the first two. The boys and girls of the 1830s, 1840s, and 1850s had defined themselves through a story of implacable differences with a hostile America. Then, as they came into their authority in the 1870s, 1880s, and 1890s, their world shifted on its axis. Events suddenly pulled them toward accommodation and eventually full integration into the union that, during their formative years, had been the defining enemy. This was more than politics. Changing the Church's orientation meant shifting the very sense of who they were. Their life-scripts suddenly had an ending badly out of character with all those scenes that led up to it.

That sort of wrenching rewrite is rarely done with anything close to full success. Historians of Mormonism might ask how, and how well, this generation managed that sudden, veering shift in their personal narratives. They might look to see whether powerful crosscurrents were at work beneath the outward reconciliation of the Saints and American society. It is intriguing, for instance, that a generation or so later Mormon youth were drafted into the missionary work previously done by older members. There were practical reasons, but the questions are worth asking: Was this a means of replicating among each generation something like the original formation of Mormon identity, sending the young out into the chancy world of nonbelievers? In the face of the ironic challenge of safety and success, was far-flung missionizing, in Pakistan or Arkansas, an impulse to keep alive what those in power considered something fundamental to becoming Mormon, finding in confrontation the chance to explore one's own resources and faith?

Pursuing questions like those might reveal the years of the late nineteenth and early twentieth centuries as some of the most deliciously complicated in the extraordinary American story of the birth, childhood, and coming of age of the Mormon Church and society.[35] If nothing else, following those lines of wondering is a healthy reminder that Mormon history is partly one of individuals learning from their past and sometimes bravely trying to transcend it. As with all histories, it is also one of a common human striving to discover meaning in our lives as individuals and as part of something larger.

Notes

An earlier version of this chapter appeared as "Becoming Mormon," *Journal of Mormon History* 28, no. 1 (Spring 2002): 31–51.

1. William G. Hartley, "Joseph Smith and Nauvoo's Youth," *Ensign* 9:9 (September 1979): 27–29; M. Guy Bishop, "Preparing to Take the Kingdom: Child-drearing Directives in Early Mormonism," *Journal of the Early Republic* 7:3 (Fall 1987): 275–90; Lyndon W. Cook, *Joseph Smith and the Doctrine of Little Children* (Provo, Utah: Grandin Book Co., 1987).

2. Austin N. Ward, *Male Life Among the Mormons; Or, the Husband in Utah, Detailing Sights and Scenes Among the Mormons; with Remarks on the Moral and Social Economy* (Philadelphia: J. Edwin Potter, 1863), 89; Davis Benton, "Zion's Rowdies: Growing Up on the Mormon Frontier," *Utah Historical Quarterly* 50 (Spring 1982): 182–95.

3. John Codman, *The Mormon Country: A Summer with the "Latter Day Saints"* (New York: United States Publishing Co., 1874), 67.

4. While historians have made only a limited effort to analyze and evaluate children's experiences and to mine them for insights into the early history of the Church, they have helped compile firsthand accounts of young Saints. Two revealing collections are Susan Arrington Madsen's *Growing Up in Zion: True Stories of Young Pioneers Building the Kingdom* (Salt Lake City: Deseret, 1996) and *I Walked to Zion: True Stories of Young Pioneers on the Mormon Trail* (Salt Lake City: Deseret, 1994). There is also a considerable literature on childhood and how children fit into the larger institutional themes of Mormon history in the nineteenth century. The following represent a sampling of topics and approaches: Martha Sonntag Bradley, "Hide and Seek: Children on the Underground," *Utah Historical Quarterly* 51 (Spring 1983): 133–53, and "Protect the Children: Child Labor in Utah, 1880–1920," *Utah Historical Quarterly* 59 (Winter 1991): 52–71; Carolyn J. Bauer and Sheridan P. Muir, "Visions, Saints, and Zion: Children's Literature of the Mormon Movement," *Phaedrus* 7 (Spring–Summer 1980): 30–38; William G. Hartley, "From Men to Boys: LDS Aaronic Priesthood Offices, 1829–1996," *Journal of Mormon History* 22 (Spring 1996): 80–136; "Childhood in Gunnison, Utah," *Utah Historical Quarterly* 51 (Spring 1983): 108–32; and "Were There LDS Teenagers in the 1870s?" paper in author's possession; Susan Staker Oman and Carol Cornwall Madsen, *Sisters and Little Saints: One Hundred Years of Primary* (Salt Lake City: Deseret, 1979); Tally S. Payne, "Education on the American Frontier: The Territory of Utah in 1870" (M.A. thesis, Brigham Young University, 2000); D. Michael Quinn, "Utah's Educational Innovation: LDS Religion Classes, 1890–1929," *Utah Historical Quarterly* 43 (Fall 1975): 379–89; Wendy Lavitt, "Children's Clothing on the Utah Frontier," *Beehive History* 15 (1989) 27–32; Bruce Lott, "Becoming Mormon Men: Male Rights of Passage and the Rise of Mormonism in 19th Century America" (M.A. thesis, Brigham Young University, 2000).

5. The scholar most associated with this approach to identity development is Dan P. McAdams. See his *The Stories We Live By: Personal Myths and the Making of the Self* (New York: William Morrow, 1993) and a volume he edited with Richard L. Ochberg, *Psychobiography and Life Narratives* (Durham, N.C.: Duke University Press, 1988).

6. Caroline E. W. W. Larrabee, "Caroline," in *Our Pioneer Heritage,* comp. Kate B. Carter, 20 vols. (Salt Lake City: Daughters of Utah Pioneers, 1958–77), 12:196.

7. Ibid., 12:196–98.

8. Lawrence Christian Mariger, Autobiography and Journal, 1879–91, Historical Department Archives, Church of Jesus Christ of Latter-day Saints, Salt Lake City (hereinafter cited as LDS Church Archives).

9. Iver Carl Magnus Nielsen, Autobiography, ca. 1911, 2, 4, MS 8351, LDS Church Archives.

10. Ibid., 2–3.

11. Charmaine A. Burdell, ed., "A Young Girl's Memory of Nauvoo: 1846–1847," *Nauvoo Journal* 7 (Spring 1995): 37.

12. Ibid.

13. Ibid.

14. Benjamin Chamberlain Critchlow, "Sketch of My Early Life," ca. 1865, typescript, MS 1662, LDS Church Archives.

15. William Moore Allred, "A Short Biographical History and Diary of William Moore Allred, 1819–1901," unpaginated typescript, LDS Church Archives.

16. Thurmon Dean Moody, "Nauvoo's Whistling and Whittling Brigade," *BYU Studies* 15 (Summer 1975): 480–90. For an account of a boy serving in the militia at Nauvoo at fourteen, see George Washington Bean, Reminiscence, n.d., L. Tom Perry Special Collections, Harold B. Lee Library, Brigham Young University, Provo, Utah (hereinafter cited as Perry Special Collections).

17. Samuel Kendall Gifford, Autobiography and Journals, 1864, 2–3, MS 8167, LDS Church Archives.

18. Naomi Melville Cottam, comp., "Journal of Mosiah Lyman Hancock," in *Chronicles of Courage,* Daughters of Utah Pioneer Lesson Committee, 8 vols. (Salt Lake City: Daughters of Utah Pioneers, 1990–97): 6:185–87, 196, 206.

19. Ibid., 6:198.

20. Ibid., 6:203–205.

21. Joseph Hyrum Moesser, "Sketch of the Life of Joseph Hiram Moesser," typescript, ca. 1921, MS 11395, LDS Church Archives.

22. Beverly Wessman, "Edwin Pettit," in *Chronicles of Courage,* 6:150–52.

23. Alma Helaman Hale, "Autobiography of Alma Helaman Hale," typescript, 1901, MS 965, LDS Church Archives; Harrison Sperry, "A Short History of the Life of Harrison Sperry Sr.," n.d., typescript, MS 722, LDS Church Archives; "Life of Charles Sperry," in *Our Pioneer Heritage,* 9:441–44; Martin Luther Ensign, Autobiography, n.d. MS 5372, LDS Church Archives.

24. Jill Jacobson Andros has provided a fine overview of the overland experience of children, in "Children on the Mormon Trail" (M.A. thesis, Brigham Young University, 1997), and in her "Are We There Yet? The Story of Children on the Mormon Trail," *Beehive History* 22 (1996): 5–10.

25. Heber Robert McBride, Journal, 9–15, Perry Special Collections.

26. Moesser, "Sketch of the Life," 3–4.

27. George Washington Bean, Reminiscence, Perry Special Collections; Barbara Gowans Bowen, "Autobiography," in *Our Pioneer Heritage*, 9:412–14.

28. Franklin Wheeler Young, Autobiography, ca. 1915–17, 8–9, MS 1148, LDS Church Archives (emphasis in original).

29. Myrtle Ballard Shurtliff, "Margaret McNeil Ballard," in *Our Pioneer Heritage*, 3:200.

30. Aaron Johnson, "Life Sketch of A. Jay," 1926, holograph, 1–7, LDS Church Archives.

31. Horace Hall Cummings, Autobiography, n.d., typescript, LDS Church Archives.

32. Johnson, "Life Sketch of A. Jay," 13–14.

33. Leonard J. Arrington, "Crisis in Identity: Mormon Responses in the Nineteenth and Twentieth Centuries," in *Mormonism and American Culture,* ed. Marvin S. Hall and James B. Allen (New York: Harper & Row, 1972), 168–84.

34. Jan Shipps, *Mormonism: The Story of a New Religious Tradition* (Urbana: University of Illinois Press, 1985), 115–16, sums up the situation nicely. The decision of Church leaders to reconcile with the U.S. government raised all sorts of practical issues that had to be wrestled with, but beneath them all was something more fundamental: "The question of concern here is what happened to Mormonism when the old order passed away." The aspect raised at the end of this essay is how that question was pursued and resolved (or not) at the level of personal identity among those who lived across the divide between the old order and the new.

35. The events covered in the first three chapters of Thomas G. Alexander's splendid history of the Church during the late nineteenth and early twentieth centuries, when set against the questions I've tried to raise here, offer some obvious starting points for such a line of investigation. See his *Mormonism in Transition: A History of the Latter-day Saints, 1890–1930* (Urbana: University of Illinois Press, 1986). Interestingly, as the Church accepted, and indeed fought for, political integration with the nation around it, the crucial work of maintaining Mormons' identity as a separate and chosen people became more of a matter of each member's perception of himself or herself. As Shipps puts it (*Mormonism,* 116), hard institutional and political boundaries now were unacceptable, so "the responsibility for boundary maintenance had to be shifted from the corporate body to the individuals within that body." The crisis of Mormon identity, that is, shifted toward issues of individual identity. This shift inevitably positions the inner conflicts and resolutions of the generation that grew out of the old order into the new close to the center of this important historical transition.

9

Listen Up

Hearing the Unheard in Western History

The board room of the Wells Fargo headquarters in San Francisco is pretty plush. The chairs are cushy, and the table stretches out like a mahogany airport runway, but the walls are the real stunner. They are covered with an enlarged circular photograph of the city taken by Eadweard Muybridge, an extraordinary 360-degree panorama of San Francisco as seen in 1878 from the top of Mark Hopkins's Nob Hill mansion. It is an urban historian's dream. Great landmarks, tailor shops, and markets are in perfect focus down to the brick and ironwork. Ships rest at their moorings along neat wharves stacked with the fruits of global trade. After a moment you notice something else remarkable: nobody is there. The photograph is completely empty of people. Wells Fargo officials puzzled over this a long time. How in the world did Muybridge manage to capture this, one the of the world's busiest cities, in full daylight, without a single soul in sight? No Sunday could be *that* dull.

The answer turns out to be obvious—once you hear it. The historian Richard Orsi saw it right away. His first clue was a headless horse—or rather a horse with a gray smudge where its head should have been. Looking closer, he saw that while the buildings were sharp and clear, the sidewalks were blurry and parts of the streets were streaked with what seemed a thin smoke. The panorama, of course, turns out to be a time-lapse photograph. The slow exposure of the film captured whatever stood still but missed everything that moved, including the people who were there all the time, hurrying along the sidewalks and crossing the streets and working the wharves.

In a way this photograph is more truthful, not less. As Orsi commented, it is a pretty accurate picture of how history is usually written. We get a sense of the outward structure of things—the grid of streets, the arrangement of neighborhoods, the lay of the economic and social landscape. The skyline is dominated by seats of government (the Hall of Records and U.S. Mint), by the stock exchange and grand hotels and office buildings, all of them creations of the sort of men who bulk large in standard histories. Those histories, like these streets, are largely empty of ordinary folks going about their daily lives. The reasons also are much the same. Great buildings are what is left of egos longing to stay forever in the world. Think of banks and mansions as stone embodiments of wealthy and powerful men posing for the future—that is, for us. Everyone else is invisible because, frankly, such people do not much care whether we see them or not. They are too busy working, seeing to their families, muddling through the day, and so they blur away into their own worlds—worlds that now seem largely beyond our sight and reach.

Largely, that is, but not entirely. The draymen and hod carriers, the farmers, sailors, and ranchers, the mothers, miners, clerks, and housewives occasionally did hold still. When they did stop, they sometimes spoke to those of us waiting in the future. We can hear them if we wish, though usually we have to listen pretty hard.

The effort is worth it, partly because, to put it bluntly, most of us are nosy. Something in us wants to use faster film and catch those people in freeze frame. We want to step into the photograph, walk up and ask them questions, then peek in windows to see what's happening in the parlor and the kitchen. Apart from our nosiness, we know down deep that the usual telling of history—history as skylines—is nowhere near complete. We wonder what is going on inside those buildings, because we sense that most people in the past have been more or less like us, and for us, history happens mostly indoors, inside those grand events happening around us that we know will later become the skyline of textbook history. Historians take this curiosity a step further. Their job is to look for patterns in what has happened and to lay them out in hopes of understanding a little better the collective experience of the past. The work is a bit like describing the terrain of a place to someone who has never been there; and to do that, they need patterns among both grand events and the daily lives of the folks who drift like smoke through Muybridge's photograph.

The patterns sometimes confirm our oldest clichés. Pioneers, for instance, are usually considered the ultimate cockeyed optimists, and a candidate for the all-time champion in the Westward Expansion Positive Thinking Competition has to be the forty-niner Thomas Forbes. "Dear Sir," he wrote in a letter written on board a ship to California: "I have seated myself to write you a few lines to let you know that I am well [and I am] hoping . . . this will find you enjoying the same. I sailed out of New York on the 17 of Feb and I have had a very good time every day since I started except on one occasion on the eleventh of March [when] we was struck by lightning."[1]

As is often the case, we hear more the closer we listen. Forbes is writing to, and asking about, his father. It is a reminder that most people's attention was not on the nation or manifest destiny, economic issues or cultural trends. People's lives centered around parents, children, wives and husbands, relatives close at hand and far away. Understanding the historical world of the ordinary might begin by appreciating that the axis of most people's worlds was the family.

The westward movement stressed and sometimes shattered American families. Pioneers bid tearful goodbyes to kinsmen and friends as they climbed into wagons or boarded trains that would take them to the new country. Pioneering, however, did not so much destroy families as reshape them. The fracturing was often along generational lines. Older parents stayed home; grown children, who had more energy and more to gain, took off for the territories. Among those young adults, more men left than women. Husbands and bachelors, as Victorian males in their prime, were expected to leave home and find their families' fortunes, while wives and single women were far more likely to stay and wait.

So if a family's older parents stayed while the grown children left, and if its young sisters stayed while the young men took off, what was left was a bunch of brothers. Westward expansion selected out and strengthened this particular family bond—that of brother to brother. Bachelor brothers might take off together for California or Arizona, or married brothers might leave their families temporarily behind as they walked or rode off to make their marks. For these men, their relations with each other became the innermost circle of their personal worlds.

Eavesdrop for a moment on the Langdon brothers of North Carolina as they headed west. Their letters reveal that two of them set out by ship with several other local sets of brothers. After crossing Panama, Robert Langdon wrote his mother that one of the young men "was taken sick . . . with a fever . . . and died last night. . . . He fell in his prime, being only twenty-two years of age. I was with him before he died . . . he said he was ready and . . . commenced singing a hymn. His brother was very much affected, threw his head on my shoulder, burst into tears, and said oh! Langdon, Albert is going to die, Oh! it will kill his mother. . . . He has preserved the body by putting it in Brandy and is going to take it home with him as soon as he arrives in California."[2]

The Langdons landed in San Francisco, safe and full of vinegar, but still looking home toward family. Robert quoted Lord Byron:

Here's a sigh to those who love me,
And a smile to those who hate;
And whatever sky's above me,
Here's a heart for every fate.[3]

Meanwhile a third brother, Paul, had headed overland and had stopped to seek his living around Fort Laramie in Wyoming. For the next five years the siblings wrote back and forth among themselves, to and from Wyoming and California and home to their relatives. Robert told of goldfield adventures and tried to lure Paul to the coast. Paul wrote of awful winters, operating his ferry, and various setbacks. Finally Paul determined to reunite with his California brothers in a common pursuit of the main chance: "I have become very tired of the slow cent-by-cent life I have been living. . . . I am determined to embark my all . . . on the soap bubble principle: swell or burst."[4]

At the end of his trip Paul Langdon was sitting beside a California river when Robert found him and stood quietly until his brother turned.

Victorian women often expressed emotions about each other in floods of effusive and sensual feelings that are contrasted with Victorian men, who supposedly lived by a kind of iron stoicism. But listen to Robert Langdon when he wrote home about the moment his brother turned and saw him after their five-year separation: "He looked up and gazed into my face for about three or four seconds when he exclaimed, 'why brother!' and quick as thought he was on his feet and we were locked in each others arms, and only separated to gaze into each others countenances for an instant, and then again and again to unite ourselves in an affectionate embrace, the tears all the time flowing silently and copiously from our eyes. The joy of meeting him was almost too intense. I felt as if my heart were bursting. Such exstacy, if continued would surely kill [me]. My feelings to me are indescribable [even now]; the pen is inadequate to the task—I must desist."[5]

The Langdon brothers were creating an emotional geography in what was to them a new country. Such emotional terrain was not always pretty. When the alignment of power in a family was different, as when the bond was not man to man but man to woman, the landscape was more likely to turn ugly, arid, rocky. It was even more so when the bond was adult to child. Everyone heading west faced new challenges and threats, but the most vulnerable by far were the children. They are also among the most historically silent. When we let them speak, they often tell us that moving west and living there made for a fine enough time and that they found in their experience what it took to make fulfilling lives as adults, but in the inherently iffy world of new settlement, children were even less in control than their elders. In such a world children relied on the family to give them what they needed more than just about anything—predictability. Among the most heart-wrenching pioneer testimony, consequently, is that from children who watched the protective structure for their lives suddenly collapse, leaving them vulnerable to whatever might come at them. In probably the most famous instance, the seven children of Henry and Naomi Sager lost both parents on the trail to Oregon in 1844. They were adopted by the missionaries Marcus and Narcissa Whitman, but in 1847 Cayuse Indians killed the Whitmans and two of the Sager boys. The surviving five Sagers thus were orphaned a second time. Theirs was by no means the only such tragedy on the overland journey. "Yesterday passed the grave of a woman, today saw husband buried, with children left to go on with strangers," a diarist wrote in 1852. Only a few weeks later he saw the same thing again:

> I was . . . traveling along and in advance of our Teams when I over took a little girl, who had lingered far behind her Company. She was crying, and as I took her into my arms [I] discovered that her little feet were bleeding by coming in contact with the sharp flint stone upon the road. I says why do you cry, does your feet hurt you, see how they bleed. No (says she) nothing hurts me now. They buried my father and mother yesterday, and I don't want to live any longer. They took me away from my sweet mother and put her in the ground."[6]

Nearly as unnerving was encountering human remains pulled by wolves and coyotes from trailside graves, grisly reminders of the terrifying turns life could take in this strange land.[7]

For women, as for children, families were the best bet for security in the chancy world of the frontier, but they had their own vulnerabilities. Law and custom left daughters and wives subject to the decisions of fathers and husbands. For women who agreed that moving west was a fine idea—and there were many of them—and who found fulfillment in traditional women's work—and there were plenty of them too—this was less of a problem. "Money could not hire me to go back [east] to live!" Carrie Williams wrote in her journal from California.[8] Many women, however, were more divided in their response. Sarah Hively seemed at least resigned to coming to Denver in 1863, but soon after her family's arrival she told her diary of their "miserable room" where "the wind blows the sand into the house all over every thing. . . . Oh how lonely I do feel here all alone with no one to keep me company." She was five months' pregnant. Three months later, close to delivery, things had not much improved: "I never was so homesick in my life. I have had a good cry and now I have got the headache for it."[9] The relative lack of women on many frontiers offered economic opportunity for those willing to play the woman's role for pay, but the workload could be oppressive. "Weary days of labor and pain," wrote Ellen Hunt from her cabin in early Denver. "Have made 175 loaves of bread and 450 pies. Taken all the care of the children and done all the housework but the washing." A bit later she told of being "nearly worked to death." Her husband would go on to become territorial governor. She would die at forty-four.[10] Many complained of husbands who were chronic movers always on the sniff for the next main chance. Most had little choice but to go along, but Edwin Bennett's mother was one who finally put her foot down. When her husband announced that the family would be leaving Creede, Colorado, she answered: "Ernest, you can move on if you have to, but I've dragged two boys and a houseful of furniture just as far as I'm going to. First it was Ohio, then Michigan again, then the Peninsula, then Minnesota, Michigan again, then Denver, Weaver and Creede, and right here I'm going to stay."[11] And she did, for the next thirty years.

The worlds of Carrie Williams, Ellen Hunt, and the Sager siblings were in a sense molded by the institutions and grand events normally studied in our classrooms, those made solid in the buildings of Muybridge's panorama of San Francisco. Law gave husbands their authority, wars and treaties opened lands to family settlement, and politics created the Homestead Act and other inducements for westering. Those developments only boxed out a crude container for the more important events of their world, however. Western history for them was losing parents, baking hundreds of pies, enjoying the pleasures of life freshly started, wondering about the where and when of the next bite of food, and forging the tight links of family that could make all this much better or worse. The men, too, had their own inner histories. They might be freer to use authority as they wished, but doing so could leave them facing other dilemmas we never find in the usual accounts, and their responses do not fit cleanly into any simple division between the powerful and powerless. Examples may be found in the earliest years of westward expansion.

No one would call John Winthrop an "unheard voice." The early governor of Puritan Massachusetts was one of those institutional shapers who dominate our texts. His voice gave us one of the most enduring phrases in American history, from his sermon on the *Arbella* in 1630. In America, he said, God's chosen people would build a "city upon a hill,

and the eyes of the world shall be set upon us." But while he was helping construct the outward America of governments and guiding values,
Winthrop was living out his own tug-of-war and, with everybody else,
was shaping the country's inner history. A few weeks before he delivered
his famous sermon, he sat on the *Arbella* at Cowes, England, waiting for
favorable winds to carry him westward. He wrote his wife, Margaret:

> And now (my sweet soul) I must . . . take my last farewell of thee in old
> England. . . . I know to whom I have committed thee, . . . to him who
> loves thee much better than any husband can, who hath taken a count
> of the hairs of thy head, and puts all thy tears in his bottle. . . . How it
> refresheth my heart to think that I shall yet again see thy sweet face in
> the land of the living: that lovely countenance that I have so much de-
> lighted in and beheld with such great content! I have been so taken up
> with business [that] I could seldom look back to my former happiness,
> but now when I [am] at some leisure, I shall not avoid the remember-
> ance of thee, nor [my] grief for thy absence. . . . I hope the course we
> have agreed upon will be some ease to us both, Mondays and Fridays
> at five of the clock at night we shall meet in spiritt till we meet in per-
> son. . . . I will . . . take thee now and my sweet children in mine arms
> and kiss and embrace you all, and so leave you with my God. Farewell,
> farewell. I bless you all in the name of Lord Jesus. Thine wheresoever,
> Jo: Winthrop[12]

Winthrop had power and position, which brought with them public duties and private expectations, which in turn left him torn in his
personal loves and longings. It was a theme that recurs throughout the
westward movement. Winthrop was pulled across the Atlantic by religious values. In late-nineteenth-century America men were obliged to
sally forth because Victorian standards required men to go into the world,
do battle in the marketplace, and find their family's fortune wherever that
might be. For tens of thousands, that was a call into the Far West. The
personal dilemma, however, remained strikingly the same. Two hundred
and nineteen years after John wrote Margaret Winthrop, the forty-niner
David DeWolf wrote his wife from a camp along the trail to California:

"I dreamt last night I was home. I thought I was mighty happy. I thought Little Sis was standing in the door. I thought she had grown tremendous, but I knew her. I was enjoying myself fine when I awoke, and behold, it was all a dream. When Little Sis begins to talk, learn her to call me, won't you? My God, how I want to see you both."[13]

DeWolf's response to pioneering was also part of the history that sits inside the outward structure of nation, economy, diplomacy, politics, and prevailing values. "In my dreams last night I was home six days—and nothing ever seemed so real," another man wrote his wife on the way to California; then he asked, "Which are the realities, the dreaming or waking moments?"[14] The answer, of course is, both. We need to bring it all into the picture. We need to chart this country where real people actually lived, where the central events concerned family, the weekly weather, and neighbors (or the lack of them), jokes and abuse, loving dreams and waking nightmares.

Such voices scarcely begin the list of the mostly unheard. Everyone quoted so far was an Anglo-American taking part in one of those east-to-west episodes, the rush for gold or settling the plains, that march through our textbooks. Tens of thousands are left out when we listen only there: European Americans who spoke something other than English, the Germans, Swedes, Russians, Italians, French, and other immigrants following the oldest paths into the West, northward out of Mexico, the men and women whose ancestors had lived in one part of the West or another for thousands of years. When we listen to them, sometimes we're surprised at how familiar they sound. Here is a free-verse poem by a man newly arrived in California:

> At the moment, I hardly have enough grub to eat.
> But I won't take it as my fate, my final destiny.
> I don't believe I will live like this till my hair turns white;
> It's only the low ebb in my life.
> When luck strikes,
> With the whole world behind me,

I will be rich in a few years' turn.
And then, I will buy property and build a Western mansion.

And this from a fellow countryman:

Not one day have I dared forget my family.
My mind is chaotic, like hemp fibers, with constant thought of home;
Each meal is hard to swallow, because of sorrow.
My dear woman:
Don't ever think your husband has betrayed your love.
It's hard enough to share my words with you in dreams;
My soul is wandering, every night, my tongue tightened.

These might have been written by Paul Langdon, he of the soap bubble principle of swell or burst, or by David DeWolf dreaming of Little Sis grown tremendous big. In fact these are translations of poems written in San Francisco's Chinatown by two Cantonese immigrants.[15]

Their voices are from one of the groups we might call the radically silent, those who have been shut almost completely out of the usual historical record. The Chinese, partly by choice, lived mostly in their own communities. They left relatively few records. Most important, perhaps, their native tongue was so alien to those around them that communication was mostly choked off. It is more than coincident that Chinese also were arguably the most abused ethnic group in the nineteenth-century West. People are most likely to brutalize those they do not talk to. Chinese do sometimes speak indirectly through documents or the words of those who wrote about them. A ledger of a ship in 1856 that hired both Chinese and white sailors shows whites were paid an average of $15 a month, Chinese anywhere from $5 down to $3.70, or roughly 12 cents a day.[16] Among items scattered through nineteenth-century newspapers, one mentions a twelve-year-old white boy who stopped his play to draw a revolver and shoot a Chinese man in the neck because the man and his burro had interrupted the boy's sledding. Another tells of men pouring kerosene over coal in a stove as a practical joke on their Chinese cook. When the cook lit the fuel, the explosion charred his face and he ran from the house screaming. The editor was amused, but he cautioned readers that "a little heavier charge of coil oil might have set the building on fire."[17]

Even in this contentious world there must have been some rare exchanges between Chinese and their neighbors, and if we keep our ears historically cocked, we occasionally have a chance to listen in. The Bancroft Library holds two Chinese-English phrase books, from 1867 and 1875. One is made up of expressions considered most necessary for English speakers talking to Chinese. The other was compiled from the opposite side: phrases that Chinese found most useful in talking to whites. Together the books document a kind of formal conversation between the cultures, bits of dialogue we can hear from 130 years ago.[18]

Some of the phrases, admittedly, are odd and unlikely, such as these, translated from Chinese to English: "Don't you have a camel?" and "Anyone who has my umbrella has my boots." Some are more practical, especially in California: "The earth is shaking." For the most part the phrases show us the yawning gap between these two groups and what they expected from each other. In the book for English speakers, here are phrases under the section on hiring and directing a house servant: "Can you get me a good boy? He wants $8.00 a month? He ought to be satisfied with $6.00. Bring him here. I think he is very stupid. Come at seven every morning. Go home at eight every night. If you want to go out you must ask me. You will take care of the baby. Light the fire. Sweep the rooms. Wash the clothes. Wash the windows. Wash the floor. Sweep the stairs. Trim the lamps. Brush my clothes. I want to cut his wages." Two phrases are nowhere to be found: "How are you?" and "Thank you."

In the book composed from the other side, the English useful for Chinese who are speaking to others, there are two phrases as answers to employers: "Yes, madam (not Mum)" and "You have made an agreement to hire me, [and] if you find that I am not suitable you can discharge me, but you must not strike me." More common are statements about the speaker's difficulties: "He does not intend to pay me my wages. He claimed my mine. He tries to extort money from me. He took it from me by violence. He assaulted me without provocation." The largest number by far are phrases about the fates of others: "The man struck the Chinese boy on the head. He came to his death by homicide. He was murdered by a thief. He was smothered in his room. He was shot dead by his enemy. He was poisoned to death. He was flogged publicly twice in the streets. He was frozen to death in the snow. He was starved to death in prison. He committed suicide."

This early Chinese-white conversation documents one of those themes unifying the broad contours of the western past, the racial divide that was so much a part of life. Look still closer and listen harder, however, and the lessons are not quite so clear. The lines blur and soften. A few precious documents show ordinary people, Chinese and others, actually talking to each other on ordinary terms. As a young girl, Grace Fisk, of a prominent Helena, Montana, family, wrote her grandmother of journeys into the Chinese quarter, of her shy approach to merchants, of their gifts of dried fruit, small cakes, firecrackers. A miner wrote home from California about visits among the Chinese, whom he called "a curious kind of beings," and he commented, with no apparent hostility, on their customs: "They are very neat in their cooking . . . they eat everything with what they call 'chopsticks' . . . which they handle very dexteriously." Another wrote of befriending a laundryman and complained bitterly of his mistreatment.[19] And there is this entry in a gold seeker's journal:

> A company of Chinese have been building a log cabin near us. They are mostly young men, apparently of good blood and very polite. I like to talk with them and ask them hundreds of questions about their native land, for they are intelligent and one of them speaks good English. . . . Here is a specimen of his writing which he gave me at my request.

This "specimen" is a short glossary of Chinese characters and their English translations. In it, we can hear what must have been a dialogue very different from the one that speaks from those two phrase books. The words in the journal include *bird, salt, fish, church, very good place, very bad place, wine, money, Stockton, Canton, pork, sugar, brandy, gold, cigar,* and "if you please."[20]

Native American women were, if anything, more radically silent than the Chinese. The rare voices we do hear are haunting. The elderly Hidatsa

Buffalo Bird Woman testified in the 1920s: "Often in summer I rise at daybreak and steal out to the cornfields; and as I hoe the corn I sing to it, as we did when I was young. No one cares about our corn songs now."[21] The Crow Pretty Shield remembered when, as an infant, her grandmother apologized on her behalf to a bushful of chickadees after she had thrown a buffalo chip at them.[22] The Papago Maria Chona was ninety when she told of her puberty rite, of being thin as a strip of yucca after running for miles, dancing all night, and eating only gruel and unsalted ash bread. We hear her feelings toward the husband she married as a girl: "It was as if we had been children in the same house. I had grown fond of him. We had starved so much together."[23]

In the sacred ground of archives are occasional small treasures, like the reminiscence of Isadora Filomena de Solano.[24] It goes back much earlier than most—she was born in 1784—and in a place largely hidden to us, northern California before the gold rush. Her vivid, scattered images are like phrases from a poem, teasing our imaginations to build them into a fuller portrait. Isadora had been wife to the Suysona Indian leader Solano, a great warrior, she said, "who made all the white world and Indians tremble." He had stolen her as a child, then later married her. He surrounded the couple with the best astrologers. His warriors fought in the nude except for *penachos* of feathers in their hair to mark allegiance and rank: captains wore black, foot soldiers white duck down, and horsemen the gray feathers of wild mountain chickens. Her people danced naked as well, with women wearing only collars and feathered crowns. Their teeth gleamed white because they scrubbed them with animal hair. They buried their dead tightly wrapped in belts of shells and in their ears were ornaments of duck bone rubbed thin with flint.

Then came invaders from the east. "I do not like the white man much," she explained, "because he is a liar and a thief. . . . Sutter lied to everyone, took everything and paid nothing." Solano died, and then "I remarried Bill, [a] man of little heart. I stopped giving birth." With Solano she had mothered eight children, but now they were all dead but one son, who gave her twenty *pesos* a month. Isadora's interviewer described her as "a woman of great dignity," snub-nosed and black-haired, who walked tall and erect on tiny feet. She asked to be buried in the wedding skirt of shells and bones given her by her kidnapper-warrior-husband. Now, in 1874, she waited. "I drink a lot of liquor and I do this because I no longer have much land full of cows, as the blonde [Sutter] stole everything. . . . I take [my] communion with brandy. I drink in order to forget."

Isadora's is another family story, hers a precious look at a woman's life before, during, and after that tumultuous, bloody time when the westering frontier washed up against the Pacific Coast. It is another variation on the stark divisions we can see elsewhere—between male and female, poor and not-so-poor, Chinese and white, black-haired and blonde. And yet, again, when we look closer, the distinctions refuse to hold still. Elijah Potter's reminiscence from these same years must be one of western history's most disturbing documents, a lengthy account of systematic roundups and confinement of California Indians, of Indian servants poisoning their masters and attacking them with axes at dinner tables, of impromptu "Indian hunts" and butcherings of Native families in their camps.[25] Potter delivers it all deadpan, with something between indifference and approval. Then suddenly in this catalog of horrors, Potter tells the story of Joseph Roff. Roff supplied hay to soldiers who were herding Indians onto reservations. "He lived with an Indian woman," Potter writes. "Our captain with a party went [to take] her and several [others] away from white men. The men all came to our camp, and wanted to marry the women, but our captain would not permit it. Roff followed us down to red bluff, and there tried to hire some men to steal her, but he could not make it work. He then followed her to Fort Bragg and married her."

Roff and his wife lived in the surrounding hills until about 1865, when things changed. Potter continues: "They had two little girls, one five and the other three. They were both taken sick about the same time. He brought them in to Mr. P. A. Witts [apparently the closest thing to a doctor]. . . . The children both died the same week, and are buried along the line fence between Mrs. Johnson's place and the Purcell place, opposite the hop house. I have forgotten their names. They were beautiful children. The mother did not survive them but a few weeks. Her people buried her. Roff sold out what he had and went away, no one knew where."

In the middle of a slaughterhouse, a peculiar love story. We watch society laboring to sort itself out according to those patterns historians are trained to find, the structures and distinctions that make up a culture. Whites go here, Indians over there. Towns are sectioned off into neighborhoods, including Irishtowns and Chinatowns, and beyond the town limits is the countryside. Countryside is divided into family domains cleanly arranged and identified as property: Mrs. Johnson's place, the Purcell place. And walking through it all are a man and a woman living their own mark into the country. Historians instinctively see the big picture of an ordering of separations and clear distinctions: lines on the land. Then we follow one of those lines, a fence; we stop and dig, and we discover, literally right under our feet, two lovely children, names forgotten, with stories that fit nowhere within the order that people were making of their world—and nowhere within the sense that historians try to bring to the past we study.

The historian's essential task—sifting through remnants of the past, setting them in this or that order, and finding in that order what seem to be the most sensible meanings—is honorable work that is necessary to understanding who we are by tracing how we have come to be. In textbook history most of the patterns and shapes of past events concern the economic, political, and social forces at work in our collective life. Such forces are crucial to understanding any past era, whether the Elizabethan Age or the West of gold rushes and Indian wars. Inside those patterns, however, inside the brick and steel structures of governments and institutions, are other settings made from the day-to-day experiences and the emotions that fill ordinary lives. We can find the raw stuff of this history in the occasional voices from the vast majority of those alive at any moment of the past. Patterns may be found there, too, and historians need to work harder at describing them and bringing them more into the wide narratives of common experience. At the least, doing so can flesh out the familiar stories, but listening to the unheard can also open the way to meanings of the past and to patterns of experience that are wholly unexpected and sometimes at odds with the standard picturing of some time and place. Pricking up the ears just a bit should convince anyone of how much is lost in the usual overarching history of the West.

Listening should be another sort of caution. If we try to force too much meaning from them, those voices might end up laughing at us. History is not only a way to make sense of the past. It is also humane entertainment. It can be read as we do our best fiction, drama, and poetry, and as such the words of plain people have a value and power that set them above the other sources from the record. Those words are part of our literature, and we should let them simply feed the pleasure that our species finds in watching the human condition display itself. Not only is the American West full of insights into how the American nation was made, but it is also a grand display of the irrepressible, breathtaking variety and unpredictability of human nature. The western story can be told best if its voices have their say on their own terms.

Notes

An earlier version of this chapter appeared as "Listen Up: Hearing the Unheard in Western History," *Southern California Quarterly* 85 (Spring 2003): 13–28.

1. Thomas Forbes to "Dear Sir," April 11, 1849, in Gold Rush Letters Collection, Bancroft Library, University of California, Berkeley.

2. R. F. Langdon to Mother, January 7, 1850, Langdon-Young-Maeres Papers, Special Collections, University of North Carolina Library, Chapel Hill.

3. R. F. Langdon to Mother, January 30, 1850, ibid.

4. P. H. Langdon to Mother, September 9, 1851; P. H. Langdon to Mother, December 16, 1851; P. H. Langdon to Brother, July 14, 1852; P. H. Langdon to Mother, September 7, 1853, ibid. The quotation is from the last letter cited.

5. R. F. Langdon to Mother, August 31, 1854, ibid.

6. John H. Clark Diary, June 11, 30, 1852, Bancroft Library, University of California, Berkeley.

7. Elliott West, *Growing Up with the Country: Childhood on the Far-Western Frontier* (Albuquerque: University of New Mexico Press, 1989), 37–38.

8. Carrie Williams journal, November 27, 1858, Beinecke Library, Yale University, New Haven.

9. Sarah Hively Journal, May 18, 21, August 30, 1863, Western History Collection, Denver Public Library.

10. LeRoy R. Hafen, ed., "Diary of Mrs. A. C. Hunt, 1859," *Colorado Magazine* 21:15 (September 1944): 169–70.

11. Edwin Lewis Bennett, *Boom Town Boy* (Chicago: Sage Books, 1966), 26.

12. Quoted in *Witnessing America: The Library of Congress Book of Firsthand Accounts of Life in America, 1600–1900,* comp. and ed. Noel Rae (New York: Penguin/Stonesong Press, 1996), 134.

13. David DeWolf to Matilda, June 17, 1849, David DeWolf Letters, Henry E. Huntington Library, San Marino, California.

14. Addison Crane diary, June 17, 1852, Henry E. Huntington Library, San Marino, California.

15. Marlon K. Hon, *Songs of Gold Mountain: Cantonese Rhymes from San Francisco Chinatown* (Berkeley: University of California Press, 1987).

16. Charles Augustus Rantlett Record Book, Henry E. Huntington Library, San Marino, California.

17. Virginia City, Nevada, *Territorial Enterprise*, February 8, 1868, June 24, 1871, transcriptions of articles in Russell M. Magnaghi Collection, Bancroft Library, University of California, Berkeley.

18. The following phrases are all from Sam Wong and Assistants, *An English-Chinese Phrase Book Together with the Vocabulary of Trade, Law, etc . . .* (San Francisco: Cubery and Co., 1875); Benoni Lanctot, *Chinese and English Phrase Book, With the Chinese Pronunciation Indicated in English, Specially Adapted for the Use of Merchants, Traders, Travelers and Families* (San Francisco: A. Roman & Co., 1867).

19. West, *Growing Up with the Country*, 72; William Carroll to Ann Buck, September 8, 1860, Henry E. Huntington Library, San Marino, California; M[atthew] G[ilbert] Upton, "Etchings in El Dorado, or the Wags and Waggeries of the Argonauts of '49," Ms. Reminiscence, Henry E. Huntington Library, San Marino, California.

20. Timothy Coffin Osborn Journal, December 26, 1850, Bancroft Library, University of California, Berkeley.

21. Peter Nabokov, ed., *Native American Testimony: A Chronicle of Indian-White Relations from Prophecy to the Present, 1492–1992* (New York: Viking, 1978), 182.

22. Frank B. Linderman, *Pretty-shield, Medicine Woman of the Crows* (Lincoln: University of Nebraska Press, 1972), 154–55.

23. Ruth Underhill, ed., "The Autobiography of a Papago Woman," *Memoirs of the American Anthropological Association* 46 (1936): 35–53.

24. Isadora Filomena de Solano, "Autobiography," Bancroft Library, University of California, Berkeley.

25. Elijah Renshaw Potter, "Reminiscences of the Early History of Northern California and of the Indian Troubles," Bancroft Library, University of California, Berkeley.

PART THREE

Myth

❀

10

Bison R Us

The Buffalo as Cultural Icon

Animals talk. They growl and bark and hoot and snarl at each other, of course, but they also speak to us. The reference here is to animals as symbol and myth. Every recorded culture has them—creatures that people select to express their values and to tell their history. A horse or serpent becomes something like a ventriloquist's dummy for an entire society. The way we picture such a creature, the traits we give it, the stories we tell about it are all really comments we are making about ourselves. And so animals talk—not only *to* us but also *for* us.

Americans have chosen many such animals, but except for one, all speak for many others, too. The eagle on our currency has also stood for power and resurrection among Chaldeans, Syrians, Zunis, and Nazis. Bears stand for our athletic prowess and remind us to protect our forests, but mythic bears walk as well through virtually every tradition of the Northern Hemisphere. The single exception is the buffalo—or, more properly, the bison. It is ours, and with the possible exception of Canada, it is nobody else's. Because we have this creature on exclusive retainer as our mythic spokesman, it gives us one of our best chances to listen to what we, as a people, have had to say about ourselves. The bison, as we have pictured and imagined it, has gone through many mutations from its first sighting by Europeans until today. Together they are a nearly five-hundred-year commentary on the meaning of America.

The first accounts are a jumble of impressions of an animal that refused to fit the writers' expectations. Its shape and form were "marvelous and laughable, or frightful," Juan de Oñate's secretary wrote of his first encounter in 1598. "No one could be so melancholy," he added, "that if he were to see it a hundred times a day he could keep from laughing . . . or could fail to marvel at the sight of so ferocious an animal."[1] The typical bison, David Ingram wrote in the sixteenth century, was twenty feet long, with the drooping ears of a giant bloodhound and hair like a goat. Fernando del Bosque downsized it to the size of a cow, but he agreed about the goat hair and added that "the hips and haunches . . . [are] like those of a hog" and its fierce, bristly expression was like a wild boar's.[2] Another Spaniard thought the mane horselike, the tail tufted like a lion's, and in between was a hump like a camel's. But no, said another, the wool was more like a sheep's, and the tail was carried erect when in flight, like a scorpion's. This observer added a reptilian touch: bison shed their hair every May, like snakes sloughing their skins.[3]

It must have been a gifted reader who could picture this terrifying and comic, divinely hideous satanic pig-goat, this camel-humped, sheepish, lionlike scorpion-cow. Early artists, most of whom had never seen a bison, produced images just as bizarre, often with faces showing a wide range of human expressions: bashful and coy, arch and offended, open and genial, petulant. All depictions, however, had a common theme: the hope of profit. Spanish observers referred to bison as "wild cattle" and "wild oxen" and visually portrayed them as curly-haired bulls with bullish horns and cows with exaggerated bovine hooves. To the French it was *le boeuf sauvage,* and the English called them "shag-haired oxen," "wild cattle," and "prairie beeves." The appeal was obvious: cattle, "wild" or otherwise, could be put to use, converted into some sort of wealth. "Their flesh is good and their hides [make] good leather," an early observer wrote, and another added hopefully, "the hides of these beasts are sold very dear."[4]

As the generations passed, misconceptions were clarified and Europeans learned what bison really looked like, but while buffalo were an economic pillar for Native peoples in western North America, colonizers never made the meat-and-hide trade pay. As an imperial asset, the bison was a bust. At the end of the eighteenth century this animal, with its shaggy hair, muscular hump, and outsized head, was a familiar bit of American exotica, but beyond that it had no particular economic or cultural heft.

Then, during the first half of the nineteenth century, the bison suddenly emerged as a central symbol of the land it occupied. It appeared
prominently in the paintings and illustrations of several artists who
toured the West from the 1820s to mid-century, including Titian Ram-
sey Peale, Peter Rindisbacher, George Catlin, Alfred Jacob Miller, Karl
Bodmer, Charles Wimar, Paul Kane, and others.[5] Each artist had his own
style, but most of their productions had two points in common—two
traits that appear with such remarkable regularity that they almost certainly mean *something*. First, bison were typically pictured with Native
Americans, usually in the bison's primary habitat, the Great Plains. And
second, almost invariably they were shown being hunted by Indians, who
are usually on horseback and in the act of shooting or spearing their giant,

Titian Ramsay Peale, *American Buffaloe,* from *The Cabinet of Natural History
and American Rural Sports,* Vol. 1 (Philadelphia: John and Thomas Doughty,
1830). Hand-colored lithograph, 8.5 × 6.5 in. Courtesy of William H. and
Mewes Goetzmann Collection, Austin, Texas.

rumbling prey. Throughout the century and even today, this image has been essential to the western artist's repertoire. It comes as close as anything to a distinctively American visual cliché.

Part of the appeal is obvious. The dynamics of form and color gave the illusion of breathtaking action. Arresting details of the hunters' dress and weaponry made the scenes interesting to look at. But the West had plenty of excitement for painters and sculptors to choose from, plenty of animals like grizzly bears and mountain lions to put in exciting poses, plenty of things that Indians did that were worth attention. What the obvious reasons cannot explain is the startling similarity of one image to the next and, at least as stunning, how often that scene has appeared and how long it has persisted, decade after decade. The tougher question, that is, is why the scene has been at the same time so enduringly popular and so relentlessly formulaic. The explanation is similar to what is behind the fictional genre born in the same years—those stories, so utterly predictable and persistently popular, that in time would be called Westerns. Like the earliest versions, these paintings seemed to speak to a widely felt need at a time of national transition.

Bodmer, Catlin, Wimar, and others painted these scenes during the first few generations of the American republic. After announcing what they were not (English and part of the British Empire), Americans began the complicated job of saying what and who they were. Defining themselves involved the creation of a political culture, a mother tongue, distinctive novelists and poets, and more than a dozen new religions. Basic to this process was also the invention of symbols and icons and images that helped Americans explain themselves to themselves and to the rest of the world.

This search for identity often came to focus on the West, partly because of timing. Early notions of national distinctiveness emerged simultaneously with two other developments. First, there were the explorations that gave outsiders their first concrete impressions of what was, to them, the Far West: the Rockies and Sierra, the deserts and plains. Second, this exploration coincided with the floodtide of European and American Romanticism, with its emphasis on Nature's purifying power, the corruptions of civilization, and the innocence of the primitive. Taking this

cultural theme, Romanticism, and applying it to that western country being suddenly revealed led to part of the answer to who Americans were.
Europeans might have deep histories and crumbled ruins, but we had this
magnificent Edenic wilderness. In expressions as varied as the landscapes
of the Hudson River School, the fiction of James Fenimore Cooper, the
poetry of Henry Wadsworth Longfellow, the travel narratives of Washington Irving, and many wildly popular comic tropes, Americans were
portrayed as a people somehow made different by the mere presence of
that idealized country to the West, over the horizon.

Thus the suddenly prolific images of bison. The recurring scene of
Indians galloping after buffalo summed up nicely this image of the West
and its part in our national meaning. The animal was long established
as the most exotic wilderness resident. The buffalo's partner was another
romantic favorite—the American Native, dressed in strange garb and dis-
playing his courage and wilderness skills. The action unfolded in the vast,
open terrain that many were coming to consider the essential western
landscape—the Great Plains.

That appeal, however, is as obvious as the scene's excitement and color,
and it slides past the same question. The paintings show basically the
same thing, the chase, and the same moment in the same chase, the point
of attack. Why? Behind the obvious allure is an element of denial. What
the paintings always show is the color and action of life in the imagined
American wild. What they never show are consequences. If the bison
and the Indian were ideal symbols of the romantic horizon, choosing this
frozen moment suggests a need to believe that their world would always
be there, with history somehow suspended. Like this moment, the wild
country, so important to being American, would be arrested and timeless. Grand sights would always be waiting. Gloriously wild people, bows
eternally drawn, would forever be in violent marriage with strange and
powerful beasts.

Written accounts of visiting easterners often hint at the same thing.
Lewis Garrard, observing an Indian bison hunt firsthand along the Santa
Fe Trail in 1846, returned to his tent and wrote: "I thought with envy
of the free and happy life [the hunters] were leading on the untamed
plains, with fat buffalo for food, fine horses to ride, living and dying in a

state of blissful ignorance. . . . What more invigorating, enlivening pleasure is there than traversing the grand prairies, admiring the beauties of
unkempt, wild and lovely nature, and chasing the fleet-footed buffalo."[6]
Garrard spoke for a kind of national reverie, and the dozens of paintings
pictured it. The bison ran with that other symbol of the land beyond history, Garrard's "free and happy" Indian. Buffalo and predator had become
icons, frozen figures that told Americans something about their imagined
selves.

From the start, however, this portrait had a problem. The Wild West
has always had a double meaning. At the same time that the West was
celebrated as a land of romantic escape, it was also looked on as country to
be subdued and transformed. The question, Who are the Americans? had
two answers. Americans were people blessed with magnificent wilderness, and they were people destined to conquer that wilderness and bring
into it the blessings of civilization. This second meaning of the West had
its own visual depictions, but here the bison and Indians play very different roles. Especially during the last third of the nineteenth century, in
illustrations like John Gast's oft-reprinted *American Progress,* bison still
appear as symbols of the wild, but now they are tiny figures dwarfed by
other images of the nation's relentless westward march—railroads, miners,
the agricultural frontier, telegraph stations, and tidy cottages, churches,
and schoolhouses. The bison are still running away, but this is no frozen
moment, no vision of timelessness. They are clearly caught up in an inexorable process that will destroy their world. They are in hopeless flight
from history.

After the Civil War, Americans seemed to be rapidly fulfilling that
second promise. These years witnessed the most renowned episodes of
westward expansion—the transcontinental web of steel, the cattle kingdom, the blossom of cities, the uncovering of a mineral empire, the agrarian march of pioneers in bib overalls. That second meaning of the West, as
a land of national progress, seemed on the verge of accomplishment. The
problem, of course, was that the triumph of America's second meaning
necessarily meant the death of the first. The West can either be wild or
subdued, but it cannot be both. In the earlier West of Catlin and Bodmer, with so much land left to be conquered, it had been easy enough to

George A. Crofutt, *American Progress* (1873). Chromolithograph after John Gast, *American Progress* (1872). Courtesy of Library of Congress.

ignore the contradiction. Fifty of sixty years later, the implications were inescapable.

Images of the imagined West began to shift and change, and so did portrayals of the animal that we had made its symbol. A strong early hint was the monumental painting completed by Albert Bierstadt in 1889. It was one more view of Indians hunting bison—but with a big difference. Herds in the distance are grazing on an open plain, but the foreground is littered with dead and dying animals. All around them are bleaching bones from earlier kills. In this painting Bierstadt moved ahead from the familiar frozen moment of attack to show what was obvious all along: when people shoot arrows and stick lances into bison, they die. And if people did that not enough, they would find themselves facing what Bierstadt named his painting: *The Last of the Buffalo.*[7]

In the late nineteenth century the death of the bison became the new focus of the animal's popular portrayal. It is all the more intriguing, then, that these same years had as their greatest American celebrity William F.

Albert Bierstadt, *Last of the Buffalo* (ca. 1888). Oil on canvas, 60.25 × 96.5 in. Courtesy of Buffalo Bill Historical Center, Cody, Wyoming (2.60; Gertrude Vanderbilt Whitney Trust Fund Purchase).

"Buffalo Bill" Cody. In the year of Bierstadt's painting Cody embarked on his second phenomenally successful European tour. By then he was what he would remain for years to come, the popular embodiment of the West and of that first, older dream of freedom, adventure, and prowess. His Wild West show included most standard dime novel vignettes, from Indian fights to sharpshooting to trick-riding cowboys. One of the most popular defining moments occurred when a herd of bison were stampeded across the arena with mounted hunters in pursuit. To the audience, of course, this moment resonated with the show's star, whose identity, like that of the earlier wild America, was summed up in that familiar image: the hunter galloping beside the bison, taking aim, in endless pursuit of this mythic beast.

By the 1890s, however, this image was profoundly ironic. Cody did not earn his nickname through some mystical union with this American icon. People called him Buffalo Bill because he had *killed* the bison by the thousands. He had killed them to help feed some of the prime agents of conquest, railroad construction crews and soldiers fighting Indians. He was called Buffalo Bill, that is, for his vigorous, enthusiastic role in destroying a living symbol and ushering in the very changes that destroyed the Wild West his audiences were celebrating and mourning as they bought tickets to his show. Cody's intuitive brilliance lay in his ability somehow to avoid that contradiction, now nearly impossible to ignore. He had a knack for somehow sustaining the old illusion that Americans could forever find adventure and freedom in the wild country even after they had conquered it.

Outside Cody's arena, however, Americans knew better. The frontier (whatever that was) was closing. Wild America was being tamed, plowed, fenced. The death of the wild made many Americans uneasy, and they looked for images to speak for that unease. They found them in the same action and in the same setting that earlier stood for an enduring, romantic West. Once again the images were of bison being hunted on the Great Plains. Now, however, the vision was not of colorful Natives but of white hunters slaughtering buffalo by the millions in the 1870s and 1880s.

Plains bison had started to disappear decades earlier, and for a number of different reasons, but in 1871 scientists found a way to process bison hide into leather that could be used to make clothing, hats, furniture, and, especially lucrative, gaskets and belts in factories. Coming at a low point in the global supply of cow leather, this discovery instantly created enormous demand for the skins of the surviving buffalo. The great hunt began. Working in teams of shooters and skinners, with the help of powerful new rifles and new railroads to ship the hides, an army of white hide hunters fanned out over the central plains, then moved south and north, killing bison at a clip of more than two million a year. By 1883 the plains herds were virtually annihilated.[8]

The meaning of the West changed, and with it the message of the bison as cultural icon. In the 1840s hunting on the plains had been a vision of Eden. By the end of the century, it had become Golgotha. That portrayal has spread and persisted ever since. The dozen-year slaughter of 1871–83 has no competition as our most infamous case of wildlife destroyed for profit. William Hornaday called it the supreme example of "reckless greed, . . . wanton destructiveness, and improvidence," and the first modern student of the bison, Joseph Asaph Allen, used nearly identical words:

an "indiscriminate, improvident, and wanton slaughter."[9] No figure in western history has been regarded with greater aversion and contempt than the men who accomplished that destruction, the hide hunters. They were "butchers drawn from the dregs of border towns," Ernest Thompson Seton wrote. Allen called them "filthy . . . a paradise for hordes of nameless parasites, conscious of their unfitness for civilized society." The historian T. R. Fehrenbach called them "rough, bearded, dirty, violent . . . men."[10] With just a little reflection, this seems odd. The hunters were only acting out the hopes of the first Europeans, fulfilling a wish three centuries old. "Their flesh is good and their hides make good leather," one of them had written, remember, and another: "the hides of these beasts [might be] sold very dear." And after all, killing a lot of animals for profit was not exactly a novelty in the nineteenth-century West.

With that obvious point in mind, it is helpful to consider another animal killer, this one from fifty years earlier—the beaver trapper or mountain man—and his very different reputation. The mountain man of the 1820s and 1830s is among the most heroized actors in the western drama. In popular novels and films like *Jeremiah Johnson* he is a romantic, almost godlike character living among nature's handiworks. The buffalo hunter, on the other hand, is seen as the essence of mindless greed, up to his elbows in gore, an irredeemable defiler of nature's bounty. He is covered, not with glory, but with flies.

Yet both men were doing basically the same thing. Both tried to make money by taking considerable risks in that part of America synonymous with opportunity—the West. Both were cogs in a vast international commerce. Both killed millions of two of the West's most prolific species and, in each case, took the skins and tossed the rest away as carrion. Their popular images do have one thing in common: both appear as men living on the far edge of society, both physically and in their values and traits. Pulled by the wilderness, mountain men were said to flee society for union with nature. Hide hunters supposedly were virtual exiles pushed to the edge by normal people because they were degenerates fit only for their own company. Still, by popular tradition, the two were alike in this one way: they were men of the fringe.

But on a closer look, the facts shift. Historians have accepted for more than thirty years that most mountain men were not social aliens but people whose values fit pretty well the society of their day. The point is made best by answering a question: where did these men end up? Very few stayed in the Wild West. Most went back east to become farmers, merchants, businessmen, ranchers, clerks, government employees. They headed west as young men not to reject their mother culture but to find quick profits that would boost them up the social and economic ladder back home.[11]

Given the mountain man's true nature, it seems that the trappers and bison hunters were different from each other—one part of the social mainstream, the other an outcast. But what about the hide hunters? Where did *they* end up? According to a modern encyclopedia of the West, they were "misfits . . . who disappeared when the buffalo had been reduced to near extinction." Others wrote that they did not vanish but lingered on the social margin and "could hardly be induced to abandon . . . the free border-life and resume the restraints of civilization."[12] The tradition persists in western fiction. In Larry McMurtry's *Anything for Billy*, hunters sit around in Greasy Corners, New Mexico, "whittling and spitting, looking sadly again and again across the empty plain, like tired old bears whose coats had worn shabby." Looking them over, the book's protagonist, Billy Bones, says: "Somebody ought to just shoot them."[13]

From the point of view of the new western society, it is a good thing nobody did, because the actual buffalo hunters, like the real mountain men, quickly re-entered the social mainstream and sometimes dominated it.[14] They founded several central Kansas counties and became ranchers, farmers, merchants, druggists, candy salesmen, county clerks, tax assessors, and judges. James Mead was a founder of Wichita, Kansas, vice president of its first bank, president of the Wichita and South Western Railroad, state representative and senator, and president of both the state historical society and the Kansas Academy of Science. Many turned to law enforcement as marshals, constables, detectives, and sheriffs. The record for bison killed in a season—well more than six thousand—was held not by Bill Cody but by Bill Tilghman, who went on to become U.S. marshal and police chief of Oklahoma City. He was also an early filmmaker, delegate to the 1904 Democratic national convention, and a successful breeder of racehorses. One of his favorites, Chant, won the 1894 Kentucky Derby.[15]

Here is a puzzle. If mountain men and hide hunters were the same sort of men doing the same sort of thing, why has one been pictured as a hero and the other as a degenerate? And if both were squarely in the American mainstream, why have both been seen as men on the fringe? Given all the evidence to the contrary, why has it been necessary to see the two as both different from *us* and different from *each other*? The reasons are found in their times. The two animal-killers did their bloody work when Americans had different mythic needs, and so Americans imagined them differently and put them, and the animals they killed, to different mythic uses.

The mythic mountain man was the white counterpart of that other wild child of the time, the horseback Indian galloping beside the running bison. Both embodied the notion of the young nation wedded to the wilderness, and in the supremely optimistic Age of Jackson, with so much of the West unmapped and nicely out of focus, it was possible to believe that far into the fuzzy future that distinctive American world might remain, out there, with the buckskinned trapper and Garrard's "free and happy Indian" joined on the hunt that would never end. By the last years of the century, however, when the tide of conquest and transformation could not possibly be missed, such a vision was far harder to sustain. Now the icon of the timeless, romantic West, the bison, was shown dead where it had endlessly run, on the Great Plains. In another turn in popular art, its earlier hunter, the mounted Indian, was ridden down and unhorsed, often in the maudlin company of the bones of his old quarry. As for the bison's new predator, the white hunter, he too reflected the new awareness of a vanishing Eden. He was shown, not in the pursuit, but with its consequences, surrounded by his grisly handiwork. Unlike the mountain man or horseback Indian, he was less a hunter than a killer, and his victim was not only an animal but the dream of the American wild.

These scenes not only looked backward to a lost paradise; they looked forward, too. The bison were slaughtered at a time when the public worried deeply that progress was bringing a new world—industrial, urban, corporate—that was alien and threatening. Americans, now uneasy about where history was taking them, once again looked westward to say what they felt. The bison as icon was caught up in the same currents that ushered in populist and Progressive politics, the literature of realism and naturalism, and the art of the Ashcan School. The point here was made not so much by the animal itself, or by its killers, but by how it died and what happened afterward.

Everything about the new images was drearily mechanistic. The hide men did not confront their prey courageously with arrow and lance; they worked from anonymous distance with modern killing tools, breech-loading high-powered rifles. With the shooters working their famous stands and dropping thirty, fifty, seventy bison, one at a time, hour after hour, the killing had a relentless feel. This was death metronomic, less like a hunt than like a forge stamping out rivets. In photographs the killers and skinners are faceless, almost robotic. Once the bison were flayed, their hides were stretched, bound, and carted off in giant wagons, then stacked like lumber or ingots, one more industrial product to be carried away by what many considered the arch villain of the new America, the railroad. Finally, the hides and ultimately even the bones were processed, sliced, ground, and transformed, not into something as individual and personal as a lap robe or garment, but into belts and gaskets for smoke-belching factories and fertilizer for mechanized agriculture. The whole operation, in fact, felt like a factory. From the first rifle shot to its end, the process seemed like one great machine. Prolific nature was not just mowed down efficiently; it was taken into the industrial maw, chewed, and absorbed. The symbol of wild America didn't simply become a trophy; it disappeared entirely into a voracious corporate America.

Seen in this light, as martyrs to a dark industrial age, the slaughtered bison might seem a biting critique of the dream of progress and a painful admission of how America—or more exactly, how *Americans*—had slain their other dream of who they were, a people wedded to the wilderness. But not so fast. Admitting that would depend on seeing the hide hunter as he truly was, a dollar-chasing westerner no different from millions of

Frenzeny & Tavernier, "Sketches in the Far West—Curing Hides and Bones" (1874). Wood engraving. First published in *Harper's Weekly,* April 4, 1874, supplement, p. 307.

countrymen from coast to coast. Instead Americans pulled off a neat trick. They reimagined future lawmen and railroad executives into misfits and outcasts. They turned mainstream westerners into men-on-the-margin who either slunk away or vanished in a poof. With that, they could distance themselves from what was, after all, a natural consequence of values and pursuits all held in common. Earlier, when they had wanted both national expansion and endless Eden, they had taken one of themselves, the mountain man, and remade him into a romantic isolate who lived in the forever wild. Now, when the death of Eden was undeniable, they took another of their own, the hide hunter, and remade him for a new purpose. They turned him into the stinking exile, then they handed him the responsibility for all the worrisome costs of what they nonetheless wanted. With that, they could turn up their noses, or rather hold them, and walk away, full of doubts about the new era while doing everything possible to push it forward and to enjoy its benefits.

Despite their brush with extinction, bison are still with us. They have rebounded nicely, breeding as vigorously as two-thousand-pound cockroaches, and they have persisted as well in popular imagery. As symbols of a national birthright and of a lost Edenic past they have grazed on our flags, coins, and currency and raced over the land in advertisements for everything from prunes to whiskey. Today we are well into another romantic revival, and with it has come a reprise of the bison's familiar poses. The 1990 film *Dances With Wolves* featured both a spectacular Indian hunt on horseback and a lingering sequence of rotting carcasses skinned by white hunters. Policy theorists who argue that we should repent for our efforts to transform the Great Plains use the phrase "buffalo commons" to invoke memories of those massive herds and to massage nostalgic yearnings for a vanished wilderness.[16] In the marketplace, where anything associated with Native America and the American wild has instant appeal, there are arguably more buffalo paintings, sculptures, T-shirts, fetishes, baseball caps, posters, neckties, boxer shorts, boot scrapers, and nose studs than there ever were actual bison. With a large enough line of credit, anyone can wear the fantasy as a coat or even run a bison ranch, with specialized periodicals for advice. At restaurants or at home we can chow down on the mythic food of rollicking mountain men and Indians running free, advertised with a contemporary twist as a kind of supermeat, high in protein but with barely a whiff of cholesterol or fat.

Our images are as ironic as ever. To venerate a preindustrial age, we buy buffalo products made and distributed through a corporate marketplace that dwarfs the one that nearly exterminated the bison. Some of our most successful captains of capital now profit from the antimodern fascination with things bison. With ranches in seven western states, totaling more than two million acres, Ted Turner is both the nation's largest landowner and proprietor of the largest bison herd in the world, more than fifty thousand animals. To the southwest of Turner's domain, near Telluride, Colorado, another eastern buckaroo, Ralph Lauren, has his own refuge from modern life, the twenty-two-thousand-acre Double RL Ranch. There he has a great family lodge, but if too pressed even there by responsibilities, Lauren can escape to his own very large tipi built of (what else?) authentic bison hides. Lauren designed it with a frontiersman's spit-in-your-eye individualism. "I don't look at anyone else's tee-pee," Lauren told a reporter. "I make my own rules about how I want to live." The interior features Navajo rugs, Edward Curtis photographs, a chandelier, and plush chairs from an English club. On the outside a local self-defined mountain man has decorated the hides, Indian-style, with simple stylized drawings of Lauren. "My goal is to keep and preserve the West," Lauren explained from his buffalo-skin lodge, with fluency in the new romantic litany. "I'm just borrowing the land," he added, surrounded by fifteen miles of tall white fence. "You can never really own it."[17]

Lauren and Turner might draw a bemused smile, but it is worth remembering that they say what they say, do what they do, and harvest their billions because they know Americans very well. Many others act out the same fantasy with contradictions that are much the same, only on a smaller scale. Americans buying Buffalo Gal Jerky might think of Kevin Costner eating pemmican, but it is still factory-processed, shrink-wrapped bison meat with some soy sauce and MSG. And they might lounge of an evening on a Thundering Herd buffalo robe ("As seen in 'Dances With Wolves'"), but they might also be eating microwave popcorn and choosing among hundreds of cable channels as they recline their way to a simpler, more basic past.

As it always has, the buffalo serves Americans as a kind of national totem. How it appears is as much of a jumble as those earliest descriptions, but the reason today is not poor reportage. The imagined bison today is a hodgepodge of contradictions because we are. Americans have always been at ease while living with irreconcilable values, celebrating a vanished age while worshipping change, taking pride in accumulation while longing for simplicity, escaping westward into a natural, untouched world that we have carefully built to our specifications. As we push into a new century, comfortable as ever in our breathtaking discrepancies, we stand as a people in high-fashion, low-cholesterol communion with this great American animal, a people in ongoing conversation with our paradoxical selves.

Notes

1. George P. Hammond and Agapito Rey, *Don Juan de Oñate, Colonizer of New Mexico, 1595–1628*, vol. 1 (Albuquerque: University of New Mexico Press, 1953), 402.

2. Quoted in J. A. Allen, *The American Bison, Living and Extinct* (New York: Arno Press, 1974), 80.

3. William Temple Hornaday, *The Extermination of the American Bison* (Washington: Smithsonian Institution Press, 2002), 374–75.

4. C. Raymond Beazley, *Voyages and Travels Mainly during the 16th and 17th Centuries* (Westminster, U.K.: Constable, 1903), 168.

5. I. S. MacLaren, "Buffalo in Word and Image: From European Origins to the Art of Clarence Tillenius," in *Buffalo*, ed. John E. Foster, Dick Harrison, and I. S. MacLaren (Edmonton: University of Alberta Press, 1992), 79–129; Brian W. Dippie, "'Flying Buffalo': Artists and the Buffalo Hunt," *Montana The Magazine of Western History* 51:2 (Summer 2001): 2–17.

6. Lewis H. Garrard, *Wah-To-Yah and the Taos Trail*, ed. Ralph P. Bieber, Southwest Historical Series, vol. 6 (Glendale, Calif.: Arthur H. Clark, 1938), 83.

7. Rena N. Coen, "The Last of the Buffalo," *American Art Journal* 5:2 (November 1973): 83–94.

8. Among the standard works are Mari Sandoz, *The Buffalo Hunters* (New York: Hastings House, 1954); Wayne Gard, *The Great Buffalo Hunt* (Lincoln: University of Nebraska Press, 1978); David A. Dary, *The Buffalo Book* (New York: Avon Books, 1974), esp. chapters 6 and 7; and Andrew C. Isenberg, *The Destruction of the Bison: An Environmental History, 1750–1920* (Cambridge: Cambridge University Press, 2000), esp. chapter 5.

9. Hornaday, *Extermination of the American Bison*, 464; Joseph Asaph Allen, "History of the American Bison," *Ninth Annual Report of the United States Geological and Geographic Survey for 1875* (Washington, D.C.: Government Printing Office), 554.

10. Ernest Thompson Seton, "The American Bison or Buffalo," *Scribner's Magazine* 40:4 (October 1906): 403–404; Allen, *American Bison*, 214; T. R. Fehrenbach, *Lone Star: A History of Texas and the Texans* (New York: MacMillan, 1968), 536.

11. William H. Goetzmann, "The Mountain Man as Jacksonian Man," *American Quarterly* 15:3 (Fall 1963): 402–15.

12. Denis McLoughlin, *Wild and Woolly: An Encyclopedia of the Old West* (Garden City, N.Y.: Doubleday, 1975), 66; Allen, *American Bison*, 214.

13. Larry McMurtry, *Anything for Billy* (New York: Simon & Schuster, 1988), 70–71.

14. David D. Dawson, "Reconsidered: The Buffalo Hunters on the Southern Plains" (M.A. thesis, University of Arkansas, 1990).

15. Zoe A. Tilghman, *Marshal of the Last Frontier: Life and Services of William Mathew (Bill) Tilghman, For Fifty Years One of the Greatest Peace Officers of the West* (Glendale, Calif.: Arthur H. Clark, 1949).

16. Anne Matthews, *Where the Buffalo Roam* (New York: Grove Press, 1992).

17. James Reginato, "Ralph's Teepee," *W* 24:12 (December 1995): 228–31.

Jesse James, Borderman

He was one of "the boldest bandits to ever plague the world," dazzling and "dashing and skillful" in his bravery and nerve. He was "the worst man, without exception, in America," coldhearted and vicious. He was a friend of the poor, an enemy to tyrants. Compared to him, "Claude Duval, Robin Hood and Brennan-on-the-moor were effeminate, sunflowered aesthetes."[1] Yet there "was nothing chivalrous in his nature," for "he lived for himself alone" and led a "gang of villains" more suited for the jungles of central Africa than the American heartland.[2] Some have said he was "cut off in his prime of strength and beauty."[3] Others have gibed that his baptizing preacher should have drowned him when he had the chance.

Jesse James always got mixed reviews. Successful criminals often do, but the range of opinions on this Missouri bandit is far greater than usual. One word, however, is scattered often throughout the range of voices: "border." In book titles, Jesse and friends were *The Border Outlaws* and *The Border Bandits* and their deeds were the *Daring Exploits . . . of Border Train Robbers.*[4] The term is sprinkled liberally among the dozens of potboilers and dime novels in which Jesse steals, murders, gives to penniless widows, and rescues swooning maids. Enemies held him high as glaring proof of the chaos waiting when society marked too poorly the border of rightful law. And after years of angry exchanges, scholars like Frederick Jackson Turner would complain about all the attention given to men like Jesse, "that line of scum [on] the waves of advancing civilization," who were consumed by "border warfare and the chase."[5]

"Border" turns out to be a useful term in describing Jesse James's life, reputation, and place in our popular culture. At the time, it described the country where Jesse, Frank, and their gang operated—western Missouri, eastern Kansas, northwestern Arkansas, and eastern Indian Territory, the far western border of the American South. If we look back, however, the term takes on other meanings. The Jesse James of fact committed his crimes along the historical boundary between two American eras, the age of sectional war and the age of industry. His myth took its shape from those same years, and as the flesh-and-blood outlaw met his bloody end, the mythic Jesse James was approaching another kind of border. He evolved neatly from a contentious legend of the first era into a national hero for the second. The western legend that emerged, and continues to ride through American dreams, was that of a borderman who had skirted the lines among many parts of American history and our understanding of who we are.

In 1841 Robert and Zarelda Cole James moved from Kentucky to Clay County in western Missouri, a neighborhood of farms and woodlands that would remain the center of the family's bloody story for the next half century. Jesse Woodson James was born in September 1847, four years after his brother, Alexander Franklin. Their father, a minister, died in 1850 while prospecting in California. Five years later, their mother married Reuben Samuel, a medical doctor and farmer. Four children followed: Archie, John, Sallie, and Fannie.[6]

"The border" in these years referred to a stretch of country from Council Bluffs, Iowa, on the north, down Missouri's western boundary, and through the land between Arkansas and Indian Territory. This region of new farms attracted a mixed population of tens of thousands during Jesse's first fifteen years and was a launching place for many people's journeys to the Pacific Coast. Life was unsettled and the general mood of the area was competitive. The border drew a lot of hard cases.

Although the word was usually not applied to it, there was another border in these years—the one between North and South. Values and lifeways in the two sections were increasingly in conflict in the 1850s, and where they merged along this line, they were chafed and raw. Emigrants heading westward moved in two broad streams, from North and South of the Ohio River Valley, converging in middle Missouri River ports like Kansas City and Atchison and in the surrounding countryside that included Clay County. Factions from North and South were tossed together along the turbulent border where East met West. As national tensions were reaching their peak, Jesse and Frank grew up at this intersection, at the crosshairs of these two American dividing lines.

Virtually nothing outside of folklore is known about the brothers' childhoods. They developed their own personalities. By tradition, Jesse was mercurial and inventive, while Frank was more solid but persistent and dogged. As they grew older, their personalities were usually complementary, but there are hints as well that the brothers clashed. They presumably worked hard at the usual chores of farm life. Their stepfather did rather well, and the family probably wanted for little. Considering their mother's prominent role in their later lives, a clearer look at Zarelda would be useful, but, except that her personality was formidable, there is not much to learn. Nothing, in fact, suggests anything for Jesse and Frank except a normal upbringing—or as normal as possible in one of the most troubled parts of America.

The Civil War exaggerated the worst of border life, and it proved to be the shaping event of Jesse's adolescent years.[7] Frank volunteered immediately for the South, the section favored by their high-tempered mother, but Jesse, only fourteen years old, stayed behind. Formal Confederate forces in the state were soon defeated. Missouri, however, remained at war, and except for Virginia, more engagements were fought there than in any other state. Southern opposition came from guerrilla forces led by men whose names would inspire remarkable hatred and loyalty: William Quantrill, William "Bloody Bill" Anderson, George Tate, and others. Frank fought on and off with these irregulars throughout the war. The guerrillas harassed troops and Unionist civilians in Missouri and Kansas and found refuge among clusters of sympathizers, as in the "Cracker Neck" neighborhood east of Kansas City. Frustrated Union regulars and militia fought back as best they could.

It was a nasty business. All sides were guilty of atrocities and innumerable petty cruelties. The lunacy reached its height in the late summer of 1863 when the Union commander, Brigadier General Thomas Ewing, tried to slow the guerrillas by arresting the wives, mothers, and sisters of some of their leaders. The maneuver failed tragically when the Kansas City Hotel, where they were confined, collapsed, killing five, including "Bloody Bill" Anderson's sister, and injuring several more. A week later, Quantrill led his infamous attack on Lawrence, Kansas. Frank James rode with him. More than 150 civilian men were murdered, some in front of their families, and the town was leveled before the guerrillas returned to their Missouri strongholds. Ewing responded on August 25 with his General Orders No. Eleven. All persons in Jackson, Cass, and Bates Counties living more than a mile from a principal town were forced to abandon their homes. Anyone who could prove his or her loyalty could stay at a military post. The rest had to leave the area within fifteen days. As usual, even those in command were not in control. Troops and militia killed some of the twenty thousand evacuees and looted and destroyed the property of many more.

Around this time, according to tradition, the war's viciousness came home to the Samuel farm. According to a well-rooted story, a clutch of Union militiamen came in search of Frank. They abused and insulted a pregnant Zarelda Samuel and whipped and beat young Jesse. After they hoisted Dr. Samuel by his neck from a tree limb, choking him to unconsciousness, he led the militia to Frank and his fellows, camped nearby in the woods. Some of Frank's companions died, but he escaped. Reuben and Zarelda were taken into custody for a week or two.[8] According to local lore, this attack turned Jesse toward a life of violence. Sometime between the fall of 1863 and the following spring, he joined the guerrillas.

A rare photograph from this time shows an open-faced, reasonably handsome boy. Writers would make a lot of his clear blues eyes, said to bore into whoever was in front of them, and, in fact, this Jesse has a direct and confident look remarkable for a sixteen-year-old. Perhaps he earned it. He rode with Anderson, now the guerrillas' prime leader, in a withering campaign against Union troops and militia. He helped in the slaughter of twenty-five unarmed soldiers in the "Centralia massacre" and in the killing of a hundred more in a battle the same day. He was shot twice. A bad chest wound left a large scar. Another bullet, either taken in battle or fired accidentally by Jesse himself, took off the end of the middle finger on his left hand. He was nicknamed "Dingus." By one account this came from his Baptist-pure exclamation after he shot off his fingertip: "That's the doddingus pistol I ever saw."[9]

Sometime in the late spring of 1865 Jesse was shot again, an injury that became entwined in his life and legend. It was another bad chest wound, and his slow recovery took place partly at the home of relatives outside Kansas City, where he was nursed by Zarelda Mimms (who went by Zee), a pretty cousin named for his mother. His attraction to her would grow into something more serious. As for the wound itself, no evidence shows how he got it, but a persistent story claims that soon after Appomattox, he and a few friends tried to surrender at Lexington, Missouri, only to be attacked by soldiers. He may in fact have been part of a group considering assaulting the town, but in the popular narrative that later evolved, the rejected overture and near-mortal wound set the conviction in Jesse that he and his fellows would never be allowed to lay down arms and live peaceably.[10]

The war did provide one sure and vital bridge between Frank and Jesse and their outlaw days. In 1862 or 1863 Frank met another Quantrill irregular, Thomas Coleman (Cole) Younger, and his brother James. All three hailed from the same area. Like Jesse, Cole claimed to have joined the guerrillas after a family member, in this case his father (ironically a Unionist), was abused and finally killed by militia. He became one of Quantrill's chief subordinates and was prominent in the Lawrence raid. By the time Jesse joined, Cole had left for California, but he returned to Missouri after 1865. Cole and James Younger and two other brothers too young to fight in the war, Robert and John, would join Frank and Jesse in their rush to notoriety.

Whatever happened in those closing days of the conflict, Jesse and Frank were back on the Samuel place by late 1865. Little is known about the next few years except that the brothers were at the farm, helping run a reasonably successful operation. That is of some importance. If, as later claimed, they were being pressed and hounded by wartime enemies, their open presence and easy movements seem a little odd. Jesse healed up and was baptized in nearby Kearney, Missouri. He developed an eye for horses and a reputation for finding, raising, and racing fine animals. A passing visitor would have seen one of many scarred veterans presumably settling in for an ordinary life. This, however, was about to change.

In 1865 there was no doubt where Jesse James stood along the borders of American regions. He was a southerner in sympathy and action. Neighbors and acquaintances would have known him as one survivor among hundreds who had ridden under the black flag of Quantrill and Anderson. That was the association made when he and Frank embarked on what would become the most widely known criminal career of the day.

Not surprisingly, border violence never stopped after Lee's surrender. There were reprisals by both sides. A minority of guerrillas also put their hit-and-run skills to new purposes. Wartime raiding became peacetime robbery. One target was especially popular—a bank. Not only were banks the most obvious concentration of money, but they also represented to many an outside authority and an invasive northern institution. These border heists were the birth of modern bank robbery. Historians later would speculate that Jesse and Frank were present when several banks were robbed in Missouri and Kentucky between 1866 and 1868, but no good evidence connects them to any crime before December 7, 1869. On that day, two men took $700 from a bank in Gallatin, Missouri, shooting and killing an unarmed cashier before heading for Clay County. The fleeing men abandoned a horse that was soon traced to the Samuel farm, and when lawmen approached the house, Jesse and Frank burst from the barn on horseback, jumped a fence, and escaped in a hot exchange of pistol fire.

The Kansas City *Times* described the pair as "very desperate and determined men" experienced in "horse and revolver work," but the search cooled after family offered alibis and locals vouched for the brothers' characters.[11] In June 1871 four robbers hit a bank barely across the Iowa line. Descriptions fit the James brothers, Cole Younger, and a man who would be an associate over the next several years, Clell Miller. Ten months later, five men grabbed $600 from a Columbia, Kentucky, bank and shot to death a clerk who raised an alarm. A furious posse pursued, but once again the thieves slipped away. The crime occurred more than five hundred miles from Clay County, but investigators concluded that

Frank, Jesse, and Younger had been posing as horse traders in the area for weeks, and authorities charged the crime to what now was considered the James-Younger gang. Over the next year, the gang was accused of two more brazen robberies: one at the Kansas City fair and the other at a bank in Ste. Genevieve, Missouri, where the bandits shouted hurrahs for Confederate guerrillas as they galloped out of town with $4,000 and the teller's watch.

These early events set a pattern for the following decade. The James brothers (if they were the culprits) chose an especially brazen crime—the daylight robbery of a bank, a town's most prominent public target. They were not reluctant to kill people; in three robberies they murdered two men, one without resistance or provocation. They had a talent for evading pursuit; outside Gallatin they kidnapped a farmer as a guide, and in Kentucky they doubled back and around the posse. They protested their innocence publicly, but from a distance—in published letters claiming they were falsely accused by wartime enemies. Back home they were protected by family and probably by some friends, but both Frank and Jesse also showed a remarkable gift for social camouflage. They almost never identified themselves to strangers, showed no interest in notoriety, and had rather forgettable faces. Long after their names were familiar throughout the nation, this pair could walk unrecognized down any street in the country, even in nearby Kansas City.

The well-worn pattern of bank robberies was broken in July 1873, when the gang pulled a rail from the tracks outside Council Bluffs, Iowa, and derailed an engine of the Chicago, Rock Island, and Pacific Railroad. After looting the train's safe and stripping passengers of all valuables, the bandits, wearing Ku Klux Klan hoods, ran for the Missouri border. This robbery claimed another life—that of the engineer, who stayed aboard to slow the train and was crushed when the locomotive ran off the rails and toppled.

Like bank holdups, train robberies were a new phenomenon that garnered much public attention. The first one had occurred a few years earlier in Indiana, but the James-Younger gang would quickly seize the title of the nation's leading train thieves. The audacious next robbery, a half year later at Gads Hill in eastern Missouri, made a special splash. Bandits seized the local depot just before the train pulled in, jumped aboard, and left with cash and loot from the express safe and from the pockets and purses of travelers. The bandits had a theatrical flair. Victims were selected from among soft-handed males—the bandits swore they would take nothing from workingmen—and as the leader left, he presented a railroad worker with a carefully worded account of the incident. In effect, the thieves issued a press release. They left a blank spot where the amount stolen could be filled in.

Ten months after this bit of bravado, the gang was suspected of another criminal flamboyance—back-to-back robberies of a bank in Tishomingo, Mississippi, on December 7, 1874, and of a train not far from Kansas City the next day. Supposedly, the James-Younger gang divided forces and coordinated the thefts, which totaled nearly $40,000. The following September they were accused of striking far to the east to rob a bank in Huntington, West Virginia, of $10,000. One of the bandits in this robbery, killed while fleeing westward, was a Missourian previously thought to be a cohort of the James brothers. The dramatic, wide-ranging crimes fed a growing popular fascination with the James-Younger gang. Newspapers from Boston to San Francisco kept readers apprised of particulars of what seemed a bold and stylish banditry. Curious readers now knew that Jesse was a family man, for word was published of his marriage in April 1874 to his cousin Zarelda (Zee). Not long afterward, Frank eloped with another Missouri girl, Annie Ralston. Most stories agreed that the brothers would be devoted husbands and fathers. The bold bandits' image took on a somewhat more human face.

Authorities, on the other hand, were not amused. Lawmen seemed incapable of finding the handful of men accused of crimes in six states, despite a consensus of opinion about who they were and the general neighborhood where they hid. The heat was increasing, however. Bankers earlier had offered rewards for the brothers' capture, but banks were, after all, local businesses with limited resources. Railroads were a different matter. Among the nation's largest and wealthiest corporations with interests spanning the continent, railroads and express companies quickly began to use their unmatched power to intensify the search for the men who had taken their money, destroyed their property, killed and injured their employees, fleeced their customers, and stung their pride. To trace down Jesse and Frank, railway officials hired the Pinkerton Detective Agency, famous as much for its tenacity and ruthlessness as for its success.

These efforts made it all the easier for the gang's admirers to celebrate their boldness and evasive skills. The outlaws "only laugh at authorities," a journalist wrote, "and seemingly invite their sleepy enterprise."[12] Using the Pinkertons also fed the belief, encouraged by Jesse and Frank, that they were simple farm lads harassed by looming outside institutions, in this case a northern firm employed by those symbols of distant, uncaring power, the railroads. The Pinkertons' failures—in a back-roads firefight, two agents (and John Younger) were killed, and another was found murdered after trying to infiltrate the Samuel household—brought derisive hoots and loud applause.

A single episode at this point did more than any other to solidify the brothers' image as the victimized underdogs. Frustrated detectives, convinced that Jesse and Frank were hiding at their mother's home, made an aggressive move. Near midnight on January 26, 1875, a flaming fabric ball was thrown through a window of the Samuel home. As Zarelda and Reuben Samuel kicked it into the fireplace, a blazing metal missile followed it, and when it too was shoved into the fire, it exploded. Shrapnel tore into the side of Archie Samuel, the young half brother to Jesse and Frank, and Zarelda's hand was horribly mutilated. Archie died at dawn; his mother's hand and part of her arm had to be amputated. If Jesse and Frank were there, they soon fled. Pinkertons later claimed that agents only tossed an "illuminating device" into the darkened house after its residents had refused to come out.[13] Whatever the facts, bloody reality now meshed with evolving myth. Anyone so inclined could easily see abusive authority assaulting a central symbol of traditional good—the home. A weapon at once cowardly and impersonal had killed an innocent boy and maimed an older woman. An explosion in the night seemed to confirm, not in fact but emotionally, the myth forming around the James boys.

Much of the Missouri press howled in outrage and contempt against the Pinkerton agency and, indirectly, its employers. The brouhaha tended to drown out the mounting evidence of the James and Younger gangs' continuing crimes. Just where the gang was at any time, of course, was a matter of contemporary conjecture and future folklore. Between the more publicized bank and train robberies from Iowa to West Virginia, the outlaws probably moved between their home ground in Missouri and northern Texas, where they had friends and family roots. Stories floated around of small-scale banditry near Denison, Texas, and of a lucrative stage robbery far to the south near San Antonio. In January 1874 another stage robbery near Hot Springs, Arkansas, added a mythic dash when one of the bandits returned a watch to a veteran of the Confederate army out of loyalty to the Stars and Bars. Almost surely there were many smaller thefts from merchants and individuals never connected with any gang members.

Who took part in any particular crime was just as hazy. By 1875 it was widely argued that the gang had a core group of eight men: Frank and Jesse James; Cole, Bob, and Jim Younger; Clell Miller, Charlie Pitts, and Bill Chadwell. In addition, they often took on young men from the neighborhood to hold their horses and for the criminal equivalent of grunt labor. Only part of the group might be present even at the major robberies, however, and in cases like the Mississippi and Kansas thefts their forces might be divided.

So the remarkable contradiction persisted. At the time of the Pinkerton attack on the Samuel home, the James brothers were the most famous outlaws in the nation. Yet the gang's shifting makeup, as well as their talent for invisibility, made it possible to argue without a smirk that Jesse, Frank, the Youngers, and others were law-abiding citizens framed by malicious enemies. In early July 1876 a train was stopped in Cooper County, Missouri, and was robbed of $15,000. The practiced style of the thieves and the location, only three counties away from the Samuel farm, made the gang the obvious suspects, and when Missourian Hobbs Kerry was arrested after flashing large wads of money, he confessed and named Jesse, Frank, and the others as his fellow culprits. "Liar," Zarelda Samuel answered, and the *Times* published yet another letter, reputedly from Jesse, denying everything and promising an alibi. The editors tacitly agreed and turned their scorn on the paid "thief-catchers" who "kill twelve-year-old boys [and] blow off the arms of old women."[14]

This situation made the news from Northfield, Minnesota, all the more stunning. On September 7, 1876, eight bandits tried to rob the Northfield bank. It quickly became a bloody botch. Two outlaws wounded a fleeing employee and shot to death a balky cashier after slitting his throat. On the street an alarm turned into a chaotic gun battle. Local shopkeepers blazed away with rifles, killing two of the bandit lookouts and wounding another. A Swedish immigrant, baffled by shouts in a foreign tongue, died under the robbers' fire. In a thorough scouring of the area, another outlaw was killed and three more were captured. The last two escaped.

Identification of the dead and apprehended seemed to confirm all charges against the gang. Clell Miller, Bill Chadwell, and Charlie Pitts were killed. Cole, Jim, and Bob Younger were wounded and subsequently captured. Somehow, the last two evaded several hundred pursuers in a southward flight through Iowa and Nebraska, and informers soon reported that the James boys were back in their home territory after a long, grueling journey. The Youngers were jailed but treated well. While in captivity, Cole proved as adept at cultivating sympathy as he was at denying guilt when he was free. He chatted with curious visitors, gave public apologies, cited scripture, and spoke fondly of Sunday school. The three corpses were turned over to medical students for dissection.

The debacle began a critical time in the brothers' lives and in the shaping of their myth. Jesse and Frank were on a desperate run without seasoned companions. With six of eight names confirmed of the gang's personnel, many who had had honest doubts concluded that the James boys had been at the center of the remarkable string of crimes all along. In his criminal career and in the way he faced the public, Jesse was about to move in another direction.

Cole, Bob, and Jim Younger pleaded guilty in the Northfield killings and were sentenced to life in the Minnesota state prison. Suddenly gangless, Jesse and Frank fled to Tennessee, where they lived with their families near Nashville as J. D. Howard and B. J. Woodson. Evidence later suggested they had moved their families there in late 1875, shaken perhaps by the Pinkerton raid. Until about 1879 Frank worked at various enterprises while Jesse farmed, did some trading, speculated in commodities, and wagered at horse racing. Their lives were inconspicuous, highly domestic, and in one way, quite productive. Zee gave birth to her first child, Jesse Edwards, several months before Northfield, and to a daughter, Mary, in July 1879. Robert Franklin, the only child of Frank and Annie, also was born during this time. It would be years before the children would learn their true last name. Jesse took the masquerade a step further, always calling his son and namesake "Tim."

This three-year hiatus offers a chance for a more probing look at the legend growing up around Jesse and the James gang. It was well entrenched by the time of Northfield, and during the following months, speculation about the brothers' whereabouts deliciously deepened the mystery surrounding them. Some said that they had run to Mexico to start a new life. Others claimed that Frank and Jesse were in the far-western mining camps, digging honestly for gold and silver. Because they were nowhere to be seen, they seemed to be everywhere. Front-porch whittlers and pickle-barrel detectives were free to stretch the limits of the absurd. By one story, Jesse the scamp was posing as a Republican and supporting Grant. By another, the ever-devout borderman had turned to preaching and was spreading the gospel from Baptist pulpits throughout the South.

The last two rumors are reminders of the setting and situation that created the legend. Years later Jesse would be called "western," but while he was alive and robbing, his myth was unabashedly southern. This myth was born out of the hatred and resentment between North and South. Its context was Reconstruction, one of the most revealing and contentious times in American history. The first robbery charged to the Jameses, that of the Gallatin bank, came soon after federal rule was firmly set and operating in the former Confederacy. The Northfield rout occurred shortly before the contested presidential election of 1876, the traditional marker for Reconstruction's end.

Missouri took no direct part in that troubled postwar process, but its many Confederate sympathizers identified with states that did. In fact, with so many citizens on either side of the issues, Missouri probably was more passionately torn over Reconstruction than states that knew it firsthand. The myth of Jesse James took its first shape in this charged atmosphere along the border between the Union and defeated Confederacy.

Most directly, the James-Younger gang was said to have been forced into anonymity by false charges from carpetbaggers and enemies from the war, some of whom, it was claimed, were the true perpetrators of the crimes. Soon after the first charges against him, Jesse wrote the Kansas City *Times* to say that he had lived by the law since leaving the guerrillas, but he would never hand himself over to his accusers, the "bloodthirsty poltroons" who meant him harm.[15] Admirers saw the brothers as striking a few final blows for the mistreated South. The cashier killed in cold blood in the Gallatin bank supposedly had been mistaken for S. P. Cox, the federal officer responsible for "Bloody Bill" Anderson's death. In an especially laughable stretch, Cole Younger later claimed that the gang chose the Northfield bank because they thought it held some funds of Benjamin Butler, hated by southerners for his administration during the Union occupation of New Orleans.

Another southern postwar theme emerged from the gang's early crimes. After the fourth robbery attributed to them, a local journalist wrote, "We are bound to admire it and revere its perpetrators."[16] These men and others like them, he added, were poetry personified, chivalrous souls who might have supped with Arthur at the Round Table. The journalist's admiration is puzzling, given the specifics of the crime—snatching a tin money box at the Kansas City fair, firing at the cashier and missing, wounding a young girl in the leg. Like much of the boys' career, however, this sordid business was cut and retrimmed to fit the South's changing perception of itself. Defeated and humiliated southerners were engaged in their own reconstruction. They were reflexively reshaping the remembered South into an idyllic land of heroic grace, honor, gallantry, and beauty. The James brothers were tailored to match this reimagined past. Men like the James brothers were criminals, it was claimed, because the "social soil" of the new America starved their kind of heroism. They were "bad because they live out of their time."[17]

The journalist who praised the gang for its tin-box heroics would play as great a role as Jesse or Frank in creating the James myth. He was John Newman Edwards. A Virginian, he had come with the human tide to Missouri in 1850, fought with the Confederate general Joseph O. ("Jo") Shelby, followed Shelby briefly into Mexico after the war, and returned to Kansas City to help found and edit the *Times* in 1868. Few ex-Confederates were less repentant. None was caught up more completely in the southern cause as romance. Edwards compared Quantrill and the border guerrillas to errant knights and to the gladiators who fought beside Spartacus. Jesse was innocent, he said, but he agreed that former guerrillas had committed the crimes. He praised their élan. They struck their blows "in the teeth of the multitudes." They stole not for money but for "the wild drama of adventure."[18] They had far less in common with ordinary thieves than they did with the Old South beau ideals of Lancelot and Ivanhoe.

The specific mood of the time colored the universal elements of the legend. Jesse James was portrayed as an American Robin Hood for giving to the weak and impoverished what he stole from the rich and powerful. The most famous story has Jesse and Frank stopping at a widow's door to buy a meal. When they learn a banker is on his way to foreclose on her house, Jesse gives her money for the mortgage and makes sure she will demand a receipt. Then he waits down the road for the banker and takes the money back. There is nothing in the record to support this story, which fits a folk pattern in many cultures. The tale of the widow's mortgage is likely an invention to testify that Jesse, similar to bandit heroes throughout history, had a tender heart and was openhanded. The particulars here are what seem significant: the duped man was a symbol of economic Yankeedom, the banks that Jesse also robbed openly. In many versions the banker is a carpetbagger to boot.

Just as vital to the James brothers' image was their deep love for—and their intense loyalty to—family and kin. Jesse supposedly had been brought into the war by the bullying mistreatment of Dr. and Mrs. Samuel. Devotion between mother and sons ran especially deep. Zarelda Samuel defended her boys on every charge and called them affectionate and dutiful. Jesse doted on Zarelda, and without getting too Freudian, something might be made of his marrying a woman named for his mother. It's also important not to miss the obvious: America's two most famous bandits were brothers—and partners with Cole, Jim, and Bob Younger. A decade after the gang's demise, the Dalton brothers were robbing trains and banks in the same area of the country.

This fraternal theme had a special appeal in the Reconstruction South. The family, like the new myth of a chivalrous South, took on an inflated significance. With the collapse of authority and the occupation by a widely distrusted government, people relied far more than usual on kinfolk and the most trusted nearby friends. This innermost circle seemed the only thing they could depend on, and for years after surrender, these bonds remained important for everyone, including thieves. This pragmatic reliance on family became another part of the ideal of the lost South. Family and neighborhood loyalty was elevated as a cardinal virtue of a vanishing world.

Every nuance of this southern myth was contrasted to the North and its people. If southerners were said to have fought with an individual flair and lived by a chivalrous code, the North was plodding ahead, machinelike, toward a future of factories and dollar chasers. Southern dedication to family and a close radius of neighbors was giving way to a faceless mass culture. The James brothers, as southern heroes, were created as exemplars of the good side of these paired opposites. The Jameses and Youngers were not thieving killers but gallant banditti striking out against powerful alien institutions—railroads and banks. They embodied a doomed romance, fierce localism, and familial loyalty thought to be under siege from corrupt and soulless authority. And their enemies helped. The Pinkerton raid could not have been better designed to show this new American order—faceless, mechanistic, unfeeling—brutally assaulting an older decency and innocence.

Of course, not all Missourians saw things that way. The James myth had an enormous visceral appeal. It was like a shouted taunt across a bitter divide. Opinions on the other side were just as passionate. To Union veterans and supporters of Reconstruction, Confederate guerrillas were not Arthurian knights but traitorous bushwhackers and cowardly renegades. Farmers who resisted development were deadweight on a nation straining toward greatness. Close-knit and clannish settlers were scorned as lazy rubes and inbred, ignorant sluggards.

In the North a minor genre of books and articles blended comedy with a withering critique of the southern border. In 1867 a northern tourist, riding through northwestern Arkansas just south of the Missouri line, met a man in a collapsing cabin who was flabbergasted to learn that Lincoln had been dead two years. "I asked him if the Arkansas Legislature had met during the winter," the visitor recalled. "He did not know, but was certain they had not met in his neighborhood." The experience led the Yankee to comment on the typical "sallow-faced, stoop-shouldered, lank, long-haired, angular and awkward" southerner in the backwoods borderland:

> What does the "native" before-mentioned care for education, so long as he can get along without it? Nature has saved him the trouble of brain or hand labor. . . . There are places where men do not live in any true or exalted sense; they simply vegetate as do the beets and carrots, lifting their heads it is true into the air and light of heaven, but rooted all the while to the sordid earth.[19]

The northern press mocked the crime wave blamed on the gang. The Chicago *Tribune* thought that the thefts and murders "are a disgrace to [Missouri], and argue a degree of inefficiency or cowardice upon the part of the state authorities." A Pittsburgh paper dubbed Missouri "the bandit state," where "notorious robbers and cut-throats" operated virtually at will.[20] Boosters warned that Missouri would never move ahead if weighed down by this reputation. When the prominent reformer Carl Schurz ran for reelection to the U.S. Senate in 1874, he argued that until the criminals were caught, ambitious immigrants would avoid Missouri, capital would flow elsewhere, and property values would drop steadily. The future would sour. All this, of course, echoed the gibes of easterners. Incompetent government and killers running loose—what else could one expect from snoozing primitives in the land of the Beet People?

Originally, the James myth found its power in the crackling tension between these sets of views. In the waning months of Reconstruction, the gang suddenly moved to the center of this impassioned conflict over current politics and the past and future meanings of the South. In March 1875 the Missouri legislature considered a joint resolution that would have granted the James and Younger brothers full amnesty and pardon for anything done during the war and guaranteed special protection and fair trials on all postwar accusations. As guerrillas, the brothers had "gallantly periled their lives and their all in defense of their principles."[21] They had tried to put war behind them, but government accusations had driven them from honest toil into hiding. The resolution hinted darkly that robberies and murders might have been done by the very officials who leveled the charges at the gang and then by "arm[ed] foreign mercenaries [Pinkerton detectives] with power to capture and kill." Jesse and Frank, in any case, were models of southern manhood: "too brave to be mean, too generous to be revengeful, and too gallant and honorable to betray a friend or break a promise."[22] Missouri should pursue the true culprits and return these wronged citizens to the bosom of family and neighbors.

The resolution would have made the James legend a legislative dictate. Within its overripe rhetoric we can see Americans still looking across the deep divide of North and South. It reveals plenty about both Reconstruction America and the popular culture of banditry. And it almost passed. A strong majority of fifty-eight to thirty-nine supported it, but a joint resolution required a two-thirds vote, so it remains a historical footnote.

The first stage of the James myth had reached its high point. At this moment, Jesse's image was of a gallant cavalier—chivalrous and bold, southern virtue saddled up and ready to ride. It had no appeal outside the region and, in fact, drew whistles and applause by flicking its chin at anyone outside the Confederacy. But that would soon change. Americans were leaving the Reconstruction era for an age of new divisions. New tensions were felt and new heroes were needed to act them out. The mythic Jesse James would ride out of the South, across boundaries of history and myth, and find his place as a national legend.

Jesse resumed his criminal career on October 8, 1879, more than three years after the Northfield raid, with the robbery of a Chicago and Alton train at Glendale, Missouri. The method and style of the robbery—locals taken and held at a station, the train stopped by an agent's signal, the express safe looted—were so familiar that the boys were immediately suspected. Sometime during the previous months Jesse apparently had decided to return to his earlier enterprise, though Frank decided to stay in Tennessee. The gang at Glendale included a collection of new faces: Tucker Bassham, James A. "Dick" Liddl, William Ryan, Robert

Woodson "Wood" Hite, and Ed Miller, whose brother Clell had died at Northfield.

The James saga ran its rapid final course over the next two and a half years. Something important yet diffuse seems to have happened with Jesse during the break in the action after Northfield. The pattern of crimes after 1879 differed in a few crucial ways. Previous robberies had been scattered from Minnesota to West Virginia, but now they were concentrated in a small radius close to the gang's home turf. Although the gang had not shied from violence before, these crimes were especially brutal and reckless. The focus and tone suggested a conscious carelessness, a "catch me" fatalism. Perhaps the bloodbath at Northfield turned Jesse and Frank into harder men. Maybe they spent the next years recognizing what they were and where they were headed.

The brothers also may have sensed the changing times. With the first easing of postwar passions, their supportive climate of opinion began to dissipate. The claim that robberies and murders were somehow defenses against Yankee persecution was wearing thin. Republicans kept ridiculing the Democratic administration for failing to catch the culprits and "for permitting a Republican state [Minnesota] to perform that duty."[23] Especially after the nasty depression of 1877 the repeated charge that this ineptitude "prevented immigration . . . , the introduction of capital and the growth and development of industries" bothered Missourians who hoped to join the march toward industry and progress.[24] These included Governor Thomas T. Crittenden, a Unionist Democrat with close ties to railroads and business leaders. Except for a few editors and, of course, John Edwards, press support for the James brothers cooled. Many journalists now demanded the crimes be stopped.

In this shifting mood, the next robbery had an especially wrenching effect. On the night of July 15, 1881, several bandits bought tickets on a Chicago, Rock Island, and Pacific train heading east from Kansas City. Not far outside the small town of Winston, one of them, dressed in a duster, rose from his seat, pulled a revolver, and shot the conductor in the back, then fired again as the dying man fell out the door. A couple of others joined the killer in firing around the car, fatally wounding an aging railroad employee named Frank McMillan. After throttling an agent, the

men rifled the express safe and fled. Missourians in general were not easily shocked, but the viciousness of this crime aroused a widespread outrage, and although Zarelda Samuel and Edwards made the usual denials,
the James brothers were widely accused. Frank probably was along this
time, as well as Dick Liddl, Wood Hite, and his brother, Clarence.

In the national uproar, with papers such as the Chicago *Tribune* calling Missouri "The Outlaw's Paradise," Governor Crittenden persuaded
railroad and express officials to offer substantial rewards for information
on the James brothers.[25] The local press admitted the criminals were an
embarrassment, and old-line Democrats, who had looked benignly on
earlier crimes (like "a medieval saint upon the sins of his devotees," Crittenden later wrote), were quiet and cowed.[26] The general response in the
weeks after the bloody robbery was startlingly different from the mood a
few years earlier.

Then, astonishingly, the gang struck again. On September 7, five years
to the day after Northfield, bandits stopped a train at Blue Cut, just east
of Independence. After pistol-whipping an agent, they terrorized and
robbed almost one hundred passengers. As wallets and watches were
taken, the tall, dark-bearded leader of the thieves, who fit closely the description of the killer in the previous robbery, strode down the aisles. He
was Jesse James, he bellowed, and he was taking vengeance on the railroad
for its offer of a bounty. After a bit of familiar flamboyance—the leader
threatened to kill the engineer, but in the end called him brave and gave
him two dollars to buy a drink—the bandits took their leave.

Crittenden deplored this "foul stain" on the state's reputation and
called on all honest Missourians to lend a hand in catching or exterminat-
ing the culprits.[27] More and more of the public agreed. Even the Missouri
convention of Confederate veterans commended the governor and called
for a return of law and order to the state. In fact, supporters much closer
to Jesse and Frank were starting to fall away. Shortly after the last crime,
William Ryan, a gang member arrested several months earlier, went on
trial for helping with the Glendale train robbery. His prime accuser was
Tucker Bassham, who had pleaded guilty to the same crime the previous
year. Now, pardoned by Crittenden and pressed by the aggressive Jackson

County prosecutor, William Wallace, Bassham told the court a detailed account of the robbery he swore was led by Jesse James. The jury sent Ryan to the penitentiary for twenty-five years.

Other, even wider cracks were appearing within the group. Ed Miller vanished, and it was generally suspected that Jesse had killed him, fearing Miller would follow Bassham in trading a confession for freedom. Three local farm boys, who were lesser lights of the gang, were arrested for the Winston robbery. Greater trouble was brewing much closer to the circle's center. The revived gang included another set of brothers, Wood and Clarence Hite, who were also cousins of Jesse and Frank. Wood and fellow gang member, Dick Liddl, apparently were rivals for the same woman's affections, and in the fall of 1881 Liddl and a companion beat and shot Wood Hite to death in the woman's house. Here was a touchy situation. In one act Liddl had killed a criminal compatriot and, much worse, had violated the sacred sanctum of border culture—the family. It was time for another line of work.

Liddl secretly surrendered in late January 1882, and authorities quickly put to use the information he spilled. When Clarence Hite was arrested soon afterward and confronted with the mounting evidence, he pleaded guilty and took a twenty-five-year sentence. The web of complicity was rapidly unraveling, and before long, the authorities followed the strands to the central characters in the drama. The end came at the hands of yet another insider who was lured by advantage and by fear for his own life. Liddl had murdered Jesse's cousin Wood Hite with an accomplice, a fresh-faced new addition to the gang named Robert Ford.

Ford and his brother, Charlie, had taken part in the last train robbery, though Robert himself did little more than watch the horses. Sometime in early 1882 they had made contact with authorities. Turning on Jesse had a triple appeal: they would escape his wrath; they could win pardon for their crimes; and they might walk away with the $10,000 offered for Jesse's capture or death. Jesse was living with Zee and their children in a cottage in St. Joseph, invisible as always even in this city close to his home base. As the gang was dying of internal hemorrhaging, Charlie and Bob were living with Jesse. Either they had won his confidence, or he distrusted them and wanted to keep them close. With a few remaining cohorts scattered around the vicinity, the three were planning a bank robbery in nearby Platte City.

The final moment of Jesse's life would become one of the most familiar in American folklore. On the morning of April 3, 1882, the day before the scheduled robbery, Jesse, Bob, and Charlie rose from the breakfast table and entered the living room. The day was warm and Jesse removed his coat, then his gun belt with two revolvers, and laid them on a bed. He noted that a favorite picture on the wall—by later tellings it was a likeness of his mother, but in fact it was a race horse—had gathered dust. Standing on a chair, he reached to straighten and clean the picture, turning his back on the Fords. Bob and Charlie edged between Jesse and his guns, drew their own, and fired. Bob was faster, and his bullet tore into the back of his target's head. Without a cry, Jesse James fell to the floor in a pool of blood. Within seconds he was dead. Zee ran to his side, screaming in fury and grief, as the Fords bolted from the house to spread the boast that they had killed America's most famous outlaw.

The James brothers had remained so anonymous that it was several days before authorities could say for sure that the corpse on the floor was Jesse's. Doubts continued, in keeping with heroic tradition, and stories still circulate about the "real Jesse" living to a ripe age and obscure death in this hollow or on that farm. The murdered body of 1882, well verified by its chest wounds and cropped middle finger, was buried on the Samuel place.

Frank surrendered the following October. His only trial was for the murder of Frank McMillan, the elderly employee shot during the Winston robbery. The only direct word against him came from Liddl, a highly compromised witness, and the jury quickly set Frank free. All other charges were dismissed or dropped. For the next thirty years Frank flitted from job to job. He came up short in the Democratic caucus vote for doorkeeper in Missouri's lower house, but he did work as doorman of a St. Louis burlesque house. He dropped the starting flag for horse races at dozens of county fairs. He died in 1915 at age seventy-two on the Samuel family farm. Frank had kept his distance from the myth, condemning the dime novels and curtain-chewing stage productions about the gang, but he did spend the 1903 season with the James-Younger Wild West Show. Before riding in the final parade of each performance, he would play a silent role in vignette, sitting in a stagecoach as it was robbed.

Convicted of murder, Bob Ford was immediately pardoned and given an undisclosed reward by Crittenden. Bob toured in a melodrama built around Jesse's demise, though, by some accounts, audiences came mainly to jeer and throw food. As his moment of fame faded, Bob turned enthusiastically to drink. He was shot to death in his Creede, Colorado, saloon in 1892, six years after brother Charlie committed suicide. Bob Younger died in prison of tuberculosis, but Jim and Cole were paroled in 1901. Jim killed himself soon afterward, asserting in his suicide note that he died a socialist and advocate of women's rights. Cole sold tombstones, traveled with a Wild West show described by one editor as "the poorest ever seen in our city," wrote an autobiography, gained considerable weight, endorsed Prohibition, and frequently delivered a canned lecture titled "Crime Does Not Pay." He died in 1916.

Zee James lived quietly with her children until her death in 1900. She never acknowledged any crime on the part of her husband. Mary grew up to live inconspicuously with her farmer husband near her father's resting place. Jesse Edwards James eventually turned to lawyering after writing *Jesse James, My Father* and being acquitted of train robbery in 1898. His grandmother, Zarelda, provided his alibi. Since Jesse's death, Zarelda had been charging twenty-five cents for a tour of the farm and her son's gravesite, complete with her tearful memories, assurances of her boys' innocence, and rages against the family's tormentors. Stones from the grave were available for a fee. The supply seemed limitless. In 1902, nine years before her death, Zarelda reburied Jesse's remains in nearby Kearney beneath an eight-foot marble monument. Thirty years later the shaft had vanished, chipped and carried away, shard by shard, by admirers and relic collectors.

By then a long shelf of books had appeared. The earliest, such as John Newman Edwards's *Noted Guerillas* (1877), defended Jesse and Frank as noble and persecuted Confederates driven from honorable lives. A spate of new titles hit the market with the gang's return to crime. Most were admiring, but all recognized that Jesse and Frank were the men behind some or all of the robberies and killings. News of Jesse's assassination brought more publications, these with titles referring to his "tragic" and "treacherous" death. One company alone produced nine titles. Dozens of dime novels fed a hungry national audience.

Not everyone was happy with this attention. Stage dramas with lurid versions of the gang's exploits were especially criticized. Twenty years after Jesse's killing, one critic went so far as to seek a court order to stop performances of *The James Boys of Missouri*. It was a question of morality, he said: "The dad-binged play glorifies these outlaws and makes heroes of them. That's the main thing I object to. It's injurious to the youth of the country. . . . What will be the effect upon these young men to see the acts of a train robber and outlaw glorified?"[28] The critic was Frank James.

Frank was asking an excellent question and implying another: why have Americans given such attention to a man who was, by any fair reading, a persistent and unrepentant criminal? In the famous folksong about Jesse's death, Bob Ford is scorned as "that dirty little coward that shot Mr. Howard." The man he killed, who hid behind the Howard alias, had a hand in murdering at least four unarmed persons, shooting one in the back and slitting another's throat. "Jesse stole from the rich and gave to the poor," the song continues, but when he was killed, he was wearing a watch taken from a middling stage passenger. A search of the premises found horses, saddles, and a cache of items lifted in petty thefts from farmers and clerks. He never admitted the slightest crime, though a mountain of evidence made him a liar. He would not come in, he said, because political authorities would deny him a fair trial—this in a state whose legislative majority formally declared that it thought him innocent. Jesse is soberly described as unconcerned with mere money, an openhanded, straight-talking man who asked only the same from others. Yet while living under a false name in Kentucky, accused of nearly a dozen major robberies, he sued a neighbor for $56, indignantly claiming the man had made deceitful statements and "acted to injure my credit."

Americans of course have not admired the Jesse James of fact—a lying, murderous, thieving hypocrite. They have invented and celebrated a character who fits the peculiar needs of their time. Jesse certainly helped create his own legend. His gifts at evading capture were impressive, and his criminal theatrics bordered on the brilliant. Flagging down trains, piling rocks on the tracks, seizing stations, galloping boldly out of towns as bank clerks stood with their eyes wide and their pockets empty—the gang's style seemed scripted for dime novels and movies. As thieves go, he was pretty successful. His total take came to about $100,000, or nearly $2,000,000 by 2009 currency standards—an average of $140,000 per crime. Personally, based on what can be said for sure, Jesse apparently had that mix of likability and menace found in other outlaw heroes.

And he was very lucky. Countless times he slipped free from pursuers by turns of fortune. He was helped by his enemies' bungles and by supportive writers who knew how to touch a public nerve. Luck's greatest gift, mythically speaking, was Jesse's death. Just as he was facing capture and the ignominy of prison, just as he was about to become ordinary, he was shot in the back by a turncoat friend. The story of the powerful hero undone through betrayal has fed mythic traditions for millennia. Americans needed their own Caesar and Brutus (or Christ and Judas). Jesse and Bob Ford answered the call.

Jesse James died as he lived: with perfect timing. The James brothers rose to prominence when southerners, stinging from defeat, needed heroes who spoke for their lingering resistance and shaken pride. The gang's image of honor, dash, and adventurous independence fit the emerging cavalier tradition of the Old South, and their victims and enemies, the banks, the railroads, and the Pinkerton agency, were perfect foils in those angry years of Reconstruction. That appeal, however, could never reach beyond the former Confederacy, and when Jesse and Frank resurfaced after the Northfield fiasco, the climate feeding the early legend was fading badly.

But just then another possibility was opening. America's transformation to a modern industrial state—increasingly urbanized, knit together by new technologies, and dominated by corporate power—generated new tensions. As Americans passed from an era of sectional hatred to an age of harsh class division, they looked again for popular figures to act out their anxieties.

And once again Jesse's timing and luck held. Most themes of his first incarnation transferred nicely to the present. Was there resentment throughout the nation toward powerful distant forces controlling every-day lives? The gang's prime targets, railroads and banks, became to many the villainous manipulators of the new America. Pinkerton detectives, seen earlier as Yankee goons, now were pictured as corporate shock troops sent against honest workers in every region. The boys' devotion to mother and home jibed nicely with the late Victorian worship of the hearth as a sacred refuge in a corrupt world. Class divisions were deepening, and the gap was widening between rich and poor—the perfect setting for Jesse's Robin Hood image. It looked as if the James gang could be retooled easily for a national constituency of discontent.

But there was a problem. The original mythic Jesse had fought to de-stroy the sacred Union. Before he could claim to be a national hero, that part of his image had to be obscured. This turned out to be fairly easy. The James brothers, after all, had always lived on the border, with frequent forays into Kansas, Indian Territory, and Texas. The James legend could survive the crossing of the chronological boundary into modern, class-ridden America by stepping over another border, that of regional identity. By shifting the angle of vision only slightly, Jesse the Confederate raider emerged as someone else. He became a westerner.

This transformation could move ahead smoothly once Jesse James was dead and no longer confusing matters by hurting actual people. Frank Triplett's *The Life, Times, and Treacherous Death of Jesse James* (1882) was in the shops only a few weeks after the assassination. Triplett spent barely twenty pages on the war, and even there he wrote that Jesse and the guer-rillas combined "the infinite physical endurance of the Western Indian and the indomitable soul and mental qualities of the Anglo-Norman." Elsewhere, he called the gang "Anglo-Norman Comanches."[29] Jesse the Confederate was blurring away. Coming into focus was a character made from the most familiar formula in our national mythology. The best of blue-eyed Europe (the "Anglo-Norman") was joined with the finest "savage" traits (the Indian's prowess and nobility) to produce a unique and superior blend—the American. From Daniel Boone and Deerslayer through countless characters in movies and novels, this fusion of civilized and primitive virtues has stood tall in the American pantheon. In one sense these heroes are regional, but in another they are national. They might live in the West, but to many they are ideal composites, the best of a common American soul.

At the same time, Jesse brought with him selected virtues from his southern past. As Americans pulled further away from the war, they looked back and saw much to like in the Old South, especially its newly romanticized version. Several traits would be grafted onto the traditional western hero, most obviously in Owen Wister's *The Virginian*, the proto-type of the modern western novel. The title character took the southern gentleman's civility and sense of honor and dressed them in chaps and boots. His famous showdown with Trampas is a Deep South duel mi-grated to a dusty western street.

Jesse James was the earliest instance of this southern intrusion into the western myth. From then on, the western hero's character displayed what were considered the best characteristics of an idealized South: an easier pace of life, an inner-directedness, an insistence on respect (the Virgin-ian's "When you call me that, smile"), and a code that placed loyalty and principle over profit and practicality. Even the hero's speech changed. The rambling monologues of Leatherstocking and other backwoods blabber-mouths gave way to the slow drawl, the "Yup," and the "Howdy, ma'am." All this stood in defiance of what many feared in the new America: a driven, regimented, colorless culture of wage slaves and indebted farm-ers who labored under the yoke of distant money-grubbers and paid-for politicians.

Jesse has played one variation of the western myth, the dashing but doomed outlaw who refuses to kneel to autocrats and bullies. Cut loose from the Confederacy, he has roamed the American nation and con-sciousness. In dime novels it was not only *Jesse James in New York; or, A Plot to Kidnap Jay Gould* (1890), but also *The James Boys in Deadwood; or, The Game Pair of Dakota* (1891) and *Jesse James at Coney Island; or, The Wall Street Banker's Secret* (1898). On the silver screen Henry King's *Jesse James* (1939) was a Depression-era morality tale that anticipated *The Grapes of Wrath* (1940), with Frank and Jesse driven to crime when callous rail-road officials force the honest farmers off their land. During the anti-establishment mood of the 1960s and 1970s, the Frank and Jesse of such movies as *The Great Northfield Minnesota Raid* (1972) do not specifically go to war against moneyed power. As in *Butch Cassidy and the Sundance Kid* (1969), the bandits are likable misfits finally crushed by a stifling social order.

Westerner and southerner, victim and avenger, ruthless killer and defender of the weak, Confederate raider and Robin Hood, the bandit king has negotiated artfully many boundaries of the American experience. Like so many mythic heroes who seem to know when to die, Jesse James is a survivor, and he shows no sign of going away.

Notes

An earlier version of this chapter appeared as "Jesse James, Borderman," in *With Badges and Bullets: Lawmen and Outlaws in the Old West*, ed. Richard W. Etulain and Glenda Riley (Golden, Colo.: Fulcrum Press, 1999).

1. William A. Settle, Jr., *Jesse James Was His Name* (Lincoln: University of Nebraska Press, 1977), 191, 105, 125.

2. Ibid., 168, 124; T. J. Stiles, *Jesse James: Last Rebel of the Civil War* (New York: Alfred A. Knopf, 2002), 260.

3. Settle, *Jesse James Was His* Name, 125.

4. James William Buel, *The Border Outlaws* (St. Louis: Historical Publishing Co., 1881); James William Buel, *The Border Bandits* (St. Louis: Historical Publishing Co., 1881); Lige Mitchell, *Daring Exploits of Jesse James and His Band of Border Train and Bank Robbers; Containing Also Some Desperate Adventures of the Dalton Brothers* (Baltimore: I. & M. Ottenheimer, 1914).

5. Frederick Jackson Turner, *The Frontier in American History* (New York: Henry Holt & Co., 1921), 3, 33n.

6. The best of the many books on James is Stiles, *Jesse James*. Others of value are Settle, *Jesse James Was His Name*, and Marley Brant, *Jesse James: The Man and the Myth* (New York: Berkeley Books, 1998). A popular but highly fictionalized account is Robertus Love, *The Rise and Fall of Jesse James* (New York: G. P. Putnam's Sons, 1926).

7. Robert Dyer, *Jesse James and the Civil War in Missouri* (Columbia: University of Missouri Press, 1994).

8. Stiles, *Jesse James*, 88–91. In other accounts Dr. Samuel did not betray Frank's whereabouts.

9. Brant, *Jesse James*, 37.

10. Stiles, *Jesse James*, 151–54; Settle, *Jesse James Was His Name*, 30–31.

11. Love, *Rise and Fall of Jesse James*, 99.

12. Settle, *Jesse James Was His Name*, 59.

13. Stiles, *Jesse James*, 281–85; Settle, *Jesse James Was His Name*, 76–78.

14. Settle, *Jesse James Was His Name*, 89.

15. Brant, *Jesse James,* 78.

16. Settle, *Jesse James Was His* Name, 45.

17. Ibid.

18. Ibid.

19. Wilson Nicely, *The Great Southwest, or Plain Guide for Emigrants and Capitalists, Embracing a Description of the States of Missouri and Kansas . . .* (St. Louis: R. B. Studley & Co., 1867), 101–102.

20. Settle, *Jesse James Was His Name,* 63.

21. Ibid., 81.

22. Ibid.

23. Ibid., 106.

24. Ibid.

25. Ibid., 109.

26. Ibid., 111.

27. Ibid., 112.

28. Ibid., 176.

29. Frank Triplett, *The Life, Times, and Treacherous Death of Jesse James* (St. Louis: J. H. Chambers & Co., 1882), 17, 28.

12

American Pathways

Trails haunt the American memory. They run through our songs and folktales. We walk them in our movies and follow them to the horizon in countless paintings. We especially celebrate them as our history. The Oregon, Santa Fe, and Lewis and Clark Trails are marked along our highways. So is the Trail of Tears. Surviving ruts, once a bane to local farmers, are lovingly preserved so visitors can behold them and wonder how many thousands of wheels it took to leave such scars. Every year born-too-late pioneers follow stretches of these old paths across the West, some of them staying at some Wagon Trail Motel or Trails West Dude Ranch. As they motor along modern highways in parallel to tracks of westering emigrants, they might find themselves humming Roy Rogers's "Happy Trails to You."

Such stubborn echoes are almost certainly trying to tell us something. Trails speak of an intimate relationship with us, both as humans and as Americans. To understand what they might have to say, we might think of a trail in each of three senses: a mark on the land, a word, and a mythic experience.

Begin by literally looking at a trail as a physical artifact that is part of the land itself. Something as simple as an eroded line draws our attention and holds it stubbornly. Part of the reason has to do with our human compulsion to connect ourselves to a collective memory. To feed that need, we look for physical residues of the past, things to see and touch as a prompt to jump backward in our imaginations. We gently handle family photographs and brooches. On family vacations we visit Mount Vernon, Gettysburg, or the Little Bighorn and devote five-minute pullovers to reading historical markers that root us briefly in the past as it lives in particular places: Colonel Whoever surrendered fifty yards north of this spot; in this farmhouse the poet What's-Her-Name wrote her "Ode to Something"; right here that dastardly You-Know-Who was hanged by the neck until dead, dead, dead.

Something about mementos and markers, however, is unsatisfying. Each represents a place and point in time that is anchored and frozen, and at some level of our minds we know that such a spot and moment cannot give us what we call history. Consciously or not, we know that history is more than buildings, battlefields, episodes, and dead people. History is all of those things set in motion over time and related to each other in a way that makes sense to us and engages our imagination. History, that is, is story.

A trail has one thing going for it that those other artifacts do not. We can stand and look in two directions. We see a trail coming and going. It is a physical sign, not of a frozen moment or of an event, but of a fluid process. It looks like history in a way that a building, no matter how well reconstructed, never can.

This bit of physical history also invites us to take part in it with a sense of completeness that other sites cannot. We can hike around Gettysburg, but the battlefield is far beyond any person's ability to grasp experientially; try as we might, we cannot trick ourselves into feeling the event's full sprawl. And Gettysburg was still a single event covering only three hot July days. Setting the battle in its larger story is an intellectual exercise, not an emotive one.

But if we walk a trail, even for only an hour, we can participate vicariously both in the event and the larger process. A trail is simple and literally straightforward. With a beginning, a middle, and an end, it is almost a spare and simple story in itself. Walking it seems a reiteration of the past much closer to the full original than tramping Gettysburg or touring Independence Hall. Something in this combination of simplicity and imaginative fullness calls us powerfully to step into the lives of the long dead.

Moving on a path made by others in fact can pull us into history as deep and ancient as our humanity. The oldest marks on the planet left by the earliest of our kind are in Tanzania, in eastern Africa. They were made 3.6 million years ago by *Australopithecus afarensis,* an upright hominid about four and a half feet tall, one of the first sprigs on the evolutionary bush that eventually sprouted *Homo sapiens.* The string of footprints were pressed into volcanic ash, turned to stone, and found in 1978 by a team of archaeologists.[1] Two sets of prints show adults, probably a male and female, walking in tandem at a steady and deliberate pace. At one point the female pauses and turns to her left, as if looking for something. A closer look reveals a smaller set of prints. This third figure has followed the male and carefully planted each step in the larger footprint just ahead.

Surely few can help but be struck by the humanness implied in the scene. We imagine this trio, a family perhaps, moving over the landscape. Maybe they are fleeing the volcanic eruption, maybe walking about for food or shifting with the seasons, or maybe taking a longer journey. The woman and man make their way through the dimness of settling ash and sulfurous mist, their attention divided between their destination and the danger and opportunity around them. Another—a son or brother?—is right behind. Perhaps he is excited to be on the move, perhaps frightened by the mountain's rumbling, and so he engages in a game most have played while tagging behind a parent or older sibling on a beach or vacant lot. He stretches to match the stride of the man ahead, playing grown-up, imagining a larger world.

This is the rankest speculation, of course—which is exactly the point. Besides the fact of three hominids walking, we know nothing about what was happening, yet the thought of footsteps following one another instantly and irresistibly engages our imagination. Like all trails, this one implies a story. That story's cues, elemental and simple, call us to picture ourselves in it. Human paths bind us together, even across the unthinkable chasm between that line of nearly four-million-year-old steps and today.

The same can be said of every trail, including the far more recent ones across Nebraska, New Mexico, Utah, or Montana. We look, and we feel the invitation to follow the line and live the story. Adding to the power of the western trails is the fact that we know something about them. We know that the mothers, fathers, and children who walked these lines across North America in the 1840s or 1860s were doing something remarkable, and that knowledge sharpens the other appealing elements— the resemblance to history, the simplicity, the call to human memory.

Such a trail elevates the commonplace to the extraordinary—and takes us with it. By following a line over the land, in our minds or on the ground, we connect with men and women more or less like us who found in themselves what it took to accomplish something close to epic, and they did it by acting out the perfect metaphor for the way each of us makes it through every day: by putting one foot in front of the other.

But, as usual, one sort of understanding leads to more questions. If trails by their nature call out a universal storytelling urge and join us with humans of all times and places, why do they seem to mean more to Americans than to others? The question here is not about the physical artifact but to the term we apply to it. Why the appeal of "trail" as a word?

In earlier vernaculars east of the Mississippi, a route created by Euro-Americans was a *road,* like the Wilderness Road Daniel Boone blazed across the Appalachians.[2] A *path* was an older way through the land laid down by migrating animals or Indians on the move, such as the Warrior's Path that Boone preempted to make the Wilderness Road into Kentucky. Whites did not make paths; like the hero of James Fenimore Cooper's *The Pathfinder,* they searched for and used the old work of others. "Path" was synonymous with "trace," the word for another invaluable gift that pioneers used to penetrate the otherwise impassable. In time it became the favored term for westward routes commandeered and renamed— Zane's Trace, from Zanesville, Ohio, to the Ohio River; and the Natchez Trace, the infamous "devil's backbone" from Nashville, Tennessee, to the grogshops of Natchez-under-the-Hill.[3]

"Trail" appeared late. In England it was something dragged behind or a mark or scent left by an animal. It was ephemeral. Here, however, it came to be another old and enduring track through otherwise treacherous and disorienting terrain, a variation of "path" and "trace." An English writer in 1835 had to explain to his readers: "A trail, I must tell you, is an Indian footpath that has been traveled perhaps for centuries."[4] A trail's relationship to white pioneers was passive, and so the word lacked its later dramatic feel. There is nothing heroic about following a well-worn groove laid down by others.

As advancing settlement crossed the Mississippi, "trace" faded quickly from common use. "Path" survived as a general term but was never used to name some prominent way west. Instead, "trail" emerged as the favorite. By the 1830s it was the word of choice in travel books by Washington Irving and Josiah Gregg. Still, its basic meaning referred to a route laid down much earlier. It was usually assumed, incorrectly, that trails began with the "wonderful sagacity" and "traditionary knowledge" of restless animals, especially bison, that found the easiest way across wild terrain.[5] A passage created by whites was still a *road*. A *trail* remained an old topographical artifact that pioneers dropped into and followed.

Then, early in the twentieth century, "trail" underwent a change, modest on its face, that profoundly altered its place in the American language and consciousness. Now the word was applied to routes made by the pioneers themselves, and not simply made but made heroically, at great risk and with a dreaming courage. Long after the last emigrants had walked them and called them roads, westward routes became trails and typically were fused with images of a quest. Jim Bridger nosed through this mountain pass; the California-bound Bidwell party first pushed across this desert stretch; John Bozeman marked this passage to the Montana goldfields. Trail as artifact and "trail" as word were converging and being imbued with larger meanings of westering and the American past. With that, "trail" was taking on its third sense—a mythic experience.

It happened during a development familiar to every American historian. Around 1900 Americans felt a crisis of identity. The United States was growing into greatness, a nation of robust industry, vibrant cities, a huge domain rich in resources, and deepening international respect. And yet these very advances seemed to threaten the national character. The virtues of individualism and self-reliance seemed compromised in a world of corporate power and urban throngs. New sorts of immigrants brought customs that jangled against older traditions. Taking part in world relations might erode our uniqueness. Rarely had national pride and national apprehension been more garbled.

Out of this wrenching national transition a story emerged that summed up this conflicted mood of mastery and doubt. That story was westward expansion. It spoke most obviously to the nation's pride. A brave and tenacious people had struggled and won the makings of an empire. Out of the struggle a distinctive American character was born as well—individualistic, democratic, resourceful, and determined. But just below the surface was a darker message. By 1900 the creative conquest was basically finished, and since our superior nature had been born of that struggle, winning it, paradoxically, seem to threaten the very essence of our hard-won collective greatness. Had America reached the outer limit of its promise and entered a time of contracting power, the Age of Dwindle? What would happen to those virtues born of pioneering once pioneering was over? Could we count on keeping the American character in a century of cities, time clocks, corporate kingpins, and immigrants who never knew a homestead? This national myth and its doubts have persisted through the twentieth century, and they show no sign of fading in the twenty-first. Always, the myth cuts both ways. It celebrates American accomplishments and spirit; it constantly measures how far we have slid from standards and virtues of the past.

An evolving American language embedded this story in new words, or rather old words given new meanings. The word historians have most recognized in this mythic vocabulary is "frontier." In England and Europe it referred to a boundary, typically between nations. Over here it came to mean the outer rim of expanding settlement—that moving zone where American virtue supposedly was forged. It thrummed with mythic implications. It suggested adventure, heroism, sacrifice, innovation, boldness. This connotation made "frontier" useful in selling everything from sports gear and cosmetics to airline tickets and a New England president's political program.

The myth and the word, however, shared a serious problem. They were diffuse and vague. The story seemed to be all over the place, on cattle ranches and in mining camps, at military posts and isolated homesteads. "Frontier" summoned up a series of potent but diverse images from the myth. A lone cowboy on horseback embodied rugged independence. A mounted Indian stood for the wild land's threat; exhausted and downtrodden, he denoted the pioneer's victory over a noble opponent. A weathered mother holding her child in front of a sod house stood for courage, perseverance, and domestic virtue transplanted. Still, each of these scattershot symbols could capture only part of the myth and its implications.

In one chapter of westward expansion, however, the frontier idea could find its focus. The overland trek of explorers and settlers had all the essentials—testing and danger and sacrifice, all arranged so that the stages of the journey and the story of transformation meshed simply and perfectly. Explorers stare at the riverbank for signs of grizzlies and Blackfeet. Men trudge beside wagons that roll slowly over an arid plain. Devastated parents stand beside a child's grave. After straining over mountain passes and down narrow canyons, a family arrives, bone weary but hardened, in a valley of tall trees and soft grasses.

Particular images along a well-defined path build neatly toward a clear destination both geographical and moral. The scattered experiences of the westering myth are distilled into the ordeal of passage. The lessons—courage triumphant, individualism confirmed, perseverance rewarded—are summed up by the end of a thousand-mile walk. An emerging national myth was calling on the supreme advantages of the trail as artifact: its resemblance to history, a simplicity that nonetheless allows a feeling of a process fully experienced, the trail's linear articulation of a story that starts and moves along and finishes, and its strong pull on the human imagination.

The result was an American version of a universal pattern. World cultures abound with mythic traditions that rely on journeys to sum up their meanings and to keep beliefs alive and vigorous. In Islam the pilgrimage to Mecca, the hajj, is both a duty and a spiritual participation in the Prophet's path toward divine connection. Christian pilgrimages similarly join sacrifice and commitment with the practice of the faith's virtues, all by following a prescribed line over the land. Hopi men annually walk an ancient path to gather salt from the floor of the Grand Canyon, stopping to commune with gods to keep their world's order finely tuned.[6] In a favorite American version, Dorothy and friends follow the yellow brick road through many ordeals and discover in themselves virtues we much admire: compassion, courage, intelligence, and simple wisdom ("There's no place like home"). Early in the twentieth century a national version of this universal impulse took form. The frontier myth found its focus in images of its central characters moving as a column along a destined road.

The earliest example is in the most famous declaration of the frontier's magic, Frederick Jackson Turner's "The Significance of the Frontier in American History." It is an essay about lines. Mostly Turner writes of the north-south line that formed a broad front and moved steadily into the continent from the Atlantic toward the Pacific. This advancing longitude was the frontier, and the stress and ferment along it, Turner argues, forged our unique institutions and character. But the frontier is difficult to picture. Turner claims that this "elastic" term "does not need sharp definition."[7] Maybe not for him, but the rest of us want something concrete, and Turner tries to give it. He uses metaphors from the natural world like "wave" and notes how the frontier lay successively along "natural boundary lines"—the Allegheny Mountains, the Mississippi River, the 99th meridian ("the line of arid lands"), and the Rocky Mountains.[8] Still, we cannot quite see it. The nether rim of civilization, the receding gift of free land, nature's savage edge: what in the world did that look like?

Then, several pages into the essay, Turner takes the frontier line, gives it a quarter turn, and sets it down east to west. Immediately it is a trail. Turner invites us to watch the action: "Stand at Cumberland Gap and watch the process of civilization, marching single-file—the buffalo following the trail to the salt springs, the Indian, the fur-trader and hunter, the cattle-raiser, the pioneer farmer—and the frontier has passed by. Stand at South Pass in the Rockies a century later and see the same procession with wider intervals between."[9] The vague "process" of the first sentence becomes something concrete and vivid—namely, the "procession" of the second, people and animals following one another along a beaten way. A fuzzy idea takes on flesh and blood. Now we see it.

Notice the rhetorical shift. For the only time in the essay, the only time in fact in all his writing on the frontier, Turner slips into the imperative mode: "Stand at Cumberland Gap." Up to that point he has held himself aloof, the professor lecturing on abstractions. Now he steps down from the lectern, takes us firmly by the arm, and leads us to the immediate and the real. His literary device reinforces what we feel anyway. He uses the elemental pull of every line over the land, 3.6 million years ago or today, as it draws us into its flow and compels us to imagine what is happening. Finally, Turner chooses the images and characters of an emerging national myth ("watch . . . the Indian, the fur-trader and hunter, the cattle-raiser") and fuses them with this ancient symbol of human passage and transformation.

In fifty-eight words Turner gave Americans their own unique version of a universal expression of their species. No wonder this passage is the most familiar and often-quoted of his works and, for that matter, one of the best known in all American historical writing.

The final linguistic piece, however, had not fallen into place when Turner wrote in 1893. He used "trail" with its established definition of something begun by animals and taken up by Natives and then by pioneers. The buffalo in his famous passage takes its trail to the salt spring, and elsewhere he wrote that "the buffalo trail became the Indian trail, and this became the trader's trace."[10] Within a generation of Turner's famous declaration, that usage had changed. The historical emphasis shifted to pioneers finding their own way over the land (though in fact they usually used routes long taken by Indians). Now they were forgers, not followers. The new role of pioneers, discovering freshly the way west, was increasingly portrayed as a heroic, transforming experience.

In the process, the newly blazed routes of passage were called by a new term: "trail." The word was lifted to its present mythic stature. To designate this elevation, the *t* was capitalized: Oregon Trail, California Trail, Mormon Trail, Santa Fe Trail, Bozeman Trail. There were exceptions to the general pattern of trails as westward-leading and as morally uplifting, but they typically proved the rule. Cattle trails like the Chisholm and Great Western ran south to north (and drew on the word's oldest meaning of a path left by moving animals), but in the larger mythic scheme they pulled civilization east to west, birthing towns that brought a cultural tide of laws, libraries, and Methodists. Southeastern tribes were forcibly removed along the Trail of Tears. This was no glory road. It was lined with the graves of thousands of innocents. It was, however, a white-made route that opened land to white society. The Trail of Tears recognized the dark side of a story that, by the national canon, still ended triumphantly. In the American myth all trails lead finally to the good.[11]

Believers in that myth now had a one-syllable linguistic symbol summing up the lessons and injunctions invoked when they were drawn onto those lines on the land. This, too, was in keeping with other traditions. *Sharia* is the Arabic word for the route of the Muslim hajj to Mecca. It also means "law" and, by its earliest definition, refers to any straight path to water. This one word links a road to a holy place, fundamental rules of living, and finding the essence of life. The equivalent word among Christians is "way." "The pilgrim's way" means a road to a shrine, lifelong spiritual education, and a defining code of behavior ("I am the way," Christ said). Its Latin equivalent, *via,* shimmers with sacred meaning. Following Jerusalem's Via Dolorosa, actually or by moving through the stations of the cross, a Christian retraces Christ's last steps toward the pivotal moment in God's relation to man. In recent years Maoist insurgents in Peru called to the oppressed to join El Sendero Luminoso, the Shining Path, a commitment both to a life of resistance and to a full complement of revolutionary ideals.

"Trail" became the American equivalent of *sharia* and "way." Like "frontier," it infused everything around it with mythic power. Because of its specificity, it has been drafted for sales pitches, mainly for items linked directly to free movement—automobiles, camping equipment, outdoor clothing, and such—but its vivid imagery has made it even more popular as a title of Western novels.[12]

In the twentieth century the story of the trail, arguably even more than that of the cowboy, has been the favored setting of the frontier idea. The movie screen's first western epic—a story linking grand western historical experiences with the birth of a national identity—was James Cruze's *The Covered Wagon* (1923), a lengthy silent film about the overland crossing. It was preceded by *Wagon Tracks* with William S. Hart (1919) and followed by many more with the same setting and plot, from B-Westerns to John Ford's *The Wagonmaster* (1950). Cruze's film was based on a novel by Emerson Hough. Hundreds of other novels and short stories, from throwaway potboilers to A. B. Guthrie, Jr.'s Pulitzer Prize–winning *The Way West* (1949), have taken as their subject the making and following of trails. In the early 1960s, with President John F. Kennedy calling for a "New Frontier" and westerns dominating prime-time television, the top-rated show was *Wagon Train.*

So firmly rooted in popular culture were a trail's images that a speaker or writer had only to string together a few key snippets—a wagon, a sunset, a family looking west—and the points were made. The rock poet Neil Young caught the spirit of the 1960s in "After the Gold Rush," a countercultural striving for a journey of spiritual rebirth:

> All in a dream,
> All in a dream,
> The loading had begun.
> We were sailing Mother Nature's silver seed
> To our new home in the sun.

Twenty years later President Ronald Reagan, drawing on experience as an actor in Westerns, offered his own version in the most frequently quoted passage of his second inaugural address: "A settler pushes west and sings his song. It is the American sound: hopeful, bighearted, idealistic—daring, decent and fair."[13]

When Ronald Reagan and Neil Young use the same images to push our buttons, we are on to something interesting. In their odd two-part harmony they are telling us that a culture had found its myth. Its idea was the frontier. Its story was of a people born again by moving into a wild continent, suffering and prevailing. Its purest symbol was the path made by that passage. This symbol looked like the story universal; it was an artifact of the story particular. Between the two it evoked beliefs perfectly embedded in mythic memory. To capture its meanings, Americans found a simple word. "Trail" crystallized the essential American identity: salvation in movement, rebirth through travail. It had been quite a trip.

Historians quite properly have given myths like ours plenty of attention. A myth defines what a particular people believe and reveals something of who they think they are. To trace how a myth came to be, as by following the evolving myth of westering and its trails, is to plot a people's path to collective identity. To study that path is to gain a sense of the events that produced the ideals, anxieties, hopes, and blindnesses that make them who they are. Once in place, the stories expressing those values and fears play a role in moving people to action and in carrying them into their next phase of becoming. Myths, that is, are both historical productions and historical forces. Myths are often dismissed as superstition; and as mischievous and ill-founded notions, such as "University professors are smarter than plumbers," myths deserve dismissal. As an evolving story of unifying character, however, a myth is neither inherently good nor inherently bad, and the impulse to shape our memory and to change our words to express how we see ourselves is fundamentally human. We might as well criticize smiling at babies.

Confusing myth and history, however, always leads to trouble. Accept the spare, straightforward stories of myth as the way things actually were, and present values seem inevitable and irreproachable, while in fact what we believe is always our own choice and often needs changing. A myth is by nature exclusive, defining its people in contrast to others, and exclusivity can easily tend toward undeserved feelings of superiority, arrogance, and, pretty soon, misbehavior toward anybody outside the mythic circle. When we allow myth to carry the forged authority of history, it leads us into lives that are smug, painfully narrow, and dangerously intolerant. When we tell and write our history in the simple patterns and clear verities of myth, our true story will be woefully incomplete, hopelessly simplistic, and shamefully neglectful of many who have rightful parts to play.

Some of the current generation's most perceptive and articulate critics have shown how the myth of westward expansion, when allowed to bleed into the craft of history, has distorted and impoverished the historical enterprise. Their focus has been on the word "frontier," but they might just as well have chosen "trail." The t-word is potentially as dangerous as the f-word.[14] Others have chastised the critics, arguing that part of the historian's job is to find in the past the stuff to inspire the current generation—to turn history to the goals of myth. Among the most successful is Stephen Ambrose, who used the primal story of western trailblazing, the Lewis and Clark expedition, to showcase the heroes he believed we lack today.

The trick is to respect both myth and history while doing our best not to jumble the two together. Like all myths, that of American trails was made by trimming down a wealth of past events into a lean story that speaks for one particular people—in this case Euro-Americans whose ancestors came into the continent from east to west. The trails of historical fact, by contrast, are to be found not by trimming but by expanding, by opening our grasp to include as many events and participants as possible. A myth draws its force from its focus and crystalline clarity. History is most fulfilling when it shows us a multitude of meanings, demands more questions of itself, and compels us to read it from as many angles as we can.

Remarkably, western trails are as beautifully suited to teaching how history works as they are to capturing the essence of national myth. No episodes of western history bring together so many lessons about the region's past. Some of the most obvious insights can be bunched around four statements.

First, trails are lines over lines over lines. In the myth of trails, pioneers made their way across a "trackless wilderness," rather like drawing a line across a smooth beach, but in fact they entered a land already crosshatched by marks from thousands of years of human history. The older American meaning of "trail"—a path made long ago by Native peoples—fits the reality much better than the word's present use. Historically, the West is the oldest part of our nation. Every route Europeans took into the West had been used long and well, and each crossed many more paths that snaked across a country deep in experience. Historical trails are reminders that the West is ancient country traveled and known by many scores of peoples, many of them long gone, with their own histories and myths.

Second, trails move within the land. "How else would they move?" you might ask. But in the mythic version, most of us would probably use the preposition "through" instead. The land crossed by mythic pioneers was a condition to be endured. They moved through it, as if running a gauntlet to reach the place where they would create new lives.[15] As the wilderness threatens and the immigrants respond, the effects are all in one direction. Travelers endure suffering, learn lessons, and grasp new abilities, but for their part they leave behind no effects, ill or good. In fact immigrants were bringing new changes to a landscape that had been evolving for thousands of years through interaction with other humans and their attempts to live within it. Once again an older meaning—trail as an evolving result of animals and people shaping the land—is closer to accuracy. Overlanders saw only the most recent of the West's many faces, and as they moved within this country, they set loose changes that were among the most convulsive in its history. The land was affected far more by the pioneers than vice versa.

Third, trails are meeting grounds. On the mythic trails, the one-way environmental action has its human dimension. As the land blows and rages at the pioneers, Indians pop up, attack, then step back until the next travelers top the horizon. There's a mechanical feel to it, as if we are watching the Overland Trail Ride at Six Flags Over Westward Expansion. When the crisis is over, the travelers go on their way, like customers with an exciting memory, as the blizzard-and-dust machine shuts down and the natives-on-tracks-and-rollers go quiet and dead-eyed, frozen in time, until some tripped switch sets them again into terrible motion. How different the picture becomes when we see historical trails as a few new lines snarled into an evolving environment and a continuous mix of many peoples. The interactions of travelers and Indians were multifaceted and multidirectional. Trade goods, diseases, perspectives, sex, attitudes, animals, plants, language, and much more were exchanged far more often than arrows and bullets. The action along the trails was a dynamic show, with everybody and everything changing everything and everybody else.

Fourth, trails run many ways. The power of mythic trails lies in their elegant, straight-ahead simplicity. The lessons are direct, linear, and above all, progressive. The pioneer is better for the journey, while his stride brings progress in its broadest sense, the coming of history's finest harvest of institutions and culture. The first three points of trails-as-history, however, build into a fourth point that offers no such assurances. As history, each of the most famous western trails is a magnificent bewilderment. Each is part of a palimpsest of lines laid down by many peoples through deep history. On each trail the effects of its travelers remind us that the western environment has never stood still. The human exchanges along each were part of a long and continuous interaction that renders preposterous any but the most general conclusions about how people have acted in the West, and therefore what it means to be "western." Everything we see along each historical trail—people, influences, environmental change, and especially moral lessons—seems to be heading in all directions. It is easy to get turned around—and turning around, looking this way and that, is exactly what we should be doing. A trail might be the ideal setting for myth, but it is also our best condensed illustration of western history's refusal to be simply summarized.

Nowhere are western history's humbling and conflicted lessons made more vivid than on the Bozeman Trail, arguably the most neglected of the West's important pathways. In its travelers' accounts we see the sense of astonishment at some of the West's most splendid country, and once its deep past is brought into the picture, the child's-eye view of Adelia French—her wonder at the open landscape, the beautiful valleys, and the water boiling from the ground—has us imagining similar impressions of awestruck travelers generations, centuries, and millennia earlier.[16] We ask how this place was admired by the Lakotas, and by the Crows they took it from, how it had changed and been used since the time of the mammoths.

Emigrant John Hackney's complaints along the Platte road in 1864 ("Poor grass, little water and wood. . . . Scarcity of everything but alkalie") fit nicely into the mythic story of hardships endured. Then, when we stand back and remember how the immigrant trains and their millions of oxen had devastated the great valley's timber and forage beds, another perspective opens. What was an irritation to Hackney was a calamity for Natives dependent on the river valley for food, shelter, and feed for their horses. When Hackney's party turned north onto the Bozeman Cutoff, they were entering land that had not yet felt any of the onslaught that had devastated the Platte road, country of generous grass beds and thick stands of timber. The powerful Lakotas (western Sioux) had pulled back from the Platte into this territory, one of their last realms of plenty.

Contrasting the two settings, the barren Platte and the lush valleys to its north, and adopting the Indians' perspective on the difference, it is easier to put into perspective the emigrant-Indian exchange along the Bozeman. It was one not of trade and curious visiting but of confrontation and bloodshed. Once again the scenes of Indian assaults on besieged pioneers seem right out of the mythic trails, and once again, when those scenes are set into their wider and longer historical perspective, the meanings turn muddy and disorienting, morally complex and much more interesting. Take Hackney's chilling entry for July 21: "[This a]fternoon we reached the north fork of the Powder River and camped. Good water and grass. Found the scalp of a man belonging to the last train that passed here."[17] Set it beside one from Richard Owens, a member of Hackney's company: "This day there was a motion put forward and carried in the morning for the indiscriminate slaughter of all Indians, but was reconsidered and acted upon in the evening and resulted in favor of letting them alone so long as they did not intrude on us."[18]

Such accounts leave us with lots of questions but no clear answers. Who are the intruders, we wonder, and who the violated? Standing with the Lakotas and Cheyennes, watching the advance of Owens's train while remembering the lessons from the past generation, feeling the perimeter of usable country tightening every year, the direction of threats and thievery seems quite the other way around. Yet Owens was no villain. For this forty-year-old Welshman, who had made his way well enough in a strange country before heading westward into country stranger still, being scared and off-balance was natural enough: "Traveling is very dangerous now . . . on account of the Sioux Indians, who are bent on murder and theft." A latecomer to America, he had laid his life on the line to save the Union in the bloodiest war the continent would ever see. Hadn't that earned him the right at least to cross that continent and work to create a better life for his family back in Pennsylvania? "The Indians are very wicked," he wrote.[19] For a husband and father risking it all for a modest betterment, it must have seemed so.

Mythic trails can push us to keep our highest aspirations before us (and, if we are honest, always to question them), but on the trails of history, like the Bozeman, the myth's uplifting vision is no more at home than an ox is in an opera house. Certainly progress, its centerpiece, becomes the shiftiest of terms.[20] What was for some an upward road to opportunity was for others a downward path to disaster. Every other trail, when we move inside its apparently spare story with honest imagination and what we can honestly know, catches as well western history's jumble of lessons, expanding insights, and multiple points of view.

Both ways of walking these American pathways, the mythic and the historic, have their rewards, and both have the power to teach and move us. We are travelers in a collective continental experience. Our responsibility is to make sure that we do not deceive ourselves into thinking we are on one trail when in fact we are walking another.

Notes

An earlier version of this chapter appeared as "American Pathways: An Exploration of Trails and the American Imagination," *Montana The Magazine of Western History* 51, no. 3 (Autumn 2001): 20–31.

1. M. D. Leakey, "The Hominid Footprints," in M. D. Leakey and J. M. Harris, eds., *Laetoli: A Pliocene Site in Northern Tanzania* (Oxford: Clarendon Press, 1987), 490–520.

2. An interesting and helpful discussion of early uses of "path," "trace," and "trail" is in Frank Gilbert Roe, *The North American Buffalo: A Critical Study of the Species in Its Wild State* (Toronto: University of Toronto Press, 1970), 119–20n.

3. There were many other examples, mostly earlier and farther east than the traces, of Indian trails and paths being preempted and renamed roads. The Iroquois Trail became the Great State Road connecting Lake Erie to the Hudson River, and the Great Trail, used by the Shawnees, Delawares, and others, became the first military road in the Ohio Valley. Nemacolin's Path in western Pennsylvania first became Braddock's Road and Forbes's Road, then a stretch of the National Road. The most extensive writing on early trails and their transition to roads is from Arthur Butler Hulbert: *Indian Thoroughfares* (Cleveland, Ohio: Arthur H. Clark, 1902); *Pioneer Roads and Experiences of Travelers* (Cleveland, Ohio: Arthur H. Clark, 1904); and *The Paths of Inland Commerce: A Chronicle of Trail, Road, and Waterway* (New Haven: Yale University Press, 1920).

4. C. F. Hoffman, *A Winter in the Far West*, quoted in Richard H. Thornton, *An American Glossary*, 2 vols. (New York: Ungar, 1962), 2:905.

5. Lewis and Clark praised the bison's "wonderful sagacity," and Washington Irving reported the animals' "traditionary knowledge," which led them to wear "hereditary paths and highways" that invariably passed through mountains via the most reliable passes and crossed the plains by the easiest valleys and surest river fords. Unfortunately for these natural historians, few if any of these routes had been used by bison or other animal herds. Bison paths, in fact, were a major frustration for those using the trails. Overland routes typically ran parallel to

rivers. Bison moving to and from the highlands to the streams wore deep ruts perpendicular to the direction of immigrant travel. Overlanders rattled crosswise over these ruts, breaking wheels and axles and coloring the air with curses. The "wonderful sagacity" used to discover the most usable routes was that of Indians, not animals. For a discussion, see Frank G. Roe, "The 'Wild Animal Path' Origin of Ancient Roads," *Antiquity* 3 (September 1929): 299–311.

6. Mischa Titiev, "A Hopi Salt Pilgrimage," *American Anthropologist* 39 (April–June 1937): 244–58.

7. Frederick Jackson Turner, *The Frontier in American History* (Tucson: University of Arizona Press, 1997), 3.

8. Ibid., 9.

9. Ibid., 12.

10. Ibid., 14.

11. As one measure of this fusion of trail with national destiny, the number of books on westward-tending routes, whatever they might be called, west of the Mississippi dwarfs that on routes east of the river. A very few of these, such as Walter McClintock's *Old Indian Trails* (Boston: Houghton Mifflin, 1923), concern the elaborate networks of Native American routes. The vast majority tell of white-made trails. The American Trails Series, published first by McGraw-Hill and later by the Arthur H. Clark Company, includes volumes on the Death Valley, Bozeman, Mormon, and Mission Trails, as well as several others among the Oregon-California Trails. The implication of this dominance by white-made trails seems clear enough. Although routes made by westering Euro-Americans made up only a tiny portion of all the trails across the West, they are the ones that define the West's historical outlines.

12. The word was a standard title device among the best and most successful writers of formula Westerns: Ernest Haycox (*All Trails Cross, Trail Smoke, Trail Town*), Max Brand (*Brothers on the Trail, The Trouble Trail*), and Louis L'Amour (*The Kiowa Trail, The Proving Trail, Ride the Dark Trail*). It was a favorite as well in titles of movie serials. One of the earliest was *The Fighting Trail* (1917). It was followed by many other week-to-week cliffhangers, such as *Vanishing Trails, Terror Trail*, and *The Oregon Trail*.

13. *New York Times*, January 22, 1985, sec. 1, p. 17.

14. The collection of essays often mentioned as the earliest statement of the New Western History critical of the frontier thesis and its limitations is *Trails: Toward a New Western History*, ed. Patricia Nelson Limerick, Clyde A. Milner II, and Charles E. Rankin (Lawrence: University Press of Kansas, 1991). It took its title from a 1989 symposium in Santa Fe, New Mexico, which in turn was spun off from a traveling exhibit on various western trails. But the naming of both symposium and book obviously drew on the unique American connotation of "trail" of pushing bravely into new territory. The essays thus enlisted a term sacred to the very myth they were challenging.

15. This view—people passing through hostile wilderness and being tested by its harshness—draws obviously on our deep cultural tradition of the exodus. The story of the Mormon trek is only the most explicit of many references in westward expansion to exiled peoples who find their identity through difficult journeys to western Zions. Always the emphasis is on how the country threatened them. There is nothing on how they might have threatened the country or changed it in any way, any more than the Bible suggests how the followers of Moses might have transformed the desert of their testing.

16. C. Adelia French reminiscence, in *Journeys to the Land of Gold: Emigrant Diaries from the Bozeman Trail,* ed. Susan Badger Doyle (Helena: Montana Historical Society Press, 2000), 235–43.

17. John S. Hackney diary, in ibid., 304, 309.

18. Richard Owens diary, in ibid., 289.

19. Ibid., 287.

20. Since this is an essay partly on etymology, here is a final example of how our evolving language speaks to us about what has been happening. This instance is especially ironic. In its earliest use, "progress" referred to a repetitive circuit, a round of movement done over and over by an official or religious seeker. It also meant a successful effort toward self-improvement, a use much closer to ours today. John Bunyan's *A Pilgrim's Progress,* for instance, carried this double meaning of a circuit journey and hard-earned improvement. Indian peoples of the plains and Great Basin were trying to improve their lot through their own annual rounds, seasonal circuits of gathering, hunting, and finding safe winter shelters, a pattern especially promising once horses were acquired from Europeans. Progress describes nicely this way of life. The westward march along the trails, soon to become the symbol of the progressive march of civilization, epitomized the changes that undercut and disrupted the Indians' well-choreographed annual movements. From the Sioux, Cheyenne, Kiowa, Comanche, and Shoshone perspective, that is, progress was precisely what the trails were bringing to an abrupt and calamitous halt. It's a one-word summary of the need to press harder and more deeply to appreciate the various lessons found along the trails.

13

On the Trail with Gus and Call

Lonesome Dove and the Western Myth

When Larry McMurtry's *Lonesome Dove* was published in 1985, virtually every review included the term "epic." "Deeply affecting" was a close
second in the flow of praise for what one critic called "the Great Cowboy
Novel." Its critical success was capped with the Pulitzer Prize and its mass
popularity with a television miniseries graced by a rare combination of
fine acting and high ratings. By then, *Lonesome Dove* was being called a
Western classic. And it is, although not for reasons that would gladden
every fan of Louis L'Amour and Zane Gray.

Lonesome Dove is most impressive as a literary balancing act. Its characters are comfortably familiar sorts who suddenly do the unexpected—
and who always speak with the most wonderfully original blather. The
story moves languidly for long stretches, then suddenly ignites in gun
battles, stampedes, and gut cuttings to satisfy the most demanding action fan. Above all, for history students, McMurtry keeps *Lonesome Dove*
centered between myth and anti-myth.

The story begins in the late 1870s in Lonesome Dove, a sunbaked
speck of a town on the Texas-Mexico border. The turmoil during and
immediately after the Civil War has subsided, and with it the need for
aging former Texas Ranger captains like the book's two primary figures,
Woodrow Call and Augustus McRae. With Pea Eye, Deets, Lippy, and
others in the Hat Creek Cattle Company, they pass time in and around
the town's one saloon, the Dry Bean, where the prostitute Lorena con-
ducts her business. Enter the handsome Jake Spoon, another ex-Ranger,
who persuades the restless Call to drive a herd of three thousand cattle

northward twelve hundred miles to the grassy valley of Montana's Yellowstone River, nearly to the Canadian border. The equivalent would be pushing a herd of balky and highly independent animals from Madrid to Helsinki, from Atlanta to beyond Ottawa, or (with a long swim) from Tunis to Moscow. Lorena, infatuated with Jake and looking for someplace cool, comes along, as does the seventeen-year-old Newt, who we learn is Call's illegitimate son.

The long drive and its adventures consume most of *Lonesome Dove*, with several subplots woven in. Except for a few terrifying freelancers like Blue Duck, the Indians by now are defeated, and their means of independent living going or gone. The plains have been swept nearly clean of bison, leaving only "roads of bones." There are vague references to Custer's recent difficulty and to the Sioux and Cheyennes' confinement to Dakota reservations. The action unfolds on the march north: Lorena is kidnapped by Blue Duck and rescued by Gus; Jake falls in with rustlers and is caught and hanged; the men pause with Gus's old flame Clara, now a ranchwoman. The outfit has barely reached Montana when Gus is wounded in an Indian skirmish. When he dies rather than have his leg amputated, Call packs his corpse in charcoal and hauls it back to Texas. The story ends where it starts, back on the border.

For readers after historical authenticity, *Lonesome Dove* is mostly accurate, at least in the term's narrowest sense. There are a few anachronisms and startling omissions. The Indians who send Gus to his deathbed with a rotting leg are presumably Blackfeet, who in fact were mostly in Canada by this time or starving on what remains today one of America's bleakest reservations. It's hard to imagine that the Hat Creek outfit sees no farmers; in western Kansas alone, sixteen counties were created during the 1870s, with more land broken to the plow than would have fit into Connecticut and Delaware combined. And where are the railroads? Every historical development in the novel's background—cattle trailing and ranching, buffalo hunting, and the Indian wars—was either spun off directly or facilitated by the first transcontinentals built during the previous decade. Montana-bound drovers would have crossed three major lines. Various characters in the novel pass time in Dodge City, Ogallala, and Miles City, towns that were creatures respectively of the Atchison, Topeka and Santa Fe; the Union Pacific; and the Northern Pacific. Except for some Mexicans and Irish, there is not much in *Lonesome Dove* to suggest that the plains West was quite an immigrant stew. The percentage of foreign-born persons in the Montana McMurtry describes was twice that of New York.

Still, given the story he chooses to tell, McMurtry is faithful in both broad strokes and detail. He catches beautifully the feel of the plains at the moment, just after the national centennial, when power tipped finally and quickly from Indians to whites. Very few have taken us more authentically into the grimy ordeal of traveling this country. River crossings and stampedes are standard stuff, but not the stunted sprawl of mesquite trees bristling with some of the nastiest thorns on the planet, or the yawning openness beyond that, an agoraphobic's nightmare, and over it all the hammering of an erratic, sometimes murderous climate. This might have been cheapened into a hyperrealism, but McMurtry balances the plains' austerity with a true loveliness equally hard for outlanders to picture, the broad rolls of low hills and "a plain of grass so huge it was hard to imagine a world beyond it."[1]

The novel gives us as well a true feeling for cowboying. Besides his own experience, McMurtry seems to have drawn heavily from two classics, Teddy Blue Abbot's memoir, *We Pointed Them North* (1939), and an early instance of what would later be called a nonfiction novel, Andy Adams's *The Log of a Cowboy* (1903), both of them accounts of similarly long cattle drives.[2] McMurtry borrows some material directly from the historical record. Call's moving epitaph to Deets after his friend is killed trying to return an Indian child is an almost exact transcription of the tribute by the Texas rancher Charles Goodnight to Bose Ikard, a former slave who was Goodnight's most trusted hand. The psychopath Blue Duck has elements of Charlie Bent—the mixed-blood son of the Cheyenne Owl Woman and the prominent trader William Bent, who preyed mercilessly on Colorado whites after the Sand Creek massacre—and perhaps of the Kiowa warrior Satanta (White Bear). Blue Duck's death, "flying" out the third-floor courthouse window just before he is to be hanged, is a mimic of Satanta's suicide by diving headfirst from the second floor of the Texas state prison hospital in 1878.

McMurtry chose the cowboy's West for his setting partly because that place and story are his and his family's. Late in the nineteenth century, his grandparents took up ranching near the North Texas town of Archer City, where McMurtry lived and worked until leaving for Rice University. He heard the stories and absorbed, but didn't share, his father's longing to have worked the country at the time of the cattle drives. McMurtry has commented that he was moved to write *Lonesome Dove* partly by the "thrill of the vernacular," the desire to re-create the speech and the dailiness of life among plainsmen of his grandfather's time.[3]

Clearly, however, he is up to much more than that. Embedded in this novel is McMurtry's vision of pioneering, of what people of his grandparents' time found, or hoped to find, and of how they and their world changed each other. This makes *Lonesome Dove* a Western in both meanings of the term. It is a wonderfully entertaining set piece from the legendary terrain of the cattleman's plains. It also wrestles with the meanings, truths, and deceptions in what amounts to our national creation myth.

Like most such myths, the Western is a deceptively simple story told by people with a common identity (many Americans in this case) to explain who they are and how they have come to be. It runs something like this: Long ago, with the first European settlement on the Atlantic Coast, people from an old world came into a new one. The old world was crowded and set in its ways. Its individuals lived within narrow possibilities. The new world was open and full of promise and essentially a social void, without cultural form or shape. It was a wilderness, full of unforeseen dangers and undreamt-of challenges. The people came brimming with hope and ideals and set out with a great determination to build new lives for themselves and to plant in the new land the first civilized order—schools, churches, government, civility broadly defined. But the wild land fought them hard. Its weather battered them; its native inhabitants (human and animal seemed often interchangeable) lashed out ferociously; its distances swallowed them. Many of the people were lost, and all suffered, but in the end they endured and the wilderness was brought under their domain.

The heart of the story, however, is not the conquest of the land but the transformation of the conquerors. The people who tamed the wilderness learned new ways, found in themselves unexpected potential, and fashioned new beliefs. As they earned a place in the country, they also grew away from the world that had first shaped them and their ancestors. It was not so much that they forged a new identity. Rather, it was forged for them out of the heat and the grinding struggle. Our western myth, then, tells of a dual metamorphosis, a violent sort of blood wedding of the people and the land, and at the end it is not always easy to say who and what is victorious. The wild country was subdued, but it absorbed and shaped the people, too; the people mastered the land, but were reborn into a life inseparable from the country that was now their home.

What this abstract thumbnail sketch cannot suggest is, first, the remarkable range of forms the myth has taken in American culture, high and low: Saturday-afternoon serials; the political appeals of Andrew Jackson, Abraham Lincoln, Theodore Roosevelt, and John Kennedy; countless potboilers and pulp paperbacks; rodeos; music from Antonin Dvorak, Gene Autry, Aaron Copland, and Johnny Paycheck; F. Scott Fitzgerald's fresh green breast of the new world; national parks; accountants from Akron wearing cowboy boots and hats of great gallonage; dozens of television series and hundreds of movies; Cather and Steinbeck and L'Amour and so much more. Nor does it hint at the myth's astonishing global appeal, once again across the intellectual spectrum. James Fenimore Cooper, who became the first American to make a living as a novelist by giving the myth its first literary expression in the Leatherstocking saga, was wildly popular from London to Jerusalem. Dumas and Tolstoy stole his plots; Conrad called him his favorite author; Goethe was so smitten he seriously considered writing a Western. One of Germany's best-selling authors of the twentieth century was Karl May, whose stories of Old Shatterhand's exploits in the Far West were the boyhood favorites of Albert Schweitzer and Adolf Hitler.

The rest of the world loves the Western because of its dramatic settings, hairbreadth action, and colorful characters. But like all cultural creation myths—the Book of Exodus, for instance, or the Navajos' perilous journey out of the earth and into what we call Arizona—it speaks to its own with an intimacy nobody else feels. *Lonesome Dove* resonates with that myth, but it is anything but a straightforward retelling of it. The book's poignant appeal, and its interest to cultural historians, lies in its ambivalence toward what that creation story tries to teach us.

Recently, McMurtry commented that while writing *Lonesome Dove*, he thought he was "demythicizing" the West.[4] This seems odd on the face. The novel is a virtually full roster of the Western's most familiar characters: cowboys and Indians, Texas Rangers, nasty renegades, bumbling deputies, rustlers, a likable and beautiful whore, a strong ranchwoman, a trapper turned buffalo hunter turned bone picker, a colorful cook, and an alcoholic doctor, just to name the most obvious. Its skeletal narrative, the cattle drive, is one of the Western's three essential storylines (the wagon train and the Indian war being the others). Like all Westerns, it is about men; women have no roles except as motivators and commentators. Its subplots and bits of business are the usual fare: Newt's coming of age through tutelage of older men, for instance, and the bantering tension between two vastly different friends sealed inseparably by the passage of years.

The Western's great army of fans know these characters and situations as well as or better than they know their families. The people and plots have been grooved into their brains. These readers do not want to be surprised, except in details of the familiar plot. They expect to respond to such a story mythically—that is, as a reiteration of patterns that feed something inside them that badly needs to be fed. The minor miracle of *Lonesome Dove* is that McMurtry stays squarely within the Western's form, yet with a novelist's magic he forces his readers to break loose from what they expect. What are normally clichés of genre fiction—the campfire gab and saloon scenes and encounters with rustlers—become the setting for a genuinely new story. We are not sure where the story is heading, because Gus and Call and most of the others are originals. McMurtry gives them humanity and inherent interest, and so it matters to us what happens to them and how the story turns out.

Here, then, is one way *Lonesome Dove* demythicizes the West, simply by giving a fresh and true voice to figures long ago kidnapped from history and held hostage to the demands of legend. That McMurtry chose the West's most clichéd setting to pull this off is truly impressive. I do not know whether it is culturally appropriate to apply "chutzpah" to a Scots-Irish Texan, but if it is, McMurtry has earned the term.

Just as surely, he means to go further than that. Implied in his fiction and more explicit in his essays is a commentary on the western character as it truly was. As original as Call and Gus are, they are also walking and riding demonstrations of what McMurtry thinks that life on the actual frontier did to those who were drawn to it. In this he moves toward the center of the western myth, the junction of history and the spirit it supposedly produced.

In the classic western myth, the frontier experience was grandly ennobling. The pioneers' trials cultivated in them a long list of virtues: self-reliance, strength, inventiveness, toleration, independence, and respect for the individual. As their characters were being transformed, westering Americans were also transplanting the best of their past. Families, schools, law and government (the pure local variety), and churches all took hold in the virgin soil of the West. As the frontier passed and communities were set in place, the finest qualities of the former were woven into the new social fabric (though Westerns never addressed in any detail how this was done). A purified America was born, a blend of pioneer virtue and values tested over the centuries. The transition from frontier to a civilized order was apparently smooth, free of bumps and contradictions.

In *Lonesome Dove*, McMurtry tells another side of this story. The frontier may have left its people strong in some ways, he says, but it took quite a toll as well. The hunger for land brought out a passion among pioneers, not simply to improve their lot, but to accomplish something truly grand, to give life to whatever dream they found inside themselves. But this passion became its own force. Soon pioneers were not drawn but driven, caught up in an unappeasable restlessness. That, more than anything, seems to define Woodrow Call. Soon after I first read *Lonesome Dove*, I loaned it to a graduate student, a fellow Texan from the ranching town of Big Spring. He returned it with a note: "This is the perfect Western novel. Everyone is in continual movement, and to no apparent purpose." Gus makes the same point about Call when they arrive in

Montana. "Now that we're here, do you plan to stop," he asks his partner, "or will we just keep going north until we get into the polar bears?"[5]

Feverish movement toward some vague goal had seemed to many to be the essence of the frontier from the time the pioneers began spilling over the Appalachians. Moses Austin, a miner, land speculator, and would-be colonizer of Texas, asked the crowds he met in 1795 what they thought was waiting for them in Kentucky: "The Answer [they gave] is Land. have you any. No, but I expect I can git it . . . did you Ever see the Country. No, but Every Body says its good land . . . here is hundreds Traveling hundreds of Miles, they Know not for what Nor Whither except its to Kentuckey."[6] Ten years later, the explorer Zebulon Pike, after crossing the treeless, wind-scoured southern plains, hoped that this country would force the relentless pioneer movers, "so prone to rambling and extending themselves on the frontiers, . . . to limit the extent on the west to the borders of the Missouri and the Mississippi."[7] The plains, that is, might require Americans at last to settle down and tend to business. It was a naïve notion, as thousands testified by flooding into the Texas colony founded by Moses Austin's son Stephen in the 1820s.

McMurtry's grandparents came to Archer County in the last stage of this push onto the plains frontier. For his father, who stayed in place, the pioneers' unscratchable itch seemed translated into a relentless drive to master the country. His few spare moments away from ranch work were spent in a hopeless campaign to push back the mesquite thickets with an ax, a spade, and a can of kerosene.[8] An urban equivalent would be marching with a flyswatter into the city dump.

In McMurtry's West the open promise of the land becomes something like a gravity field that distorts some virtues and crushes others. Men like Gus become ramblin' boys, fond of daytime whiskey and whorehouse pokes, likable and garrulous but irresponsible and hopeless as material for decent society. For others, an honest day's work becomes a life exhausted by the pursuit of what cannot be had or even defined. A comically surreal variation in *Lonesome Dove* is Aus Frank collecting bison bones, literally night and day, and piling them into gigantic pyramids, not to sell them but apparently just to do it. Honor becomes an excuse to continue what would otherwise be pointless or destructive. When Call sets off to carry Gus's body back to Texas, we know he has found one more occasion just to keep moving, even though his son, Newt, badly needs his attention. "A promise is a promise," Call tells Clara when she upbraids him, but she throws his true duty back in his face: "A promise is words—a son is a life."[9]

McMurtry is hinting here of other costs hidden within the idealized myth. The almost unimaginable load of work of settlement left little time or room for anything else. The basics of human community suffered, starting with simple talk. "This is the longest conversation I've had in 10 years. Goodbye," the rancher Charles Goodnight tells Call, using the last 11 of the 187 words he takes time to speak.[10] The western myth might celebrate the planting of the family, but McMurtry's frontier wore them down and ripped them apart. Except for Clara's household, where her husband lies in a permanent coma, there is not one nuclear family in *Lonesome Dove*, but rather a spraying of solitaires, runaways, castoffs, orphans, bastards, and parents who take the modern term "dysfunctional" to an entirely new dimension. This familial abrasion survived in the cattle country of McMurtry's own youth. The emptiness, loneliness, and grind, he writes elsewhere, took the heaviest toll on the women. Although his paternal grandmother lived with his family until she died, in his eighth year, he cannot recall her speaking a single word to him.[11]

And despite the army of schoolmarms in hundreds of popular Westerns, the legacy he remembers valued reading and literature about as much as modern dance and ice sculpture. By his own account McMurtry grew up intellectually starved, gobbling what few books he found at home and in the drugstore's rack of paperbacks, before leaving for college and reading his way eastward toward the cultural life of the Atlantic Coast and Europe.[12] In *Lonesome Dove* it is important to notice what is *not* there. Its characters would be flabbergasted to hear that anything they chose to do had the slightest civilizing purpose, with the possible exception of killing Indians. This frontier is a place of almost total cultural atrophy. Perhaps that is the joke behind the motto Gus adds to the sign for the Hat Creek Cattle Company: "Uva uvam vivendo varia fit." It is faux Latin gibberish, a mockery of cultural pretense.

So there is lots here to demythicize the West: near-neurotic obsessive-ness, cultural erosion, hardening of character and dimming of sensibility, a flight from true responsibility that hides in the guise of manly purpose. Others have made the same points. A. B. Guthrie, Jr.'s *The Big Sky* is to mountain men what *Lonesome Dove* is to cowboys and rangers. Its pro-tagonist, Boone Caudill, is drawn to the roaming life of the trapper but ends up killing his best friend and smothering his own humanity.[13] Why, then, are we drawn so powerfully to the Caudills and Gus McCraes and Woodrow Calls? *Lonesome Dove,* to McMurtry's surprise, has become "an American Arthuriad."[14] What is it that its readers find heroic? What do they see to connect these characters' destructive, dead-end lives to some grander vision of the West and America?

To start with, these men are free and they are brave, at least in facing physical dangers that would turn most of our bowels to jelly. McMurtry's West was a testing ground for courage, and this was the last time in our history when, for the cost of a ticket or a long hike down the road, you could break into country twice the size of Europe and move virtually unfettered and act without concern for any but the most immediate risks. At this irreducible core, he is saying, the mythic and the real West were the same. More to the point, the West was free as a realm of perceived possibilities, a seductive sense of limitless options that inspired an ex-traordinary determination, energy, and imagination among those pulled into it.

To McMurtry, this imaginative passion must always be given a respect equal to the frustration, the destructive self-deception, and the spiritual gnarling. Look far enough behind the apparent lunacies—chopping mes-quite, moving cattle from one end of the country to the other, building pyramids of bones—and you will find the great dream. The dream itself was largely illusion, but as an inner reality it was undeniable. At the heart of the Western is that vision of cutting loose from the settled to the wild, of shaping new country to the individual will. Whether we should be ashamed or proud of that emotional force is another question. The point here is that the dream was truly there, and because as Americans we instinctively recognize it, it continues to give Westerns an undeniable power.

And that in turn makes Westerns ultimately tragic. Whatever reality the dream held, the end was bound to come. The transition from frontier to full settlement was not smooth and unrumpled; it was a painful jolt. In the cattleman's West, the end came quickly. Longhorns were first driven to Kansas the year before Grant was elected. By the time he left office, ranching was shifting to the northern plains and the Indians were defeated. In another decade, barbed wire had mostly closed the open range and ranching had become a corporate enterprise. Twenty-five years, tops, and whatever true freedom had ever been there was fenced and mortgaged.

Lonesome Dove holds us with such a grip because we feel the dream in Call and Gus, and so we also feel the awful sadness as we watch it all slipping away. If a myth is a story we tell to say who we are, there is something in that telescoping of time, and in the longing for what is given and then snatched back, that speaks from the heart of the American experience. The variations run through our national library: Fitzgerald's receding green light, Leatherstocking sent into exile from his beloved forest, and Steinbeck's Okies taking the road to the golden land and getting their heads cracked in its orchards. McMurtry adds to this literature the long trek to Montana and Call's return in an evening's gathering dark to Lonesome Dove, where his house is full of rats and the Dry Bean has burned down.

As with the historical details of his view of the plains, we can peck at McMurtry's portrayal of men forced to watch the dream pulled out of their reach. Plainsmen frequently did all they could to hustle in the settled world of towns and fences. Christopher Columbus Slaughter used the money made driving longhorns to Kansas to start a cattle empire west of the McMurtry ranch. After squeezing out smaller competitors, he moved to Dallas, bankrolled the First Baptist Church (until recently the largest Southern Baptist congregation in the country), built houses for himself and his sons on fashionable Cole Avenue, and spent his last years spying on his children through binoculars. No free-roaming, live-and-let-live ranger here.[15] After the beaver ran out, mountain men became farmers, merchants, and government employees. Buffalo hunters often went on to be not the flyblown misfits McMurtry describes in *Anything for Billy*, but businessmen, county commissioners, and railroad executives.

And always, of course, it is crucial to keep in mind that chasing one dream usually involves shutting down another. Women, who McMurtry knows were blighted by the ranching life, often had little or no say in the choice to take it up. The plains West, furthermore, was not an unpeopled cultural void when pioneers showed up. The newcomers' expanding possibilities came at the expense of the rapidly contracting worlds of Comanches, Cheyennes, Sioux, Arapahos, Kiowas, and other Indian peoples. Every historian must throw their disaster into the balance when weighing the myth and its role in our continental story.

But McMurtry is a novelist, not a historian, and so he is freer to choose where to place his emphasis. His choice is for the dreaming—its beauty and its terrible costs and the tension between the two. It is a theme that runs strongly through American fiction, though the West sometimes seems its special home. *Lonesome Dove*, whatever its limits as a narrative of fact, manages something doubly remarkable as a novel within that mythic vein. In a tradition we have come to know as clichéd and austere, it charms us with a story with flesh and humor. Doing that, it causes us to see all the clearer the yearning, loss, and illusion that sit at the heart of our spiritual history.

Notes

An earlier version of this chapter appeared as "On the Trail with Gus and Call: *Lonesome Dove* and the Western Myth," in *Novel History: History and Novelists Confront America's Past (and Each Other)*, ed. Mark C. Carnes (New York: Simon & Schuster, 2001).

1. Larry McMurtry, *Lonesome Dove* (New York: Simon & Schuster, 2010), 628. All quotations are taken from this twenty-fifth-anniversary edition.

2. E. C. "Teddy Blue" Abbott and Helena Huntington Smith, *We Pointed Them North: Recollections of a Cowpuncher* (1939; repr., Norman: University of Oklahoma Press, 1955); Andy Adams, *Log of a Cowboy: A Narrative of the Old Trail Days* (Boston: Houghton, Mifflin and Company, 1903).

3. Larry McMurtry, *Walter Benjamin at the Dairy Queen: Reflections at Sixty and Beyond* (New York: Simon & Schuster, 1999), 187.

4. Ibid., 55.

5. McMurtry, *Lonesome Dove*, 539.

6. Ellen Eslinger, ed., *Running Mad for Kentucky: Frontier Travel Accounts* (Lexington: University Press of Kentucky, 2004), 179.

7. Elliott Coues, ed., *The Expeditions of Zebulon Montgomery Pike* . . . (New York: F. P. Harper, 1895), 2:525.

8. McMurtry, *Walter Benjamin,* 190–91.

9. McMurtry, *Lonesome Dove,* 845.

10. Ibid., 848.

11. McMurtry, *Walter Benjamin,* 20.

12. Ibid., 98–99.

13. A. B. Guthrie, Jr., *The Big Sky* (New York: William Sloane Associates, 1947).

14. McMurtry, *Walter Benjamin,* 55.

15. David J. Murrah, *C. C. Slaughter: Rancher, Banker, Baptist* (Austin: University of Texas Press, 1981).

Stories

Once again, Westerns are in. With big-name stars Ed Harris and Viggo Mortensen, the film *Appaloosa* (2008) revived the dependable plot of hired lawmen, buddies with well-tested killing skills, who tame a town and best the rancher, a snotty Englishman to boot, who has tyrannized it. There are other predictables—feckless town fathers, loutish bullies, and a faithless coquette (Renée Zellweger) who tries, and fails utterly, to pry the heroes apart. In 1995 *Toy Story* began a trend of blockbuster animated features (once called cartoons). It starred a cowboy hero, Woody, who saddled up again in two fabulously successful sequels, the latter, *Toy Story 3* (2010), released just prior to *Rango* (2011), another town-taming Western, this time with an animated chameleon as sheriff and the familiar comic trope of mistaken identity. Actual humans rode across the screen in *True Grit* (2010). Wonderful dialogue and splendid performances gave a freshness to a story featuring standard types—an aging, drunken, rules-bending marshal (Jeff Bridges), a spunky young heroine (Hailee Steinfeld), and a cocky Texas Ranger (Matt Damon). In *Cowboys and Aliens* (2011), on the other hand, the familiar gunslingers and feuding ranchers showed a new wrinkle, doing battle in 1873 with invaders from outer space bent on conquering the world, starting with Arizona.

Here is yet another flowering of a national infatuation. The seeds of the Western were planted in the early nineteenth century in the novels of James Fenimore Cooper, the poetry of Henry Wadsworth Longfellow, the art of the Hudson River School, and the politics of Andrew Jackson. The plots and characters evolved over the decades and in the early twentieth century emerged in their modern form, set in the Far West with the cowboy, lawman, and gunfighter heading the cast. The Western's popularity has risen and fallen since then. During its slack times some have always proclaimed that it is gone for good, but then, twenty or so years later, there it is again. The previous blossoming was in the early 1990s, when *Dances with Wolves* and *Unforgiven* won Academy Awards for best film in 1991 and 1993, and three multipart documentaries on the Old West appeared on television. *Architectural Digest* devoted an entire issue to palatial houses with plenty of bare timbers, adobe, cowhide, and Native ceramics in Telluride, Jackson Hole, and several southwestern spots; and a handsome model, buck naked except for his Stetson, sat atop a mechanical bull on the cover of *Naturally,* America's foremost nudist periodical.[1]

The obsession has never been only ours, of course. Westerns have appealed across a remarkable range of cultures, yet in some ways they have always been uniquely American.[2] They express our anxieties, our aspirations, and our distinctive notions of violence and rebirth, authority and rebellion, honor and responsibility.[3] In fiction, fashions, drama, political bunkum, arena performances, movies, songs, and advertisements, stories set in our unofficial fifty-first state, the imagined Western State of Mind, say something basic about America. Westerns are something like the nation's Greek chorus, and it won't shut up.

For students of western history, the importance of the Western goes far beyond that. It has had a considerable and continuing influence on the West of reality. For stories have power. They are woven through with assumptions about what a particular place is and is not, what can and cannot be done there, and how its people are expected to behave. Imagined narrative and human action fade into and feed one another. Each part of the West, then, is what it is, in part because of the tales people have told about it; and because the land west of the Missouri has been the special playground of the mass imagination, the stories that have been spun off in the process, the ones we call Westerns, have walked through the country with a John Wayne swagger, changing it profoundly.

Westerns have not been the only stories to shape the country, however—not by a long shot. Others have been alive and working in the West as long as people have. Because these other stories have been wildly at odds with Westerns, they have naturally pushed and bumped against them. The region's history consequently is not only about people fighting over who controls resources and whose institutions and values should be honored, but also about conflicting narratives over what the West means and how it should be treated.

It's natural to assume that Westerns have come out of the West and expressed the actual experience of living there. That notion is exactly backwards. The modern Western took its modern shape from the yearnings and stresses of late-nineteenth-century America east of the Missouri River. That part of the country has always provided most of the demand; its values are the ones reflected, its interests the ones entertained. Westerns did not arise in the West and go eastward to tell the world about that country and its people. They were born in the East, then they marched beyond the Missouri and proceeded to change things.

Homesteaders and town builders in a sense were among the first performers in modern Westerns. They acted out eastern perceptions, starting with the impression that the West was radically, dramatically apart from the world they were leaving. It was the nation's geographical "other." Its landscapes, scale, and life forms seemed not just different but startlingly alien. Today outsiders on their first visits usually feel the same perceptual jolt. The West is not bizarre per se, of course, only strange in relation to what those viewers, then and now, have considered normal. Everyone's standards, whether of moral behavior or for bigness, are necessarily grounded in what he or she first knew. It can be no other way. The historical geographer Eric Dardel has made the point:

> Before any choice, there is this place which we have not chosen, where the very foundation of our earthly existence and human condition establishes itself. We can change places, . . . look for [another] place, but for this we need . . . a base to set down Being—a *here* from which the world discloses itself, [before there can be] a *there* to which we can go.[4]

For everybody heading west, the "here," those deepest assumptions about what the world normally was, was elsewhere. That sense of the

West as fundamentally apart was the nearest thing to a common denominator among the varied writings of that generation that came into the country—the diaries and letters, novels and journalistic dispatches, doggerel and travel accounts. That perspective has considerable power to reveal. Many of our most vivid physical descriptions of the plains are from gawking newcomers who set the West against mental landscapes of other places, then wrote from the shock of differences.

Few writers, for instance, have described the Great Plains in more engaging detail than Richard Francis Burton during his passage in 1860. Drawing on his experience as one of the great travelers of the age—he compared buffalo chips to assorted animal dung of Switzerland, Armenia, Tibet, and India—Burton wrote like a precocious and erudite child. He was driven to look at, tell about, and if possible pick up and sniff each piece of this new world—the clotted clay soil, asters and wild parsnips, fossils, beetles, and Native artifacts. He described the northern lights and how cooking with sagebrush flavored meat like camphor and turpentine.[5] Several more recent books about the plains have continued the tradition of the spellbound outsider. Some of these writers have not just passed through, like Burton, but have stayed and worked awhile, yet their outlanders' point of view, wide-eyed tone, and ability to see the plains freshly and perceptively rank them with the best professional travelers of the nineteenth century. One is Ian Frazier, staffer for the *New Yorker* whose *Great Plains* received a wide readership and well-deserved awards, but there are several others, among them Gretel Ehrlich, Merrill Gilfillan, Dayton Duncan, Pete Davies, and Kathleen Norris. Nobody, not even Burton, has captured better the unsettling, exhilarating impact of the openness of the plains than a friend of Frazier's who telephoned home at the end of her first day driving around the Montana flatlands: "It's amazing here! The sky is like a person yawned and never stopped!"[6]

Outlanders then and now have brought other expectations, not topographical but cultural and social, and through them they have projected deeper meanings onto the physical West they describe so vividly. The new country was not simply an interesting place to look at. Differences of terrain were messages, and usually imperatives, about what ought to be done there.

Newcomers saw in the West two broad and opposing sets of possibilities. In the first, the country's difference invited them to change it,
to transform the West into places like the ones they had left behind. Because the West was "there," they felt compelled to change it into "here."
This response was the most common and had the most widespread, visible consequences. The Great Plains grasslands were corn and wheat fields
that needed only to be laid out, plowed, planted, cultivated, weeded, and
cropped. A sagebrush flat was a town in embryo, with houses, schools,
churches, and theaters anxious to bud into life. The desert only needed
irrigation to be made to bloom. However startling, the new country was
social potential waiting to be shaped by imported ideals. The West was an
economic and cultural order asking to happen.

But the second impulse of the West's promise lay in its remaining
different and fundamentally apart. The West was "there," and it ought to
keep on being "there." Newcomers praised the land for its lack of what
they had left behind. Two attributes of the plains, size and emptiness,
were especially beguiling. Climbing a bluff above the Platte, William
Lockwood looked west and saw a measureless and open land "as level as
a frozen lake." The vista was "right welcome [but] strange," not beautiful
exactly, but stunning in "its vast extent, its solitude and its wilderness."
For Julia Holmes, on her way to Colorado in 1858, the "grandeur" of the
"silent, uninhabited plains . . . made my heart leap with joy." Some slipped
into unintentional irony. "O solitude, how I love it," a young woman wrote.
"If [only] I had about a dozen of my acquaintances to enjoy it with me."
Indians, the obvious exceptions to this human absence, were something
like rare fauna, moving around with the whims common to all predators,
no more participants in history than antelopes and gophers.[7]

These two impulses, starkly different in obvious ways, had one thing
in common. In both, the new country was essentially empty of human
experience. The West was the West because of what had not happened. It
was the Land of Isn't, the Empire of Gonna Be. Maybe this was the larger,
truly compelling meaning of the famous phrase that Frederick Jackson
Turner used to define the frontier: "free land." Economically—the way
it is usually taken—the term referred to untapped resources ripe for the
taking by settlers coming out of the East. That implied that nobody was

already there making a living on the land being taken, notwithstanding the tens of thousands of Indians about to be tossed off country that had fed their people for thousands of years. More broadly, "free land" denied the human experience that lay centuries deep in the West. As white invaders saw it, the West had no stories of its own, nothing to listen to and learn from. It was land free of memories and lessons, free to be made over to resemble other places or free to be kept simple and free of complications: a land free of ghosts.

The Western's two traditions—of a land demanding to be made over, and of country forever wild—have extraordinary staying power. As lived-out narratives they have persisted through political upheavals, vast shufflings of population, half-a-dozen boom-and-bust cycles, revolutions in technology and transportation, and five generations of social change. The first story has had the most obvious consequences. Most of the West has been transformed, specifically to resemble places that sent forth those who have done the transforming. The results are obvious, ranging from the grandest overarching views—for instance, that of the rectilinear survey of farmland as seen from an airplane window at thirty thousand feet—to details on the ground, such as homes and motels and insurance offices with faux Georgian facades in mimic of Atlantic coastal colonials. Vast stretches of the semiarid West were turned green with eastern crops—wheat and corn, cotton and sorghum, almonds, grapes and oranges—with water diverted from rivers and pumped from aquifers. Towns were laid out by the classic eastern grid born in Philadelphia, often with streets with names that looked longingly backward across time and space. In southwestern Kansas, largely treeless except for cottonwoods and willows along the Arkansas River, Dodge City streets include Oak, Elm, Mulberry, Hickory, Ash, and Magnolia. "Harvard" and "Yale" are names of prominent streets in Tulsa (and, with "Princeton," of mountains in the Collegiate Range of the Colorado Rockies).

The second story, about a West of untouched natural beauty where rugged pioneers confronted the untamed, has been just as tenacious. Its obvious conflict with the first tradition, however, poses a problem. As the first story increasingly reshaped and built upon the land, there was less and less that could be imagined as wild, and the second story has seemed increasingly imperiled. One response has been to try to keep alive a semblance of the dreaming time when pioneers arrived to confront, often violently, that imagined West. Towns like Tombstone, Arizona, and Virginia City, Nevada, have made themselves over to satisfy outsiders on the hunt for that earlier, rawer West. In Dodge City the eastward-looking Elm, Mulberry, and Magnolia Streets are bounded on the north and south by Comanche and Gunsmoke Streets. The town's main thoroughfare is Wyatt Earp Boulevard. The popular need for a wild West has considerable economic advantages. "It's a product that you don't have to get funding for," observed one authority, Joe Bowlin, owner of Bowlin's Big Red Indian store in Billy the Kid country near Fort Sumner, New Mexico.[8] While resources like oil, cattle, wheat, and timber are subject to erratic swings in demand, this one has an allure that is remarkably stable and apparently bottomless. This resource is the happy opposite of the others in another way. Oil and wheat are mined and harvested in the West and marketed elsewhere, but the dream of touching a wilder, freer time originates elsewhere and can only be truly converted to income in the West. Dude ranching has exploited this edge since the 1920s. In a recent variation, the "City Slicker" phenomenon, some ranchers have learned that instead of shipping out cattle, they can invite white-collar outlanders to head west with their fantasies. Then the money comes to them.[9]

Watching reenactments and even taking part, of course, only goes so far in feeding the urge for another time. Ultimately the customer has to face the fact that the imagined early West has slipped beyond his or her grasp. That nostalgic ache, however, creates its own demand. It has produced one of the most familiar subgenres of popular western writing. It might be called "Old Geezer" fiction. In these stories the Geezers are men who were there at that moment when people came from the East to reproduce their own world in the innocent, unstoried western paradise— men who then lived long enough to be able to look back and tell us how heavenly it was in that lovely day before history arrived and spoiled everything. Larry McMurtry's novels are a veritable gallery of Geezers: Sam the Lion in *The Last Picture Show;* Wild Horse Homer Bannon in *Horseman, Pass By;* Gus McCrae and Captain Call in *Lonesome Dove;*

and Calamity Jane, a kind of Geezerette, in *Buffalo Girls.* The ultimate
Geezer is Jack Crabb in Thomas Berger's *Little Big Man,* the 111-year-
old resident of a nursing home who spins a tale of coming west as a boy,
being captured and adopted by Cheyennes, then meeting and witnessing
most of the mythic characters and events of the plains frontier. With this
device, Berger portrays the West as two utterly distinct worlds of the two
opposing narratives—the static and timeless one of the Cheyennes and
the expanding, dynamic, transforming, irresistible one of the whites.[10] As
we follow Crabb shuttling between the two, we watch the second one
triumph and the first disappear.

The tension between the two stories has played out as well in some of
the great showplaces of the West, its national parks and monuments. They
have had many purposes. Yellowstone at first was something of a geological freak show, and others over time have been devoted to scientific research and the preservation of what remains of ancient cultures. Early on,
however, one goal was to set aside what were perceived as islands of the
virginal West, the timeless, unlayered, and storyless country at the heart
of the second imported narrative. Creating these wildlands meant getting
rid of what did not fit the imagined landscape, including people. The Far
West has had a dual policy of Indian removal compelled by its two dominant stories. As Indians were being taken off land meant to become fields,
towns, and cattle pastures, they were also evicted from national parks like
Yellowstone, Yosemite, Glacier, and the Black Hills as human clutter that
had no place in Eden. This was done with the support of well-known
sympathizers of Native peoples such as George Bird Grinnell and Helen
Hunt Jackson. On a visit to Yosemite, Jackson complained of "filthy" and
"uncouth" Indians marring the valley's primordial beauty.[11]

Parks, paradoxically, have been groomed to look natural, or rather what
is thought to be natural. Stephen Mather, director of national parks from
1916 to 1929, promoted idyllic, game-filled scenes conforming to preconceptions of untouched beauty. Park workers snuffed out fires and battled
insect infestations so visitors would be sure to see the trees they expected,
apparently robust and healthy but in fact denied effects of forces essential
to their long-term survival. As a result, the settings seem to contrast with
the surrounding developed country, while in fact they are themselves, at

least in part, constructed landscapes. The overall effect perpetuates that old illusion of a dichotomized West, a land divided between the built and the wild, history and Eden. When tourist-consumers enter a park, one historian writes, they participate in a time-polished westering ritual. Like the early pioneers, they cross a "perceptual threshold," an "imaginative border," based on their "faith in radical difference, a perception that the 'undeveloped' spaces on the far side of the frontier [the park boundary] constitute an exotic other" in stark contrast to the East and to the developed West.[12]

The ironic work of updating the West to fit current illusions of the past, whether the imagined Wild West or an even earlier time before history, is vital to the region's economy. Isolated Tombstone, well more than an hour's drive through the desert from Tucson, nevertheless draws nearly half a million tourists every year. The annual count of visitations to the four most popular national parks in the West (Grand Canyon, Yellowstone, Yosemite, and Olympic) is greater than the population of New England. Death Valley, the western wild space with the most daunting and inhospitable reputation, draws nearly eight hundred thousand persons a year. It is as if all of Columbus, Ohio, came out to take a look. In 1955, the last year before restrictions were imposed on rafting through the Grand Canyon, 16,428 people braved the rapids, more than the entire overland migration to Oregon and California before 1849.[13]

The two stories—one about getting history under way and replicating distant places, the other about stalling history or keeping it wholly at bay—have shaped the West profoundly. Imported and acted out for a century and a half, they have proved resilient and endlessly seductive. They are as clear a case as we have of the power of stories to shape the land, its people, and their history.

They are also lies. The West is certainly physically different from the East—from the perspective of outlanders it is definitely "there"—but it is not what both versions of the Western say it is, a country without a significant past and thus without stories that give it meaning. The code word for that fantasized West, unhistoried and storyless, is "wilderness."

Westerns have opposite views toward wilderness—they either praise the pioneers for getting rid of it or they lament its loss—but they agree that it was there in the first place. But in fact the invaders from the East were, if anything, creating wilderness. Europeans first brought contact diseases that swept away millions of native residents of the Western Hemisphere. That made it possible to imagine the land as largely empty and barely touched by human presence, which in turn opened the way to projecting onto that newly emptied land those twin needs, to find both a wilderness demanding change and a wilderness of escape, an Edenic dreamspace.

In fact, the West has a history reaching back at least five thousand years before the earliest cities of Mesopotamia. It was the first part of the current nation to feel a human footfall, and it holds North America's oldest continuously inhabited sites. The invasions of the last century and a half were only the most recent of many human waves that have washed over that country, all with their own stories, each of which has been shaped over time to reveal its own particularity.

Most obvious are narratives of western Indian peoples, accessible as oral traditions and as transcriptions and descriptions by nonnative observers, some taken recently and others from previous generations.[14] All have their limitations. They are imprecise or entirely opaque in locating events chronologically. Oral traditions evolve over time, absorbing new influences and spinning off variations, leaving the original versions uncertain or unknowable. Many are parables and so can be read differently (and probably are meant to be) by different individuals. One thing, however, is starkly clear: Indian stories, as told now and recorded along the way, are fundamentally different from pioneer narratives in their stance, their messages, and the meanings they take from the country.

There is nothing static about these stories, despite the persistent impression of Natives living timeless, changeless lives. They are full of dynamic changes—rivalries and collective squabbles, alliances, victories and calamitous losses, adaptations, and shifting relations among spirits and men. The Kiowas tell of leaving the Yellowstone Valley over a fight with another tribal faction over some antelope udders.[15] There followed friendly relations with the Crows, bitter conflict with the Sioux, and a mixed history with the Comanches before a long-term alliance around 1790. Nor is there much to suggest people living in peace and in balance with the world around them. In these stories tomorrow's conditions depend on today's decisions, and there are plenty of foul-ups. Ancestors of the Hidatsas, having climbed from the underworld via a great root, suffered a terrible flood because of their arrogant behavior toward a bison and a bird.[16] Relations with the nonhuman world are as dynamic as those with other people, and they need close attention precisely because they can so easily go awry.

Above all, Indian stories are about particular places. For that matter, they are not merely *about* places; the stories are inseparably *from* them. That is literally the case in creation stories of peoples emerging from an underworld into ours, such as those of the Diné (Navajos), Hidatsas, and many others. The earth—and more to the point, a specific spot on the earth—is mother, less metaphorically than in fact. The kivas of Pueblo peoples, circular sacred ceremonial spaces, have a hole at the center of their floors, a *sipapu,* representing their place of emergence. The Hopis know where their original *sipapu* is. Today a spring bubbles from it. The opening is something of both a birth canal and, since sustaining spirits and rain-bearing clouds come and go from it, an umbilicus. Hopis are anchored at that spiritual center. Each year men make a pilgrimage to it and gather salt nearby, along the way visiting sites vital to the Hopi story and doing what is needed, including feigning copulation with a large rock, to renew proper relations with their world and its sacred power.[17]

The Hopis, and Indian peoples generally, would find it impossible to consider who they are apart from densely detailed specific locations and from the stories that tie it all, people and places, together. Western Apaches express moral beliefs through stories set in precise spots. Each begins, "It happened at . . . ," and one person can make an ethical point to another simply by mentioning the story's locale.[18] Their system of values is woven through the landscape of home, so anyone who leaves is morally unmoored. Native American identities are grounded inextricably in places, and the stories of those places express and reinforce these identities. In the Great Basin, wrote John Wesley Powell after years of living close to its Indians, two strangers would never ask each other what tribe they were from but rather, "To what land do you belong and how are you and your land named?"[19]

This perspective is behind one of the most persistent patterns in contemporary Native American fiction. In such stories the protagonists have left the place of their origins, frequently to chase success or to meet some duty prescribed by white American mores. They become soldiers and lawyers, or they just take off to look for a job or drift between reservation and white towns. Most stories open with them sick, physically or spiritually, usually both, but they are drawn back irresistibly to their beginnings. The "tribal past," as William Bevis puts it, is "a gravity field stronger than individual will."[20] Among the best-known examples are Abel in N. Scott Momaday's *House Made of Dawn,* Sylvester Yellow Knife and the narrator in James Welch's *The Indian Lawyer* and *Winter in the Blood,* and Tayo in Leslie Marmon Silko's *Ceremony.* The plots center on a character's dawning understanding that his identity—in a basic sense, his very meaning—can exist only in the nexus of a particular place in its many parts and in relation to the people bound to that place by common history. That pattern has its contemporary expression in movies, like *Powwow Highway* and *Smoke Signals,* produced by Indians and about present-day Indian life.

This pattern is the mirror image of a common one in white narratives set in the West. White protagonists are forever leaving home to seek fortune and adventure or to escape family, society, and history. The impulse has given us one of American literature's most famous phrases, from the final line of what often is cited as the essential American novel, when Huckleberry Finn turns his back on settled life and chooses to "light out for the territory." In contrast to the Indian characters, however, leaving home does not make these whites a spiritual mess. To the contrary, heading west is a way to "find themselves," something possible only by cutting loose from kin and culture, the very act that causes Indian protagonists to lose identity and meaning. White characters run away to the West to pursue what might be done in country stripped of entanglements. Indian characters return to the West to reintegrate their individuality in old and complex webs of places, people, memories, and traditions.

These modern Indian stories, though unfolding in New Mexico or Montana, arguably are not set in the West at all. The very name "the West" assumes a perspective from the outside, specifically from where the land in question lies westward, that is, the East. Indian stories are not told in reference to anywhere else. They sit in particular places, and they remain literally in place. There is no gawking at surroundings, as in pioneer accounts with narrators forever pointing at the land, reminding us that everything is new and alien. To Indian narrators the particulars are just there, part of the neighborhood.

The differences drawn so far, between stories about coming into strange terrain and ones rooted in place, are ones of ethnicity. The first stories are of whites, the second of Indians. That distinction has steadily eroded. For decades now there has been a flourishing of stories from the descendants of nineteenth-century white newcomers. They are part of the West's continuing, sequential aging. The sod turners, herders, town makers, and their children and grandchildren have come to their own terms with the country. The new land has become the home place, and with that change the perspective has shifted around. The West is no longer a destination but the initial vantage point, in Dardel's term the "*here* from which the world discloses itself."

We can hear such voices in many places, starting with archives throughout the West. In their vaults are hundreds of reminiscences and oral histories, from a page or so of dimly penciled scrawlings to book-length manuscripts. With titles like "Father Came West" and "Prairie Children," they look back to childhoods in country their parents settled decades earlier. Their details and points of view hint of a perspective distinct from those of their elders—a sense of discovery and vivid descriptions free of preconceptions, an intimate acquaintance with immediate surroundings, and most striking, a deep ambivalence toward the forces transforming the worlds they grew up in. Some accounts, slightly more polished, are more readily available. Virtually every western state has its small private presses that over the past fifty years have published dozens of memoirs. The titles are often overly cute, the style folksy, and the contents sugared with sentiment, but these books are nonetheless a reservoir of material on what it was like to live across those years that connected the frontier, the invaded West, with the West of today.

During the past few decades one of the most heartening developments in American literature has been a flowering of new western writing. Its forms run from fiction and essays to natural history and, among the most notable, memoirs set in the ranch and farming country that was the most common setting of frontiering narratives. The authors are from various parts of the region: Mary Clearman Blew, Ivan Doig, Teresa Jordan, Cyra McFadden, and Ruth McLaughlin from the northern plains and Rockies; William Kittredge and Sallie Tisdale from the Northwest; and Terry Tempest Williams from the Great Basin.[21] In the proper praise for their powerful evocations of life in the twentieth-century West, they are sometimes described, improperly, as if they have come out of nowhere. In fact, they are just a few among hundreds of native voices, most of them muted in the archives, calling out for our attention.

These are daughters and sons and grandchildren of the Geezers, but the stories they tell are not Geezerish ones of paradise lost, but ones of places known from the ground up. Reading through them, some in best-selling books and some in Big Chief tablets, a few themes appear again and again. One is family. Blew's paired memoirs present five generations of Montana ranch families so tangled that the most determined genealogist would be tested in untwining them. The emotional knots are just as snarled. McLaughlin's story is of three interlocking farming families trying to make a go of it over ninety-seven years dug in along the Montana–North Dakota border. Jordan's memoir is subtitled *A Western Family Album* and Williams's *An Unnatural History of Family and Place.* The frontier myth involved running away from families; these stories tell us that life outside families was a contradiction in terms.

Families in turn are bound intimately and sensually to particular places, and their stories are grounded in settings utterly their own. The unique details are inextricable from the characters' memories and identities. One remembered detail for Blew was a sandbar in the Judith River where as a child she saw (or did she?) a sow and her babies about to be swept into the swollen current; for Kittredge it was spots in the scab rock and irrigated pastures of his family ranch in the Warner Valley of southeastern Oregon; for McLaughlin it was her grandfather's windbreak of imported blue spruces that she and her brother hoed and watered as children; for Jordan it was "the Point," the highest spot on some breaks above Chugwater Creek on her family's Wyoming ranch. The writers may give these details a brush of explanation, but they go mostly unremarked, exactly because they are so naturally part of who the narrator is, so embedded that without them the wider memories of their lives do not exist.

A reader of these stories will find no fantasies, no expansive imaginings, no hopes of ultimate wisdom and boundless possibilities. The memoirs in fact are dominated by failure. Farms and ranches go belly-up. The Kittredge ranch at first prospered, but "then it all went dead, over time, but swiftly," both economically and in the environmental havoc it wreaked. [22] McLaughlin's family teetered on the edge for close to a century before her father finally sold the place for a song. No lilting *Little House* uplift here. "Montana is the land of beginning," McLaughlin's grandfather wrote of the homestead he called Surprise Ranch. Her grandmother's diary, however, detailed the reality. "Cleaned more in corral. At 10 I started to bake—not done till 5—bread, pie, 2 cakes, chicken. So tired." And at seventy-one: "Cleaned one room chicken house, 11 tubs, so tired. I wish I was a horse."[23] The compulsive effort to make over the land had costs that went well beyond the financial and physical. "I was raised to be Western, which is to say stoic," Jordan writes.[24] McLaughlin's father, left alone much of the time from the age of nine to tend an isolated farm, sleeping at night with a gun, scarcely connected with his own children. Her first hug from her mother was when she came home at the end of her fall freshman college semester. People living as they did learned "to imitate prairie grass: keeping their most vital parts deep and protected underground."[25]

These memoirists know far better than the rest of us that aching dream that drew their parents and grandparents into the country. They respect it and at some level may even share it. But they understand, too, that all who persist in living it out will endure only if they let realities hammer the dream into shapes the firstcomers would scarcely recognize. Survivors of the dream live by an iron, hard-earned lesson: if you want to make it over the long haul, you better pay both dues and attention. They have a deep but wary affection for beautiful places that sometimes will turn around and slap you silly. What they learn sits close to the center of who they are. "Verities have to be earned, and they take time in the earning," Kittredge writes, and "once earned, they inhabit you in complex ways you cannot name."[26]

These memoirs' similarities with Indian stories are obvious. They are densely situated and could not have happened anywhere else than where they did. Because they sit firmly like tubs on their own bottoms, they are no more Westerns than the stories of Kiowas, Apaches, Nez Perces, or Zunis. They are not about coming into the country but about looking outward from it. Like characters in modern Indian fiction, these white natives often leave home in search of something, usually education and accomplishment. As in Westerns, they hope to escape, but not to flee the stifling East for the freedom of the West. They run away from the provincial West to the East's excitement and sophistication. Kittredge felt a "sour envy" watching the Beatles on his television's one channel: "I wanted to be somewhere else, nearby to that mysterious frenzy of energy."[27]

Like their Indian counterparts, however, the escapees instead feel disoriented and ill-placed until they return home on what turns into a journey of self-discovery. A prime example is Wallace Stegner, whose success and example helped clear the way for these modern western narrators. After growing up in Saskatchewan, Montana, and Utah, he headed eastward. "I wanted to hunt up and rejoin the civilization I had been deprived of," Stegner recalled, but after rising to the cultural ozone of Harvard, he decided he had lost his bearings and could find them only back in the West. The distinguished career that followed was essentially epilogue, he wrote: "I grew up Western, and the very first time I moved out of the West I realized what it meant to me. The rest is documentation, detail."[28] Coming home has moments of primal reintegration. "I feel my body tugged toward each landmark," McLaughlin writes of the homesteader shack, a rare cottonwood, and the fence posts, "gray as bone," she passes while driving the last miles to the charred ruin of her girlhood house. When Stegner returned to the Saskatchewan town of his boyhood, a whiff of streamside wolf willow sent him instantly back to those years, reconnected not through his head but his gut. A middle-aged Kittredge climbed a cliff he had not seen since he was fourteen. He remembered every handhold, but only as he reached for and touched it: "It was if I was the lost piece falling into the puzzle."[29]

Stegner, Kittridge, Blew, Doig, and their literary kin are the most accessible of indigenous voices, white and Indian, that speak in counterpoise to the East-into-West stories that have held the floor for so long. The difference is no abstraction. It is acted out in public policy—for instance, in the flap over a proposal for a "buffalo commons." The brainchild of Rutgers professors Frank and Deborah Popper, it calls for vacating about 140,000 square miles of ten states of the Great Plains, an area larger than New York, Pennsylvania, and Virginia combined, and allowing it to revert to an earlier condition. With indigenous grasses and vast numbers of bison, pronghorns, coyotes, and other critters, it would be the world's largest natural preserve. The Poppers argue that the current way of life cannot sustain itself. Most counties are losing population as thousands of residents have gone bust. A sensible answer, they say, is to return the plains to what they had been when the army of hopeful farmers moved there in the nineteenth century.[30]

From one angle the proposal is a hardheaded critique of the present situation, as farms and ranches fail by the thousands. In that way the Poppers are taking on one of the two traditional Western narratives, the dream of transforming the plains by a vision from somewhere else. That hasn't worked, they say. Give it up. Their answer, however, is just another version of the other narrative, the dream of a West in stasis and largely free of human touch. The West they see is empty. "There is *nothing here*," Frank Popper exclaimed while riding through the Texas Panhandle. "This is un-country." But of course things are there—families, for instance, some into their fourth or fifth generation of hanging on. They justify staying with a mix of tenacity, faith in ingenuity, and most of all, an emotional rootedness. "That's my mama's country there, Ellis County!" a Kansan called out during one of the Poppers' lectures. Another summed up a widespread response: "Maybe a hundred years ago this would make sense, now, no."[31]

The clash of views is an ironic reprise of events a century and a half ago. In the 1860s white newcomers told native Plains Indians that their lives were outmoded and unproductive and would have to give way to something more sensible, namely the vision of the plains that would turn un-country into a bucolic garden and pasture. Now the native plainsmen are white, but the story that threatens them is the same. Once again the Western stomps out of the East, this time wearing not its make-the-land-over but its back-to-nature hat, and once again hard-pressed natives, whites this time, are told that they will simply have to go. The story demands it. Today's families, some with pasts running deeper into the country than those of Indians when they were ordered onto reservations, answer much as the Cheyennes and Lakotas did. There may be better lives, they say, but this one is ours, and we want to keep it.

Controversies like that over the buffalo commons are a key to part of the modern West's distinctiveness. Besides all the other tusslings—economic, ethnic, subregional, and the rest—there is this conflict between sources of narrative power. Westerners today live with opposed ways of thinking about the region itself: the West as place, old and tangled in lessons, and the West as space, as empty room where anyone can escape old limits, lose the past, dance with wolves. There is not the slightest reason to think the conflict will be resolved. As their regular revivals show again and again, Westerns are harder to kill than the Terminator. They were born elsewhere, and elsewhere is where their strongest appeal remains, and as long as that appeal stays vigorous, Westerns will be with us. Whatever happens in the land they pretend to be about is largely irrelevant. If the West were suddenly sealed off and all its gateways boarded and padlocked, with no one allowed to enter or leave or even to peek in, the Western would keep sailing along, buoyed by a level of loyalty, its popularity dipping and rising with puffs of fashion. Millions would hum its tunes, wear its duds, and ape its postures. Truck drivers, hairdressers, accountants, and presidents would still devour gargantuan numbers of pulp paperbacks about steely-eyed strangers under skies of brass.

But nobody can seal off the West, so Westerns will continue to come in and do what they have for generations. They have plenty of power. They continue to shape the country, and westerners themselves turn that power to profit. In one way, however, Westerns are impotent. They have not the slightest power to help westerners figure out, literally, who in the world they are. They can be brought into the West, but, as Barry Lopez reminds us, "the imposed view, however innocent, always obscures." To truly imagine any place, he adds, we have to work hard "to understand why a region is different, to show an initial deference toward its mysteries."[32] For that work, Westerns are useless. They have no inherent kinship to the country, so they just sit there, extraneous, like syrup on a rump roast.

Other stories are available, however. Native American narratives old and new, white post-frontier reminiscences and memoirs, some of the recent historical and naturalist writing all offer other visions of the West. They speak with an awareness of the frontier West, but it is a haunting presence, "the phantom limb of the American psyche," as Larry McMurtry puts it, "not there, but not forgotten."[33] Their voice is of a West matured into an understanding of how to live more sensibly in the region's countless particular places. They are stories about limits as well as a seasoned sense of possibilities and about liberties that come only by seeing any place through intricate bonds of families, society, history, and a peculiar natural setting, all forming a mesh in which everyone, like it or not, is implicated.

Perhaps the Western itself might in time be infected. After all, *True Grit* at its heart is about family and the moral call to stick with it and to meet its obligations, and it ends not in nostalgia or a gaze into a rosy future but with a one-armed tough-minded spinster running a bank and accepting life as time has confined it. In any case such stories are the only ones that can show the way to that meeting ground where people and their places are in common identity. They give westerners the power to know where they stand.

Notes

An earlier version of this chapter appeared as "Stories: A Narrative History of the West," *Montana The Magazine of Western History* 45, no. 3 (Summer 1995): 64–76.

1. "The Wild West!" special issue of *Architectural Digest* 49 (June 1992).

2. On European fascination with western themes, see Ray Allen Billington, *Land of Savagery/Land of Promise: The European Image of the American Frontier in the Nineteenth Century* (New York: W. W. Norton, 1981); Rob Kroes, ed., *The American West As Seen by Europeans and Americans* (Amsterdam: Free University Press, 1989); Gerald D. Nash, "European Images of America: The West in Historical Perspective," and Julian Crandall Hollick, "The American West in the European Imagination," both in *Montana The Magazine of Western History* 42 (Spring 1992): 2–16, 17–20.

3. See Richard Slotkin's trilogy, *Regeneration through Violence: The Mythology of the American Frontier, 1600–1860* (Middletown, Conn.: Wesleyan University Press, 1973); and Slotkin, *The Fatal Environment: The Myth of the Frontier in the Age of Industrialization, 1800–1890* (New York: Atheneum, 1985).

4. Eric Dardel, *L'homme et la terre: Nature de réalité géographique* (Paris: Presses Universitaires de France, 1952), 56, quoted in E. Relph, *Place and Placeness* (London: Pion Limited, 1976), 41.

5. Richard F. Burton, *The City of the Saints and Across the Rocky Mountains to California* (New York: Alfred A. Knopf, 1963).

6. Ian Frazier, *Great Plains* (New York: Farrar, Straus, Giroux, 1989); Gretel Ehrlich, *The Solace of Open Spaces* (New York: Viking Penguin, 1985); Merrill Gilfillan, *Magpie Rising: Sketches from the Great Plains* (Boulder, Colo.: Pruett, 1988; New York: Vintage Books, 1988); Dayton Duncan, *Miles from Nowhere: Tales from America's Contemporary Frontier* (New York: Viking Penguin, 1993); Pete Davis, *Storm Country: A Journey through the Heart of America* (New York: Random House, 1992); Kathleen Norris, *Dakota: A Spiritual Geography* (New York: Ticknor & Fields, 1993). Quote from Frazier, *Great Plains*, 15.

7. William Lockwood Diary, June 18, 1866, quoted in transcript of Samuel Finley Blythe Diary, 1866, Nebraska State Historical Society, Lincoln; Julia Archibald Holmes, *A Bloomer Girl on Pike's Peak, 1858*, ed. Agnes Wright Spring (Denver: Denver Public Library, 1949), 15; Helen Stewart Diary, May 1, 1853, Lane County Historical Society, Eugene, Oregon.

8. Duncan, *Miles from Nowhere*, 91.

9. The "City Slicker" phenomenon followed the popular film comedy of the same title (1991). When D. L. Taylor, stymied by declining beef prices and poor grass, began charging tourists to work and "act out their cowboy fantasies on his property" on his ranch near Moab, Utah, his fortunes changed dramatically. "I don't really like doing it," he said, "but it sure pays." "New Feud on the Range: Cowman vs. Tourist," *New York Times* (September 18, 1994), 1, 15. Continuing economic difficulties in ranching have sustained the trend. See, for instance, "A State That Never Was in Wyoming," *New York Times* (July 24, 2008).

10. Larry McMurtry, *The Last Picture Show* (New York: Dial Press, 1966), *Horseman, Pass By* (New York: Harpers, 1961), *Lonesome Dove: A Novel* (New York:

Simon & Schuster, 1985), and *Buffalo Girls: A Novel* (New York: Simon & Schuster, 1990); Thomas Berger, *Little Big Man* (New York: Dial Press, 1964).

11. Mark David Spence, *Dispossessing the Wilderness: Indian Removal and the Making of the National Parks* (New York: Oxford University Press, 1999), 109. See also Theodore Catton, *Inhabited Wilderness: Indians, Eskimos, and National Parks in Alaska* (Albuquerque: University of New Mexico Press, 1997); Robert H. Keller and Michael F. Turek, *American Indians and National Parks* (Tucson: University of Arizona Press, 1998); and Philip Burnham, *Indian Country, God's Country: Native Americans and the National Parks* (Washington, D.C.: Island Press, 2000).

12. Kerwin L. Klein, "Frontier Products: Tourism, Consumerism, and the Southwestern Public Lands, 1890–1990," *Pacific Historical Review* 62 (February 1993): 43–44.

13. Roderick Nash, *Wilderness and the American Mind* (New Haven: Yale University Press, 1973), 271.

14. On Native American literature, one might begin with A. LaVonne Brown Ruoff, *American Indian Literatures: An Introduction, Bibliographic Review, and Selected Bibliography* (New York: Modern Language Association, 1990); Kenneth Lincoln, *Native American Renaissance* (Berkeley: University of California Press, 1983); Louis Owens, *Other Destinies: Understanding the American Indian Novel* (Norman: University of Oklahoma Press, 1992); Gerald Vizenor, ed., *Narrative Chance: Postmodern Discourse on Native American Indian Literatures* (Albuquerque: University of New Mexico Press, 1980); Arnold Krupat, *For Those Who Come After: A Study of Native American Autobiography* (Berkeley: University of California Press, 1985); Brian Swann and Arnold Krupat, eds., *Recovering the Word: Essays on Native American Literature* (Berkeley: University of California Press, 1987).

15. Mildred P. Mayhall, *The Kiowas* (Norman: University of Oklahoma Press, 1962), 11.

16. Martha Warren Beckwith, *Mandan and Hidatsa Tails* (Poughkeepsie, N.Y.: Vassar College, 1934), 18–21.

17. Micha Titiev, "A Hopi Salt Expedition," *American Anthropologist,* new series, 39:2 (April–June, 1937): 244–58.

18. Keith H. Basso, *Wisdom Sits in Places: Landscape and Language among the Western Apache* (Albuquerque: University of New Mexico Press, 1996), 90–91.

19. Quoted in Don D. Fowler and Catherine S. Fowler, *Anthropology of the Numa: John Wesley Powell's Manuscripts on the Numic Peoples of Western North America, 1868–1880,* Smithsonian Contributions to Anthropology 14 (Washington, D.C.: Smithsonian Institution Press, 1971), 38.

20. William W. Bevis, *Ten Tough Trips: Montana Writers and the West* (Seattle: University of Washington Press, 1990), 97.

21. Mary Clearman Blew, *All but the Waltz: A Memoir of Five Generations in the Life of a Montana Family* (New York: Penguin Books, 1991), and *Balsamwood: A Memoir* (New York: Viking Penguin, 1994); Ivan Doig, *This House of Sky: Land-*

scapes of a Western Mind (New York: Harcourt, Brace, Jovanovich, 1978); Teresa Jordan, *Riding the White Horse Home: A Western Family Album* (New York: Pantheon Books, 1993); Cyra McFadden, *Rain or Shine* (New York: Random House, 1986); Ruth McLaughlin, *Bound Like Grass: A Memoir From the Western High Plains* (Norman: University of Oklahoma Press, 2010); William Kittredge, *Hole in the Sky: A Memoir* (New York: Alfred A. Knopf, 1992); Sallie Tisdale, *Stepping Westward: The Long Search for Home in the Pacific Northwest* (New York: Henry Holt, 1991); Terry Tempest Williams, *Refuge: An Unnatural History of Family and Place* (New York: Pantheon Books, 1991).

22. William Kittredge, *Owning It All: Essays* (St. Paul: Graywolf Press, 1987), 61.

23. McLaughlin, *Bound Like Grass,* 100.

24. Jordan, *Riding the White Horse Home,* 13.

25. McLaughlin, *Bound Like Grass,* 80.

26. Kittredge, *Owning It All,* 89.

27. Ibid., 34.

28. Wallace Stegner, "Finding the Place: A Migrant Childhood," in *Where the Bluebird Sings to the Lemonade Springs: Living and Writing in the West* (New York: Random House, 1992), 4, 19.

29. McLaughlin, *Bound Like* Grass, 3; Wallace Stegner, *Wolf Willow: A History, a Story and a Memory of the Last Plains Frontier* (New York: Viking Press, 1955), 18; Kittredge, *Hole in the Sky,* 233.

30. For the fullest account of the Poppers, their ideas, and responses to them, see Anne Matthews, *Where the Buffalo Roam* (New York: Grove Press, 1992).

31. Matthews, *Where the Buffalo Roam,* 12–13, 122–23.

32. Barry Lopez, *Arctic Dreams: Imagination and Desire in a Northern Landscape* (New York: Charles Scribner's Sons, 1986), 176.

33. Quote in Elliott West, "On the Trail with Gus and Call: *Lonesome Dove* and the Western Myth," in Mark C. Carnes, ed., *Novel History: Historians and Novelists Confront America's Past* (New York: Simon & Schuster, 2001), 131.

Index

References to illustrations appear in italic type.

Milton Keynes UK
Ingram Content Group UK Ltd.
UKHW040816090224
437518UK00001B/112